RailsSpace

RAILSSPACE

Building a Social Networking Website with Ruby on Rails™

Michael Hartl

Aurelius Prochazka

Upper Saddle River, NJ • Boston • Indianapolis • San Francisco

New York • Toronto • Montreal • L

Capetown • Sydney • Tokyo • Singa

The publisher offers excellent discounts on this book when ordered in quantity for bulk purchases or special sales, which may include electronic versions and/or custom covers and content particular to your business, training goals, marketing focus, and branding interests. For more information, please contact:

U.S. Corporate and Government Sales
(800) 382-3419
corpsales@pearsontechgroup.com

For sales outside the United States please contact:

International Sales
international@pearsoned.com

This Book Is Safari Enabled

The Safari® Enabled icon on the cover of your favorite technology book means the book is available through Safari Bookshelf. When you buy this book, you get free access to the online edition for 45 days.

Safari Bookshelf is an electronic reference library that lets you easily search thousands of technical books, find code samples, download chapters, and access technical information whenever and wherever you need it.

To gain 45-day Safari Enabled access to this book:

- Go to http://www.awprofessional.com/safarienabled
- Complete the brief registration form
- Enter the coupon code G9GD-Z5BI-7BRS-T5IH-D1JR

If you have difficulty registering on Safari Bookshelf or accessing the online edition, please e-mail customer-service@safaribooksonline.com.

Visit us on the Web: www.awprofessional.com

Library of Congress Cataloging-in-Publication Data
Hartl, Michael.
    RailsSpace : building a social networking website with Ruby on Rails / Michael Hartl, Aurelius Prochazka.
        p. cm.
    Includes index.
    ISBN 13: 978-0-321-48079-8 (pbk. : alk. paper)
    ISBN 10: 0-321-48079-1
    1. Web site development. 2. Ruby (Computer program language) 3. Online social networks. I. Prochazka, Aurelius.
II. Title.
    TK5105.888.H374 2007
    006.7—dc22   2007011979

ISBN 13: 978-0-321-48079-8
ISBN 10:   0-321-48079-1
Text printed in the United States on recycled paper at RR Donnelley in Crawfordsville, Indiana.
First printing, July 2007

To our parents

Contents

Figures

Acknowledgments

Thanks to Debra Williams Cauley for shepherding us through the publishing process. We would also like to thank our technical reviewers, Francis Hwang and Michael Vanier, for their careful reading and critiques.

CHAPTER 1
Introduction

RailsSpace teaches you Ruby on Rails by developing a real-world application: RailsSpace, a social networking website aimed at the Rails community itself. We take you step by step, from the virtually static front page, through user registration and authentication, up to a highly dynamic site with user profiles, image upload, simple blogs, full-text and geographical search, and a friendship request system. Though certainly not intended as a serious competitor to the social networking heavyweights, RailsSpace is not a toy; it's designed to show how to use Rails to make a web application suitable for deployment into a production environment.

1.1 Why Rails?

Ruby on Rails is a tool for making web applications—and it's freakishly good at it. If you're reading this (which, evidently, you are), you're probably wondering what makes Rails so special. When you ask this of a programmer who has already fallen in love with Rails, maybe he'll tell you it's "agile," and you'll have to read up on what that means to coders. Or maybe you'll be bombarded by a list of acronyms like ORM, MVC, or DRY. While these are all cool features of Ruby on Rails, the real reason Rails rocks is not about vocabulary; it's about the philosophy of efficient design.

There's that word: *design*. It's a slippery concept, yet unmistakable. Good design is like pornography: You know it when you see it. Rails is like very, very good pornography. What makes the design of Rails so good is difficult to pin down, but we'll do our best. We think the heart of it is *free productivity*.

1.1.1 Productivity wants to be free

The essence of free productivity is the eerie ability Rails has to anticipate your needs as a web programmer. That's not very concrete, though, so let's get a flavor for the free productivity Rails provides by looking at a list of examples. Not all of these will make sense to you right now, but they should help you develop an intuition for the kinds of things Rails is good at.

- **Ruby:** Rails applications, as well as Rails itself, are written in Ruby, a dynamic, object-oriented programming language. Ruby comes out of the Perl tradition, and Yukihiro "Matz" Matsumoto, the creator of Ruby, calls it "a better Perl than Perl." In our experience, most programmers with exposure to both languages agree. We'd add that, for web programming, embedded Ruby (ERb) is a better PHP than PHP. Being able to tap into the power and elegance of Ruby is a major advantage of Rails.

- **Mapping of database tables to Ruby objects:** There are no messy SQL[1] calls in most Rails applications—instead you'll find Ruby objects and methods. Rails does the dirty database work behind the scenes. (If, by some chance, you do want to execute some raw SQL, Rails lets you do that, too.)

- **Automatic conversion of data models into HTML and back:** There is seamless integration between the code for modeling objects in your system and the code to display them to the user. This is nowhere clearer than in data validations; for example, if your data model requires users to put in an email address, but the user submits a form without one, Rails can automatically catch the error and put it in a variable for display back to the user.

- **Built-in support for automated testing of data models and web pages:** Rails makes it easy to write test suites that verify the integrity of your data model and the correctness of the pages on your site, allowing you to be confident that changes to your code will not break your application.

- **Database-independent creation and alteration of database tables:** Rails *migrations* make it easy to create your data models, make changes to them, and roll them back if necessary, all in a way that makes it possible to use the same model for different databases.

---

[1] SQL, or Structured Query Language, is the language of relational databases.

1.1.2 This productivity ain't free

Now that we've given a sense of what free productivity is, it's important to explain what free productivity is not. Many frameworks come with lots of built-in functionality: a slick administrative interface, fancy role-based authentication and authorization, or the ability to write certain applications with virtually no code. Even Rails has this capability; a feature called *scaffolding* renders certain kinds of form-database interactions trivial— leading, among other things, to the infamous "15-minute blog engine."[2]

That's not free productivity. Built-in authentication or 15-minute blog engines might make for great marketing, but between us friends we can probably agree that any serious software application is going to take more than 15 minutes, no matter how brilliant the framework. Don't get us wrong; if, by some chance, the application you have in mind is rendered trivial by some existing framework, by all means use it. But if, as is more likely, you want to build something new, you need a framework that will help you when you need it and will get out of your way when you don't. You need a tool that will help you realize your vision; a tool flexible enough to change as your vision changes; a tool that, in the end, mutates into a new framework—one that feels as if it were custom-made to write your exact application.

This is where Rails excels. Rails is great at making *custom* applications—Rails helps you make the application *you* want. You don't switch to Rails because of the cool message board or blog software available. You switch because the process of creating your own custom apps is so much easier using Rails.

1.2 Why this book?

There's a tension in any educational book between the two extremes of pure tutorial and pure reference. We land firmly on the tutorial side of this spectrum, which has many advantages. Because our application is real, you get to learn Rails as it is actually used. You'll see for yourself all the great ways that Rails makes writing web applications easier, from its elegant model-view-controller architecture to the brilliance of embedded Ruby. You also get the advantage of artful repetition: You see the most important ideas the most. The result is learning by osmosis.

In the process of building RailsSpace, we'll also see how Rails makes it easy to write automated tests to make sure our application does what we wanted it to do. Because of our tutorial approach, we will be able to develop the tests incrementally in parallel with

---

[2] http://media.rubyonrails.org/video/rails_take2_with_sound.mov

the application, just as you do (or should do) in real life. As our application evolves, you'll see how great having a test suite is: Whenever we modify a feature or add a new one, we can run the tests to make sure that we haven't broken some other part of the application.

Of course, while good for learning, a tutorial approach is not as good for looking things up. As a counterbalance to *RailsSpace*, we recommend *Agile Web Development with Rails* by Dave Thomas and David Heinemeier Hansson (from Pragmatic Programmers), the original introduction to Rails. *AWDwR* contains a wealth of reference material documenting most aspects of the Rails framework. For learning Ruby we recommend *Programming Ruby, Second Edition*, by Dave Thomas et al. (Pragmatic Programmers), and *The Ruby Way, Second Edition*, by Hal Fulton (Addison-Wesley).

1.3 Who should read this book?

Since you're reading this, the chances are good that you should read this book. *RailsSpace* is an introductory book, so we don't assume any knowledge of the Ruby programming language or of the Rails framework. Of course, any previous exposure to either will be beneficial. Even if you have some prior experience with Rails, we hope you can learn something from our book, especially since we use several features (such as migrations, form generators, REST, and Ajax support) introduced in the more recent releases of Rails.

To get the most out of *RailsSpace*, you should probably know at least one programming language, and familiarity with object-oriented programming would be especially helpful. Java is probably sufficient background,[3] and it's even better if you are familiar with a dynamically typed language such as Perl, Python, or PHP (or Ruby!). It would be especially good if you've used one of these languages to make dynamic websites. Some exposure to JavaScript and Cascading Style Sheets (CSS) would also be good. At the very least, you should be familiar with making static websites using HTML. Finally, we assume a certain level of computer sophistication, so that when we say "Go download MySQL and install it" you're confident that (given enough time and coffee) you can probably do it, even if you've never installed a database before.

All of these supposed prerequisites are really beside the point, though. By far the most important factor is your enthusiasm for learning how to make web applications with Rails. If you're excited about putting something cool on the web, this book is for you, no matter what your background is.

---

[3] If Java is the only programming language you know, you might get tripped up by the lack of static typing in Ruby. If you find yourself freaking out, just take a deep breath and try to have faith that dynamic typing works.

1.3.1 How to read this book

RailsSpace is designed to be read from start to finish, and you'll get the most out of it if you code along with us, but we've designed the book to be instructive and interesting even if you're not sitting in front of the computer. Also, it's important to be patient. If you don't get something right away, keep pressing forward, and give the ideas a little time to sink in. You'll be amazed at how something that confuses you at the beginning of a chapter will seem trivial by the end. You're training your personal neural network how to recognize Ruby on Rails patterns, and there's no substitute for practice and perseverance.

1.3.2 How to watch this book

The accompanying website for this book can be found at

```
http://RailsSpace.com/book
```

There you'll find errata, sample data, and downloadable source code for *RailsSpace*. You'll also find links to screencasts for each chapter—narrated movies of the book's source code coming to life.

1.4 A couple of Rails stories

We've given you a bunch of reasons why Rails rocks, but there's no substitute for a couple of good, old-fashioned testimonials. These are our personal roads to Rails.

1.4.1 Aure

Way back in 1994 some friends and I in the Graduate Aeronautical Laboratories at Caltech discovered that we had a department webserver that would serve our own content at /~user_name/URLs. We started out by competing with each other for hits and instead of personal sites we put up content about our favorite musicians and airplanes. One of us was the teaching assistant for the lab and had control of the ~ta account. We rechristened the initials to stand for "The Asylum" and instead of competing, we pooled our resources to build a crazy place on the web where anyone could log on and contribute content. Some of the apps we created were a public bookmarks repository (precursor to del.icio.us), a public writing forum (precursor to wikis), and a web-based Lite-Brite emulator and gallery (sort of a primitive single-celled ancestor of Flickr!).

We gained a lot of attention for these sites and soon film studios and record companies were calling the lab tracking us down to hire us to build dynamic websites for them. It was certainly awkward to get phone calls from Universal Pictures while your Ph.D.

thesis advisor was in the lab, so we started a business and opened an office with a phone number of its very own.

We spent a few years building custom websites in Perl/CGI while getting our degrees (which we all managed to do; take that you Yahoo! millionnaire Stanford dropouts!). Slowly the stress of building websites from scratch in Perl wore us out and the company disbanded. I looked back at the websites and realized that many of them were very similar, so I began offering standard web components to my clients. Meanwhile, Philip Greenspun was running Photo.net and getting many requests from people wanting the code that the site ran on. Philip assembled his friends to beef up the Photo.net code and together we founded ArsDigita and open-sourced our code as ACS (ArsDigita Community System), comprised of standard web components and written mostly in Tcl. We used ACS to get exposure among poor developers, which led us to be found by rich companies who wanted customizations to the toolkit. Unfortunately, venture capitalists also eyed ArsDigita and once we accepted their money they also had influence; you can read about what happened after that on fuckedcompany.com.

Even with ArsDigita gone from the landscape, the toolkit lived on as "OpenACS" at openacs.org. But, as an independent contractor, could I really convince my clients that a toolkit started by a defunct company was definitely a long-term solution? Also, I was pretty sick and tired of programming in Tcl, so I turned to the prettiest language I knew—Python. That pretty much meant using Zope, and at first Zope was awesome. Indeed, there are still some applications for which Zope is a great choice. But Zope has many annoyances as well, and my clients yearned for standard version control, filesystem access, and better relational database support.

One of my favorite ex-employees was now working for Caltech and one day sent me an email about some emerging frameworks she was considering instead of Zope for her next project. Django and Ruby on Rails were on her list, and after a few hours of research I knew Zope was history. Initially I leaned toward Django because it was in Python, but Ruby on Rails was a bit further along, and it had one thing that Django will never have— David Heinemeier Hansson, the creator of Rails. From my experience with ArsDigita and Philip Greenspun I knew the importance of having a compelling, intelligent, and opinionated central figure representing the framework. Back then, and through the time of this writing, DHH has prescribed the philosophy of what Rails is and what it is not.

While DHH is its "creator," Rails clearly is the product of the evolution of web application development. Here's what struck me about Rails:

- **Ruby, mostly:** Web application development always requires some mastery of many fields. You're going to have to know at least a little about templating languages, database access, and procedural programming. But there's no denying it takes energy to constantly switch back and forth between languages, especially when languages mix within one file. Rails minimizes this—templating language: Ruby; database access: Ruby (mostly); procedural programming: Ruby (duh).

- **Data modeling, improved:** The old way I started a project was to brainstorm everything that might be needed and write a data model in SQL that would hold the final state of the data. Then I would have to write the code to populate the database tables and write the error detection to prevent bad data from going into the database. With Rails migrations, I can now incrementally augment the data model, and with validations I write rules that almost automatically show up in my web application as error reports. Also, migrations are database agnostic, so I don't have to write a new SQL file for the various available databases.

Oh, and there are many more things I have learned about Rails that I love, but frankly, you don't need a long list of great things about Rails to know it's for you. In fact, if you need a long list, then maybe you're not convinced. It's like when I bought my 2001 Nissan Frontier truck: It could carry my dog, it was fast, and it looks like a spaceship—sold!

With Ruby on Rails I can offer clients sites that are completely customized for their needs while still being fun for me to program in. Everyone is happy!

1.4.2   Michael

When I was at Caltech for graduate school, my friend Sumit Daftuar and I ran a local NCAA basketball tournament pool, which initially involved a small but important web component. Sumit used a simple Perl script to generate the results after each round of the tournament, which got posted to a website. Even though it was ridiculously simple, people loved it. In 2001 I decided to take the next step by using PHP to write a full web interface for our pool, complete with bracket entry and scoring reports. I reasoned that this would force me to learn web development, and, several 20-hour days later, it did.

PHP seemed great at first, but as the size of my projects grew, PHP became increasingly cumbersome. After graduating, Sumit and I started a company that ran unique weekly fantasy sports games and produced an improved version of our NCAA site called BracketManager. I didn't want to use PHP for the company sites, so I started looking around for something new. I had learned Perl and Python in the course of my Ph.D. research, and I looked at several frameworks in those languages.

I eventually settled on Zope, which is written in Python, even though it wasn't particularly well-suited for our primary purpose—namely, writing a large custom web application. Like many frameworks, Zope uses a watered-down template language to generate HTML, but many web applications (including ours) generate such complicated HTML that they really need a full-strength language under the hood. We ended up writing most of our HTML in pure Python and coupling it to Zope using "external methods," which got the job done but were rather cumbersome. I also found Zope's documentation to be spotty at best, due in large part to Zope's relatively small user base. Finally, Zope has weak support for relational databases; in particular, the Zope MySQL database adapter provided no support for generating the often comically verbose queries required by SQL, forcing me to write a custom MySQL library in Python.

Despite all these problems with Zope, Python is so much better than PHP that it was worth the trouble. Unfortunately, our fantasy games never reached a critical mass, and the final straw came when the NFL Players Association started (and the MLB Players Association threatened) to sue any fantasy sports companies using the players' names without a license. Unable to get licenses, we decided to shut the company down. This was unfortunate, but it did give me a chance finally to abandon my Zope codebase and take a look at a new framework I had been reading about called Ruby on Rails. I had a mental checklist of things I needed in a web development framework, and I was curious to see if Rails might meet those needs.

During all this time, I had kept in touch with Aure Prochazka, a tall, quiet, scruffy-looking guy I had met while singing in the Caltech Glee Club. He seemed to know a lot about web development, so back in my PHP days I talked with him a bit about that language. He'd looked at it a little, he said, and it seemed fine. I talked to him maybe a year later, and he told me that he had taken a good look at PHP and decided that it sucked; he had gone with Python and Zope instead. I replied that I had also switched to Zope. After another year or so, I mentioned that I had become dissatisfied with Zope and was looking at Ruby on Rails. He replied that he had recently switched from Zope to Rails, and loved his new framework.

In an effort to jump-start my Rails education, I took a Pragmatic Studio course offered by Dave Thomas and Mike Clark, spending my own hard-earned cash despite Mike's best efforts to convince me not to take the class. I'm glad that Mike was not more persuasive, because I sat in amazement as one item after another on my mental list got checked off:

- An elegant programming language with flexible data structures and powerful abstractions: *check*

- Good documentation, with a relatively large (and rapidly growing) user base: *check*

- Mature relational database support, with a good object-relational mapping library: *check*

- HTML-embedded templates with, for the love of God, a full-strength programming language: *check*

After working on a few personal projects in Rails, and doing a Rails demo site for a friend's company to show how it could replace their legacy Perl system, I was convinced that Rails was the framework I had been searching for. When Aure asked me if I might be interested in submitting a proposal to write a book on Rails with him, I leapt at the opportunity.

There's no turning back now. And there's no stopping Ruby on Rails.

PART I

Foundations

## CHAPTER 2

Getting started

It's time to start building RailsSpace, a social networking website for Ruby on Rails enthusiasts (and whoever else shows up). Eventually, RailsSpace will have many of the features associated with popular social networks such as Facebook and MySpace, with searchable user profiles, an email system, and friends lists. The first part of the book lays a foundation by developing a system for registration, login, and authentication. This system is essential for our purposes, but it's also needed for virtually any user-based web application. In the second part, we'll build a social network on this foundation. Of course, in the process of making this specific type of application, we'll develop many general techniques useful for building other kinds of websites as well.

In this chapter, we'll get started with the application by making the front page of our site, together with a couple of other static pages. Much of what we do in this chapter could be done quite easily with plain HTML files, but even in this extremely simple case Rails still proves surprisingly convenient. It also makes for a gentle introduction to some of the core concepts behind Rails, including embedded Ruby and the model-view-controller architecture.

2.1 Preliminaries

Choosing a platform

Although we suppose there are alternatives, everyone we know uses either Windows, Macintosh, or Linux for Rails development. Your choice of platform will probably be dictated more by what you are currently familiar with than anything else. In *Rails-Space*, we strive to support all three of these platforms. Your humble authors use Mac (Aure) and Linux (Michael), and Michael learned to develop Rails apps on Windows specifically to support this book. Because we like the Apple look, all screenshots in

> *RailsSpace* are from the Macintosh platform, but we can report from personal experi-
> ence that Rails is unambiguously cross-platform; you can build great Rails applications
> no matter which operating system you choose.

We bet that many of you have, in your excitement, already installed Rails, but if you haven't (or if you're using an older version[1]) you should do that now. Once you've chosen a platform (see the sidebar "Choosing a platform"), head over to the Ruby on Rails download page (`http://www.rubyonrails.org/down`) for instructions on how to install Rails. There are many different ways to get rolling with Rails; here is one basic sequence:

1. Install Ruby

   - **Windows:** Download the Windows installer (the first `.exe` file at `http://rubyforge.org/frs/?group_id=167`) and double-click on it.

   - **Linux:** Download the Ruby source code from `http://www.ruby-lang.org/en/downloads/`. Linux users, you know the drill: extract with

     ```
     $ tar zxf <filename>
     ```

     and install with

     ```
     $ ./configure; make; sudo make install
     ```

     If you don't have `sudo`[2] enabled, you'll have to log in as root for the final step:

     ```
     $ ./configure
     $ make
     $ su
     # make install
     ```

   - **OS X:** There are some issues with the Ruby that ships with OS X 10.4, so you might want to take a look at this:[3] `http://hivelogic.com/articles/2005/12/01/ruby_rails_lighttpd_mysql_tiger`

2. Install RubyGems, the standard Ruby package manager

   - **Windows:** Download the first RubyGems `.zip` file from `http://rubyforge.org/frs/?group_id=126` and unzip it, extracting the files to a directory on your

---

[1] For this book, you should have Ruby 1.8.5 or later and Rails 1.2 or later.

[2] How do you do the `sudo` that you do so well?

[3] Also consider Locomotive (`http://locomotive.sourceforge.net/`), a prepackaged Rails bundle for OS X.

local disk. Using a command prompt (DOS window), navigate to the directory where you extracted the files and run

```
> ruby setup.rb
```

- **Linux and OS X:** Download the first RubyGems `.tgz` file from `http://rubyforge.org/frs/?group_id=126`, extract it, and run

```
$ ruby setup.rb
```

  inside the source directory.

3. Install Rails at the command line:[4]

```
> gem install rails --include-dependencies
```

Now go get a cup of coffee while Rails and all of its associated files are automagically installed.[5]

2.1.1 Setting up your development environment

Your specific development environment will depend somewhat on the platform you choose, but since Rails applications are written in Ruby, at the very least you'll need a text editor for writing source code. As we'll see, Rails projects have a lot of different files and directories, so it's useful to have an editor or integrated development environment (IDE) able to navigate the directory tree and switch between files quickly.

We particularly recommend RadRails,[6] a free (as in beer and speech) cross-platform Rails IDE based on Eclipse (which will be familiar to many Java developers out there). For Rails developers working on OS X, the most popular choice seems to be TextMate,[7] a text editor with lots of nice Rails macros and good directory navigation.[8]

2.1.2 Running with `rails`

Now that you've installed Rails, it's time to get started with RailsSpace. Rails comes with a program called (appropriately enough) `rails`, which automatically creates a bunch

---

[4] Throughout the rest of *RailsSpace*, we'll use > to indicate the prompt in a cross-platform manner; for Windows users, this will be the > in a command prompt (DOS) window, while for Mac OS X and Linux users, it will be the $ in a terminal window.

[5] If Rails is already installed, run `gem update rails --include-dependencies` and `gem update --system` to update your installation.

[6] `http://www.radrails.org/`

[7] `http://macromates.com/`

[8] Lamentably, TextMate is free in neither the beer nor the speech senses of the term.

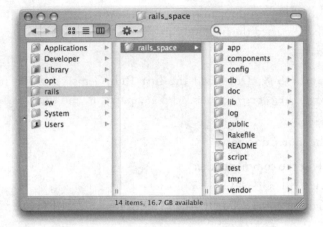

Figure 2.1 Top-level directory structure.

of files and directories to get you started with a new project. For a site with a name like RailsSpace (written in CamelCase), the Rails convention is to create a project with the corresponding name in underscore format (so we would use camel_case for project CamelCase); in our case that means making `rails_space`:

```
> rails rails_space
```

The `rails` command creates lots of files and folders, which comprise a skeleton of the project.[9] Let's take a look at it in our file browser (Figure 2.1). One of the great things about Rails applications is that they all share this common directory structure (depicted as a pie chart in Figure 2.2). It may look a little overwhelming at first, but once you've spent a little time navigating the Rails directory tree it will sink in fast. We've found that having the directory structure decided for us eliminates a lot of headaches since we don't have to spend any time agonizing about what to call our directories or where to put our new files.

Importing projects into RadRails

Here's how to import a Rails project into RadRails:

1. Go to `File -> New -> Rails -> Rails Project` and click `Next`
2. Uncheck the `Generate Rails application skeleton` and `Create a WEBrick server` boxes

---

[9] If you are using RadRails, you should import the Rails project at this point (see the sidebar "Importing projects into RadRails").

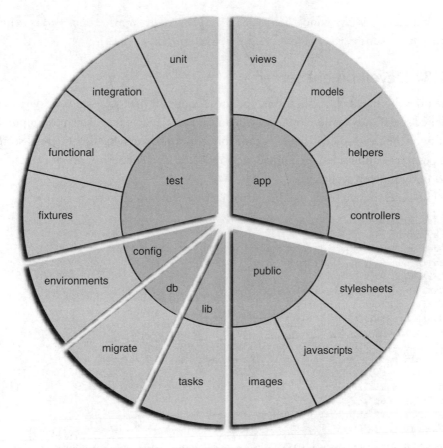

Figure 2.2 Rails, as a pie chart. (Mmm…pie.)

3. Edit the default location if it is not the parent directory of your Rails project (you will have to uncheck the box next to `Use default location` to do this)
4. Enter the name of your project (`rails_space` in this case) in the box and click `Finish`

An alternative to this is to skip the original `rails rails_space` command and then follow the steps above without unchecking `Generate Rails application skeleton`. In this case RadRails will run the `rails` command automatically.

In case it's not self-explanatory, we should note that all of the directories in this book will be relative to the base directory created by the `rails` command. For example, if your

project directory is created in `/home/user/rails_space`, `app/views/index.rhtml`
means `/home/user/rails_space/app/views/index.rhtml`.

2.1.3 Development server

When developing Rails applications, the most common practice is to use a webserver
designed specifically for development, run on your local machine.[10] The most important
quality of the development server is probably an immediate reloading of code, so that
changes to the application are immediately reflected on the website, which makes for a
short development-debug cycle.

The development server can be started using a standard script:[11]

```
> cd rails_space
> ruby script/server
=> Booting Mongrel (use 'script/server webrick' to force WEBrick)
=> Rails application starting on http://0.0.0.0:3000
=> Call with -d to detach
=> Ctrl-C to shutdown server
** Starting Mongrel listening at 0.0.0.0:3000
** Starting Rails with development environment...
** Rails loaded.
** Loading any Rails specific GemPlugins
** Signals ready.  TERM => stop.  USR2 => restart.  INT => stop
   (no restart).
** Rails signals registered.  HUP => reload (without restart).
   It might not work well.
** Mongrel available at 0.0.0.0:3000
** Use CTRL-C to stop.
```

(Under Linux or Macintosh OS X, you can omit the `ruby` command and write simply
`script/server`, but it does no harm, so we included it for the convenience of Windows
users typing commands into their DOS terminals.)

The development server runs on port 3000[12] of `localhost` by default, so you can
access the Rails start page at `http://localhost:3000/`. You should see something like
the screenshot in Figure 2.3. Clicking on the "About your application's environment"
link shows information about your site's local environment (Figure 2.4).

---

[10] The specific server depends somewhat on your configuration and platform. Until recently, the development
server was a lightweight HTTP server called WEBrick; nowadays some installations use Mongrel instead, a
production-quality server written in Ruby. Either one works.

[11] Since the server takes over the window in which it is started, we recommend opening a new terminal to act
as a dedicated server window.

[12] The standard port number for websites is port 80, but special privileges are needed to run on low-numbered
ports, so the Rails development server runs on port 3000 by default.

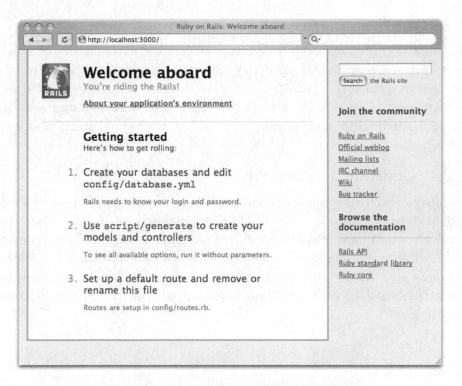

Figure 2.3   Here's proof that your server is running.

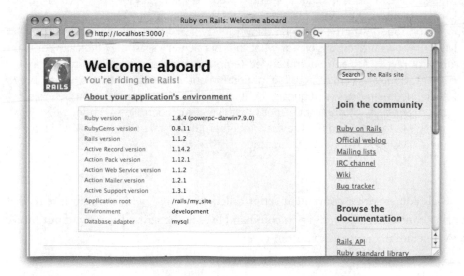

Figure 2.4   Information about the Ruby on Rails environment.

2.2 Our first pages

Now that we've got those boring but necessary preliminaries out of the way, it's time to get started on RailsSpace. Our goal in this section is to make the front page of our site, so that if we go to `http://localhost.com:3000/` it says something like "Welcome to RailsSpace!" Since we know that we'll want more than just a front page, we'll add "About Us" and "Help" pages as well.

2.2.1 Generating a controller

The first step in creating pages for our site is to make a site *controller*. The controller is the C in MVC, the design architecture used by Rails (see the sidebar "Easy as 1-2-3"); you can think of the controller as a container for a group of related pages. Rails controllers are pure Ruby code, with Ruby functions, called *actions*, which correspond roughly to individual pages. (Don't worry if this seems overly abstract at this point; the only real way to understand the MVC architecture is to absorb it by osmosis, and that might take some time.)

Easy as 1-2-3

Rails uses the *model-view-controller* architecture, also known as MVC (Figure 2.5). Models contain "business logic," including representations of the objects (users, personal data, friendships, etc.) used by your web application; models are responsible for communicating with the back-end data store, typically a relational database such as MySQL. Views are responsible for what the user actually sees; they typically contain a mix of raw HTML and an embedded template language for generating dynamic content. Controllers are responsible for figuring out what to do with user input: They handle incoming browser requests, call the appropriate functions on model objects if necessary, and—through the *actions* that live inside controllers—render views into pure HTML for return to the browser. Together, these three components make for a natural division of labor in web applications.

Rails comes with a convenient script called `generate`, which we can use to make our first controller. The `generate` command lives in the script directory of our project, so to generate the controller you can type[13]

```
> ruby script/generate controller <ControllerName> [optional actions]
```

---

[13] You can add the flag `--help` to the end of any Rails script to display help information.

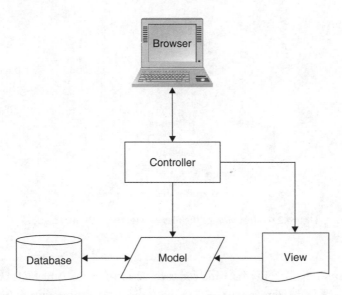

Figure 2.5   Simple representation of the MVC architecture.

Let's call our initial, generic controller `Site`. While we're at it, let's generate some of the actions we know we'll need. We'll start with an `index` action for our front page,[14] together with `about` and `help` actions for the two other pages on our (proto)site. Making sure that you're still in your new `rails_space` directory, create the Site controller and the actions as follows:

```
> ruby script/generate controller Site index about help
      exists  app/controllers/
      exists  app/helpers/
      create  app/views/site
      exists  test/functional/
      create  app/controllers/site_controller.rb
      create  test/functional/site_controller_test.rb
      create  app/helpers/site_helper.rb
      create  app/views/site/index.rhtml
      create  app/views/site/about.rhtml
      create  app/views/site/help.rhtml
```

Note that `generate` creates a bunch of files (Figure 2.6).[15] Probably the most important is a controller corresponding to our controller name, `app/controllers/site_controller.rb`, which is a Ruby file (hence the `.rb` filename extension). It also

---

[14] The name "index" is based on the (somewhat obscure) convention of using index.html as the default page on static HTML sites.

[15] In case you ever need to undo the work done by `generate`, you can use `ruby script/destroy controller <ControllerName>`. That's certainly a lot easier than deleting a bunch of files by hand.

Figure 2.6   Tree view of the files we created with `generate`.

makes an *rhtml* ("Ruby HTML") file for each action (`index.rhtml`, `about.rhtml`, and `help.rhtml`) in the `app/views/site/` directory; these rhtml files are templates for our site's pages (Section 2.3). The `generate` script also creates a test file (`test/functional/site_controller_test.rb`), which we'll learn more about in Chapter 5, and a site helper file (`site_helper.rb`), which will contain any utility functions that we write in the course of filling in the pages on our site (the first example of which is in Section 4.4.1).

2.2.2 The Site controller

Now that we've generated it, let's take a look at the Site controller:

Listing 2.1 app/controllers/site_controller.rb

```
class SiteController < ApplicationController

  def index
  end

  def about
  end

  def help
  end
end
```

This is our first example of a Ruby file. Each of the actions we wanted (`index`, `about`, and `help`) shows up as a blank Ruby function (defined using the `def` keyword).[16] Eventually, we'll fill in these functions, but for now we'll leave them alone.

Perhaps the most important feature of this file is the strange-looking line

```
class SiteController < ApplicationController
```

Ruby uses the < character to indicate *inheritance*; what this line means is that our Site controller automatically has all the functionality of ApplicationController. But what does that mean? We can find out by looking at the Application controller file:

Listing 2.2 app/controllers/application.rb

```
class ApplicationController < ActionController::Base
  .
  .
  .
end
```

Now we've gotten to the bottom of it. `ActionController::Base` is a Ruby class defined by Rails, which contains functions for performing many common web-programming tasks, such as accessing form parameters and session variables. The top controller (`ApplicationController`) for our application inherits from this base class, thereby inheriting all of that functionality; SiteController, in turn, inherits from `ApplicationController`. We won't need any of the functions or variables defined by `ActionController::Base` in this chapter, but starting in Chapter 3 we will see many examples. Impatient readers can dig into `ActionController::Base` by looking it up in the Rails API at

```
http://api.rubyonrails.org/classes/ActionController/Base.html
```

(see the sidebar "The Rails API").

The Rails API

The entire Rails API (application programming interface) is available online at

```
http://api.rubyonrails.org/
```

---

[16] If you ever want to add more actions to a particular controller, don't try to do it using `generate`; just add another function definition for each new action by editing the controller file directly.

Figure 2.7   The default view for the Site controller.

When programming Rails, you may find that (like us) you consult the API frequently. To search for something in the API (such as `ActionController::Base`), we usually just use the "find" feature of our browsers.

By the way, if you want to have the Rails API and other documentation available on your local machine, install the docs using[17]

```
> gem rdoc --all
```

and then start the gem documentation server using

```
> gemserver
```

Now all of the documentation is available on your local machine on port 8808:

```
http://localhost:8808
```

2.2.3   Rails URLs

Even though we've hardly done anything, we actually already have a working site, which we can see at `http://localhost:3000/site/index` (Figure 2.7). Notice that the URL contains the base of our site (i.e., `localhost:3000` when in development mode) followed by the controller (`site`) and the action (`index`). Many Rails URLs follow this general form, which we can write abstractly as

```
http://localhost:3000/<controller>/<action>
```

From this template, you can infer that `http://localhost:3000/site/index` goes to the `index` action in the `site` controller. In our case, since `index` is the default action in Rails, we can omit its name—that is, `http://localhost:3000/site/index` and `http://localhost:3000/site` go to the same page.

---

[17]Warning: This takes a *long* time.

At this point, if you're used to static HTML pages or even dynamic pages generated by, say, PHP or ASP, you may be wondering why we write `http://localhost:3000/site/index` instead of `http://localhost:3000/site/index.rhtml`. There are several reasons. First, it's probably a mistake to expose our choice of web application framework by putting "rhtml" in the URL. Rails programmers (among others) consider the appearance of the filename extension (say, `.php` or `.asp`) in the URL to be a design flaw, since those site's users almost certainly don't care about which technology was used to make the site; moreover, any site that decides to convert from ASP to PHP will regret having to break all its former URLs. Also, we want to think of the `index` as something more general than a web page; since Rails is designed to make web applications, it's likely that many of our URLs will lead to some sort of calculation or database call. We think of our URLs as pieces of a computer program rather than simply pages on a website.

There's also an aesthetic aspect to Rails URLs: The Rails community values "pretty URLs," with human-readable and -guessable words in the URL and without a lot of filename extensions and punctuation mucking it up. An example of an ugly URL is something like

`http://example.com/blog/post.asp?val=1047`

This is just ugly.[18] If `example.com` used Rails, the URL would be

`http://example.com/blog/post/1047`

In this URL you might guess that `blog` is a controller and `post` is the action. (We'll see in Section 9.1.1 how Rails handles things like the `1047` at the end.) Much better, no?

2.2.4 Changing the route

Of course, there are two major things wrong with our front page. First, we don't want the URL to be `http://localhost:3000/site`; we want it to be `http://localhost:3000/`, so that the public site will live at `http://RailsSpace.com/`. And second, we want the page to contain some (possibly) useful information. Let's take care of the URL first.

The machinery that Rails uses to make nice URLs relies on a configuration file called `routes.rb`. For our case, all we need to do is make the Site controller handle the root

---

[18] It's possible to make these URLs pretty, but it typically requires digging into the webserver and using something such as the `mod_rewrite` module for Apache. That's kind of a pain, and the profusion of `.asp` extensions on the web shows that even a minor annoyance can be enough to prevent people from doing something. In any case, with Rails pretty URLs come for free.

of the site. The way to do this is to open the `config/routes.rb` file and uncomment[19] the line

```
# map.connect ", :controller => "welcome"
```

and change it to this:

```
map.connect ", :controller => "site"
```

This should look like magic at this point (that is to say, this is probably confusing). Routing requests is a fairly advanced topic, and it's unfortunate that we have to introduce it so early, but we think it's important to make our URLs look good right from the start. (When we were Rails newbies, it made us nervous to have `http://localhost:3000/` be some funky default Rails page rather than what *we* wanted it to be.) We'll talk more about routes in Section 9.1.1, and we'll explain the syntax `:controller => "site"` in Section 2.4.3; for now, just take it on faith. You'll see momentarily that it works.

Unfortunately, even with all that work we're not quite done, since Rails looks for a file called `index.html` in the `public` directory. If that file is there, Rails will return the default page, as seen in Figure 2.3, so we have to delete it to get the behavior we want:

```
> rm public/index.html
```

2.3 Rails views

We are finally ready to change the content of the index page by editing `app/views/site/index.rhtml`, which is a Rails *view* (the V in MVC):[20]

Listing 2.3 app/views/site/index.rhtml

```
<!DOCTYPE HTML PUBLIC "-//W3C//DTD XHTML 1.0 Strict//EN"
  "http://www.w3.org/TR/xhtml1/DTD/xhtml1-strict.dtd">
<html>
  <head>
    <title>RailsSpace</title>
  </head>
  <body>
    <h1>Welcome to RailsSpace!</h1>
    <p>This is going to be the best site ever!</p>
  </body>
</html>
```

---

[19] Ruby (like Perl, Python, and Unix shell languages) uses the "#" character for comments.
[20] Recall from the introduction that all the source code for RailsSpace is available for download at `http://RailsSpace.com/book`.

Figure 2.8   Our front page.

Now the default page appears at `http://localhost:3000/` with our own customized content (Figure 2.8).

2.3.1   Embedded Ruby

We mentioned rhtml files in our discussion of the `generate` script in Section 2.2, and `index.rhtml` is our first concrete example. In general, rhtml files consist of HTML combined with embedded Ruby (ERb) commands. Our example is the simplest possible kind of rhtml file—it's just static HTML. We will see a less trivial example containing some ERb in Section 2.4.

Since we've defined a couple of other actions, let's go ahead and flesh out their corresponding views (see Figures 2.9 and 2.10):

Figure 2.9   About Us page.

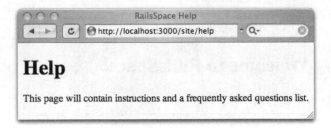

Figure 2.10   Help page.

Listing 2.4   app/views/site/about.rhtml

```
<!DOCTYPE HTML PUBLIC "-//W3C//DTD XHTML 1.0 Strict//EN"
  "http://www.w3.org/TR/xhtml1/DTD/xhtml1-strict.dtd">
<html>
  <head>
    <title>About RailsSpace</title>
  </head>
  <body>
    <h1>About Us</h1>
    <p>RailsSpace is a social networking website for Ruby on Rails
enthusiasts (and whoever else shows up).</p>
  </body>
</html>
```

Listing 2.5   app/views/site/help.rhtml

```
<!DOCTYPE HTML PUBLIC "-//W3C//DTD XHTML 1.0 Strict//EN"
  "http://www.w3.org/TR/xhtml1/DTD/xhtml1-strict.dtd">
<html>
  <head>
    <title>RailsSpace Help</title>
  </head>
  <body>
    <h1>Help</h1>
    <p>This page will contain instructions and a frequently asked questions
list.</p>
  </body>
</html>
```

2.4 Layouts

So far, we haven't done anything that we couldn't do just as easily with static HTML files. You might notice, though, that a lot of the HTML is the same in these three files.

We can use Rails to eliminate the repetition by using *layouts* to handle the redundant boilerplate HTML on the top and bottom of our pages. We simply create a new rhtml file in the `app/views/layouts/` directory and place the repeated code there. Then we add a magic word or two (explained momentarily) to reconstruct the original pages. You can give the layout file any name you please (see the sidebar "Alternate layouts"), but Rails will find a layout automatically if it has the same name as the controller:

Listing 2.6 app/views/layouts/site.rhtml

```
<!DOCTYPE HTML PUBLIC "-//W3C//DTD XHTML 1.0 Strict//EN"
  "http://www.w3.org/TR/xhtml1/DTD/xhtml1-strict.dtd">
<html>
  <head>
    <title><%= @title %></title>
  </head>
  <body>
    <%= @content_for_layout %>
  </body>
</html>
```

Alternate layouts

To use a different layout for the Site controller, create a file called `app/views/layouts/different.rhtml` for example, and then add a line after the Site-Controller class declaration referring to it:

Listing 2.7 app/controllers/site_controller.rb

```
class SiteController < ApplicationController
  layout "different"
  .
  .
  .
end
```

Now we can pare down the views considerably:

Listing 2.8 app/views/site/index.rhtml

```
<h1>Welcome!</h1>
<p>This is going to be the best site ever!</p>
```

Listing 2.9 app/views/site/about.rhtml

```
<h1>About Us</h1>
<p>RailsSpace is a social networking website for Ruby on Rails enthusiasts
(and whoever else shows up).</p>
```

Listing 2.10 app/views/site/help.rhtml

```
<h1>Help</h1>
<p>This page will contain instructions and a frequently asked questions
list.</p>
```

Keeping your code DRY?!?

In general, Ruby on Rails developers take particular pride in not repeating code. This is not a new idea, of course; eliminating repetition by using appropriate abstractions is as old as computer programming itself. But, from a cultural point of view, Rails programmers are particularly vigorous supporters of code reuse. There's even an acronym for the principle, which has gained some popularity in Rails circles: DRY = Don't Repeat Yourself.

   This laudable principle leads to some rather egregious abuses of the English language, in phrases such as "Rails is a DRY framework" and "Now let's DRY out our code." We'll try to avoid inflicting such violence on our native tongue, but we will not hesitate to use the many wonderful features that Ruby and Rails provide to reduce duplication.

Notice how much less code there is now. Although programmer productivity is often measured in lines of code produced per unit time, often the greatest productivity comes from eliminating repetition (see sidebar "Keeping your code DRY?!?"), which makes programs much more maintainable and extensible. (Still, we don't recommend that you brag to your manager or client that you "wrote negative 1,000 lines of code yesterday.")

2.4.1   ERb, actions, and instance variables

The layout in the previous section introduces our first example of the ERb template language mentioned briefly in Section 2.3.1. In rhtml files, wrapping an expression in <%=...%> evaluates the expression as Ruby code and then inserts the resulting value into the page. For example, if the variable @foo (pronounced "at foo") contains the string "bar", then <%= @foo %> would insert the word "bar" into the file. (We'll explain the funny "@" symbol at the front of the variable name later in this section.)

The real magic of the layout is in the line <%= @content_for_layout%>, which you now know inserts the value of the variable @content_for_layout into the layout. But where does this variable come from? When Rails processes the URL http://localhost:3000/site/about/, it puts the results of processing about. rhtml into @contentforlayout; in our case, @contentforlayout contains the string <h1>Help</h1>\n<p>This page will contain instructions and a frequently asked questions list.</p>.[21] Rails then processes the layout, thereby substituting the content into the page at the appropriate place.[22]

A second example of ERb in our layout is <%= @title %>, but, unlike @content_for_layout, @title is not created automatically by Rails. As you might guess, we want @title to be a string with the title of the current page, but where does it come from? We define @title in the actions inside the Site controller as follows:

Listing 2.11 app/controllers/site_controller.rb

```
class SiteController < ApplicationController
  def index
    @title = "Welcome to RailsSpace!"
  end

  def about
    @title = "About RailsSpace"
  end

  def help
    @title = "RailsSpace Help"
  end
end
```

You've probably noticed by now that both of the variables we've seen inside embedded Ruby begin with the "@" symbol. This is no accident; a variable defined

---

[21] In Unix, the line break is represented as the newline character, which is written as \n.

[22] This isn't quite what happens; Rails uses a more advanced feature of Ruby called *blocks* to process templates. In fact, the currently favored method for implementing layouts uses <%= yield %> in place of <%= @content_for_layout %>, which is a big hint to the Ruby cognoscenti that blocks are involved, since the yield keyword is characteristic of blocks. We will switch to yield in future chapters, but for now @content_for_layout is much easier to understand (and in fact may still be more common in Rails code than yield in this context).

in the controller is automatically available in the view (including the layout) as long as its name starts with "@." In Ruby, these are known as *instance variables*, but for our purposes their relevant property is their availability in the view. We will see many examples of instance variables throughout the book.

2.4.2   Recap: slicing up a page

Let's take a moment to review where we started and where we've gone. Consider, for example, the help page, which started like this:

Listing 2.12   app/views/site/help.rhtml

```
<!DOCTYPE HTML PUBLIC "-//W3C//DTD XHTML 1.0 Strict//EN"
  "http://www.w3.org/TR/xhtml1/DTD/xhtml1-strict.dtd">
<html>
  <head>
    <title>RailsSpace Help</title>
  </head>
  <body>
    <h1>Help</h1>
    <p>This page will contain instructions and a frequently asked
questions list.</p>
  </body>
</html>
```

We've now effectively split this page into three different pieces:

- A title, which we've placed in the Site controller (`app/controllers/site_controller.rb`)
- The HTML skeleton, which we've placed in the site layout (`app/views/layouts/site.rhtml`)
- The body content, which has stayed in the view (`app/views/site/help.rhtml`)

This may seem like an awful lot of trouble, and it would be if there were only one page on the site. But since we expect RailsSpace to have many pages, partitioning our application in this way gives us a great deal of flexibility. For a concrete example, we need look no further than the common task of adding site-wide navigation.

2.4.3   Adding navigation

Having now used the layout to capture the structure common to each page, adding site-wide navigation is simple, since any navigation links we add will automatically be included on every page. We'll create these links using the Rails `linkto` function and separate them using the vertical bar character (|):

Listing 2.13 app/views/layouts/site.rhtml

```
<!DOCTYPE HTML PUBLIC "-//W3C//DTD XHTML 1.0 Strict//EN"
  "http://www.w3.org/TR/xhtml1/DTD/xhtml1-strict.dtd">
<html>
  <head>
    <title><%= @title %></title>
  </head>
  <body>
    <%= link_to("Home",     { :action => "index" }) %> |
    <%= link_to("About Us", { :action => "about" }) %> |
    <%= link_to("Help",     { :action => "help"  }) %>
    <%= @content_for_layout %>
  </body>
</html>
```

This makes our front page look like Figure 2.11.

`link_to` is our first example of a Rails function for HTML generation. Even this simple example introduces a lot of new material, so let's break it down into bite-sized pieces.

We know that code between <%= and %> is evaluated as Ruby code, and the value returned is inserted into the page at that point; based on its name, you should be able to guess that `link_to` is a function that returns a string corresponding to an HTML link tag a (also called an anchor tag). The first argument to `link_to` is the text of the link as displayed in the browser, so `link_to("About Us")` returns the string <a href="/">About Us</a>. That's not the right address, though; we need to tell `link_to` which action to use when constructing the URL. For this purpose `link_to` takes a second, optional argument, which is a Ruby *hash*.

Figure 2.11 A navigation bar now appears at the top of each page.

Hashes are an essential part of Ruby and Rails, so let's take a moment to understand them.

2.4.4 Hashes

A hash (short for *hash table*), also called an *associative array* or a *dictionary*, is a data type consisting of key-value pairs; you can think of a hash as a sort of generalized array, with the index type not limited to integers. Probably the best way to understand hashes is to look at a few examples using the interactive Ruby program irb.[23] We'll start with an empty hash {}, try to access a nonexistent element, and then add several key-value pairs:

```
> irb
irb(main):001:0> h = {}
=> {}
irb(main):002:0> h["foo"]
=> nil
irb(main):003:0> h["foo"] = "bar"
=> "bar"
irb(main):004:0> h["foo"]
=> "bar"
irb(main):005:0> h["baz"] = "quux"
=> "quux"
irb(main):006:0> h[17] = 123.5
=> 123.5
irb(main):007:0> h
=> {17=>123.5, "baz"=>"quux", "foo"=>"bar"}
```

Note that we access a hash value by putting the key in square brackets; if the hash doesn't have a value corresponding to a particular key, it returns nil, which is a special Ruby value for "nothing at all." We can also add elements to the hash using square brackets, as in h["foo"] = "bar". If we type the name of the hash (h in this case), irb prints the key-value pairs. Ruby hashes can contain multiple types; you probably recognize strings, integers, and floating-point numbers in the examples above. Also note that hashes have no intrinsic sense of order, so your version of irb might print out the key-value pairs in a different order.

Always having to build up hashes using the bracket notation would be cumbersome, so Ruby lets us define a hash explicitly using curly braces and key-value pairs as follows:

```
irb(main):008:0> h = { :action => "help", :controller => "site"}
=> {:action=>"help", :controller=>"site"}
```

Each key in this example is a *symbol*, which may be unfamiliar to many readers since few languages have this type. Of course, it's just our luck that this is precisely the syntax that occurs in link_to.

---

[23] irb comes bundled with Ruby; just run irb from the command line.

2.4.5 Symbols

A Ruby symbol is just a label, formed in the same way as a string except with a single colon instead of quotes. Most languages use strings as labels, especially in hashes, but a string has a lot of properties that have nothing to do with its role as a label—you can find a string's length, access a substring, compare it to a regular expression, reverse it, and so on. Ruby takes the next logical step and creates a separate data type for labels; you can think of symbols as strings without all those other unnecessary attributes. As a result, symbols can be compared very quickly, whereas comparing strings requires that you walk down both strings character by character. Efficient comparison makes symbols ideal for use as hash keys.

2.4.6 Polishing up `link_to`

We're now in a position to understand the expression

```
link_to("About Us", { :action =>"about" })
```

The `link_to` function makes an HTML link tag by taking the string in its first argument and putting it inside the `a` tag, and it constructs the appropriate URL defined by the optional hash in its second argument, which it puts after the `href` inside the opening tag. In other words,

```
link_to("About Us", { :action =>"about" }}
```

returns the string

```
<a href="/site/about">About Us</a>
```

Since

```
<%= link_to("About Us", { :action =>"about" }) %>
```

inserts the result of evaluating the enclosed Ruby code, once the rhtml has been processed, the source code for the home page appears as follows (this is what you see if you use the "view source" feature of your browser):

```
<!DOCTYPE HTML PUBLIC "-//W3C//DTD XHTML 1.0 Strict//EN"
  "http://www.w3.org/TR/xhtml1/DTD/xhtml1-strict.dtd">
<html>
  <head>
    <title>Welcome to RailsSpace!</title>
  </head>
  <body>
    <a href="/">Home</a> |
    <a href="/site/about">About Us</a> |
    <a href="/site/help">Help</a>
    <h1>Welcome!</h1>
<p>This is going to be the best site ever!</p>
  </body>
</html>
```

What link_to is doing may not seem too amazing at this stage, but it is actually constructing the appropriate URL using rules set in the routes.rb file that we introduced in Section 2.2.4. This means that link_to is more flexible than hard-coding the URL; for example, if we decided to change the address for "About Us" to about_us, we could use routes.rb to ensure that a request for about would be handled by the about_us action. It is true, though, that for this simple example hard-coding the address isn't difficult; the fact of the matter is that using Ruby code rather than HTML to create links is a nearly universal Rails convention—due in part to the flexibility mentioned above, to be sure, but it's also an aesthetic judgment, a matter of style.

2.4.7 Some matters of style

Before leaving link_to, we should mention two more important matters of style. Several aspects of Ruby syntax are optional, depending on context; in particular, parentheses are optional in function calls, and curly braces are optional in hashes when they are the final argument to a function. The usual style used by Rails programmers omits these optional characters in many cases, including our link_to example. Although the code we produced is perfectly valid, it is not idiomatically correct; most Rails programmers would write instead

Listing 2.14 app/views/layouts/site.rhtml

```
<!DOCTYPE HTML PUBLIC "-//W3C//DTD XHTML 1.0 Strict//EN"
  "http://www.w3.org/TR/xhtml1/DTD/xhtml1-strict.dtd">
<html>
  <head>
    <title><%= @title %></title>
  </head>
  <body>
    <%= link_to "Home",     :action => "index" %> |
    <%= link_to "About Us", :action => "about" %> |
    <%= link_to "Help",     :action => "help"  %>
    <%= @content_for_layout %>
  </body>
</html>
```

This is the convention we will use in this book.

We should also note that, in the context of Rails programming, "good style" is a moving target, both because Rails is a young framework and because web development itself is a young and rapidly changing field. Reflecting on the large number of code changes in the second edition of *Agile Web Development with Rails*, Dave Thomas writes in the preface that "In the time since the first book [i.e., the first edition] was released, we'd all gained a lot more experience of just *how* to write a Rails application. Some stuff that seemed like a great idea didn't work so well in practice, and other features that initially seemed peripheral turned out to be significant." We expect this process to continue; as Rails evolves, the practices and conventions constituting good Rails style will evolve as well.

2.4.8 Polishing navigation

There is another reason to use Ruby to create links beyond those cited above: For a proper navigation system, we shouldn't link to the page that is currently displayed. This is a very common pattern on websites—and you'll often find that if a particular pattern is common, Rails has made it trivially easy to do. In the present case, it turns out that Rails provides a function for exactly the feature we want; we just change the `linkto` function to `link_to_unless_current`:

Listing 2.15 app/views/layouts/site.rhtml

```
<!DOCTYPE HTML PUBLIC "-//W3C//DTD XHTML 1.0 Strict//EN"
  "http://www.w3.org/TR/xhtml1/DTD/xhtml1-strict.dtd">
<html>
  <head>
    <title><%= @title %></title>
  </head>
  <body>
    <%= link_to_unless_current "Home",     :action => "index" %> |
    <%= link_to_unless_current "About Us", :action => "about" %> |
    <%= link_to_unless_current "Help",     :action => "help" %>
    <%= @content_for_layout %>
  </body>
</html>
```

Now Rails will automatically use the address of the current page to decide whether or not to make a link (Figure 2.12).

2.4.9 Finding things for yourself

You might be getting nervous about something at this point. If we didn't tell you about `link_to_unless_current`, how might have you discovered it for yourself? Well, there was a time when we didn't know about it either. Here's how we found out. We knew that Rails adheres to a naming convention whereby a group of related

Figure 2.12   The effect of using the `linktounlesscurrent`.

functions have related names, usually of the form `original_function_name` and `original_function_name_with_modification` (and now you know about this convention, too!). In the present case, we suspected that `link_to` might have a related function to do what we wanted, so we went to the Rails API at `http://api.rubyonrails.org/` and looked it up; in the process, as hoped, we found several `link_to`-type functions:

```
link_to
link_to_if
link_to_image
link_to_remote
link_to_unless
link_to_unless_current
```

It doesn't take a couple of rocket scientists to figure out that `link_to_unless_current` is what we were looking for.

2.5 Developing with style

Some programmers like to isolate themselves completely from the aesthetic side of web development. While we can certainly understand this tendency, we don't recommend it. Inserting stylistic elements into the code, even if they are fairly primitive by the standards of real graphic designers, will in fact help the project along. A site that looks more like a finished project is a great source of motivation; moreover, since the final product will have a graphical user interface, programmers should start thinking about site design, page length, form simplicity, and layout as soon as possible. If you build in design from an early stage, it will feel like a natural part of the application rather than an add-on.

As you may have guessed from the DOCTYPE declaration in all our HTML files, we are fans of web standards, including valid XHTML and Cascading Style Sheets[24]; those of you familiar with web standards won't be surprised that we will be adding styles using a CSS file. You also probably won't be surprised that Rails has a helper function (called stylesheet_link_tag) for including CSS files into Rails applications; here's how to include a file called "site.css":

```
<%= stylesheet_link_tag "site" %>
```

The proper place to put this is inside the `<head></head>` tag of our site layout:

Listing 2.16 app/views/layouts/site.rhtml

```
<!DOCTYPE HTML PUBLIC "-//W3C//DTD XHTML 1.0 Strict//EN"
   "http://www.w3.org/TR/xhtml1/DTD/xhtml1-strict.dtd">
<html>
  <head>
    <title><%= @title %></title>
    <%= stylesheet_link_tag "site" %>
  </head>
  <body>
    <div id="whole_page">
      <div id="header">RailsSpace</div>
      <div id="nav">
        <%= link_to_unless_current "Home",     :action => "index" %> |
        <%= link_to_unless_current "About Us", :action => "about" %> |
        <%= link_to_unless_current "Help",     :action => "help" %>
      </div>
      <div id="content">
        <%= @content_for_layout %>
      </div>
    </div>
  </body>
</html>
```

Note that in addition to adding the style tag, we wrap the navigation, header, and content sections in `<div></div>` tags so that we can style those sections separately. In addition, there is a whole_page wrapper for all of the page content.

To make use of the CSS ids, create the site stylesheet in the directory public/stylesheets/ and add a few style rules:

---

[24] Cascading Style Sheets provide a unified way to apply styling to web pages. See http://www.w3.org/Style/CSS/ for more information.

Listing 2.17   public/stylesheets/site.css

```
body {
  font-family: sans-serif;
  background: gray;
  margin: 0;
  text-align: center;
}
#whole_page {
  width: 50em;
  margin: auto;
  padding: 0;
  text-align: left;
  border-width:  0 1px 1px 1px;
  border-color:  black;
  border-style:  solid;
}

#header {
  color: white;
  background: maroon; /* No "ruby" defined in HTML color names! */
  font-size: 24pt;
  padding: 0.25em;
  margin-bottom: 0;
}

#nav {
  color: black;
  font-size: 12pt;
  font-weight: bold;
  background: #ccc;
  padding: 0.5em;
}

#nav a, #nav a:visited  {
  color: maroon;
  text-decoration: none;
}

#nav a:hover {
  border-bottom: 2px dotted maroon;
}

#content {
  height: 100%;
  background:  white;
  padding: 1em;
}
#content h1 {
  font-size: 18pt;
}
```

Our pages now look like Figures 2.13–2.15.

Figure 2.13   The main page with CSS defined.

Figure 2.14   The about page with CSS defined.

Figure 2.15   The help page with CSS defined.

CHAPTER 3

Modeling users

Having a front page up and running is a good start, but now it's time to get to the core of any social networking site: a database of registered users. In the process, we'll experience the remarkable power of *models*—the M in MVC—which, perhaps more than anything else, sets Rails apart from other frameworks.

The purpose of this chapter is to build a User model to represent RailsSpace users, deciding which attributes (such as screen names, email addresses, etc.) we want them to have. The User model will rely on Active Record, a library for communicating between Ruby objects and relational databases. We'll spend much of the chapter exploring Active Record using the *console*, which is essentially a command line for Rails. We'll also learn about *migrations*, which provide a convenient and flexible way to manage our data models using pure Ruby.

3.1 Creating the User model

In this section we'll get started with data modeling by creating a basic User model. As a prelude to this, we'll install and configure a database and some associated tools. Then we'll use Rails migrations to create the table and columns for the User model.

3.1.1 Setting up the database

Since we want to store our users in a database, we first need to install one. Its advocates often describe Rails as being *database agnostic*, which means that almost all Rails database functions will work for a variety of databases,[1] but we still have to pick one to get started

---

[1] So shouldn't it be *database polytheistic*?

43

(see the sidebar "Choosing a database").[2] Since we're lazy, we'll go with the Rails default database, MySQL.

> **Choosing a database**
>
> Rails works with MySQL, Oracle, PostgreSQL, and SQLite, among others. We use MySQL, which is the default, but we have heard especially good things about Post-greSQL (which everyone calls simply Postgres), and the reader is warned that the authors have never met a Postgres user who didn't look down on MySQL. The con-tempt that Postgres users have for MySQL might have made sense a few years ago, but MySQL has come a long way in that time, and we're not embarrassed to use it. Nevertheless, we still sometimes secretly worry that those Postgres users know some-thing we don't. You might want to give it a try.
>
> By the way, MySQL is pronounced "My-Ess-Cue-Ell." If you insist on pronouncing it "My-Sequel," Aure won't hold it against you, but Michael will.

At this point you need to download and install MySQL (version 5 or later) for your platform.[3] You might also look into getting the MySQL query browser[4] (cross-platform), PHPMyAdmin[5] (cross-platform), CocoaMySQL[6] (OS X), or HeidiSQL[7] (Windows), which provide graphical user interfaces for interacting with MySQL databases. Once you've done that, you'll be ready to create the database[8] that we will use for RailsSpace.

Rails uses a convention of separate databases for development, production, and test-ing; that way, if you happen to write some action that clobbers the database, you won't accidentally destroy your production machine. There's also a standard convention for the database names: the project name in underscore format (that is, `rails_space` in-stead of `RailsSpace`), followed by an underscore, followed by the type of database. In our case, the development database will be called `rails_space_development`.

---

[2] Though it's a bit of a pain, you can actually run Rails without a database, in which case you are a *database atheist*.

[3] `http://dev.mysql.com/downloads/`

[4] `http://www.mysql.com/products/tools/query-browser/`

[5] `http://www.phpmyadmin.net/home_page/`

[6] `http://cocoamysql.sourceforge.net/`

[7] `http://www.heidisql.com/`

[8] In a bit of confusing but standard usage, the word "database" refers both to the overall program (such as MySQL) and to the separate data stores maintained within the program.

You can create this database using a GUI tool, but we're in the habit of using the command line; for MySQL, the command is[9]

```
> mysqladmin create rails_space_development --user=root --password=my_password
```

This uses the `mysqladmin` command to create the database using the root[10] user, assuming that the password is "my_password" (but you should, of course, choose a more secure password than this; see the database documentation for instructions on how to do this).

There's one more step before we can start building our User model: We need to tell Rails how to talk to the database. Rails uses a configuration file written in the YAML format located in `config/database.yml` (see the sidebar "Rhymes with 'camel'"). Let's take a look at it:[11]

Listing 3.1   config/database.yml

```
# MySQL (default setup).   Versions 4.1 and 5.0 are recommended.
#
# Install the MySQL driver:
#   gem install mysql
# On MacOS X:
#   gem install mysql -- --include=/usr/local/lib
# On Windows:
#   There is no gem for Windows.   Install mysql.so from RubyForApache.
#   http://rubyforge.org/projects/rubyforapache
#
# And be sure to use new-style password hashing:
#   http://dev.mysql.com/doc/refman/5.0/en/old-client.html
development:
  adapter: mysql
  database: rails_space_development
  username: root
  password: my_password
  host: localhost

# Warning: The database defined as 'test' will be erased and
# re-generated from your development database when you run 'rake'.
# Do not set this db to the same as development or production.
```

Continues

---

[9] Depending on your platform, you might have to start MySQL first, and you might have to type in the full path name of `mysqladmin` (e.g., `/usr/local/mysql/bin/mysqladmin`).

[10] The term comes from Unix, where `root` is the name of the administrative *superuser* allowed to do basically anything on the system.

[11] You can ignore the stuff at the top of the `database.yml` file about installing the MySQL driver; we just took care of that by installing MySQL.

```
test:
  adapter: mysql
  database: rails_space_test
  username: root
  password:
  host: localhost

production:
  adapter: mysql
  database: rails_space_production
  username: root
  password:
  host: localhost
```

Focus on the part under `development:`. You can see that we've told Rails the username and password to use to connect to the `rails_space_development` database.[12] (Also note that since we followed the conventional naming scheme, Rails already knew the name of our database.) With that bit of configuration done, we're now ready to roll with our data modeling.

> ### Rhymes with "camel"
>
> The `.yml` configuration files used by Rails are written in YAML, a lightweight plain-text language for storing data in a convenient, human-readable format. Its name is a shamelessly geeky two-layer joke. Most computer terms that start with "ya" are "yet another" something; `yacc`, for example, is "yet another compiler-compiler." One might guess, therefore, that YAML is "Yet Another Markup Language." In this case it's a bit of misdirection, though, because YAML uses another common hacker naming tradition, the *recursive acronym*: "YAML Ain't a Markup Language."

3.1.2 Migrations and the User model

Now that we have a database, it's time to make a data model for our users. We will use the standard method for database-backed websites and create a `users` table, with table columns corresponding to the user attributes. We'll start with three attributes: `screen_name`, `email`, and `password`, but (as we'll see in Section 3.2.6) Rails makes it easy to add more attributes later if we want.

---

[12] If you have databases for multiple projects, you might want to create a different user for each one instead of using root for all of them. Go ahead and create a `rails_space` MySQL user at this point if using root makes you unhappy.

As in the case of controllers, the Rails `generate` command is the most convenient way to make a new model, which we'll call `User`:[13]

```
> ruby script/generate model User
      exists   app/models/
      exists   test/unit/
      exists   test/fixtures/
      create   app/models/user.rb
      create   test/unit/user_test.rb
      create   test/fixtures/users.yml
      create   db/migrate
      create   db/migrate/001_create_users.rb
```

The final file created by `generate`, `db/migrate/001_create_users.rb`, is the first file we need to edit. It contains a migration that creates the first version of our users table. It used to be necessary to learn the SQL DDL (Structured Query Language Data Definition Language) in order to create database tables, but migrations provide a way to manipulate databases using Ruby instead. In addition to saving you the trouble of learning SQL DDL, migrations make it possible to use the same files to create tables in Oracle, MySQL, or whatever supported database you're using.[14] They also make it very easy for your data model to evolve and devolve as needed so that it matches the code.

3.1.3   The first user migration

The `generate` script creates a skeleton migration file for creating the users table:

Listing 3.2   db/migrate/001_create_users.rb

```ruby
class CreateUsers < ActiveRecord::Migration
  def self.up
    create_table :users do |t|
      # t.column :name, :string
    end
  end

  def self.down
    drop_table :users
  end
end
```

---

[13] As with controller names, it's conventional to use CamelCase for the model name—which, also as in the case of controllers, `generate` promptly converts to underscore format.

[14] This is part of what it means to be database agnostic.

The file has two functions, `self.up` and `self.down`, which represent migrations up from version 0 to version 1 or down from version 1 to version 0.[15] In the case of the skeleton file, the `self.up` function creates an empty `users` table, while `self.down` undoes the action of `self.up` by dropping the `users` table from the database. The line under `create_table`, which is commented out, serves as an example of how to create a column in the database table of type `string` and with name `name`.

We want a nonempty `users` table, so we have to define columns of data types to store the information about our users. Let's expand the `self.up` function to create columns for each user's screen name, email address, and password:

Listing 3.3 db/migrate/001_create_users.rb

```ruby
class CreateUsers < ActiveRecord::Migration
  def self.up
    create_table :users do |t|
      t.column :screen_name, :string
      t.column :email,       :string
      t.column :password,    :string
    end
  end

  def self.down
    drop_table :users
  end
end
```

If the syntax for table creation looks strange, that's not surprising: It's our first example of a remarkable Ruby construct called a *block*, which is a way of bundling together a group of statements (in this case, all the code between `do` and `end`). Since we want to get on with our data modeling, it would take us too far afield to explain blocks in detail now, but we'll return to the subject in Section 4.2.3.

Rails table names

The detail-oriented reader may have noticed that we (or, more accurately, the `generate` command) called our user table `users` instead of `user`. This is an aspect of Rails design philosophy, which uses natural language to help us store the data model in our heads as well as in our computers: It just makes more sense to say

```
SELECT screen_name FROM users WHERE id=1
```

---

[15] Don't worry about what `self` means at this point.

> than
>
> ```
> SELECT screen_name FROM user WHERE id=1
> ```
>
> Rails has a powerful *inflector* that properly pluralizes virtually all the table names you are likely to need. If you come across a word that Rails can't pluralize, or if you decide not to use the default convention, you should do a web search on `Rails set_table_name` to learn about the facilities Rails provides for alternate table naming (including using Rails with legacy database schemas whose tables already have names).

3.1.4   Raking the migration

We make the migration happen using the Ruby utility Rake, which is kind of like a Make command for Ruby (see the sidebar "Make and Rake"):

```
> rake db:migrate
(in /rails/rails_space)
== CreateUsers: migrating ======================================================
-- create_table(:users)
   -> 0.0995s
== CreateUsers: migrated (0.1013s) =============================================
```

This creates a bare-bones user table that contains the columns for screen name, email address, and password.[16] If you take a look at the database with your favorite GUI, you'll see that it now has the `users` table, which in turn has three columns corresponding to those we defined in the migration, as well as an `id` column that Rails creates automatically to identify our users (Figure 3.1). (You also might notice `schema_info`, which is a table that Rails uses for its own internal purposes—see the sidebar "Wiping the database.")

> **Make and Rake**
>
> Readers coming from outside the Unix tradition may not be familiar with Make. The `make` program is most often used to build executables by selectively compiling source code files. Perhaps its best-known use is handling dependencies (defined in a *Makefile*), so that, if source file `foo.c` changes, only files that depend on `foo.c` get recompiled. Make is actually far more general than this, though, and more advanced Makefiles often define commands such as `make doc` to make documentation and `make clean` to remove non-source files (such as object files and executables) that

---

[16] If the `rake` command fails, check to make sure you put the password for your database in `database.yml`.

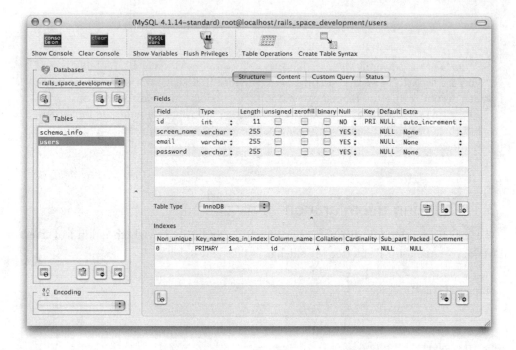

Figure 3.1   Users schema as displayed by CocoaMySQL.

can be rebuilt from the source. The Ruby system Rake (with the associated *Rakefile*) incorporates both the dependency-based build and general utility aspects of its cousin Make.

We referred above to the `self.down` function, which undoes the actions performed by `self.up`. This is a hint about one of the benefits of migrations: We can roll back any changes to the database if desired, simply by reverting to a previous version using a command-line argument to `rake`.[17] For example, to migrate our database back to version 0, we would use

```
> rake db:migrate VERSION=0
(in /rails/rails_space)
== CreateUsers: reverting =======================================
-- drop_table(:users)
   -> 0.0077s
== CreateUsers: reverted (0.0085s) ==============================
```

---

[17] Migrating down potentially destroys data in your database, so it can be helpful to have a mechanism for loading some standard sample data; see Section 10.2 for one possible approach.

Go ahead and play around with rolling back to previous versions now if you like, but be sure to run

```
> rake db:migrate
```

before moving on to the next section.

Wiping the database

Sometimes, in the process of making database migrations, you'll completely screw up the database, especially if you edit the migrations to make them follow a logical progression (perhaps, to pick a random reason, because you're writing a book on Rails). One common symptom is an error message like this:

```
> rake db:migrate VERSION=0
.
.
.
rake aborted!
Mysql::Error <something really scary-looking>
```

It's hard to be more specific than that; trust us when we say that you'll know it when it happens. The main indication is that you will just want to wipe the damn thing clean, and then possibly throw your computer across the room.

Luckily, it's easy to rebuild your database from scratch. The trick is to empty out the `schema_info` table, which stores the migration and version information; once your migrations and database get out of sync, everything goes haywire unless you wipe `schema_info` clean. So, here's what to do if you need to reset your database:

1. Using your favorite GUI or the command line, drop all the tables
2. `rake db:migrate`

Now your database should be squeaky clean. (If you throw your computer across the room, you're on your own.)

3.2 User model validations

It's nice to see that the migration created our table and columns, but what good does it do us? How do we use the database in the context of Rails? Let's take a look at the User model:

Listing 3.4 app/models/user.rb

```
class User < ActiveRecord::Base
end
```

It looks virtually empty, but notice that our user class inherits from something called `ActiveRecord::Base`. This is a big hint that User is more than meets the eye: Because of inheritance, it automatically has all the functionality associated with the ActiveRecord::Base class. Active Record is a large library for interacting with the database in a convenient way, known as an object-relational mapping (ORM).

The heart of an ORM library is a mapping between database tables and classes, where each row maps to an instance of the class (i.e., an object) and each column value is an attribute of the instance. More concretely, in the context of Rails this simply means that instead of writing SQL code to deal with a `screen_name` column in the `users` table, we can just use Ruby code to deal with `user.screen_name`. With Active Record, we can easily create Ruby objects that model our users, validate their properties, save them to the database, and retrieve them at our leisure. The best part is that we (almost) never have to get down-and-dirty with messy SQL; virtually all of our interactions with a database can be done in pure sweet, sweet Ruby.

3.2.1   The console

The best way to understand Active Record is to see a bunch of examples. This is quite difficult in the context of a web page, since most of what Rails does goes on behind the scenes. Happily, Rails comes with a remarkable utility called the console, which is basically the interactive Ruby interpreter `irb` (which we saw when we learned about hashes in Section 2.4.4) run in a Rails environment, so that it has access to all of the standard Rails functions as well as any classes or functions that we write. You can think of the console as a command line for Rails.

In addition to being useful for developing an intuition for Rails functions by interacting with Rails in a concrete way, the console is also an industrial-strength tool: Many a nasty Rails bug has been squashed using the console, and we've even heard that David Heinemeier Hansson, the originator of the Rails framework, relies on the console to administer the popular Basecamp web application. Let's take a look at what it can do:

```
> ruby script/console
Loading development environment.
>> user = User.new(:screen_name => "me",
?>                     :email => "",
?>                     :password => "a")
=> #<User:0xb76fadd0 @new_record=true,
    @attributes={"screen_name"=>"me", "password"=>"a", "email"=>""}>
>> user.screen_name
=> "me"
```

```
>> user.save
=> true
```

Because the console gets started in our Rails development environment, we have access to the `User` class from `user.rb`. In this example, we use the `new` method that automatically comes with any Active Record class, including our `User` class. Using a hash of values, `User.new` initializes a new *instance* of class `User`, which we have called `user`.

To save or to save()

Parentheses are optional on Ruby methods, including those that take no arguments. If you want to, you can certainly use parentheses, which means you can save a user with `user.save()` instead of `user.save`. This might make you Java/Python/PHP programmers out there happier, since `user.save` might look a little bit too close to a regular class attribute for your comfort. On the other hand, leaving off the parentheses in this context is very Rubyish; putting them back on will immediately mark you as a Java/Python/PHP programmer.

The console shows how to access the `screen_name` attribute using the same dot notation used for Ruby method calls. In the final line, we use the `save` method to write the user information to the database (see the sidebar "To save or to save()"), which returns `true` to indicate success.

How can we be sure that the user got saved? We could use our favorite GUI to check the status of the database, but we can also use Active Record to prove that the new user is actually there. First, we'll clear out the `user` variable by setting it to `nil`, and then we'll use a find method called `find_by_screen_name` to fetch our user from the database:

```
>> user = nil
=> nil
>> user = User.find_by_screen_name("me")
=> #<User:0xb76b6e50 @attributes={"id"=>"1",
                                  "screen_name"=>"me",
                                  "password"=>"a",
                                  "email"=>""}>
>> user.password
=> "a"
```

Notice that Rails somehow knew that our user had an attribute called `screen_name`, and constructed the `find_by_screen_name` method based on that attribute just for us. This is but one example of the wonderful magic of Rails (see the sidebar "Reflection and metaprogramming").

Reflection and metaprogramming

Rails takes advantage of the power of Ruby in many ways, none so dramatic as the dynamic creation of database `find` methods. By *reflecting on* (reading) the names of the columns from the database, Rails is able to synthesize functions on the fly using Ruby *metaprogramming,* which basically means generating methods based on information discovered at runtime. In our case, Rails effectively looks in the database and sees that there's a column called `screen_name`; it then uses powerful incantations to tell Ruby to make a function called `find_by_screen_name`. There are dark forces at work here, but if you're curious and brave, you can learn more about these incantations at

`http://blog.hasmanythrough.com/articles/2006/08/13/how-dynamic-finders-work`

3.2.2 A simple validation

In a certain sense we're now "done" with the user data model—after all, the `users` table now exists in the database, and we can read and write user objects using the User class. That's not the full story, though; in the example above we were able to create a user with an absurdly short screen name and password and with a blank email address. We would like to be able to impose restrictions on the kind of user objects we save to the database; for instance, we probably want to limit the length of screen names and passwords—say, at least 4 characters long but no more than 40. We would also like to make sure that screen names and email addresses are unique. Finally, we'd like to make sure that there is a nonempty email address which is at most (say) 50 characters long.

Rails makes it easy to impose these sorts of constraints on our models by applying *validations* before anything gets saved to the database:

Listing 3.5 app/models/user.rb

```
class User < ActiveRecord::Base
  validates_uniqueness_of :screen_name, :email
  validates_length_of     :screen_name, :within => 4..20
  validates_length_of     :password,    :within => 4..40
  validates_length_of     :email, :maximum => 50
  validates_presence_of   :email
end
```

This code probably looks like magic, and that's pretty much what it is. These validations are function calls, but you don't have to think of them that way; instead, think of them as instructions to the User class itself, telling it about the properties that it should have. Rails runs these validations when it tries to save the user to the database, and the save only succeeds if all the validations pass. If any validation fails, it gives an error message which can be returned to the user. We'll see several examples of this shortly.

The `validates_uniqueness_of` function takes in one or more symbols and, before saving the model to the database, makes sure that there isn't already an entry matching any attribute corresponding to one of the symbols. In other words, if you try to register with screen name `foobar`,

```
validates_uniqueness_of :screen_name
```

won't let the save go through if screen name `foobar` is already in use. By the way, the uniqueness check is case-insensitive, so we don't have to worry that we'll have two different users called "foobar" and "FooBar."

Inside the length validations we've used the `:within` and `:maximum` options. As you can probably guess, validating the screen name with `:within => 4..20` makes sure that the screen name is no shorter than 4 characters and no longer than 20; this uses the Ruby `..` syntax, which creates a kind of Ruby object called a *range*. Meanwhile, `:maximum => 50` makes sure that the corresponding attribute (email, in this case) is no more than 50 characters long. The `validates_length_of` function accepts several other options; see the Rails API for more possibilities.

Since their origins are often obscure, hard-coded numbers like 4 or 20 (so-called *magic numbers*) can make for confusing code. Let's take this opportunity to bind those numbers to more descriptive constants. We'll see later that we can reuse these constants (in keeping with the DRY principle), but the increased readability alone is probably worth the trouble. In Ruby, constants must begin with a capital letter and are conventionally written in ALL CAPS, so we can introduce constants for screen name, password, and email validations as follows:

Listing 3.6 app/models/user.rb

```
class User < ActiveRecord::Base

  # Max & min lengths for all fields
  SCREEN_NAME_MIN_LENGTH = 4
  SCREEN_NAME_MAX_LENGTH = 20
  PASSWORD_MIN_LENGTH = 4
  PASSWORD_MAX_LENGTH = 40
  EMAIL_MAX_LENGTH = 50
  SCREEN_NAME_RANGE = SCREEN_NAME_MIN_LENGTH..SCREEN_NAME_MAX_LENGTH
  PASSWORD_RANGE = PASSWORD_MIN_LENGTH..PASSWORD_MAX_LENGTH

  validates_uniqueness_of :screen_name, :email
  validates_length_of :screen_name, :within => SCREEN_NAME_RANGE
```

Continues

```
  validates_length_of :password, :within => PASSWORD_RANGE
  validates_length_of :email, :maximum => EMAIL_MAX_LENGTH
  validates_presence_of :email
end
```

Though the names may seem comically verbose in the context of the User model, when we use them in other areas of RailsSpace we'll be glad that they are so descriptive, since their meaning will be apparent at a glance. What we lose in brevity we gain in clarity,[18] and our efforts in defining these constants will be put to excellent use in Section 4.2.4, Section 5.6, and Section 6.2.4.

3.2.3 Validations in action

Let's take a look at what happens now when we try to save an invalid user. We first need to reload the Rails environment (using the perhaps overly excited-looking `reload!` command) so that the User model will be equipped with the validations we just defined. Then we'll take a look at the errors on the user object after we try to save it:

```
>> reload!
>> user = User.new(:screen_name => "me",
?>                  :password => "a",
?>                  :email => "")
=> #<User:0xb76fadd0 @new_record=true,
    @attributes={"screen_name"=>"me", "password"=>"a", "email"=>""}>
>> user.save
=> false
>> user.errors.on(:screen_name)
=> ["is too short (minimum is 4 characters)", "has already been taken"]
>> user.errors.on(:email)
=> ["can't be blank", "has already been taken"]
>> user.errors.on(:password)
=> "is too short (minimum is 4 characters)"
```

It looks like our validations caught a bunch of invalid entries. We can see the errors by calling `errors.on` on the attribute label; they correspond either to the default error message used by Rails (e.g., "has already been taken") or to error messages that we define ourselves (as we'll see in the next section).

---

[18] We won't dispute that using Ruby constants is rather LOUD, but they nevertheless seem like the right tool for the job. You can actually have the best of both worlds by using a remarkable Ruby feature called `method_missing`, which can be used to make model constants look like regular (and much quieter) object attributes. `method_missing` is beyond the scope of this book, but if your curiosity is piqued, a little web searching will no doubt lead you in the right direction.

Let's see if we can construct a user that passes the validations:

```
>> user = User.new(:screen_name => "the dude",
?>                    :email => "dude_at_example.com",
?>                    :password => "foobar")
=> #<User:0xb7707c10 @new_record=true,
    @attributes={"screen_name"=>"the dude",
                  "password"=>"foobar",
                  "email"=>"dude_at_example.com"}>
>> user.save
=> true
```

3.2.4 Improving validations

We intentionally picked very simple validations, but of course we want to be more restrictive than this. We got away with saving a screen name that has spaces in it, and an email address that doesn't even have the "@" symbol. Rails doesn't provide predefined validations for these cases, but if we define a function called `validate`, then Rails knows to call that function before saving to the database:

Listing 3.7 app/models/user.rb

```
class User < ActiveRecord::Base
  .
  .
  .
  def validate
    errors.add(:email, "must be valid.") unless email.include?("@")
    if screen_name.include?(" ")
      errors.add(:screen_name, "cannot include spaces.")
    end
  end
end
```

Here we have an example of a string method, combined with a couple of conditionals (`unless` and `if`). You should be able to figure out from context what they do; for example,

```
errors.add(:email, "must be valid.") unless email.include?("@")
```

adds an error string corresponding to the `:email` symbol to an internal Rails object called `errors`, unless the email string includes "@." (Notice that the `include?` method ends with a question mark; this is a Ruby convention for boolean functions, which return either true or false.)

Since we're now doing at least a minimal format check on the email address, we no longer need the `validates_presence_of` test, so let's remove it:

Listing 3.8 app/models/user.rb

```
class User < ActiveRecord::Base
  .
  .
  .
  validates_length_of :screen_name, :within => SCREEN_NAME_RANGE
  validates_length_of :password, :within => PASSWORD_RANGE
  validates_length_of :email, :maximum => EMAIL_MAX_LENGTH

  def validate
    errors.add(:email, "must be valid.") unless email.include?("@")
    if screen_name.include?(" ")
      errors.add(:screen_name, "cannot include spaces.")
    end
  end
end
```

And now let's take our new validations out for a spin:

```
>> reload!
>> user = User.new(:screen_name => "the dude abides",
?>                  :email => "the_dude_at_example,com",
?>                  :password => "foobar")
=> #<User:0xb7707c10 @new_record=true,
     @attributes={"screen_name"=>"the dude abides",
                  "password"=>"foobar",
                  "email"=>"the_dude_at_example,com"}>
>> user.save
=> false
>> user.errors.full_messages
=> ["Screen name cannot include spaces.", "Email must be valid."]
>> user = User.new(:screen_name => "the_dude/abides",
?>                  :email => "the_dude@example,com",
?>                  :password => "foobar")
>> user.save
=> true
```

That's a lot better. We caught some errors that slipped by in the previous example, and using the `errors.full_messages` method, we're able to see the full error messages. We did still manage to get a couple of invalid values past our validations: we put a slash in the screen name, and (in a diabolically subtle modification) we substituted a comma for the dot in the email address.[19] It would be really nice if we could get the computer to check for these things automatically.

---

[19] We put the comma in ,com.

3.2.5 Full-strength validations

Our previous examples show how you sometimes start with validations that seem good to begin with but which end up being too weak for real-world use. The time has come to implement some real, industrial-strength validations. We'll follow a common convention for screen names by allowing only letters, numbers, and underscores. Also, we discovered above that simply checking for the "@" sign is not good enough email validation, and we'll see how Rails makes it easier to enforce a more stringent requirement.

Like virtually all modern programming languages, Ruby includes support for *regular expressions*,[20] and they're just the tool we need. We could put some regular expression tests in the `validate` function, but we don't need to; Rails provides the `validates_format_of` function to make it easy to use regular expressions in validations:

Listing 3.9 app/models/user.rb

```
class User < ActiveRecord::Base
  .
  .
  .
  validates_length_of :email, :maximum => EMAIL_MAX_LENGTH

  validates_format_of :screen_name,
                      :with => /^[A-Z0-9_]*$/i,
                      :message => "must contain only letters, " +
                                  "numbers, and underscores"
  validates_format_of :email,
                      :with => /^[A-Z0-9._%-]+@([A-Z0-9-]+\.)+[A-Z]{2,4}$/i,
                      :message => "must be a valid email address"
end
```

We've kept the uniqueness and length requirements, but now we're also validating the format of the screen name and email with regular expressions—including a fairly scary regexp in the second case.[21] Regular expressions are a huge subject, constituting essentially a mini-language for text pattern-matching, and whole books have been written on the subject. Everyone we know knows enough about regular expressions to get by, with much of their knowledge coming from doing web searches to find patterns relevant to the problem they're trying to solve.

---

[20] Ruby regular expressions are virtually identical to those from Perl and PHP. And there was much rejoicing.

[21] Note that even though regular expressions are powerful enough to do both the format and length tests at the same time, we left in the length test for the screen name so that a friendly length-related error message gets reported to the user if that validation fails.

Since the screen name regular expression is basically a subset of the one we used for email validation, let's take a detailed look at the latter:

```
/^[A-Z0-9._%-]+@([A-Z0-9-]+\.)+[A-Z]{2,4}$/i,
```

We constructed this beast based on a few web pages we found and on our own experience. It's a regular expression that matches the beginning of the line (^); at least one of a list of valid characters: any capital letter, number, dot, underscore, or hyphen; the "@" sign; at least one string of capital letters, numbers, or hyphens separated by periods; between two and four capital letters; and then the end of line ($). Since email addresses are case-insensitive, we included a trailing i to tell Ruby to do the comparison in a case-insensitive way, which is also why we only needed to include capital letters in our regular expression.

This email regular expression is not a perfect test: It still lets through invalid addresses such as foo@bar.baz or bar@baz.quux, but virtually all commonly used valid email addresses match the pattern, and at the same time it catches many invalid ones.[22] The regular expression for screen names is even better: since we have complete control over the format of screen names, every valid screen name will match our regular expression, and no invalid screen name will. Let's take a look at them in action:

```
>> reload!
>> user = User.new(:screen_name => "rails/rocks",
?>                  :email => "rails@example,com",
?>                  :password => "foobar")
=> #<User:0xb7707c10 @new_record=true,
     @attributes={"screen_name"=>"rails/rocks",
                  "password"=>"foobar",
                  "email"=>"rails@example,com"}>
>> user.save
=> false
>> user.errors.full_messages
=> ["Screen name must contain only letters, numbers, and underscores",
    "Email must be a valid email address"]
>> user = User.new(:screen_name => "rails_rocks",
?>                  :email => "rails@example.com",
?>                  :password => "foobar")
=> #<User:0xb7707c10 @new_record=true,
     @attributes={"screen_name"=>"rails_rocks",
                  "password"=>"foobar",
                  "email"=>"rails@example.com"}>
>> user.save
=> true
```

---

[22] It is possible to write a perfect regular expression test for email addresses, but it is more than 6,000 characters long! For the gory details, go to www.regular-expressions.info/email.html.

Now our validations are looking pretty good. Of course, we haven't really tested them all that thoroughly; if your spidey sense is tingling, that's a good sign, and we'll return to this subject with a vengeance in Chapter 5.

Password encryption (?)

Starting in Chapter 6, we'll use the combination of screen name and password to authenticate the users of RailsSpace and grant them access to protected pages. In the process, we'll be comparing the password submitted on a login form to passwords in our database. At this point, the alert reader may have noticed that we're storing the user password as cleartext—that is, the password is unencrypted, which means that anyone gaining access to our user database would be able to see all of the passwords.

Why not encrypt the user password, store the encrypted version in the database, and then compare encrypted versions? The answer is, we could, but (in addition to increasing code complexity on the back-end) it would cost us the ability to send the user a login reminder if he forgets his password. As is often the case, there is a tension between security and convenience; for RailsSpace, we've elected to err on the side of convenience. (The RailsSpace password reminder function appears in Section 13.1.2 as part of an introduction to email in Rails.)

3.2.6 Magic columns

When we made the User model, we created columns for the bare minimum of attributes, but it would be nice to be able to keep track of our users by keeping a record of when they joined RailsSpace and, later on, when they have updated their user information. That way, we can follow the growth and activity of our site membership. Happily, Rails makes it easy to add such attributes using *magic columns*.

We've already made the basic User model, so to keep track of user creation and update, we have to add a couple of columns to the current model. In principle, we could use any names for these columns, but we want to take advantage of the magic columns `created_at` and `updated_at`. If we make columns with these names and associate them with the SQL `datetime` type, Rails will automatically fill them with the current date and time when a user is created (Section 4.5) or updated (Chapter 8).[23]

---

[23] The related magic columns `created_on` and `updated_on` are the same as their _at cousins, except they are of type `date`.

Rails migrations make it easy to respond to changes in project requirements such as this one, a flexibility that lowers the barrier to getting started on a model in the first place.[24] Let's generate a new migration to add the new magic columns:

```
> ruby script/generate migration AddUserTimestamps
      exists  db/migrate
      create  db/migrate/002_add_user_timestamps.rb
```

Next, we'll use the `add_column` function, which takes three symbols as arguments:

```
add_column :table_name, :column_name, :type
```

In our case, we want to make a migration to add `created_at` and `updated_at` columns to the `users` table,[25] both of type `timestamp`:

Listing 3.10 db/migrate/002_add_user_timestamps.rb

```
class AddUserTimestamps < ActiveRecord::Migration
  def self.up
    add_column :users, :created_at, :timestamp
    add_column :users, :updated_at, :timestamp
  end

  def self.down
    remove_column :users, :created_at
    remove_column :users, :updated_at
  end
end
```

Following the usual practice for migrations, we've been sure to add commands to remove the columns added so that we can migrate backward if desired.

```
> rake db:migrate
  (in /rails/rails_space)
  == AddUserTimestamps: migrating ============================================
  -- add_column(:users, :created_at, :timestamp)
     -> 0.7265s
  -- add_column(:users, :updated_at, :timestamp)
     -> 0.6017s
  == AddUserTimestamps: migrated (1.3293s) ===================================
```

Let's use the console to take a look at how magic columns work. First, we'll create a new user and save it to the database:

---

[24] This is part of what makes Rails an *agile* framework. (See the Agile Manifesto at http://agilemanifesto.org/ for more on what it means to be agile.)

[25] Recall that Rails table names are plural by default.

```
> ruby script/console
Loading development environment.
>> user = User.new(:screen_name => "example",
?>                      :email => "example@example.com",
?>                      :password => "example")
=> #<User:0x2758e3c @new_record=true,
    @attributes={"updated_at"=>nil,
                 "screen_name"=>"example",
                 "password"=>"example",
                 "created_at"=>nil,
                 "email"=>"example@example.com"}>
>> user.save
=> true
>> user.created_at
=> Wed Dec 06 20:00:59 PST 2006
>> user.updated_at
=> Wed Dec 06 20:00:59 PST 2006
```

Rails has automatically filled the magic columns with appropriate values. In this case, since an initial save is both a creation and an update, the `created_at` and `updated_at` timestamps are the same. Let's see what happens if we save again a few seconds later:

```
>> user.save
=> true
>> user
>> user.created_at
=> Wed Dec 06 20:00:59 PST 2006
>> user.updated_at
=> Wed Dec 06 20:01:18 PST 2006
```

As expected, this time only the `updated_at` timestamp changed. Pretty cool, no?

3.3   Further steps to ensure data integrity (?)

Model validations give us great protection from bad data originating from the web. Traditionally, though, maintaining data integrity was the job of the database. In our case, we have a large number of constraints enforced by model validations; some of these constraints are (relatively) easy to implement at the database level:

- Screen name cannot be null, longer than `SCREEN_NAME_MAX_LENGTH` characters, or the same as any other screen name

- Email address cannot be null, longer than `EMAIL_MAX_LENGTH` characters, or already be used for another login

- Password cannot be null or longer than `PASSWORD_MAX_LENGTH` characters

Throughout RailsSpace, we will elect not to implement rules of this kind at the database level. The main reason is because it significantly reduces our ability to change the constraints on our data in the face of new requirements (in other words, it's not agile). For example, if we decided to restrict screen names to no more than 15 characters, all we have to do now is change SCREEN_NAME_MAX_LENGTH in the User model. If we enforced this constraint at the database level, we would also have to remember to muck around in the database to make the corresponding change there.

In short, the Rails Way is to have the database take care of basic integrity issues such as the ACID[26] properties (for which it is well suited), and to enforce more sophisticated data model rules at the application level using validations.

---

[26] Atomicity, Consistency, Isolation, and Durability; see http://en.wikipedia.org/wiki/ACID.

CHAPTER 4

Registering users

Now that we've built the database back-end to store RailsSpace user information, it's time to make a registration page to collect it. This will involve all three parts of the MVC architecture. The registration view will be dynamically generated by embedded Ruby using a Rails function specialized for producing HTML forms to interact with models. Once the form is submitted, the controller will use the form data to create a User model object. What happens next depends on whether the user is valid according to the criteria that we set in Section 3.2 when creating the User model: Valid users will be saved, resulting in a successful registration, while invalid users will be sent by the controller back to the registration view, with error messages suitable for display in the browser.

Because it touches on so many parts of Rails, user registration is fairly complicated but highly instructive. Mastering registration will take you a long way toward understanding Rails and being able to use it to make practical applications.

4.1 A User controller

Recall from Section 2.2.1 that a controller contains actions for a group of related pages. In Chapter 2, we created the Site controller for the generic pages in our application (such as "Help" and "About Us"), which are available to any visitor to RailsSpace and have nothing to do with any particular user. Starting in this chapter, and going through Chapter 7, we'll be developing actions for creating and authenticating users: registration, login, and logout, together with a User index, which we'll use as a hub for the features of RailsSpace available to each user. Since these features all center on users, it's time to create a new User controller to contain them.

The object of this chapter is to give people a way to sign up for RailsSpace, so let's create a `register` action, together with the controller's default `index` action:

```
> ruby script/generate controller User index register
      exists  app/controllers/
      exists  app/helpers/
      create  app/views/user
      exists  test/functional/
      create  app/controllers/user_controller.rb
      create  test/functional/user_controller_test.rb
      create  app/helpers/user_helper.rb
      create  app/views/user/index.rhtml
      create  app/views/user/register.rhtml
```

Let's take a look at our new User controller:

Listing 4.1 app/controllers/user_controller.rb

```
class UserController < ApplicationController

  def index
  end

  def register
  end
end
```

Based on our controller and action names, our registration page will live at `http://localhost:3000/user/register`; in Section 2.2.3 (pretty URLs), we learned that a URL of this form calls the `register` action in the `user` controller. That action then renders the template in the corresponding rhtml file, `register.rhtml`. That's where we'll put the registration form.

4.2 User registration: The view

To make the registration form, we need to edit `register.rhtml`. Eventually, we'll process the data submitted from this form using the register action (Section 4.3), but we can develop the registration form independently since even a blank action is sufficient to render a view.

4.2.1 The registration view: Appearance

For the registration view, we could go the traditional route used by some other frameworks and create text and password elements in a form, and then use the names and values from those elements to update a user table in a database, basically doing everything by hand.

This approach is cumbersome and error-prone, so Rails provides a helper function called `form_for`, which makes it easy to make a form for our User model. Underneath the hood, `form_for` does use form element names and values, but it uses a few tricks to make interacting with the database much cleaner and more elegant than the standard approach. (By the way, we'll also use a little-known but convenient HTML tag called `fieldset`.) The following code introduces a lot of new material, so don't panic; we'll explain it momentarily (Section 4.2.2):

Listing 4.2 app/views/user/register.rhtml

```
<h2>Register</h2>
<% form_for :user do |form| %>
  <fieldset>
    <legend>Enter Your Details</legend>

    <label for="screen_name">Screen name:</label>
    <%= form.text_field :screen_name %>
    <br />

    <label for="email">Email:</label>
    <%= form.text_field :email %>
    <br />

    <label for="password">Password:</label>
    <%= form.password_field :password %>
    <br />

    <%= submit_tag "Register!", :class => "submit" %>
  </fieldset>
<% end %>
```

The resulting page (Figure 4.1) looks pretty bad, though, so let's clean it up before moving on. In Section 2.4 we went to the trouble of creating a nice layout for the Site controller, and it would be nice to use the same layout for the User controller. One way to do this is to use the `layout` function to invoke the Site controller's layout explicitly:

Listing 4.3 app/controllers/user_controller.rb

```
class UserController < ApplicationController
  layout "site"

  def index
  end
```

Continues

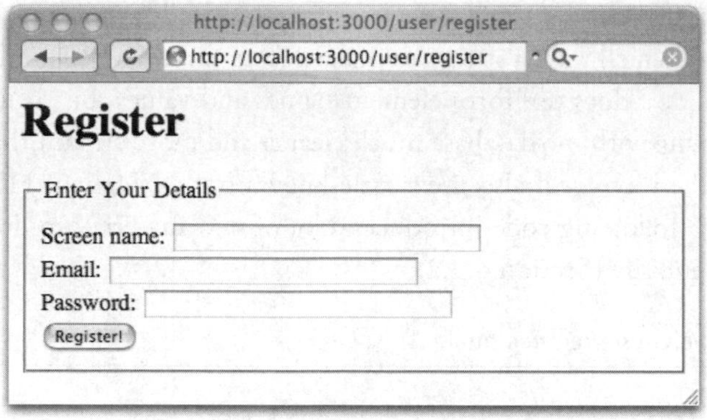

Figure 4.1   Registration page.

```
  def register
    @title = "Register"
  end
end
```

It turns out that we can do even better; we expect to use the site layout for all our controllers, and we can avoid having to put `layout "site"` everywhere by moving `site.rhtml` to `application.rhtml`:[1]

```
> mv app/views/layouts/site.rhtml app/views/layouts/application.rhtml
```

This layout file is used by default, so that we can write simply

Listing 4.4   app/controllers/user_controller.rb

```
class UserController < ApplicationController

  def index
  end

  def register
    @title = "Register"
  end
end
```

and automatically get a nice layout for every controller.

We can add another minor bit of polish to the register page by wrapping each form field in a `<div>` tag so that they can be styled with CSS:

---

[1] Here DOS users should use `rename` in place of `mv`.

Listing 4.5 app/views/user/register.rhtml

```
<h2>Register</h2>
<% form_for :user do |form| %>
  <fieldset>
    <legend>Enter Your Details</legend>
    <div class="form_row">
      <label for="screen_name">Screen name:</label>
      <%= form.text_field :screen_name %>
    </div>

    <div class="form_row">
      <label for="email">Email:</label>
      <%= form.text_field :email %>
    </div>

    <div class="form_row">
      <label for="password">Password:</label>
      <%= form.password_field :password %>
    </div>
    <div class="form_row">
      <%= submit_tag "Register!", :class => "submit" %>
    </div>
  </fieldset>
<% end %>
```

Finally, let's add the form styles to the site stylesheet:[2]

Listing 4.6 public/stylesheets/site.css

```
body {
  font-family: sans-serif;
}
.
.
.


/* Hack to get IE to display fieldset/legend correctly */

html fieldset {
  position: relative;
}
html legend {
  position:absolute;
  top: -1em;
```

Continues

---

[2] Note the hack needed to get Internet Explorer to display fieldsets and legends correctly. Experienced web developers will recognize in this a sadly familiar pattern.

```
    left: .5em;
}
html fieldset {
  position: relative;
  margin-top:1em;
  padding-top:2em;
  padding-bottom: 2em;
}


/* Form Styles */

fieldset {
  background: #ddd;
}
legend {
  color: white;
  background: maroon;
  padding: .4em 1em;
}
label {
  width: 10em;
  float: left;
  text-align: right;
  margin-right: 0.2em;
  display: block;
}
.form_row {
  white-space: nowrap;
  padding-bottom: .5em;
}
.submit {
  margin-left: 15em;
}
```

That's better (Figure 4.2)!

4.2.2 Understanding the registration view

The registration view introduces several new ideas, so let's break it down into pieces.
The basic structure of our use of form_for looks like this:

```
<% form_for :user do |form| %>
code that uses the form variable
<% end %>
```

We've seen several examples of embedded Ruby using <%=...%>; here we see a sec-
ond syntax, which omits the equals sign: <% form_for :user do |form| %>. When
we put code inside <%...%>, instead of evaluating the code and inserting its value,

Figure 4.2   A more stylish registration page.

Rails only evaluates it. This makes it possible for Rails templates to incorporate arbitrary chunks of Ruby code. As we mentioned in the introduction, this is a major advantage of Rails: Unlike many frameworks, instead of using a watered-down language to make templates, Rails uses full-strength Ruby.

Now we know that Rails evaluates Ruby code inside of `<% ...%>`, but what is the result of evaluating `<% form_for :user do |form| %>`? The first part is just a function call with the parentheses omitted; `form_for :user` is equivalent to `form_for(:user)`. In Section 3.1.3, we created a model for the users of the site, each of whom is a `user`, so in this case we pass `form_for` the `:user` symbol.

That's all well and good, but what is that `do |form|` part doing? The previous Rails functions we've seen, such as `link_to`, take an ordinary list of arguments, but `form_for` is different: In addition to normal arguments, it requires another argument, which must be a *block*. Apart from a brief encounter during database migrations (Section 3.1.3), chances are you haven't seen anything like blocks before. Blocks are a way of creating one-shot unnamed ("anonymous") functions on the fly, whose local variables stay around only as long as we need them. Don't worry if you aren't quite able to wrap your head around blocks right away—they're a characteristic feature of Ruby, and Rails uses them heavily. You'll have plenty of chances to see them again.

The code `form_for :user do |form|` shows the `form_for` function taking in the `:user` symbol, which, as mentioned before, is an ordinary function call. The next part is a block of code (between `do` and `end`), with a new variable called `form` that is local to the block. We can use that local variable until the block is ended using the `end` keyword, at which point the local variable goes away. (It's important to note that the variable name in the vertical lines is up to us; we could just as easily write

```
<% form_for :user do |foo| %>
code that uses foo
<% end %>
```

and it would do exactly the same thing. It would, of course, be more difficult for a human to understand.) By ending the block, the `end` keyword causes `form_for` to *yield* the contents of the block—which will turn out to be just a string—and insert the result into the template.

The variables local to blocks can be any kind of Ruby object; in the case of `form_for`, the block variable (which we've called `form`) comes equipped with methods[3] specialized for the creation of fields inside an HTML form tag. In the present example, we use two different methods on the `form` object to create text fields and a password field. When we call

```
<%= form.text_field :screen_name %>
```

in the context of `form_for :user`, Rails produces

```
<input id="user_screen_name" name="user[screen_name]" type="text" />
```

and similarly for the password field. It's not important to understand everything here; in fact, it's probably important not to understand everything here, in the sense that it's a good idea to ignore the actual values in the raw HTML. The `id` and `name` attributes are magic values used by Rails to make it easy to create a User object from the form submission, but exactly how that magic happens isn't particularly important at this stage.[4]

4.2.3   Registration form refinements

We are basically done with the registration view at this point, but there are a couple of HTML refinements we ought to make. First, we've gone with the default size for HTML text and password fields, but we can customize the size by specifying the `:size` option. Second, when accepting input from the user, it's good practice to put a limit on the size of the input by using the `maxlength` property of the HTML `input` tag. In the context

---

[3] A *method* is just a function attached to an object. Like most object-oriented languages, Ruby uses a dot syntax to indicate method calls; `foo.bar()` calls the `bar()` method on the `foo` object. (It would be more idiomatic in this case to omit the parentheses, writing instead `foo.bar`.)

[4] It turns out that it's never important.

of embedded Ruby, all we need to do is specify the `:maxlength` option. The updated register view then appears as follows:

Listing 4.7   app/views/user/register.rthml

```
<h2>Register</h2>
<% form_for :user do |form| %>
  <fieldset>
    <legend>Enter Your Details</legend>
    <div class="form_row">
      <label for="screen_name">Screen name:</label>
      <%= form.text_field :screen_name, :size => 20, :maxlength => 40 %>
    </div>

    <div class="form_row">
      <label for="email">Email:</label>
      <%= form.text_field :email, :size => 30, :maxlength => 50 %>
    </div>

    <div class="form_row">
      <label for="password">Password:</label>
      <%= form.password_field :password, :size => 10, :maxlength => 40 %>
    </div>

    <div class="form_row">
      <%= submit_tag "Register!", :class => "submit" %>
    </div>
  </fieldset>
<% end %>
```

Notice that the maximum lengths are exactly those from the User model validations in Section 3.2. We hope that hard-coding those lengths makes you violently (or at least mildly) unhappy, since it means we have to keep the User model and the registration form in sync by hand. Avoiding this situation is the essence of the DRY principle, and we've already laid the foundation by defining constants for the relevant lengths:

Listing 4.8   app/models/user.rb

```
class User < ActiveRecord::Base

  # Max & min lengths for all fields
  SCREEN_NAME_MIN_LENGTH = 4
  SCREEN_NAME_MAX_LENGTH = 20
  PASSWORD_MIN_LENGTH = 4
  PASSWORD_MAX_LENGTH = 40
  EMAIL_MAX_LENGTH = 50
```

Continues

```
SCREEN_NAME_RANGE = SCREEN_NAME_MIN_LENGTH..SCREEN_NAME_MAX_LENGTH
PASSWORD_RANGE = PASSWORD_MIN_LENGTH..PASSWORD_MAX_LENGTH

# Text box sizes for display in the views
SCREEN_NAME_SIZE = 20
PASSWORD_SIZE = 10
EMAIL_SIZE = 30
  .
  .
  .
end
```

Note that we've added constants for the sizes of the boxes as well.

The way we use these constants in our view is simple: We can get access to class constants outside of the model by prefixing them with the name of the model (followed by two colons). In other words, inside the User model we write SCREEN_NAME_SIZE, and outside we write User::SCREEN_NAME_SIZE. Updating our view with the class constants gives us the (nearly) final form of our register view:[5]

Listing 4.9 app/views/user/register.rthml

```
<h2>Register</h2>
<% form_for :user do |form| %>
<fieldset>
  <legend>Enter Your Details</legend>

  <div class="form_row">
    <label for="screen_name">Screen name:</label>
    <%= form.text_field :screen_name,
                        :size => User::SCREEN_NAME_SIZE,
                        :maxlength => User::SCREEN_NAME_MAX_LENGTH %>
  </div>

  <div class="form_row">
    <label for="email">Email:</label>
    <%= form.text_field :email,
                        :size => User::EMAIL_SIZE,
                        :maxlength => User::EMAIL_MAX_LENGTH %>
  </div>

  <div class="form_row">
    <label for="password">Password:</label>
    <%= form.password_field :password,
```

---

[5] We'll add one last refinement, password confirmation, in Section 8.5.

```
                                   :size => User::PASSWORD_SIZE,
                                   :maxlength => User::PASSWORD_MAX_LENGTH %>
    </div>

    <div class="form_row">
      <%= submit_tag "Register!", :class => "submit" %>
    </div>
  </fieldset>
<% end %>
```

4.2.4   Fun with forms—and `debug`

That's a lot of new material to absorb, so let's play around with the page a bit to get used to it. If you're anything like us, when you see a submit button on a page, even one you just created, you're tempted to click on it. Go ahead and try it.

Alas, nothing happens—or so it would seem. There's actually a lot going on. We can peek under the hood by adding a few lines to the layout:

Listing 4.10   app/views/layouts/application.rhtml

```
<!DOCTYPE HTML PUBLIC "-//W3C//DTD HTML 4.01//EN"
  "http://www.w3.org/TR/html4/strict.dtd">
<html>
  <body>
    .
    .
    .
      <% if ENV["RAILS_ENV"] == "development" %>
        <%= debug(params) %>
      <% end %>
    </div>
  </body>
</html>
```

This makes use of the wonderful Rails `debug` function, which returns nicely formatted HTML describing the structure of the variable in its argument—in this case, `params`, a key Rails variable which we will learn a lot more about momentarily.[6] In order to set the debug information off from the rest of the site visually, add the following style to the end of the site stylesheet:

---

[6] Rails sets an environment variable to `"development"` when in development mode, which is the default mode when we start the server with `ruby script/server`. We put the `if` in our layout so that the debug information will automatically disappear when we deploy the application to a production environment (at which point the environment variable will be set to `"production"`).

Listing 4.11   public/stylesheets/site.css

```
     .
     .
     .
/* Debug Style */

.debug_dump  {
  text-align: left;
  border-top: 1px dashed black;
  background: #ccc;
  margin: 0;
  padding: 0.5em;
}
```

Let's take a look at what happens when we fill in the fields—let's use "foo," "bar,"
and "baz"—and then click "Register!" again. At the bottom of the page you will see
the debug information for the params variable (Figure 4.3). You might guess from the
somewhat mysterious HashWithIndifferentAccess that params is a sort of hash, and
so it is. The debug information says that the params hash has a user associated with it,

Figure 4.3   Registration page after submission with foo, bar, and baz in the three fields.

which is a result of the `:user` symbol that we passed to `form_for`.[7] Furthermore, that user itself is a hash with three attributes, corresponding to the text fields (`:screen_name`, `:email`) and password field (`:password`) we defined in the view.

Notice that we are using symbols to refer to the different attributes; this is part of a general rule: *Rails nearly always uses symbols as hash keys.* We will make use of this knowledge in Section 4.3, when the `params` variable will play a key role in creating new users.

4.3   User registration: The action

In the previous section, we used the Rails debug information to see the contents of the `params` variable, but we haven't done anything with it yet. It's time to change that, and in the process we'll make a functional registration page with minimal effort.

GET POSTal

The hypertext transfer protocol (HTTP) provides a standardized method of communication between *clients* (typically web browsers) and *servers* (typically servers :-). Part of the standard includes eight different kinds of *requests* that clients can make; by far the two most common are GET and POST.[8] A GET request just gets a page, possibly supplying some data (such as an id number) needed to retrieve the resource; a normal hit by a browser on a web page is a GET request. A POST request, on the other hand, typically submits data to be processed, as in a form submission.

The Rails class `ActionController::Base` contains a large number of utility functions for dealing with HTTP requests, thereby granting (through inheritance) the same functionality to all Rails controller classes. Among these are

`request.get?`

which returns true for a GET request and

`request.post?`

which returns true for a POST request.

Recall that we used the `form_for` function to construct our registration form. By default, `form_for` makes a form that submits to the same page that constructed it—in other words, a *self-handling* form. Ordinary hits to a web page are GET requests, while forms submissions are typically POST requests, so we can use the `request.post?` method to tell if the user has submitted the form (see the sidebar "GET POSTal").

---

[7] In other words, if we'd passed the symbol `:foo` to `form_for`, it would be the `foo` hash.

[8] We'll meet two more in Chapter 15.

Let's fill in the `register` action in the User controller with code to create a new user object and save its attributes to the database:

Listing 4.12 app/controllers/user_controller.rb

```
def register
  @title = "Register"
  if request.post?
    @user = User.new(params[:user])
    if @user.save
      render :text => "User created!"
    end
  end
end
```

If the request isn't a POST (i.e., if it's a GET), then all `register` does is define the title of the page and then drop through to the bottom of the function, at which point Rails performs the default action: render the page `register.rhtml`. If, on the other hand, the request *is* a POST, indicating a user submission, we create a new user using the `User.new` function we saw in Section 3.2.1. Note that we create our user object as an instance variable, `@user`, which is therefore available in the view (`register.rhtml`); this will be important for displaying error messages when the user submission is invalid (Section 4.3.1). Once we've created a Ruby variable for the user, we try to save the user to the database, just as we did from the console. If successful (i.e., if `@user.save` is `true`), then we render some text using the `render` function indicating that the user was created.

If you take a closer look at the creation of the user, you'll see that we use the `params` variable to initialize the user attributes:

```
@user = User.new(params[:user])
```

Recall that, in the context of the Rails console, we called `User.new` with an explicit hash of initial values (Section 3.2.1), but now we don't have to. Looking at the debug information on the bottom of the page (Figure 4.3), we can guess that `params[:user]` is exactly the initialization hash we're looking for—and indeed it is. (For an even more explicit demonstration of this, see the sidebar "inspecting variables.")

inspecting variables

Using `debug` lets you see the contents of, say, `params[:user]`, but it's in a slightly abstract form; it's not the same format you would use to type it in directly. There is a way to see a variable in the standard human-readable format, though, using the `inspect` method available on all Ruby objects.

```
$ tail -12 log/development.log

Processing UserController#register (for 127.0.0.1 at 2006-10-25 03:24:56) [POST]
  Session ID: 952d0038ec59a4e1e66f039af1d31793
  {"user"=>{"screen_name"=>"foo", "password"=>"baz", "email"=>"bar"}, "commit"=>"Register!",
  "action"=>"register", "controller"=>"user"}
  User Columns (0.001354)   SHOW FIELDS FROM users
  SQL (0.000311)   BEGIN
  User Load (0.001029)   SELECT * FROM users WHERE (users.screen_name = 'foo') LIMIT 1
  User Load (0.000940)   SELECT * FROM users WHERE (users.email = 'bar') LIMIT 1
  SQL (0.000317)   COMMIT
Rendering  within layouts/site
Rendering user/register
Completed in 0.04698 (21 reqs/sec) | Rendering: 0.03100 (65%) | DB: 0.00395 (8%) | 200 OK
[http://localhost/user/register]
```

Figure 4.4 The development log (with user params `foo`, `bar`, `baz`).

One way to do this is to use the Ruby `logger` function in your action and then look for the output in your development log file `logs/development.log`:

Listing 4.13 app/controllers/user_controller.rb

```ruby
def register
  .
  .
  .
  if request.post?
  # Output goes to log file (logs/development.log in development mode)
  logger.info params[:user].inspect
  .
  .
  .
end
```

The development log spits out a lot of lines of text (Figure 4.4), so sometimes it's hard to find the result of our custom logger command. An even more definitive way to view the contents of a variable, which has no chance of getting lost in the log messages, is to `raise` its contents as an *exception*:[9]

```ruby
def register
  .
  .
  .
```

_____

[9] An exception is a change in the normal execution of a program (often an error). For example, division by zero results in a `ZeroDivisionError` exception. Ruby indicates exceptions with the `raise` keyword. Exceptions are a fairly complicated subject and take some getting used to; we recommend *Programming Ruby* by Dave Thomas for more about Ruby exceptions.

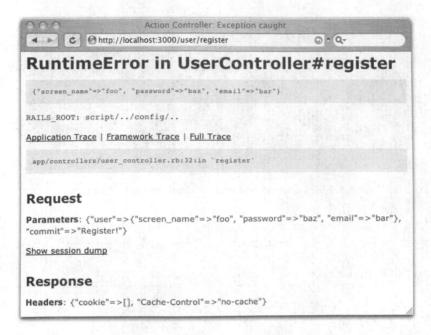

Figure 4.5   Exception created by `raise params[:user].inspect`.

```
  if request.post?
   # Output goes to browser
   raise params[:user].inspect
   .
   .
   .
end
```
This will stop the execution of your program at that line and dump the contents to your browser screen (Figure 4.5). It's a heavy-handed debugging approach, but sometimes that's exactly what the situation calls for.

Before moving on, there's one refinement we'd like to make. Although our method of handling form submission using a test for a POST request is common, we don't think it's sufficient. What we really want to test for is a POST request *along with* a non-nil `params[:user]` variable.[10] Otherwise, the register page will break if someone visits it with a POST request from anywhere other than the register page itself—which would happen, for example, if we decided to make a *button* link to RailsSpace registration from somewhere else on the site.[11] We can incorporate this additional requirement on `params` as follows:

Listing 4.14 app/controllers/user_controller.rb

```
def register
  @title = "Register"
  if request.post? and params[:user]
    @user = User.new(params[:user])
    if @user.save
      render :text => "User created!"
    end
  end
end
```

You may wonder why we wrote

```
if request.post? and params[:user]
```

instead of

```
if request.post? and params[:user] != nil
```

or even[12]

```
if request.post? and not params[:user].nil?
```

The answer is we could have, but we don't have to: `nil` is false in a boolean context (see the sidebar "This `"statement"` is true"). In general, which comparison form we use—an explicit comparison to `nil` or an implicit conversion to `true` or `false` based on the boolean context—will depend on which one we think is more readable. In this case, we think that

```
if request.post? and params[:user]
```

---

[10] The `params` variable is just a hash; recall from Section 2.4.4 that a hash returns `nil` if no value corresponds to the given key.

[11] Rails makes this easy with the `button_to` function, which works just like `link_to` but creates a button instead of a normal link. See the Rails API for more information.

[12] All Ruby objects have a `nil?` method that returns true if the object is `nil` and false otherwise; see `Object#nil?` in the Ruby documentation at `http://www.ruby-doc.org/core/classes/Object.html#M000204`.

succinctly expresses the idea "if the request is a POST and there are user parameters . . ."
(If you prefer "if the request is a POST and the user parameters are not nil. . . " feel free
to use the not params[:user].nil? construction.)

This "statement" is true

Every Ruby object evaluates to either true or false in a boolean context, that is, in a
conditional statement such as if *object* or unless *object*. This sort of behavior
is fairly common for high-level languages, but Ruby is unusual in that the number
0, the empty array [], the empty hash {}, and the empty string "" are all *true*.
(This might take some getting used to.) In fact, virtually all Ruby objects (including,
for example, the string "statement") are true in a boolean context; the *only* false
objects are nil and false itself.

4.3.1 Form error messages

At this point, if we go to the page and don't fill in any fields and just hit submit, at
first nothing happens. But suppose we put in an extra line in our register view using the
error_messages_for function:

Listing 4.15 app/views/user/register.rhtml

```
<h2>Register</h2>
<% form_for :user do |form| %>
  <fieldset>
    <legend>Enter Your Details</legend>

    <%= error_messages_for "user" %>
    .
    .
    .
<% end %>
```

Now some magic happens (Figure 4.6)—Rails catches the errors and puts the error
messages on the screen. Notice that these are exactly the errors from the errors.full_
messages method we saw in our validations (Sections 3.2.4–3.2.5). (This is no coinci-
dence; in fact, we have to confess that we found out about the errors.full_messages
method by looking at the source code for error_messages_for in the Rails API.)

But wait, there's more! If we look at the HTML source of the page, the offending
form elements are enclosed within <div class="fieldWithErrors"> and </div>,
so we can edit the stylesheet to highlight items with errors:

Listing 4.16   public/stylesheets/site.css

```
/* Error Reporting Styles */

.fieldWithErrors {
  margin:   2px;
  padding: 2px;
  background-color: red;
  display: table;
}

#errorExplanation {
  border: 2px solid red;
  padding: 7px;
  padding-bottom: 12px;
  margin-bottom: 20px;
  background-color: #f0f0f0;
}

#errorExplanation h2 {
  text-align: left;
  font-weight: bold;
  padding: 5px 5px 5px 15px;
  font-size: 12pt;
  margin: -7px;
  background-color: #c00;
  color: #fff;
}

#errorExplanation p {
  color: #333;
  margin-bottom: 0;
  padding: 5px;
}

#errorExplanation ul li {
  font-size: 11pt;
  list-style: square;
}
```

Now if we again hit submit without filling in any information, we see a nicely formatted error page (Figure 4.7).

Let's try using the text "rails rocks" for all three fields. As expected, it no longer complains about screen name and password length, but it doesn't accept the screen name with spaces (Figure 4.8). Even better, notice that the text boxes are filled with the values from the previous submission, so that (for example) if you accidentally put a space

Figure 4.6   Errors reported by a blank submission.

in the screen name, you can just delete it rather than retyping the whole thing. Rails accomplishes this trick by filling in the form with values from `@user`—which, as you'll recall from Section 2.4.1, is visible in the views by virtue of being an instance variable. (If we called the variable `user` instead of `@user`, Rails wouldn't have known how to fill in the form values, thereby forcing the user to reenter all of his information if he made even one error on the registration form—not very friendly behavior.)

Finally, use the screen name "foobar," together with a valid email address and password. You should see a one-line response, "User foobar created!" That's pretty good, but we don't want the registration experience to leave the user at such a dead end. Let's

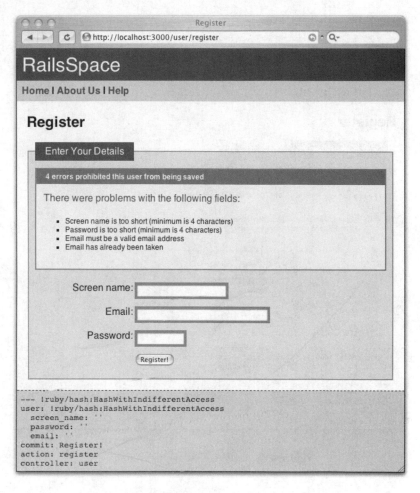

Figure 4.7   Pretty error reporting.

follow a common convention by sending the user back to the site front page with an indication that indeed the registration was successful.

4.3.2   Flash

The standard Rails way to give user feedback after a successful event is to put a message in a special container called the `flash`. This might sound like it's named after a superhero in a red suit, but it's more likely that the name is inspired by "flash memory"—memory that is temporary and can easily be wiped clean. The flash acts essentially as a hash that

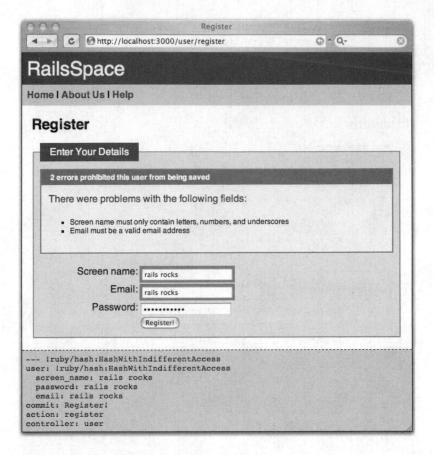

Figure 4.8   A different set of errors found.

lasts for only one request, so that we can put a notice on a page which, when the page is reloaded, disappears. Having a flash notice is so common that it has become conventional to add a snippet to the layout itself between the header and the content:

Listing 4.17   app/views/layouts/application.rhtml

```
    .
    .
    .
  <div id="header">RailsSpace</div>
  <div id="content">
    <% if flash[:notice] -%>
      <div id="notice"><%= flash[:notice] %></div>
    <% end -%>
```

```
  <%= @content_for_layout %>
</div>
```
.
.
.

Here we've wrapped the flash message in a `div` tag with class `"notice"` so that we can give it a "notice"able style by adding some rules to the site stylesheet:

Listing 4.18 public/stylesheets/site.css

```
/* Flash Notice Style */

#notice {
  border: 1px solid green;
  padding: 1em;
  margin:  1em;
  margin-bottom: 2em;
  background-color: lightgray;
  font: bold smaller sans-serif;
}
```

We also slipped in one new little piece of embedded Ruby syntax here: We used `<% if flash[:notice] -%>`...`<% end -%>`, with minus signs before the final percent signs, instead of `<% if flash[:notice] %>`...`<% end %>`. The only difference is that, without the minus signs, the embedded Ruby inserts a newline into the page. It shouldn't matter, since HTML is supposed to be insensitive to whitespace, but some browsers actually are whitespace sensitive in some contexts.[13] Moreover, sometimes you might want to generate plain text (such as in a text email), and it's important to be able to suppress the newline in this case.

With our new flash notice, the layout becomes

Listing 4.19 app/views/layouts/application.rhtml

```
<!DOCTYPE HTML PUBLIC "-//W3C//DTD XHTML 1.0 Strict//EN"
  "http://www.w3.org/TR/xhtml1/DTD/xhtml1-strict.dtd">
<html>
  <head>
    <title><%= @title %></title>
    <%= stylesheet_link_tag "site" %>
  </head>
```

Continues

---

[13] We're looking at you, Internet Explorer.

```
<body>
  <div id="whole_page">
    <div id="header">RailsSpace</div>
    <div id="nav">
      <%= link_to_unless_current "Home",     :action => "index" %> |
      <%= link_to_unless_current "About Us", :action => "about" %> |
      <%= link_to_unless_current "Help",     :action => "help" %>
    </div>
    <div id="content">
      <% if flash[:notice] -%>
        <div id="notice"><%= flash[:notice] %></div>
      <% end -%>
      <%= @content_for_layout %>
    </div>
    <% if ENV["RAILS_ENV"] == "development" %>
      <%= debug(params) %>
    <% end %>
  </div>
</body>
</html>
```

4.3.3 The finished `register` function

With the flash notice in the layout, upon successfully registering a user we can personalize it with the screen name instead of just rendering generic text. We just put the personalized note into the flash variable and redirect to the User index page:

Listing 4.20 app/controllers/user_controller.rb

```
def register
  @title = "Register"
  if request.post? and params[:user]
    @user = User.new(params[:user])
    if @user.save
      flash[:notice] = "User #{@user.screen_name} created!"
      redirect_to :action => "index"
    end
  end
end
```

Here the #{...} syntax is Ruby variable interpolation (see the sidebar "Variable interpolation"), so that a user with screen name foobar will see the text "User foobar created!"

> **Variable interpolation**
>
> The Ruby programming language supports *variable interpolation*, a feature that will be familiar to Perl and PHP programmers (among others). In both of those languages, if we define `$title = "RailsSpace"`, then `"Welcome to $title!"` becomes `"Welcome to RailsSpace!"`: The variable is *interpolated* into the string. Ruby has a similar construct, but with different syntax; let's take a look at it in an `irb` session:
>
> ```
> irb(main):001:0> title = "RailsSpace"
> => "RailsSpace"
> irb(main):002:0> "Welcome to #title!"
> => "Welcome to RailsSpace!"
> irb(main):003:0> 'Welcome to #title!'
> => "Welcome to #title!"
> ```
>
> Notice that (as in Perl and PHP) Ruby only interpolates when the variable is inside a double-quoted string; single-quoted strings don't work.

4.3.4   A hub stub

The redirect to the `index` action at the end of a successful registration works fine, but the page itself is currently blank. Let's fill it in with a stub indicating its eventual likely use. While we don't have much for users to do yet, we can imagine what should exist at the URL `http://www.RailsSpace.com/user`. Basically, if `/` is the opening page for the general public, then `/user` will be the hub for users, where we'll link to the things that users can do at the site. Let's just put a note to that effect:

Listing 4.21 app/views/user/index.rhtml

```
<h1>Welcome!</h1>
<p>This page will serve as the hub for users of RailsSpace.</p>
```

And let's give the page a title by assigning it in the index action of the User controller:

Listing 4.22 app/controllers/user_controller.rb

```
def index
  @title = "RailsSpace User Hub"
end
```

Now, registering the user "foobar" we get redirected to the hub (Figure 4.9).

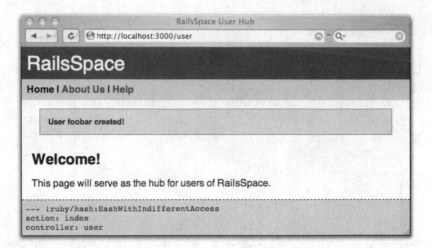

Figure 4.9   Flash notice announcing successful user creation.

4.4 Linking in registration

If you ever start a social networking website, you could rely on people randomly typing in the URL for your registration page, but that might put a damper on your site's growth. Let's make sure that this doesn't happen to us by adding a registration link to the layout:[14]

Listing 4.23   app/views/layouts/application.rhtml

```
<!DOCTYPE HTML PUBLIC "-//W3C//DTD XHTML 1.0 Strict//EN"
  "http://www.w3.org/TR/xhtml1/DTD/xhtml1-strict.dtd">
<html>
  <head>
    <title><%= @title %></title>
    <%= stylesheet_link_tag "site" %>
  </head>
  <body>
    <div id="whole_page">
      <div id="header">RailsSpace</div>
      <div id="nav">
        <%= link_to_unless_current "Home",     :action => "index" %> |
        <%= link_to_unless_current "About Us", :action => "about" %> |
```

---

[14] We switch here from `@content_for_layout` to the `yield` keyword, which is the current recommended (if slightly obscure) way to insert content into layouts.

```
      <%= link_to_unless_current "Help",      :action => "help" %> |
      <%= link_to_unless_current "Register", :action => "register",
                                             :controller => "user" %>
    </div>
    <div id="content">
      <% if flash[:notice] -%>
        <div id="notice"><%= flash[:notice] %></div>
      <% end -%>
      <%= yield %>
    </div>
    <% if ENV["RAILS_ENV"] == "development" %>
      <%= debug(params) %>
    <% end %>
    </div>
  </body>
</html>
```

Note that there is an extra argument to link_to_unless_current which specifies that the register function is contained within the User controller. The embedded Ruby tag spans two lines, which is fine, and the :controller definition is tabbed to match :action only for readability.

Upon reloading the register page, we see that links now appear, but if you click on "Help," you'll find that you actually end up at http://localhost:3000/user/help, which throws an error because the User controller does not have a help action. Home, About Us, and Help should link to the Site controller, and we need to state that explicitly since we're now on the registration page, which lives in the User controller:

Listing 4.24 app/views/layouts/application.rhtml

```
<!DOCTYPE HTML PUBLIC "-//W3C//DTD XHTML 1.0 Strict//EN"
  "http://www.w3.org/TR/xhtml1/DTD/xhtml1-strict.dtd">
<html>
  <head>
    <title><%= @title %></title>
    <%= stylesheet_link_tag "site" %>
  </head>
  <body>
    <div id="whole_page">
      <div id="header">RailsSpace</div>
      <div id="nav">
        <%= link_to_unless_current "Home",     :action => "index",
                                               :controller => "site" %> |
        <%= link_to_unless_current "About Us", :action => "about",
                                               :controller => "site" %> |
```

Continues

```
    <%= link_to_unless_current "Help",     :action => "help",
                                           :controller => "site" %> |
    <%= link_to_unless_current "Register", :action => "register",
                                           :controller => "user" %>
  </div>
  <div id="content">
    <% if flash[:notice] -%>
      <div id="notice"><%= flash[:notice] %></div>
    <% end -%>
    <%= yield %>
  </div>
  <% if ENV["RAILS_ENV"] == "development" %>
    <%= debug(params) %>
  <% end %>
  </div>
 </body>
</html>
```

4.4.1 Helper files

At this point, you might have noticed a little repetition in the code for the navigation links. If we ever want to change those links—say, restoring the original `link_to` usage or adding a CSS class to each link—we have to make the change in each one. Let's create a navigation link function so that we only have to make changes in one place.

Rails provides a *helper* file for situations like this: any function defined in

`app/helpers/application_helper.rb`

will automatically be available in all of the controllers.[15] We'll put our navigation link function there:

Listing 4.25 app/helpers/application_helper.rb

```
module ApplicationHelper

  # Return a link for use in layout navigation.
  def nav_link(text, controller, action="index")
    return link_to_unless_current text, :controller => controller,
                                        :action => action
  end

end
```

---

[15] The application helper is a *module*, which is a collection of functions designed to be *mixed in* to a class. A single module can be mixed into many different classes; Ruby modules thereby constitute a convenient way to collect a group of related functions in one place.

Here we've used the `return` keyword to return the link, but in Ruby you don't actually have to return values explicitly: The last statement in the function is automatically the return value. Thus, it's more idiomatically correct to write

Listing 4.26 app/helpers/application_helper.rb

```ruby
module ApplicationHelper

  # Return a link for use in layout navigation.
  def nav_link(text, controller, action="index")
    link_to_unless_current text, :controller => controller,
                                 :action => action
  end

end
```

The one bit of this code that might be a little confusing is `action="index"`, which is a Ruby *optional argument*, with (in our case) default value `"index"`. In other words, if we call `nav_link` with only two arguments, Ruby knows to make the `action` variable `"index"` automatically.

There's one more important thing to note about our `nav_link` function. We put a comment line describing the function right above the declaration. This is a *documentation comment*, and Rails rewards you richly for making them (see the sidebar "Site documentation").

Having finished our utility function, we can tidy up our layout, which is now in its final form:

Listing 4.27 app/views/layouts/application.rhtml

```html
<!DOCTYPE HTML PUBLIC "-//W3C//DTD XHTML 1.0 Strict//EN"
  "http://www.w3.org/TR/xhtml1/DTD/xhtml1-strict.dtd">
<html>
  <head>
    <title><%= @title %></title>
    <%= stylesheet_link_tag "site" %>
  </head>
  <body>
    <div id="whole_page">
      <div id="header">RailsSpace</div>
      <div id="nav">
        <%= nav_link "Home",     "site" %> |
        <%= nav_link "About Us", "site", "about" %> |
```

Continues

```
      <%= nav_link "Help",     "site", "help" %> |
      <%= nav_link "Register", "user", "register" %>
    </div>
    <div id="content">
      <% if flash[:notice] -%>
        <div id="notice"><%= flash[:notice] %></div>
      <% end -%>
      <%= yield %>
    </div>
    <% if ENV["RAILS_ENV"] == "development" %>
      <%= debug(params) %>
    <% end %>
    </div>
  </body>
</html>
```

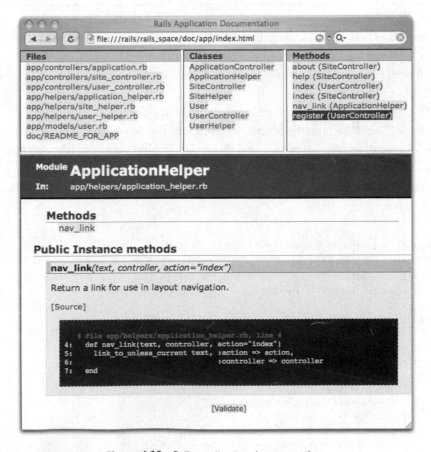

Figure 4.10   Rails application documentation.

> **Site documentation**
>
> To see the virtue of documentation comments (which appear immediately before function definitions), add `nav_link` to the Application helper as described in the text and then run the following command:
>
> ```
> > rake doc:app
> ```
>
> This creates HTML documentation for your application and puts it in `doc/app/index.html`, so you can view it in your browser at
>
> ```
> file:///pathtorailsspace/doc/app/index.html
> ```
>
> replacing `path_to_rails_space` with the path on your machine. From Figure 4.10, you can see that the documentation comment appears under the name of the function, so by consistently adding documentation comments, you get great site documentation practically for free.

4.5   An example user

Now that we have finished the `register` action and the associated site changes, let's create a hypothetical user called Foo Bar:

1. If the `users` table is not empty, empty it now using your MySQL GUI of choice (or the command line), or even better yet, `rake db:migrate VERSION=0` followed by `rake db:migrate` so that you start from a completely blank slate.

2. Go to `http://localhost:3000/user/register` and register Foo Bar with the following information:

    (a) Screen name: `foobar`

    (b) Email: `foobar@example.com`

    (c) Password: `bazquux` (or a password of your choice)

We'll learn how to log Foo in starting in Chapter 6. Before moving forward, though, we should address a most pressing matter: We are currently performing no tests on our application. Most frameworks don't provide automated testing facilities at all, of course, but the Rails community generally considers testing a necessity. We agree—so let's get started.

CHAPTER 5

Getting started with testing

If you've spent much time developing web applications, you've no doubt experienced the pain of making a form handler (for, say, registration), filling it out to test it, making some changes (say, adding some fields), filling it out again, having it break, filling it out again, fixing one problem but having it break for a second unrelated reason, filling it out again—well, you get the idea. What a disaster! What's a developer to do?

Rails to the rescue! By using automated *testing*, we don't have to do any of those things by hand—Rails does them all for us. Rails *unit* tests let us check our model validations and make sure that the database is working. *Functional* tests let us simulate a browser hitting the controller actions and verify responses, redirects, variable assignments, and HTML tags. Finally, *integration* tests let us see how different parts of the application interact by simulating a browser hopping from page to page. In this chapter, we cover unit and functional tests; we introduce integration testing in Section 7.4.

By taking time now to write tests for our models, views, and controllers, we effectively stop moving forward with our application and instead take a step sideways. If you're skeptical that this is a good idea, you're not alone (see the sidebar "*Aure says*: Don't panic!"). In our experience, though, tests make for better, cleaner code, and end up saving time in the long run by exposing flaws in the current application and catching bugs as the application evolves. Put simply, the Rails testing facilities are the greatest thing since sliced bread, and we strongly recommend taking advantage of them.

> **Aure says: Don't panic!**
>
> There are going to be some developers who get to this chapter and say "Oh no, not testing already!" and I want to commiserate with you. I skipped testing when I first learned Rails because the chapter was long and the tests seemed trivial. So, having been there, I want to implore you not to skip this chapter. We'll keep it relevant and to-the-point, and the payoff is great.
>
> I think you'll be a convert like me.... Now, whenever I check out new Rails-based software, I go straight to the tests to see if I can really trust the developer.

5.1 Our testing philosophy

Testing is a huge part of Rails. Some people even use "Test-Driven Development" (TDD) when creating applications, which involves writing a (failing) test for each new feature even before implementing the feature itself. (This might sound like a rather *extreme* programming technique, but we know people who swear by TDD.) Our approach is to work on each piece of an application until we think that it's unlikely to change in a fundamental way (at least in the short run). At that point, we write some tests to anchor the state of the project. Then we can continue developing the application (adding new tests as necessary) while occasionally running the test suite to make sure we haven't broken anything.

This is the point we find ourselves at now with RailsSpace. We've defined the User model and made a registration form to manipulate that model by saving submitted information to the database. The front-end interface and back-end data model are both fairly stable, so now is a good time to write some tests.

By the way, we will show plenty of examples of tests being run at the command line, but you should feel free to run the tests as little or as often as you like. In particular, if you've added several tests and you start to worry about whether they'll pass or not, that's a sign that it's time to run the tests again.

5.2 Test database configuration

If testing is so great, you may be wondering why we didn't introduce it sooner—maybe even in Chapter 2. The main reason is that Rails requires a database to run its tests, even if the tests don't need a database, and setting up a database just to test a handful of mostly static pages seemed like a lot of overhead. (Actually, it is possible to set up Rails to run tests without a database, but it's nearly as much trouble as setting up a database.) Now that we've set up our database for the User model, though, there's no excuse for not testing the Site controller.

Since testing can potentially destroy or alter data, we'll need to create a testing environment that is nondestructive to data in either the development database or the (yet-to-be-created) production database. For this purpose, Rails uses a dedicated testing database, which in our case will be called `rails_space_test`. Create a database with that name using whichever command line or GUI interface you prefer. (As we'll see momentarily, we don't need to create the tables or columns, just the database itself.)

We'll configure the test database the same way we configured the development database. Recall from Section 3.1.1 that Rails uses the `database.yml` file to get the login and authentication information for the development database; the same file has a place for test database configuration, so let's put that in now:

Listing 5.1 config/database.yml

```
test:
  adapter: mysql
  database: rails_space_test
  username: root
  password: <your password>
  host: localhost
```

We need to prepare the test database with the `rake` utility (which we saw before in Section 3.1.4 in the context of migrations):

```
> rake db:test:prepare
(in /rails/rails_space)
```

This copies the schema (i.e., the tables and columns) from the development database into our new test database.

5.3 Site controller testing

You may recall that the first `generate controller` created a Site controller test file (Section 2.2.2). This is our first example of a functional test. Let's take a look at it:

Listing 5.2 test/functional/site_controller_test.rb

```
require File.dirname(__FILE__) + '/../test_helper'
require 'site_controller'

# Re-raise errors caught by the controller.
class SiteController; def rescue_action(e) raise e end; end
```

Continues

```
class SiteControllerTest < Test::Unit::TestCase
  def setup
    @controller = SiteController.new
    @request    = ActionController::TestRequest.new
    @response   = ActionController::TestResponse.new
  end

  # Replace this with your real tests.
  def test_truth
    assert true
  end
end
```

You can see that Ruby is require-ing test helper functions at the top of the file and then creating a unit test class using the Test::Unit::TestCase, which comes from Ruby's own unit testing facility. It's not important to understand everything that's going on in this file; what you need to know is that if you make functions that start with test_ and then run the file with the ruby command, it will execute each of those tests.

The default file has a test that is utterly trivial but serves as an example for the actual tests. In general, tests use the assert function to assert the truth of certain conditions; the default trivial test simply asserts that true is true. A test suite passes if all the assertions in all the test functions are true. Since the test file is simply a Ruby file, you can run it from the command line as follows:

```
> ruby test/functional/site_controller_test.rb
Loaded suite test/functional/site_controller_test
Started
...
Finished in 0.035964 seconds.

1 tests, 1 assertions, 0 failures, 0 errors
```

Woo hoo! It passed. (If the trivial test failed—D'oh!—more than likely your database was not properly created or you have incorrect connection information in the database.yml file.)

5.3.1   A nontrivial test

We'll replace the trivial test with a test for each action defined in the Site controller. The structure of each test is the same.

- Simulate the user hitting the page with a GET request using the Rails get function.
- Verify that the action defines the title instance variable and fills it with the correct value.

- Check for the proper HTTP response for success.[1]

- Make sure that the action renders the proper rhtml templates.

  Implementing these steps in code gives us the following tests:

Listing 5.3   test/functional/site_controller_test.rb

```ruby
require File.dirname(__FILE__) + '/../test_helper'
require 'site_controller'

# Re-raise errors caught by the controller.
class SiteController; def rescue_action(e) raise e end; end

class SiteControllerTest < Test::Unit::TestCase
  def setup
    @controller = SiteController.new
    @request    = ActionController::TestRequest.new
    @response   = ActionController::TestResponse.new
  end

  def test_index
    get :index
    title = assigns(:title)
    assert_equal "Welcome to RailsSpace!", title
    assert_response :success
    assert_template "index"
  end

  def test_about
    get :about
    title = assigns(:title)
    assert_equal "About RailsSpace", title
    assert_response :success
    assert_template "about"
  end

  def test_help
    get :help
    title = assigns(:title)
    assert_equal "RailsSpace Help", title
    assert_response :success
    assert_template "help"
  end
end
```

---

[1] HTTP uses a numeric code to indicate the response type; the code happens to be 200 for success. You don't have to remember this, though, since Rails lets you use the symbol `:success` instead.

Note that we're using `assigns` to get the value of the `@title` instance variable defined in each action. The `assigns` function takes in a symbol and looks for the corresponding instance variable in the action; e.g., `assigns(:title)` returns the value of `@title` (or `nil` if `etitle` is undefined).

The `assert_equal` function is a bit of an oddball: The first argument is the value you expect, while the second value is the unknown quantity. To the authors this seems backward; we'd prefer to say things like "We assert that the car's color is blue," but instead we have to say, "We assert that we're expecting blue to be the car's color." That's the way it is, though, so we'll just suck it up and deal.

Let's run the test to see how we did:

```
> ruby test/functional/site_controller_test.rb
Loaded suite test/functional/site_controller_test
Started
..F
Finished in 0.123532 seconds.

1) Failure:
test_index(SiteControllerTest) [test/functional/site_controller_test.rb:18]:
<"RailsSpace"> expected but was
<"Welcome to RailsSpace!">.

3 tests, 7 assertions, 1 failures, 0 errors
```

Oops! Two of our tests passed, but one failed. The output tells us on which line the error occurred (line 17). If we look there, we see that we expected the title to be `"Welcome to RailsSpace!"`, but it is actually just `"RailsSpace"`. Of course, in the future we expect that the most useful test failures will involve correct tests catching bugs introduced into our site, but when you're writing tests, most of the failures will (as in this case) lead to debugging the test code first.

Notice that under the word "`Started`", there is a letter "`F`" and two periods, indicating one failed test and two passed tests. The order might seem mysterious, since it was the first test in the file that failed, but it turns out that the tests run in alphabetical order. We would have to keep our tests in alphabetical order in order to take full advantage of this, but we'd rather let logical structure dictate the order of the tests in the file. Because of this choice, in general we'll use the line number to find the place where the error occurred.

Let's fix the test by correcting the title:

Listing 5.4   test/functional/site_controller_test.rb

```
def test_index
  get :index
  title = assigns(:title)
  assert_equal "RailsSpace", title
  assert_response :success
  assert_template "index"
end
  .
  .
  .
```

We can run just the `test_index` test by passing the `-n` (name) flag, which takes the name of the test as an argument:

```
> ruby test/functional/site_controller_test.rb -n test_index
Loaded suite test/functional/site_controller_test
Started
...
Finished in 0.090368 seconds.

1 tests, 3 assertions, 0 failures, 0 errors
```

5.3.2   Test overkill?

We claimed that testing is the greatest thing since sliced bread, so you might be underwhelmed at our first test suite. Why would you possibly want to test that Rails can respond to a request for a page successfully? Isn't this test overkill?

Well, that's a matter of judgment, but the reason we test things like this is that sometimes the small things that go wrong are the hardest to find. After this site gets more complex, will we ever feel like checking if the help page is working, or if the title on that page is correct? Probably not, and then one day someone will send us a nasty email saying the help page doesn't even respond, and therefore the whole site must suck. But if we make testing the help page part of our standard test suite, we'll probably catch any breakage before our users do. And even if someone does write to complain, by running the test suite in response, we can pinpoint the problem and fix it.

5.4   Registration testing

So far, the Site controller testing we've done has allowed us to feel secure that our (nearly) static pages can be tested at any time. The next step is to test the registration process. This is where we really kick things into high gear.

5.4.1   Running functional tests

Before we get started with the registration functional tests, we'd like to mention an alternate technique for running tests, one that doesn't require using the Ruby interpreter explicitly: Rails provides a rake shortcut that you can use to run all of your functional tests automatically. Let's give it a whirl:

```
> rake test:functionals
Started
....
Finished in 0.207734 seconds.

4 tests, 10 assertions, 0 failures, 0 errors
```

There are only three tests in our Site controller test suite; where does the "4" come from? Well, `rake test:functionals` runs *all* the test suites—including the trivial test in `test/functional/user_controller_test.rb` (which got created automatically when we generated the User controller). That makes four tests total.

By making a habit of running `rake test:functionals` as you build the tests in this section, you will catch typos and other errors in the tests immediately, which will save you a lot of time in the long run. This general style of programming is called *incremental development*, and we recommend it strongly.

5.4.2   Basic registration tests

Let's start our registration testing by replacing the trivial test with the same basic test that we had for the Site controller:

Listing 5.5   test/functional/user_controller_test.rb

```
require File.dirname(__FILE__) + '/../test_helper'
require 'user_controller'

# Re-raise errors caught by the controller.
class UserController; def rescue_action(e) raise e end; end

class UserControllerTest < Test::Unit::TestCase
  def setup
    @controller = UserController.new
    @request    = ActionController::TestRequest.new
    @response   = ActionController::TestResponse.new
  end

  # Make sure the registration page responds with the proper form.
  def test_registration_page
    get :register
```

```
    title = assigns(:title)
    assert_equal "Register", title
    assert_response :success
    assert_template "register"
  end
end
```

That's great, but Rails testing lets us do a lot more. Using the `assert_tag` function, we can probe the actual tags on the page to make sure that they have the proper form. For example, we know that there should be a form tag with four input tags—one each for the screen name, email address, password, and submit button. Let's take a look at some of the HTML generated by the registration form to figure out how to test it:[2]

.

.

.

```
<form action="/user/register" method="post">
<fieldset>
  <legend>Register</legend>



  <div class="form_row">
    <label for="screen_name">Screen name:</label>
    <input id="user_screen_name" maxlength="20" name="user[screen_name]" size="30"
    type="text" />
  </div>

  <div class="form_row">
    <label for="email">Email:</label>
    <input id="user_email" maxlength="50" name="user[email]" size="20"
    type="text" />
  </div>

  <div class="form_row">
    <label for="password">Password:</label>
    <input id="user_password" maxlength="40" name="user[password]" size="20"
    type="password" />
  </div>
  <input class="submit" name="commit" type="submit" value="Register!" />
</fieldset>
```

---

[2] The Rails functions for testing HTML structure are very sensitive to invalid (X)HTML; if you are getting strange errors, you might want to validate your markup. We recommend the HTML validator plugin for Firefox (`https://addons.mozilla.org/firefox/249/`). Edit its settings so that only local pages get validated and you'll be able to tell at a glance when your markup goes astray.

```
</form>
.
.
.
```

We see here that there is an HTML form tag with two attributes, an action pointing to `"/user/register"` and a method indicating an HTTP POST request. There are also three input tags, each with five attributes: a type, a size, a maximum length, and rather complicated id and name attributes.[3] Let's use `assert_tag` to test for the presence and correctness of these attributes:

Listing 5.6   test/functional/user_controller_test.rb

```ruby
# Make sure the registration page responds with the proper form.
def test_registration_page
  get :register
  title = assigns(:title)
  assert_equal "Register", title
  assert_response :success
  assert_template "register"
  # Test the form and all its tags.
  assert_tag "form", :attributes => { :action => "/user/register",
                                      :method => "post" }
  assert_tag "input",
             :attributes => { :name => "user[screen_name]",
                              :type => "text",
                              :size => User::SCREEN_NAME_SIZE,
                              :maxlength => User::SCREEN_NAME_MAX_LENGTH }
  assert_tag "input",
             :attributes => { :name => "user[email]",
                              :type => "text",
                              :size => User::EMAIL_SIZE,
                              :maxlength => User::EMAIL_MAX_LENGTH }
  assert_tag "input",
             :attributes => { :name => "user[password]",
                              :type => "password",
                              :size => User::PASSWORD_SIZE,
                              :maxlength => User::PASSWORD_MAX_LENGTH }
  assert_tag "input", :attributes => { :type => "submit",
                                       :value => "Register!" }
end
```

---

[3] Don't worry about exactly where these come from; they are part of the `form_for` magic that Rails uses to manipulate the User model.

Note that we test both the `size` and `maxlength` attributes using the respective constants from the User class, prefixed with `User::` so that we can use them outside of the model. Also note that we don't have to test all the attributes for every tag, but we do have to give enough attributes so that the tag is identified uniquely (otherwise, the test wouldn't know how to find it). For example, to test the screen name text box, we can specify either the name or the id attribute, but we don't need both—either one specifies the tag uniquely, and we don't have to test both since their form is determined by the `form_for` function. We do, however, test the type, size, and maximum length, since an errant keystroke could potentially break those attributes.

5.4.3 Testing successful registration

Here, we finally get the chance to address the nightmare scenario from the chapter introduction: We get to automate form submission. First, we'll test a successful registration:

Listing 5.7 test/functional/user_controller_test.rb

```
# Test a valid registration.
def test_registration_success
  post :register, :user  => { :screen_name => "new screen_name",
                              :email       => "valid@example.com",
                              :password    => "long_enough_password" }
  # Test assignment of user.
  user = assigns(:user)
  assert_not_nil user
  # Test new user in database.
  new_user = User.find_by_screen_name_and_password(user.screen_name,
                                                   user.password)
  assert_equal new_user, user
  # Test flash and redirect.
  assert_equal "User #{new_user.screen_name} created!", flash[:notice]
  assert_redirected_to :action => "index"
end
```

Let's take this function step by step. We first need to simulate the user entering values into our registration form and then hitting the submit button to produce an HTTP POST request; we do this with the Rails `post` function. Since the registration form is generated by the `form_for` function using the `:user` symbol, we pass `post` a hash argument with key `:user`. The value of that hash is another hash with key-value pairs corresponding to the variables generated by the form: In our case, these are the screen name, email, and password.

Once we've posted the user information, we use `assigns` to initialize a `user` variable from `@user` in the `register` action. We make sure it's not `nil`, but, more importantly, we make sure that a new user has actually been created in the database based on the information we posted. Finally, we make sure that the flash variable has the proper value, and we test the redirect to the index page of the User controller.

Notice how we were able to grab the user out of the database based on screen name and password. Anticipating our every need, Rails has magically created the `find_by_screen_name_and_password` function inside the `User` class to make it easy to find users by, well, screen name and password. We saw an example of this before when we were playing with the console in Section 3.2.1, where we used a function called `find_by_screen_name`. Ruby has the remarkable ability to create new functions at runtime; that is, we don't need to define the function explicitly—it's created on-the-fly based on the column names in our database. We will put this function to good use again in Chapter 6, where we'll use it to log a user in.

At this point it may be bothering you that we seem to be creating a new user each time we run the successful registration test. It's important to emphasize that the new user is created in the *test* database, `rails_space_test`; our development (and, later, our production) databases remain untouched. Moreover, Rails prepares a fresh database for each run of the test, so the user created during this test is automatically destroyed when it finishes (whether it passes or not).

5.4.4 Testing unsuccessful registration

Now that we've created a test for successful registration, let's make a test for some of the things that can go wrong. We'll post the attributes of an invalid user with screen name `aa/noyes` and email address `anoyes@example,com`. This produces the following HTML:

```
.
.
.
<fieldset>
  <legend>Register</legend>

  <div class="errorExplanation" id="errorExplanation"><h2>3 errors prohibited this
user from being saved</h2><p>There were problems with the following fields:</p>
<ul><li>Screen name is too short (minimum is 4 characters)</li><li>Password is too
short (minimum is 4 characters)</li><li>Email must be a valid email address</li>
</ul></div>

  <div class="form_row">
    <label for="screen_name">Screen name:</label>
```

```
    <div class="fieldWithErrors"><input id="user_screen_name" maxlength="20" name=
    "user[screen_name]" size="20" type="text" value="aa/noyes" /></div>
</div>
    <div class="form_row">
    <label for="email">Email:</label>
    <div class="fieldWithErrors"><input id="user_email" maxlength="50" name=
    "user[email]" size="20" type="text" value="anoyes@example,com" /></div>
</div>

<div class="form_row">
    <label for="password">Password:</label>
    <div class="fieldWithErrors"><input id="user_password" maxlength="40" name=
    "user[password]" size="20" type="password" value="" /></div>
</div>

<input class="submit" name="commit" type="submit" value="Register!" />
</fieldset>
.
.
.
```

This might seem like a mess, but it's not as bad as it looks. At the top, there is a `div` tag for the error messages, which contains a list with an element tag `li` for each of the errors. The rest of the form is the same as the unsubmitted version, except that the input boxes with errors are wrapped inside of a div with class `"fieldWithErrors"`.

We can test this HTML by asserting the presence of the top error div, identified by its id and class (both of which are `"errorExplanation"`). Then we'll check each of the list element tags for the proper content; we won't bother to type in the entire error message to check the content of the error list, but `assert_tag` can do a partial match, which we'll use to make sure that the list elements start with the names of the corresponding attributes (`"Screen name"`, `"Email"`, and `"Password"`). Finally, the trickiest test is making sure that the input boxes are wrapped in the `fieldWithErrors` div tag; we do it by using the `:parent` option for `assert_tag`, which tests the value of a tag's "parent" tag (the one wrapping it). Rolling all of these together gives us the following test for registration failure:

Listing 5.8   test/functional/user_controller_test.rb

```
# Test an invalid registration
def test_registration_failure
  post :register, :user  => { :screen_name => "aa/noyes",
                              :email       => "anoyes@example,com",
                              :password    => "sun" }
```

Continues

```
assert_response :success
assert_template "register"
# Test display of error messages.
assert_tag "div", :attributes => { :id => "errorExplanation",
                                    :class => "errorExplanation" }
# Assert that each form field has at least one error displayed.
assert_tag "li", :content => /Screen name/
assert_tag "li", :content => /Email/
assert_tag "li", :content => /Password/

# Test to see that the input fields are being wrapped with the correct div.
error_div = { :tag => "div", :attributes => { :class => "fieldWithErrors" } }

assert_tag "input",
           :attributes => { :name => "user[screen_name]",
                            :value => "aa/noyes" },
           :parent => error_div
assert_tag "input",
           :attributes => { :name => "user[email]",
                            :value => "anoyes@example,com" },
            :parent => error_div
assert_tag "input",
           :attributes => { :name => "user[password]",
                            :value => "sun" },
           :parent => error_div
end
```

Notice for the last three tests we use only the `name` attribute to find the tag, ignoring the type and size of the tag since those properties are already tested by `test_registration_page`.

5.4.5 Running the tests

Of course, we've been developing incrementally by running the tests every time we add a few lines, but it's still deeply satisfying to run them all at the end:

```
> rake test:functionals
Started
......
Finished in 0.208865 seconds.

6 tests, 30 assertions, 0 failures, 0 errors
```

Sweet!

5.4.6   More registration tests?

Just because we say that we are "at the end" doesn't make it so. We can think of lots more things to test in the registration page, such as the exact error messages and enforcement of the validations. But these are really tests of the model, and Rails provides a separate facility dedicated to model testing.

5.5   Basic User model testing

Now that we've tested our site's controllers, let's take a look at the User model we created in Chapter 3. It has two kinds of code: *magic code* and *hairy code*.[4] The magic code consists of functions like "validates_uniqueness_of," which Rails somehow knows how to enforce, and the hairy code is the stuff that uses complicated regular expressions. Now that we're in the testing state of mind, we've become a little bit paranoid (tinfoil hats optional), and so we don't trust that either magic or hairy code will always work.

By now you are no doubt catching on to how testing-centric Rails is, so you won't be surprised (and you may even recall) that `generate` created a sample test at the same time that it created our model. If you look back at what we did (Section 3.1.2), you'll see that `generate` also created a YAML file in one of the test directories:

```
test/unit/user_test.rb
test/fixtures/users.yml
```

Like `site_controller_test.rb`, `user_test.rb` file starts out with only a trivial test:

Listing 5.9   test/unit/user_test.rb

```
require File.dirname(__FILE__) + '/../test_helper'

class UserTest < Test::Unit::TestCase
  fixtures :users

  # Replace this with your real tests.
  def test_truth
    assert true
  end
end
```

---

[4] These are the technical terms.

The first line under the class is important here; it tells the test to load a *fixture*, which contains data to help us make our tests. The `fixtures` function takes a symbol and uses the data in the corresponding YAML file to make objects for the test. In this case, the data file is precisely the `users.yml` file created by `generate`. Let's take a look at it:

Listing 5.10   test/fixtures/users.yml

```
# Read about fixtures at http://ar.rubyonrails.org/classes/Fixtures.html
first:
  id: 1
another:
  id: 2
```

The line `fixtures :users` reads this file and creates two User objects with ids 1 and 2. Within the context of the user test, these objects can be accessed by `users(:first)` and `users(:second)`.

Of course, we'll want to edit `users.yml` so that the fixtures are more interesting, but first let's see if we can get the trivial test to pass:

```
> rake test:units
  (in /rails/rails_space)
  Started
  .
  Finished in 0.092606 seconds.

  1 tests, 1 assertions, 0 failures, 0 errors
```

By the way, throughout this section we could type `ruby test/unit/user_test.rb`, but we've elected to use the convenient rake task `test:units`, which is the unit test version of the `test:functionals` task we used in Section 5.4. As you can probably guess, `rake test:units` runs all of our unit tests. There's only one unit test file for now, of course, but, as in the case of the functional tests, we'd like to get in the habit of comprehensive testing.

Now that we've gotten the trivial test to pass, let's create a couple of more interesting users (with more than just ids). In `users.yml`, define one user that the system should accept as valid and a second that is all kinds of bad:

Listing 5.11   test/fixtures/users.yml

```
valid_user:
  id: 1
  screen_name: millikan
  email: ram@example.com
  password: electron
```

```
invalid_user:
  id: 2
  screen_name: aa/noyes
  email: anoyes@example,com
  password: sun
```

Notice that we kept the ids but gave the users names more descriptive than "first" and "another," while filling in the screen name, email, and password attributes.

Now let's run the test again just to make sure everything still works:

```
> rake test:units
  (in /rails/rails_space)
  Started
  .
  Finished in 0.092606 seconds.

  1 tests, 1 assertions, 0 failures, 0 errors
```

The fixtures file does load, and the trivial case still passes.

5.5.1   Basic validation testing

Now, we'll start making the tests a little tougher to pass:

Listing 5.12   test/unit/user_test.rb

```
require File.dirname(__FILE__) + '/../test_helper'

class UserTest < Test::Unit::TestCase
  fixtures :users

  # This user should be valid by construction.
  def test_user_validity
    assert users(:valid_user).valid?
  end

  # This user should be invalid by construction.
  def test_user_invalidity
    assert !users(:invalid_user).valid?
  end
end
```

```
> rake test:units
Started
..
Finished in 0.119358 seconds.

  2 tests, 2 assertions, 0 failures, 0 errors
```

All we did here was attempt to validate the two users, asserting that the (supposedly) valid user actually is valid and the invalid one not so much. Pretty trivial, eh? Well, it actually does quite a lot, since having those tests pass means that we've configured the database correctly, successfully loaded the fixture, extracted the users by passing the appropriate symbol to the `users` function created by the fixture, and successfully executed the validation code for each user. Those are a lot of steps that had to go right for these tests to pass.

We can clean up the code a bit by making use of the `setup` function to define instance variables. We can also beef up our invalidity test by checking that each one of the invalid user's bad traits is invalid by looping over them:

Listing 5.13   test/unit/user_test.rb

```
require File.dirname(__FILE__) + '/../test_helper'

class UserTest < Test::Unit::TestCase
  fixtures :users

  def setup
    @valid_user = users(:valid_user)
    @invalid_user = users(:invalid_user)
  end

  # This user should be valid by construction.
  def test_user_validity
    assert @valid_user.valid?
  end

  # This user should be invalid by construction.
  def test_user_invalidity
    assert !@invalid_user.valid?
    attributes = [:screen_name, :email, :password]
    attributes.each do |attribute|
      assert @invalid_user.errors.invalid?(attribute)
    end
  end
end
```

Here we define instance variables for the users fixture and for the invalid user, and we loop over each of the potentially damaging column names while asserting that the user fails validation each time by testing the `errors` attribute of our user (which you can read about in the Rails API under `ActiveRecord::Errors`). Note that we've used the `errors` attribute, which has a boolean method `invalid?` that takes in a symbol and returns true if the corresponding attribute is invalid. As we'll see in Section 5.6, `errors` also contains the actual validation error messages.

We actually snuck in some new Ruby here, but we bet that it looks so natural you barely even noticed: `attributes = [:screen_name, :email, :password]` is our first example of a Ruby *array*. We presume that you're familiar with arrays from your prior computer experience; Ruby arrays are much the same as in other languages, but they are distinguished by the distinctly Rubyish way of iterating through them. Arrays have a method called `each` that accepts a block as an argument, with the block variable stepping through the array elements one by one:[5]

```
> irb
irb(main):001:0> attributes = [:screen_name, :email, :password]
=> [:screen_name, :email, :password]
irb(main):002:0> attributes.each do |attribute|
irb(main):003:1*   puts attribute
irb(main):004:1> end
screen_name
email
password
=> [:screen_name, :email, :password]
```

As you can probably infer, the `puts` here is Ruby's "put string" command; when you `puts` a symbol, Ruby just converts it to the corresponding string and then prints it out (along with a newline).

5.6 Detailed User model testing

The testing in the previous section seems a bit generic. Running those tests gave us a sense that our code is working, but it didn't rigorously test everything about our model. That is the goal of this section.

5.6.1 Testing uniqueness

We'll start with the first validation in the User model, which says:

Listing 5.14 app/model/user.rb

```
validates_uniqueness_of :screen_name, :email
```

---

[5] This is basically what would be called a *for each* loop in some other languages. In fact, in Ruby `for element in array do` is the same as `array.each do |element|`, though the latter is the more Rubyish way to iterate.

So, in the test we check as follows:

Listing 5.15   test/unit/user_test.rb

```
def test_uniqueness_of_screen_name_and_email
  user_repeat = User.new(:screen_name => @valid_user.screen_name,
                         :email       => @valid_user.email,
                         :password    => @valid_user.password)
  assert !user_repeat.valid?
  assert_equal "has already been taken", user_repeat.errors.on(:screen_name)
  assert_equal "has already been taken", user_repeat.errors.on(:email)
end
```

Here the `user_repeat` object is a copy of the valid user from the fixture file. Since the User model does not allow repeated screen names or email addresses, we assert that the repeat user is invalid with `assert !user_repeat.valid?`[6] When we call `valid?` on `user_repeat`, it automatically fills up the `errors`, which we then check to make sure that the proper error messages have been recorded.

You might feel a little uncomfortable with using the string "has already been taken" to check the error message. After all, you may misremember it as "is already taken," or it may even change in a future version of Rails. So, instead, you can look up the hash of all available error messages and assign it to an instance variable `@error_messages` in the setup function.[7] The default error message for the value that has already been taken is then found using `@error_messages[:taken]`:

```
def setup
  @error_messages = ActiveRecord::Errors.default_error_messages
  @valid_user = users(:valid_user)
  @invalid_user = users(:invalid_user)
end
```

so that the uniqueness test becomes:

```
def test_uniqueness_of_screen_name_and_email
  user_repeat = User.new(:screen_name => @valid_user.screen_name,
                         :email       => @valid_user.email,
                         :password    => @valid_user.password)
```

---

[6] This uses the boolean negation operator `!`, which is essentially the same as `not` except that it has a higher precedence. We could use `not` instead (as we have in previous chapters), but the rules of operator precedence in Ruby would require us to write `assert(not user_repeat.valid?)`. (See http://phrogz.net/ProgrammingRuby/language.html#table_18.4 for a Ruby operator precedence table.)

[7] We have to admit that we learned about `ActiveRecord::Errors.default_error_messages` from *Agile Web Development with Rails* (Dave Thomas and David Heinemeier Hansson).

```
    assert !user_repeat.valid?
    assert_equal @error_messages[:taken], user_repeat.errors.on(:screen_name)
    assert_equal @error_messages[:taken], user_repeat.errors.on(:email)
  end
```

5.6.2 Testing screen name length

Now let's test the length validation for the screen name:

Listing 5.16 app/model/user.rb

```
    SCREEN_NAME_RANGE = SCREEN_NAME_MIN_LENGTH..SCREEN_NAME_MAX_LENGTH
    .
    .
    .
    validates_length_of :screen_name, :within => SCREEN_NAME_RANGE
```

In this case, we are actually validating both minimum length and maximum length, so we'll write two tests:[8]

Listing 5.17 test/unit/user_test.rb

```
# Make sure the screen name can't be too short.
def test_screen_name_minimum_length
  user = @valid_user
  min_length = User::SCREEN_NAME_MIN_LENGTH

  # Screen name is too short.
  user.screen_name = "a" * (min_length - 1)
  assert !user.valid?, "#{user.screen_name} should raise a minimum length error"
  # Format the error message based on minimum length.
  correct_error_message = sprintf(@error_messages[:too_short], min_length)
  assert_equal correct_error_message, user.errors.on(:screen_name)

  # Screen name is minimum length.
  user.screen_name = "a" * min_length
  assert user.valid?, "#{user.screen_name} should be just long enough to pass"
end
```

Continues

---

[8] Note that, as we did in the register view (Section 4.2.3), we get access to the User model class constants by prefixing the constant names with `User::`.

```
# Make sure the screen name can't be too long.
def test_screen_name_maximum_length
  user = @valid_user
  max_length = User::SCREEN_NAME_MAX_LENGTH

  # Screen name is too long.
  user.screen_name = "a" * (max_length + 1)
  assert !user.valid?, "#{user.screen_name} should raise a maximum length error"
  # Format the error message based on maximum length
  correct_error_message = sprintf(@error_messages[:too_long], max_length)
  assert_equal correct_error_message, user.errors.on(:screen_name)

  # Screen name is maximum length.
  user.screen_name = "a" * max_length
  assert user.valid?, "#{user.screen_name} should be just short enough to pass"
end
```

Note that we could have written this as one test, but then if we got an error, it would be hard to see which part failed. Also, note that each test completely tests the boundary conditions: 3 characters is too short but 4 characters is okay, and 20 characters is okay but 21 is too long.[9]

The only new Ruby in these tests is `sprintf` and string multiplication. How do they work? *Use the Console, Luke.*

5.6.3 Detour: "Use the Console, Luke."

You may very well be confused by the function `sprintf` in the previous section's tests. This brings up an important question: What should you do when you encounter code you don't understand? We saw a hint of it in Section 5.5.1, but the particular technique we talk about here is so important that we're devoting an entire subsection to it. And that technique is: Use the console.

The Rails console utility gives us a great way to test in an interactive way any bits of code that look confusing. In this case, we have a line like

```
correct_error_message = sprintf(@error_messages[:too_short], 4)
```

which probably looks quite mysterious. Let's demystify it by dropping it into the console:

```
> ruby script/console
Loading development environment.
```

---

[9] Assuming, as is currently the case, that `User::SCREEN_NAME_MIN_LENGTH = 4` and `User::SCREEN_NAME_MAX_LENGTH = 20`. In addition to being more readable, using the class constants means that our tests will still pass even if we decide to change the lengths we allow.

```
>> @error_messages = ActiveRecord::Errors.default_error_messages; 0
=> 0
>> @error_messages[:too_short]
=> "is too short (maximum is %d characters)"
>> sprintf(@error_messages[:too_short], 17)
=> "is too short (maximum is 17 characters)"
>> sprintf(@error_messages[:too_short], 4)
=> "is too short (maximum is 4 characters)"
```

(See the sidebar "Suppressing long output" for an explanation of the trailing `;  0` in the first line.) So it turns out that the error message for `:too_short` is not a normal string, but rather has a `%d` (for "digit") in it, making it a template that accepts an integer, converts the integer to a string, and uses that string to replace `%d`. The way we accomplish the replacement is to use "string printf," or `sprintf`.[10]

Suppressing long output

The command

```
>> @error_messages = ActiveRecord::Errors.default_error_messages; 0
=> 0
```

shows a useful trick for keeping the console (or irb) from printing a long output line (such as a list of all the Active Record default error messages). It works because Ruby allows multiple statements on a line separated by a semicolon, and the console only prints the last one (which in this case we chose to be 0 for simplicity).

A similar console session demystifies string multiplication:

```
> ruby script/console
Loading development environment.
>> min_length = 4
=> 4
>> "a" * min_length
=> "aaaa"
>> "d" + 5 * "u" + "de!"
TypeError: String can't be coerced into Fixnum
        from (irb):4:in '*'
        from (irb):4
>> "d" + "u" * 5 + "de!"
=> "duuuuude!
```

---

[10] Kids these days may not know about `printf`. If this is the case for you, drop "printf" into a search engine and read up on it (noting especially its origins in the C programming language). It will be good for your programming, and good for your soul.

(Evidently, string "multiplication" is not commutative. That's okay—string "addition" (concatenation) isn't either.)

5.6.4 Testing password length

Now that we know the secret console path to knowledge, it's time to test the password length validation:[11]

Listing 5.18 app/model/user.rb

```
PASSWORD_RANGE = PASSWORD_MIN_LENGTH..PASSWORD_MAX_LENGTH
.
.
.
validates_length_of :password, :within => PASSWORD_RANGE
```

The password tests are similar to those for the screen name:

Listing 5.19 test/unit/user_test.rb

```
# Make sure the password can't be too short.
def test_password_minimum_length
  user = @valid_user
  min_length = User::PASSWORD_MIN_LENGTH

  # Password is too short.
  user.password = "a" * (min_length - 1)
  assert !user.valid?, "#{user.password} should raise a minimum length error"
  # Format the error message based on minimum length.
  correct_error_message = sprintf(@error_messages[:too_short], min_length)
  assert_equal correct_error_message, user.errors.on(:password)

  # Password is just long enough.
  user.password = "a" * min_length
  assert user.valid?, "#{user.password} should be just long enough to pass"
end

# Make sure the password can't be too long.
def test_password_maximum_length
  user = @valid_user
  max_length = User::PASSWORD_MAX_LENGTH
```

---

[11] If you haven't gotten in the habit of running `rake test:units` after each new test, now would be a good time to start.

```
  # Password is too long.
  user.password = "a" * (max_length + 1)
  assert !user.valid?, "#{user.password} should raise a maximum length error"
  # Format the error message based on maximum length.
  correct_error_message = sprintf(@error_messages[:too_long], max_length)
  assert_equal correct_error_message, user.errors.on(:password)

  # Password is maximum length.
  user.password = "a" * max_length
  assert user.valid?, "#{user.password} should be just short enough to pass"
end
```

Finally, we need to test the email maximum length validation:

Listing 5.20   app/model/user.rb

```
validates_length_of :email, :maximum => EMAIL_MAX_LENGTH
```

The only tricky part here is constructing an email address that is just barely too long but also valid. Our method is to replace `max_length + 1` (which we used in the screen name and password tests to guarantee that they were barely too long) with `max_length - user.email.length + 1`, and then add the resulting string to the original (valid) user email. Given the fixture file we defined in Section 5.5, this means replacing `ram@example.com` with `aaa...aaaram@example.com`, where there are just enough `"a"`s to make the address 51 characters long:[12]

Listing 5.21   test/unit/user_test.rb

```
# Make sure email can't be too long.
def test_email_maximum_length
  user = @valid_user
  max_length = User::EMAIL_MAX_LENGTH

  # Construct a valid email that is too long.
  user.email = "a" * (max_length - user.email.length + 1) + user.email
  assert !user.valid?, "#{user.email} should raise a maximum length error"
  # Format the error message based on maximum length.
  correct_error_message = sprintf(@error_messages[:too_long], max_length)
  assert_equal correct_error_message, user.errors.on(:email)
end
```

---

[12] Recall that EMAIL_MAX_LENGTH = 50.

5.6.5 Testing regexps

Having tested the magic (although relatively straightforward validation) code, it's time
to take a look at the very hairy regular expression validations from our User model. Let's
take a look at the hairiest of the hairy to start with:

Listing 5.22 app/model/user.rb

```
validates_format_of :email,
                    :with => /^[A-Z0-9._%-]+@([A-Z0-9-]+\.)+[A-Z]{2,4}$/i,
                    :message => "must be a valid email address"
```

This definitely qualifies as hairy code, maybe even hirsute. Experienced regexp wizards
know that a single errant keystroke can wreak havoc, so let's write some tests for this
beast.

In principle it's possible to prove that a particular regexp is correct, but verifying
that it works on a bunch of test cases is probably good enough—possibly even better.[13]
So, we'll use Ruby to construct a bunch of valid and invalid email addresses, and then
assign each address to our user, which will allow us to test the email address for validity
with the User model validation. We could create the addresses in the fixture, since you
can actually put embedded Ruby in the YAML file, but we think it's clearer to put them
in the test. Let's do the valid addresses first:

Listing 5.23 test/unit/user_test.rb

```
# Test the email validator against valid email addresses.
def test_email_with_valid_examples
  user = @valid_user
  valid_endings = %w{com org net edu es jp info}
  valid_emails = valid_endings.collect do |ending|
    "foo.bar_1-9@baz-quux0.example.#{ending}"
  end
  valid_emails.each do |email|
    user.email = email
    assert user.valid?, "#{email} must be a valid email address"
  end
end
```

---

[13] As Donald Knuth once said, "Beware of bugs in the above code; I have only proved it correct, not tried it."

There's a little Ruby prestidigitation in this test, especially in the construction of the valid email list, `valid_emails`. Let's apply our newfound console wisdom to figure it out:

```
> ruby script/console
Loading development environment.
>> valid_endings = %w{com org net edu es jp info}
=> ["com", "org", "net", "edu", "es", "jp", "info"]
>> valid_endings.collect do |ending|
?>   "foo.bar_1-1@baz-quux0.example.#{ending}"
>> end
=> ["foo.bar_1-1@baz-quux0.example.com", "foo.bar_1-1@baz-quux0.example.org",
    "foo.bar_1-1@baz-quux0.example.net", "foo.bar_1-1@baz-quux0.example.edu",
    "foo.bar_1-1@baz-quux0.example.es", "foo.bar_1-1@baz-quux0.example.jp",
    "foo.bar_1-1@baz-quux0.example.info"]
```

You can see from this console session[14] that

```
%w{com org net edu es jp info}
```

produces an array of strings.[15] Incidentally, delimiters other than { also work, with

```
%w(com org net edu es jp info)
```

and even

```
%w/com org net edu es jp info/
```

giving the same result.

In the test, we use the array's `collect` method to take `valid_endings` and use it to make a list of valid email addresses (as shown in the console above), and then we test each one in turn. (If this style of programming is new to you, you may want to read more about `collect` and meditate on it awhile; `collect` is an example of *functional programming* in Ruby.)

Our final email test is probably the most important, since it tests for a bunch of common (and not-so-common) errors in email addresses. In this example, in addition to checking to make sure that the email address is invalid, we also check that the error string produced is the same as the one we defined in the User model validation:

Listing 5.24   test/unit/user_test.rb

```
# Test the email validator against invalid email addresses.
def test_email_with_invalid_examples
  user = @valid_user
```

Continues

---

[14] The code in question is actually pure Ruby, so you could use `irb` for this example as well.

[15] Perl programmers will know this better as `qw`.

```
    invalid_emails = %w{foobar@example.c @example.com f@com foo@bar..com
                        foobar@example.infod foobar.example.com
                        foo,@example.com foo@ex(ample.com foo@example,com}
    invalid_emails.each do |email|
      user.email = email
      assert !user.valid?, "#{email} tests as valid but shouldn't be"
      assert_equal "must be a valid email address", user.errors.on(:email)
    end
  end
```

Note that, as in the test for valid emails, we included a string as a second argument to our assertion:

```
assert !user.valid?, "#{email} tests as valid but shouldn't be"
```

This string will be printed out if the test fails, as you can verify by putting a valid email address in the list of invalid emails. Also note that in `assert_equal` we put the expected value first; otherwise, the error messages don't make sense.

Finally, we have the screen name validation:

Listing 5.25   app/model/user.rb

```
    validates_format_of :screen_name,
                        :with => /^[A-Z0-9_]+$/i,
                        :message => "must contain only letters, numbers, " +
                                    "and underscores"
```

which we test in the same way we tested email addresses:

Listing 5.26   test/unit/user_test.rb

```
  def test_screen_name_with_valid_examples
    user = @valid_user
    valid_screen_names = %w{aure michael web_20}
    valid_screen_names.each do |screen_name|
      user.screen_name = screen_name
      assert user.valid?, "#{screen_name} should pass validation, but doesn't"
    end
  end

  def test_screen_name_with_invalid_examples
    user = @valid_user
    invalid_screen_names = %w{rails/rocks web2.0 javscript:something}
    invalid_screen_names.each do |screen_name|
      user.screen_name = screen_name
```

```
      assert !user.valid?, "#{screen_name} shouldn't pass validation, but does"
    end
  end
```

At this point, it's worthwhile to take a look at the whole User test file to get a sense of what we've accomplished so far:

Listing 5.27   test/unit/user_test.rb

```
require File.dirname(__FILE__) + '/../test_helper'

class UserTest < Test::Unit::TestCase
  fixtures :users

  def setup
    @error_messages = ActiveRecord::Errors.default_error_messages
    @valid_user = users(:valid_user)
    @invalid_user = users(:invalid_user)
  end

  # This user should be valid by construction.
  def test_user_validity
    assert @valid_user.valid?
  end

  # This user should be invalid by construction.
  def test_user_invalidity
    assert !@invalid_user.valid?
    attributes = [:screen_name, :email, :password]
    attributes.each do |attribute|
      assert @invalid_user.errors.invalid?(attribute)
    end
  end

  # One test that checks the uniqueness of both screen name and email
  def test_uniqueness_of_screen_name_and_email
    user_repeat = User.new(:screen_name => @valid_user.screen_name,
                           :email       => @valid_user.email,
                           :password    => @valid_user.password)
    assert !user_repeat.valid?
    assert_equal @error_messages[:taken], user_repeat.errors.on(:screen_name)
    assert_equal @error_messages[:taken], user_repeat.errors.on(:email)
  end

  # Make sure the screen name can't be too short.
  def test_screen_name_minimum_length
```

Continues

```ruby
  user = @valid_user
  min_length = User::SCREEN_NAME_MIN_LENGTH

  # Screen name is too short.
  user.screen_name = "a" * (min_length - 1)
  assert !user.valid?, "#{user.screen_name} should raise a minimum length error"
  # Format the error message based on minimum length
  correct_error_message = sprintf(@error_messages[:too_short], min_length)
  assert_equal correct_error_message, user.errors.on(:screen_name)

  # Screen name is minimum length.
  user.screen_name = "a" * min_length
  assert user.valid?, "#{user.screen_name} should be just long enough to pass"
end

# Make sure the screen name can't be too long.
def test_screen_name_maximum_length
  user = @valid_user
  max_length = User::SCREEN_NAME_MAX_LENGTH

  # Screen name is too long.
  user.screen_name = "a" * (max_length + 1)
  assert !user.valid?, "#{user.screen_name} should raise a maximum length error"
  # Format the error message based on maximum length
  correct_error_message = sprintf(@error_messages[:too_long], max_length)
  assert_equal correct_error_message, user.errors.on(:screen_name)

  # Screen name is maximum length.
  user.screen_name = "a" * max_length
  assert user.valid?, "#{user.screen_name} should be just short enough to pass"
end

# Make sure the password can't be too short.
def test_password_minimum_length
  user = @valid_user
  min_length = User::PASSWORD_MIN_LENGTH

  # Password is too short.
  user.password = "a" * (min_length - 1)
  assert !user.valid?, "#{user.password} should raise a minimum length error"
  # Format the error message based on minimum length.
  correct_error_message = sprintf(@error_messages[:too_short], min_length)
  assert_equal correct_error_message, user.errors.on(:password)

  # Password is just long enough.
  user.password = "a" * min_length
  assert user.valid?, "#{user.password} should be just long enough to pass"
end
```

```ruby
# Make sure the password can't be too long.
def test_password_maximum_length
  user = @valid_user
  max_length = User::PASSWORD_MAX_LENGTH

  # Password is too long.
  user.password = "a" * (max_length + 1)
  assert !user.valid?, "#{user.password} should raise a maximum length error"
  # Format the error message based on maximum length.
  correct_error_message = sprintf(@error_messages[:too_long], max_length)
  assert_equal correct_error_message, user.errors.on(:password)

  # Password is maximum length.
  user.password = "a" * max_length
  assert user.valid?, "#{user.password} should be just short enough to pass"
end

# Make sure email can't be too long.
def test_email_maximum_length
  user = @valid_user
  max_length = User::EMAIL_MAX_LENGTH

  # Construct a valid email that is too long.
  user.email = "a" * (max_length - user.email.length + 1) + user.email
  assert !user.valid?, "#{user.email} should raise a maximum length error"
  # Format the error message based on maximum length.
  correct_error_message = sprintf(@error_messages[:too_long], max_length)
  assert_equal correct_error_message, user.errors.on(:email)
end

# Test the email validator against valid email addresses.
def test_email_with_valid_examples
  user = @valid_user
  valid_endings = %w{com org net edu es jp info}
  valid_emails = valid_endings.collect do |ending|
    "foo.bar_1-9@baz-quux0.example.#{ending}"
  end
  valid_emails.each do |email|
    user.email = email
    assert user.valid?, "#{email} must be a valid email address"
  end
end

# Test the email validator against invalid email addresses.
def test_email_with_invalid_examples
  user = @valid_user
  invalid_emails = %w{foobar@example.c @example.com f@com foo@bar..com
                      foobar@example.infod foobar.example.com
                      foo,@example.com foo@ex(ample.com foo@example,com}
```

```
      invalid_emails.each do |email|
        user.email = email
        assert !user.valid?, "#{email} tests as valid but shouldn't be"
        assert_equal "must be a valid email address", user.errors.on(:email)
      end
    end

    def test_screen_name_with_valid_examples
      user = @valid_user
      valid_screen_names = %w{aure michael web_20}
      valid_screen_names.each do |screen_name|
        user.screen_name = screen_name
        assert user.valid?, "#{screen_name} should pass validation, but doesn't"
      end
    end

    def test_screen_name_with_invalid_examples
      user = @valid_user
      invalid_screen_names = %w{rails/rocks web2.0 javscript:something}
      invalid_screen_names.each do |screen_name|
        user.screen_name = screen_name
        assert !user.valid?, "#{screen_name} shouldn't pass validation, but does"
      end
    end
end
```

Running this beast from the command line should result in the following:

```
> rake test:units
  Started
  ...........
  Finished in 0.450406 seconds.

  12 tests, 53 assertions, 0 failures, 0 errors
```

Damn, that's a lot of assertions!

5.6.6   Running all tests

So far in this book, we've used the `rake` utility many times, for many tasks. It has always taken some sort of argument, as in `rake test:units`. But what if you run `rake` without any arguments? The answer is a big indication of how test-centric Rails is—`rake` with no arguments runs all the tests:

```
> rake
(in /rails/rails_space)
/usr/local/bin/ruby -Ilib:test "/usr/local/lib/ruby/gems/1.8/gems/rake-
0.7.1/lib/rake/rake_test_loader.rb" "test/unit/user_test.rb"
```

```
Loaded suite /usr/local/lib/ruby/gems/1.8/gems/rake-0.7.1/lib/rake/rake_test_loader
Started
...........
Finished in 0.332547 seconds.

12 tests, 53 assertions, 0 failures, 0 errors
/usr/local/bin/ruby -Ilib:test "/usr/local/lib/ruby/gems/1.8/gems/rake-0.7.1/lib/
rake/rake_test_loader.rb" "test/functional/user_controller_test.rb" "test/
functional/site_controller_test.rb"
Loaded suite /usr/local/lib/ruby/gems/1.8/gems/rake-0.7.1/lib/rake/rake_test_loader
Started
......
Finished in 0.207768 seconds.

6 tests, 30 assertions, 0 failures, 0 errors
/usr/local/bin/ruby -Ilib:test "/usr/local/lib/ruby/gems/1.8/gems/rake-0.7.1/lib/
rake/rake_test_loader.rb"
```

Already we have 18 tests with 81 assertions! If we're curious about just how good our test coverage is, there's one more `rake` task worth running:

```
> rake stats
(in /rails/rails_space)
+--------------*-------+--------+-------+---------+---------+-----+-------+
|Name                  | Lines  |  LOC  | Classes | Methods | M/C | LOC/M |
+--------------------+-------+-------+----------+---------+-----+-------+
|Controllers           |     39 |    30 |       3 |       5 |   1 |     4 |
|Helpers               |     12 |    10 |       0 |       1 |   0 |     8 |
|Models                |     30 |    23 |       1 |       0 |   0 |     0 |
|Libraries             |      0 |     0 |       0 |       0 |   0 |     0 |
|Components            |      0 |     0 |       0 |       0 |   0 |     0 |
|Integration tests     |      0 |     0 |       0 |       0 |   0 |     0 |
|Functional tests      |    127 |   104 |       4 |      10 |   2 |     8 |
|Unit tests            |    161 |   113 |       1 |      13 |  13 |     6 |
+--------------------+-------+-------+----------+---------+-----+-------+
|Total                 |    369 |   280 |       9 |      29 |   3 |     7 |
+--------------------+-------+-------+----------+---------+-----+-------+
   Code LOC: 63      Test LOC: 217      Code to Test Ratio: 1:3.4
```

Our test code is over three times larger than our application code! Does that seem a bit ridiculous? It's certainly a little on the high side—we're erring on the side of caution at the start—but it's not insane. In general, a high test-to-code ratio is a sign that the application is thoroughly tested.

CHAPTER 6

Logging in and out

In Chapter 4, we implemented a rudimentary default user page, and we promised to restrict access to this page based on the user's login status. This is the first of two chapters fulfilling that promise. In this chapter, we develop a basic login and authentication system, and in Chapter 7 we implement a more advanced system with cookie-based "remember me" functionality.

While it's certainly possible to implement a simple login system using relatively little code, taking the time to build an industrial-strength authentication system is well worth the effort. After all, virtually every web application requires some sort of login machinery for its operation. Moreover, authentication offers a rich variety of problems whose solutions touch virtually every aspect of web programming: forms, database interaction, sessions, cookies, request variables, and more. Of course, the requirements for an authentication system depend on the nature of the application; we hope that the code in these next two chapters can serve as a foundation for whatever sort of login system fits your needs.

Because of the complexity of the RailsSpace authentication system, these two chapters taken together also offer a chance to see the value of keeping our code shiny and beautiful through *refactoring*, which involves changing the appearance of the code without altering what it does. As part of this effort, we'll write tests for all of our new actions and views, thereby giving us confidence that the essential function of RailsSpace remains unchanged even as we change its form.

6.1 Maintaining state with sessions

Logging a user in is a specific example of the more general problem of maintaining state from page to page. If a user logs in on one page, for example, somehow we need to keep track of that information, so that when he tries to access a protected page his logged-in status will allow him to see it. Rails provides a special variable called `session` for just this purpose. To the programmer, `session` looks like a hash, and you can assign to it like this:

```
session[:user_id] = user.id
```

(Note that we follow the Rails convention of using Ruby symbols for hash keys.) Once we've put a value in the session, it will be available to us even when our user visits another page on the site.

6.1.1   Setting up database sessions

By default, Rails uses disk-based sessions—that is, the session information is written to a file on the server's local disk and then retrieved using a special session cookie that Rails places on the user's browser. In other words, when you assign a value to a session key, Rails writes that information to the server's hard disk with a session label and puts the same label into a cookie on the user's browser. When the user visits another page, Rails uses that cookie to look up the session information from the disk. This creates the illusion of a variable that persists from page to page.

Rails sessions work right out of the box; you can use the session variable without any special configuration. We prefer to use database-based sessions, which are faster than files under heavy load and can be used easily with multiple webservers (Figure 6.1).[1] (Disk-based sessions won't work well with multiple servers, since one request might hit server A while a second request might hit server B—thereby losing the session, which is stored in a file on server A.) Though a single server is sufficient for many applications, setting up a session mechanism that works for multiple servers is quite easy, and it unties that knot in the pit of your stomach that comes from worrying what happens when you're so successful that you have to set up a bunch of servers. When sessions are stored in the database, all the webservers can talk to the same database server, so all requests will have access to the session information.[2]

Rails provides a method (called ActiveRecordStore) to make it easy to store sessions in the database using Active Record. Here's how:

---

[1] For very heavy loads, Rails supports the *memcached* system; see `http://wiki.rubyonrails.com/rails/pages/MemCached`.

[2] Eventually, if your site is very successful, you will need multiple database back-ends as well, but this is beyond the scope of a web application framework. That's a problem you have to solve by scaling out your database infrastructure.

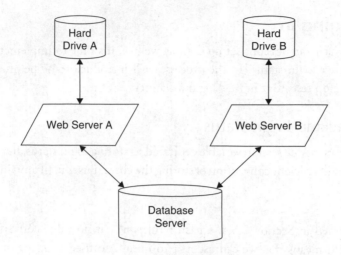

Figure 6.1 A typical multiple webserver, single database server setup.

1. Run `rake db:sessions:create`

   ```
   > rake db:sessions:create
     (in /rails/rails_space)
           exists   db/migrate
           create   db/migrate/003_add_sessions.rb
   ```

2. In `config/environment.rb`, uncomment the line

   ```
   config.action_controller.session_store = :active_record_store
   ```

3. Run `rake db:migrate`

   ```
   > rake db:migrate
     (in /rails/rails_space)
     == AddSessions: migrating ==================================================
     -- create_table(:sessions)
        -> 0.3567s
     -- add_index(:sessions, :session_id)
        -> 0.4498s
     == AddSessions: migrated (0.8079s) =========================================
   ```

4. Restart the webserver.

You'll note that step 3 creates a new table in your database called `sessions`. In the future, *if random weird stuff having anything to do with sessions goes wrong, try emptying the* `sessions` *table*. This simple trick could save you much pain and hand-wringing.

6.2 Logging in

Now that we have our sessions set up the way we like, it's time to implement a method for tracking user login status. In the process, we'll introduce some helpful debugging hints and develop tests for our new login machinery.

6.2.1 Tracking login status

We could use a separate session variable dedicated to storing login status, but we'll follow the common and efficient convention of storing the current user id (if any) in the session, like so:

```
session[:user_id] = user.id
```

As we mentioned in Section 2.4.4, a hash returns nil if no value corresponds to the given key. This means that we can use nil to mean "no user is logged in." If, on the other hand, we've put the user id in the session, then the value will not be nil and we'll know that the user has logged in. Moreover, we can use the value itself to retrieve the user's information from the database (the first example of which is in Section 8.2).

6.2.2 Registration login

We'll create a separate login page shortly, but we can apply our login-tracking technique immediately by updating the register action so that newly registered users are automatically logged in:

Listing 6.1 app/controllers/user_controller.rb

```ruby
class UserController < ApplicationController
  def index
    @title = "RailsSpace User Hub"
  end

  def register
    @title = "Register"
    if request.post? and params[:user]
      @user = User.new(params[:user])
      if @user.save
        session[:user_id] = @user.id
        flash[:notice] = "User #{@user.screen_name} created!"
        redirect_to :action => "index"
      end
    end
  end
end
```

We should also test this code by adding a couple of lines to the registration test, one to check that the user id in the session is not `nil`, and another to verify that session user id matches the actual user id:

Listing 6.2 test/functional/user_controller_test.rb

```
# Test a valid registration.
def test_registration_success
  post :register, :user => { :screen_name => "new_screen_name",
                             :email       => "valid@example.com",
                             :password    => "long_enough_password" }
  # Test assignment of user.
  user = assigns(:user)
  .
  .
  .
  # Make sure user is logged in properly.
  assert_not_nil session[:user_id]
  assert_equal user.id, session[:user_id]
end
```

6.2.3 Debugging with the session variable

When developing Rails applications, it is sometimes useful to be able to see the contents of the session. Recall from Section 4.2.4 that we put the `params` variable debug information in the layout; we can do the same with `session`:

Listing 6.3 app/views/layouts/application.rhtml

```
<!DOCTYPE HTML PUBLIC "-//W3C//DTD XHTML 1.0 Strict//EN"
  "http://www.w3.org/TR/xhtml1/DTD/xhtml1-strict.dtd">
<html>
  <body>
    .
    .
    .
    <% if ENV["RAILS_ENV"] == "development" %>
      <%= debug(params) %>
      <%= debug(session) %>
    <% end %>
    </div>
  </body>
</html>
```

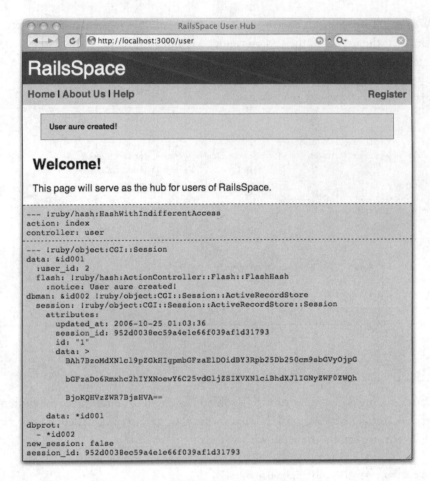

RailsSpace User Hub

http://localhost:3000/user

RailsSpace

Home I About Us I Help   Register

User aure created!

Welcome!

This page will serve as the hub for users of RailsSpace.

```
--- !ruby/hash:HashWithIndifferentAccess
action: index
controller: user
--- !ruby/object:CGI::Session
data: &id001
  :user_id: 2
  flash: !ruby/hash:ActionController::Flash::FlashHash
    :notice: User aure created!
dbman: &id002 !ruby/object:CGI::Session::ActiveRecordStore
  session: !ruby/object:CGI::Session::ActiveRecordStore::Session
    attributes:
      updated_at: 2006-10-25 01:03:36
      session_id: 952d0038ec59a4e1e66f039af1d31793
      id: "1"
      data: >
        BAh7BzoMdXN1cl9pZGkHIgpmbGFzaElDOidBY3Rpb25Db250cm9sbGVyOjpG

        bGFzaDo6Rmxhc2hIYXNoewY6C25vdGljZSIXVXNlciBhdXJlIGNyZWF0ZWQh

        BjoKQHVzZWR7BjsHVA==

    data: *id001
dbprot:
  - *id002
new_session: false
session_id: 952d0038ec59a4e1e66f039af1d31793
```

Figure 6.2   Session information when registering a new user.

Now Rails dumps a human-readable representation of the session when running in development mode. Let's register a new user and take a look at the resulting session (Figure 6.2). Note that there is now a key called `:user_id` with value equal to 2 (or some higher number if you've created more users in the process of experimenting with registration).

Unfortunately, the session information is typically long enough that it really clutters up the screen. Let's add a refinement to our debug information by making a link to each debug dump and only displaying it if we click on the link:

Listing 6.4 app/views/layouts/application.rhtml

```
<!DOCTYPE HTML PUBLIC "-//W3C//DTD XHTML 1.0 Strict//EN"
  "http://www.w3.org/TR/xhtml1/DTD/xhtml1-strict.dtd">
<html>
  <head>
    <title><%= @title %></title>
    <%= stylesheet_link_tag "site" %>
    <%= javascript_include_tag :defaults %>
  </head>
  <body>
    .
    .
    .
    </div>
    <% if ENV["RAILS_ENV"] == "development" %>
      <div id="debug">
        <a href="#" onclick="Element.toggle('params_debug_info');return false">
        params</a> |
        <a href="#" onclick="Element.toggle('session_debug_info');return false">
        session</a>
        <fieldset id="params_debug_info" class="debug_info" style="display:none">
          <legend>params</legend>
          <%= debug(params) %>
        </fieldset>
        <fieldset id="session_debug_info" class="debug_info"
                  style="display:none">
          <legend>session</legend>
          <%= debug(session) %>
        </fieldset>
      </div>
    <% end %>
    </body>
  </html>
```

Be sure to note the line `<%= javascript_include_tag :defaults %>`, which loads
the default JavaScript files included with Rails (including the `Element` function we use
here).[3] Also note that we're taking the debug information out of the content div element
so that the development information is clearly separated from the regular page. Once

---

[3] We'll use many more of the Rails JavaScript functions in Chapter 16.

you've added these lines to the layout, you can style the debug output by putting the following lines in the site CSS file:

Listing 6.5   public/stylesheets/site.css

```
/* Debug Style */

#debug {
 margin-top: 1em;
 margin-left: auto;
}
#debug a, #debug a.visited {
 text-decoration: none;
 color: maroon;
}
fieldset.debug_info {
  text-align: left;
  margin: 1em;
  background: #eee;
}
```

Together, the extra layout markup and CSS rules give us debug links at the bottom of the page (Figure 6.3), which can be clicked to open and close the corresponding debug displays (Figure 6.4).

6.2.4   Login view and action

Now that we've decided on a method for keeping track of user login status, let's put the login function on the site. First, we'll change the top navigation in the layout file to make a link to the login function:

Figure 6.3   Debug links appear at the bottom, separated from the content.

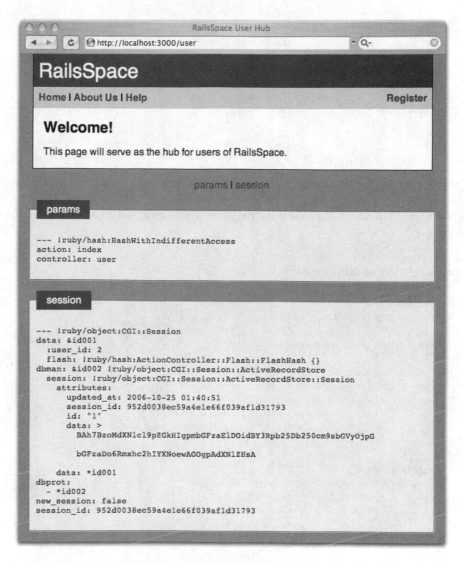

Figure 6.4 Debug information display when both params and session are clicked.

Listing 6.6 app/views/layouts/application.rhtml

```
.
.
.
<div id="nav">
```

Continues

```
<span style="float: right">
  <%= nav_link "Register", "user", "register" %> |
  <%= nav_link "Login",    "user", "login" %>
</span>
<%= nav_link "Home",     "site" %> |
<%= nav_link "About Us", "site", "about" %> |
<%= nav_link "Help",     "site", "help" %>
</div>
.
.
.
```

Next, we'll make a login view using the same basic idea as the register function from Chapter 3:

Listing 6.7 app/views/user/login.rhtml

```
<h2>Log in</h2>
<% form_for :user do |form| %>
<fieldset>
  <legend>Enter Your Details</legend>

  <div class="form_row">
    <label for="screen_name">Screen name:</label>
    <%= form.text_field :screen_name,
                        :size => User::SCREEN_NAME_SIZE,
                        :maxlength => User::SCREEN_NAME_MAX_LENGTH %>
  </div>

  <div class="form_row">
    <label for="password">Password:</label>
    <%= form.password_field :password,
                            :size => User::PASSWORD_SIZE,
                            :maxlength => User::PASSWORD_MAX_LENGTH %>
  </div>

  <div class="form_row">
    <%= submit_tag "Login!", :class => "submit" %>
  </div>

</fieldset>
<% end %>

<p>
  Not a member?  <%= link_to "Register now!", :action => "register" %>
</p>
```

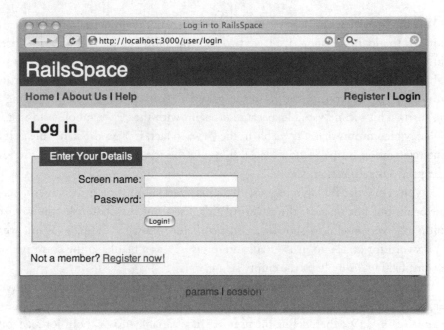

Figure 6.5 Login page.

The result appears in Figure 6.5.

The login action also resembles its registration counterpart:

Listing 6.8 app/controllers/user_controller.rb

```
def login
  @title = "Log in to RailsSpace"
  if request.post? and params[:user]
    @user = User.new(params[:user])
    user = User.find_by_screen_name_and_password(@user.screen_name,@user.password)
    if user
      session[:user_id] = user.id
      flash[:notice] = "User #{user.screen_name} logged in!"
      redirect_to :action => "index"
    else
      # Don't show the password in the view.
      @user.password = nil
      flash[:notice] = "Invalid screen name/password combination"
    end
  end
end
```

You might notice one subtle difference between the login action and the register action: In the login function, we have two user variables—`user` and `@user`—instead of just `@user`. Their uses are quite different. The `user` variable is retrieved from the database; it's either `nil` or a valid registered user. In contrast, `@user` can be virtually anything, since it is constructed from the parameters submitted by the user using the login form. This second variable, because it begins with the "@" symbol, is an instance variable, which means that it is visible in the view. In fact, it plays the same role as it did in the registration form (Section 4.3.1), filling in the screen name field with the result of the previous submission.

A typical practice for login pages with an incorrect submission is to show the screen name again but not to show the password (it's just a bunch of asterisks anyway, so it wouldn't be very useful to show it again), so before showing the page again, we set the password for `@user` to `nil`.[4] Rails interprets `nil` as a blank, so the corresponding password field will simply be the empty string.

As in the case of the register function, we use `request.post?` and `params [:user]` to tell if the user submitted a POST request with a non-nil value for `params[:user]`. We then define the user instance variable `@user`, both for readability and for reuse in the login view if the authentication is not successful. To authenticate the user's submission, we look in the database to find a user with a matching screen name and password:

```
user = User.find_by_screen_name_and_password(@user.screen_name, @user.password)
```

We saw this function in the test for successful registration in Section 5.4.3, where we used it to verify that the user that was created in-memory by the registration action matched the user saved to the database, which we retrieved with this function.

Here, we use `find_by_screen_name_and_password` for essentially the same purpose, only in this case we also use the results to test whether the user is in the database at all. The Rails `find_by` functions return `nil` if they are unable to find a matching record in the database, so `user` is `nil` if the login is unsuccessful.

6.2.5   Testing valid login

Now that we have functioning login views and actions, it's time to apply our hard-won testing expertise from Chapter 5 to test them. We're going to need a valid user object for these tests, so it makes sense to use the fixtures file from the User model test (Section 5.5)

---

[4] It's important to understand that `@user` is a Ruby variable that exists in memory, so setting its password attribute to `nil` doesn't affect the database at all.

to create a user instance variable. That means we need to include the users fixture into the User controller test with `fixtures :users`, and then make an `@valid_user` variable in the setup function using

```
@valid_user = users(:valid_user)
```

With these additions, the first part of the User controller test looks like this:

Listing 6.9 tests/functional/user_controller_test.rb

```ruby
require File.dirname(__FILE__) + '/../test_helper'
require 'user_controller'

# Re-raise errors caught by the controller.
class UserController; def rescue_action(e) raise e end; end

class UserControllerTest < Test::Unit::TestCase
  fixtures :users

  def setup
    @controller = UserController.new
    @request    = ActionController::TestRequest.new
    @response   = ActionController::TestResponse.new
    # This user is initially valid, but we may change its attributes.
    @valid_user = users(:valid_user)
  end
  .
  .
  .
```

The test for the login page itself is nearly identical to the corresponding registration test from Section 5.4.2, including tests for both the `size` and `maxlength` attributes using the constants from the User model:

Listing 6.10 tests/functional/user_controller_test.rb

```ruby
  # Make sure the login page works and has the right fields.
  def test_login_page
    get :login
    title = assigns(:title)
    assert_equal "Log in to RailsSpace", title
    assert_response :success
    assert_template "login"
    assert_tag "form", :attributes => { :action => "/user/login",
                                        :method => "post" }
```

Continues

```
    assert_tag "input",
            :attributes => { :name => "user[screen_name]",
                             :type => "text",
                             :size => User::SCREEN_NAME_SIZE,
                             :maxlength => User::SCREEN_NAME_MAX_LENGTH }
    assert_tag "input",
            :attributes => { :name => "user[password]",
                             :type => "password",
                             :size => User::PASSWORD_SIZE,
                             :maxlength => User::PASSWORD_MAX_LENGTH }
    assert_tag "input", :attributes => { :type => "submit",
                                         :value => "Login!" }
end
```

Along with the standard flash and redirect tests, testing login success simply involves making sure that the relevant session variable (session[:user_id]) is both not nil, indicating that a user is logged in, and equal to the correct user id:

Listing 6.11 tests/functional/user_controller_test.rb

```
# Test a valid login.
def test_login_success
  try_to_login @valid_user
  assert_not_nil session[:user_id]
  assert_equal @valid_user.id, session[:user_id]
  assert_equal "User #{@valid_user.screen_name} logged in!", flash[:notice]
  assert_redirected_to :action => "index"
end

private

# Try to log a user in using the login action.
def try_to_login(user)
  post :login, :user => { :screen_name => user.screen_name,
                          :password    => user.password }
end
```

Note that we've created a function that tries to log a user in by posting to the login action (labeled private since it is only used internally by the User controller test). We could have put the raw post code in the test itself, of course, but we anticipate that many tests will need the same function—and, indeed, this little try_to_login function will be put to good use immediately in the next section.

We can run our new login tests by passing a regular expression to Ruby to run all the tests whose names match the pattern test_login:

```
> ruby test/functional/user_controller_test.rb -n /test_login/
Loaded suite test/functional/user_controller_test
Started
..
Finished in 0.123146 seconds.

2 tests, 11 assertions, 0 failures, 0 errors
```

6.2.6   Testing invalid login

Having verified that a valid user can log in successfully, we need to test for a login failure. There are two failure modes for logging in: an invalid screen name and an invalid password. Let's test both cases:

Listing 6.12   tests/functional/user_controller_test.rb

```ruby
# Test a login with invalid screen name.
def test_login_failure_with_nonexistent_screen_name
  invalid_user = @valid_user
  invalid_user.screen_name = "no such user"
  try_to_login invalid_user
  assert_template "login"
  assert_equal "Invalid screen name/password combination", flash[:notice]
  # Make sure screen_name will be redisplayed, but not the password.
  user = assigns(:user)
  assert_equal invalid_user.screen_name, user.screen_name
  assert_nil user.password
end

# Test a login with invalid password.
def test_login_failure_with_wrong_password
  invalid_user = @valid_user
  # Construct an invalid password.
  invalid_user.password += "baz"
  try_to_login invalid_user
  assert_template "login"
  assert_equal "Invalid screen name/password combination", flash[:notice]
  # Make sure screen_name will be redisplayed, but not the password.
  user = assigns(:user)
  assert_equal invalid_user.screen_name, user.screen_name
  assert_nil user.password
end
```

This gives

```
> ruby test/functional/user_controller_test.rb -n /test_login_failure/
Loaded suite test/functional/user_controller_test
```

```
Started
..
Finished in 0.119785 seconds.

2 tests, 8 assertions, 0 failures, 0 errors
```

At this point we can also check our progress by running only the recently changed test files (those that have changed within the last ten minutes):

```
> rake test:recent
(in /rails/rails_space)
Started
.......
Finished in 0.21661 seconds.

7 tests, 42 assertions, 0 failures, 0 errors
```

Your results may vary depending on how quickly you're working through the chapter.

6.3 Logging out

Having given users a way to log in, we certainly need to give them a way to log out as well. The logout action is very simple; since we're using `nil` to indicate that no one is logged in, we just need to set `session[:user_id]` to `nil`, fill the flash with an appropriate message, and then redirect to the index page of the site:

Listing 6.13 app/controllers/user_controller.rb

```
  def logout
    session[:user_id] = nil
    flash[:notice] = "Logged out"
    redirect_to :action => "index", :controller => "site"
  end
```

Since logged-in users no longer need to register or log in but do need to be able to log out, let's change the top navigation bar to reflect that:

Listing 6.14 app/views/layouts/application.rhtml

```
  .
  .
  .
<div id="nav">
  <span style="float: right">
    <% if session[:user_id] -%>
```

```
      <%= nav_link "Hub", "user", "index" %> |
      <%= nav_link "Logout", "user", "logout" %>
    <% else -%>
      <%= nav_link "Register", "user", "register" %> |
      <%= nav_link "Login",    "user", "login" %>
    <% end -%>
  </span>
  <%= nav_link "Home",     "site" %> |
  <%= nav_link "About Us", "site", "about" %> |
  <%= nav_link "Help",     "site", "help" %>
</div>
.
.
.
```

Here we've also added a link to the user hub for convenience. Now when you log in, you see the login and registration links disappear, with the hub and logout links taking their place (Figure 6.6).

6.3.1 Testing logout

The logout test is fairly straightforward; after logging in (and checking that `session [:user_id]` is initially not `nil`), we get the logout action, check for the proper redirect

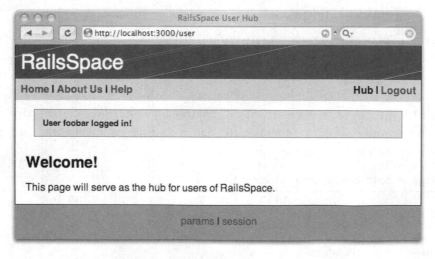

Figure 6.6 Login-dependent navigation bar.

and flash notice, and finally check to make sure that `session[:user_id]` has been set to `nil`:

Listing 6.15 test/functional/user_controller_test.rb

```
    .
    .
    .
  # Test the logout function.
  def test_logout
    try_to_login @valid_user
    assert_not_nil session[:user_id]
    get :logout
    assert_response :redirect
    assert_redirected_to :action => "index", :controller => "site"
    assert_equal "Logged out", flash[:notice]
    assert_nil session[:user_id]
  end
```

This gives

```
> ruby test/functional/user_controller_test.rb -n test_logout
Loaded suite test/functional/user_controller_test
Started
.
Finished in 0.099663 seconds.

1 tests, 5 assertions, 0 failures, 0 errors
```

6.3.2 Testing navigation

Since we want to make sure that our navigation links actually change appropriately based on login status, we should (as always) write some tests. First, we'll test the navigation before logging in. We'll use the index page of the Site controller, checking to make sure that the register and login links are both present, and that there is no link for "Home" (since `link_to_unless_current` should suppress any links to the current page). We can do this with the `:content` option to `assert_tag`, which matches the content of the tag against the given regular expression:

Listing 6.16 test/functional/site_controller_test.rb

```
  # Test the navigation menu before login.
  def test_navigation_not_logged_in
    get :index
    assert_tag "a", :content => /Register/,
               :attributes => { :href => "/user/register" }
```

```
  assert_tag "a", :content => /Login/,
          :attributes => { :href => "/user/login" }
  # Test link_to_unless_current.
  assert_no_tag "a", :content => /Home/
end
```

(If this test doesn't pass, make sure you put it in the test file for the Site controller, not the User controller.)

Second, we'll test the changes to navigation after logging in (as implemented in Section 6.3). We'll have to log in as a valid user; since the User controller test file already has such a user, we'll put the test there. Although we could use `try_to_login` to log the user in, instead we'll define a second function, `authorize`:

Listing 6.17 test/functional/user_controller_test.rb

```
private
.

.

.
# Authorize a user.
def authorize(user)
  @request.session[:user_id] = user.id
end
```

The `authorize` function introduces an essential idea for writing tests involving the session variable: in tests, assignments to the session variable *must* use `@request.session`, not simply `session`. (Refer to Section 7.4.2 to see the kind of mischief this can cause.)

Having `authorize` in addition to `try_to_login` helps to distinguish between two cases: (1) tests that require actually posting to the login action (which may or may not successfully log a user in) and (2) tests that require a valid user to be logged in (as indicated by the value of `session[:user_id]`). In addition to making a useful conceptual distinction, separating trying to log in from user authorization will pay dividends starting in Chapter 9, where the tests require a logged-in user but are unable to call the `login` action.[5]

With the `authorize` function in hand, we are now in a position to write the test for the post-login changes to the navigation menu. The changes we need to verify are

---

[5] Functional tests can only call actions inside the controller they test.

very simple—make sure that a logout link has appeared, and that both the register and login links have disappeared:

Listing 6.18 test/functional/user_controller_test.rb

```
# Test the navigation menu after login.
def test_navigation_logged_in
  authorize @valid_user
  get :index
  assert_tag "a", :content => /Logout/,
             :attributes => { :href => "/user/logout" }
  assert_no_tag "a", :content => /Register/
  assert_no_tag "a", :content => /Login/
end
```

Runing the test gives

```
> ruby test/functional/user_controller_test.rb -n test_navigation_logged_in
Loaded suite test/functional/user_controller_test
Started
.
Finished in 0.539325 seconds.

1 tests, 3 assertions, 0 failures, 0 errors
```

Of course, we could test all of the other navigation links as well. We could also test the navigation on all our other pages, and also check to make sure that the current page never has a link to itself. The testing facilities included with Rails are so powerful that, at a certain point, you realize you could just go completely nuts and test every nook and cranny of the site. Deciding where to stop is a matter of judgment; we think we've covered everything in the site that could plausibly break, so we've decided to stop here (for now).

6.4 Protecting pages

The principal use for login and authentication is to restrict access to certain pages on a site. Let's create a stub protected page, which we will use expressly for the purpose of implementing page protection separate from any other functionality. We plan to use the index page as the hub of the user's logged-in experience, so let's protect it first:

Listing 6.19 app/controllers/user_controller.rb

```
def index
  @title = "RailsSpace User Hub"
  # This will be a protected page for viewing user information.
end
```

6.4.1   Protecting pages the stupid way

Our basic strategy for protecting pages will be to check to see if the user is logged in and, if not, redirect to the login page. The quick-and-dirty way to protect the `edit_profile` action is to put the protection machinery right in the function:

Listing 6.20   app/controllers/user_controller.rb

```
def index
  unless session[:user_id]
    flash[:notice] = "Please log in first"
    redirect_to :action => "login"
    return
  end
  @title = "RailsSpace User Hub"
  # This will be a protected page for viewing user information.
end
```

Notice that we have an explicit call to `return`; this is a subtle point which could bite you some day (see the sidebar "Redirecting and returning"). Also note that, as in Section 6.2.4, we're relying on `session[:user_id]` being `nil` when a user is not logged in, so that `unless session[:user_id]` is false when there is no user logged in.

Redirecting and returning

You may have noticed that in the protected index page we have an explicit call to `return` after redirecting:

```
redirect_to :action => "login"
return
```

This is because a redirect does not immediately return (which is a property of HTTP and not a limitation of Rails). So far in this book, we've always used redirects in a context where the next line of the function executed was simply the end of the function, which contains an implicit return. In the present case, though, anything after the `unless` block would be executed:

```
def index
  unless session[:user_id]
    flash[:notice] = "Please log in first"
    redirect_to :action => "login"
    # Uh oh, no return!
  end
  @user = User.find(session[:userid])
  @title = "RailsSpace User Hub"
  # This will be a protected page for viewing user information.
end
```

> This code will break, since if the session's user id is `nil`, there will be no valid user to find and `User.find` will raise an exception.
>
> We can avoid such brittle code by putting the authentication code in a function and calling it with a `before_filter`—a technique we cover in Section 6.4.2.

6.4.2   Protecting pages the smart way

Since any site with one protected page is likely to have many, putting the authentication machinery on every protected page would be a tremendous waste of effort and a blatant violation of the DRY principle.

Rails has a facility to accomplish just this sort of task much more elegantly using a function called `before_filter`.[6] By placing our authentication code in a function called `protect`, and then putting `before_filter :protect` inside the User controller, Rails will know to call the authorization function before serving up any actions in the controller:

Listing 6.21   app/controllers/user_controller.rb

```
class UserController < ApplicationController

  before_filter :protect
  .
  .
  .

  def index
    @title = "RailsSpace User Hub"
    # This will be a protected page for viewing user information.
  end
  .
  .
  .

  private

  # Protect a page from unauthorized access.
  def protect
```

---

[6] The `before_filter` function is but one piece of a more general filter framework, which makes it possible to execute a chain of functions before and after actions in a controller. Additional functions following the same basic syntax as `before_filter` include `after_filter` and `around_filter` (a combination before/after filter); see http://rubyonrails.org/api/classes/ActionController/Filters/ClassMethods.html for more information.

```
    unless session[:user_id]
      flash[:notice] = "Please log in first"
      redirect_to :action => "login"
      return false
    end
  end
end
```

Note that the line `unless session[:user_id]` works since `nil` is false, but this code is suspect for several reasons (see the sidebar "A rough edge").

It's also important to note that we've included `return false` after the redirect in `protect`. This is because Rails uses `before_filter` to build up a *chain* of filters, executing each one in turn. In later chapters, we will sometimes have more than one function in the chain, and these functions might require a logged-in user; it's therefore important for `protect` to *break* the chain if the user isn't logged in. The way to do this is to return false.

A rough edge

You may recall from Section 6.2.4 that `nil` is false in a boolean context, which is why we can write

`unless session[:user_id]`

in `protect` instead of

`unless session[:user_id] == nil`

or

`unless session[:user_id].nil?`

This could conceivably bite you someday, and you can make a good argument for using `session[:user_id].nil?`, even if it seems a bit pedantic. The problem with saying `unless session[:user_id]` is that it doesn't say what we really mean: We wish to use `nil` *and only* `nil` as a special value to indicate "nothing." Moreover, it exposes unnecessarily our mechanism for keeping track of login status. As a result, it doesn't read at all like sensible English (which is how Ruby should read in the ideal case). This sort of rough edge may not bother you, but it does bother us,[7] and we'll clean things up in Section 6.6.

---

[7] Especially Michael.

This protection machinery may look fine, but it won't work quite right. By default, a before_filter will be run on *all* actions in a controller, which in our case would include register and (even more perversely) login itself. Rails anticipates this situation by allowing us to pass an optional hash to before_filter, which can either specify which pages to filter, or which pages *not* to filter. We can include particular pages explicitly like so:

```
before_filter :protect, :only => :index
```

Or we can exclude one or more pages:

```
before_filter :protect, :except => [ :login, :register ]
```

By the way, we can specify the included pages using symbols (as shown) or as strings; either will work (see the sidebar "Symbols vs. strings").

Since our only protected page right now is index, we'll go with the :only formulation for now; if the number of protected pages gets too large, we'll switch to the :except option:

Listing 6.22   app/controllers/user_controller.rb

```
class UserController < ApplicationController

  before_filter :protect, :only => :index
  .
  .
  .
```

Symbols vs. strings

In our before filter code, we wrote

```
before_filter :protect, :only => :index
```

but

```
before_filter :protect, :only => "index"
```

works just as well. In fact, there are many places in Rails where symbols and strings are interchangeable; another example is in the link_to function, where

```
link_to "Login", :controller => "user", :action => "login"
```

and

```
link_to "Login", "controller" => "user", "action" => "login"
```

are equivalent.

Our tendency is to use symbols when possible, but you will encounter a variety of conventions in Rails code. Ultimately, the decision is a matter of personal taste.

6.4.3   Testing protection

Testing our protection machinery is simple. First, we'll get a protected page, and then make sure that we are prompted to log in:

Listing 6.23   test/functional/user_controller_test.rb

```
# Test index page for unauthorized user.
def test_index_unauthorized
  # Make sure the before_filter is working.
  get :index
  assert_response :redirect
  assert_redirected_to :action => "login"
  assert_equal "Please log in first", flash[:notice]
end
```

Second, we'll get the same protected page as an authorized user and assert a :success response instead of a redirect:

Listing 6.24   test/functional/user_controller_test.rb

```
# Test index page for authorized user.
def test_index_authorized
  authorize @valid_user
  get :index
  assert_response :success
  assert_template "index"
end
```

Here are the results:[8]

```
> ruby test/functional/user_controller_test.rb -n /test_index_/
Loaded suite test/functional/user_controller_test
Started
..
Finished in 0.315019 seconds.

2 tests, 5 assertions, 0 failures, 0 errors
```

---

[8] The assertions here don't add up. For reasons we don't understand, at the time of this writing assert_redirected_to counts as two assertions in this context.

6.5 Friendly URL forwarding

There's one final flourish we'd like to add to our basic login functionality. One of our pet peeves is when we go to the front page of a site, click on a link for a protected page, are prompted to log in, and then get forwarded back to the front page rather than the protected page we originally requested. This is lame, lame, lame. Obviously, the site should remember the protected page we requested and then forward us *there* after logging in. Let's implement (and test) this feature, which we call "friendly forwarding."

6.5.1 The `request` variable

In order to pull this trick off, we have to figure out which page the user is trying to view. This is a job for HTTP, which maintains a bunch of variables with information about each request, including the browser type (`HTTP_USER_AGENT`), the IP number where the request is coming from (`REMOTE_ADDR`), and the address of the page requested (`REQUEST_URI`). We've used `request` many times now to test for GET versus POST requests, but there's a lot more to it; we can view all the information in the request variable by putting it at the bottom of the debug section of the layout:

Listing 6.25 app/views/layouts/application.rhtml

```
<!DOCTYPE HTML PUBLIC "-//W3C//DTD XHTML 1.0 Strict//EN"
  "http://www.w3.org/TR/xhtml1/DTD/xhtml1-strict.dtd">
<html>
  <body>
    .
    .
    .
    <% if ENV["RAILS_ENV"] == "development" %>
      <div id="debug">
        <a href="#" onclick="Element.toggle('params_debug_info');return false">
        params</a> |
        <a href="#" onclick="Element.toggle('session_debug_info');return false">
        session</a> |
        <a href="#" onclick="Element.toggle('env_debug_info');return false">
        env</a> |
        <a href="#" onclick="Element.toggle('request_debug_info');return false">
        request</a>
        <fieldset id="params_debug_info" class="debug_info" style="display: none">
          <legend>params</legend>
          <%= debug(params) %>
        </fieldset>
        <fieldset id="session_debug_info" class="debug_info" style="display: none">
          <legend>session</legend>
          <%= debug(session) %>
```

```
      </fieldset>
      <fieldset id="env_debug_info" class="debug_info" style="display: none">
        <legend>env</legend>
        <%= debug(request.env) %>
      </fieldset>
      <fieldset id="request_debug_info" class="debug_info" style="display: none">
        <legend>request</legend>
        <%= debug(request) %>
      </fieldset>
    </div>
  <% end %>
  </body>
</html>
```

Now visit (say) the "About Us" page and click on the `request` link. The resulting data dump is rather intimidating (Figure 6.7), but with experience you can learn to parse this visually and find all manner of useful things. In particular, if you use your browser's text search to look for `REQUEST_URI`,[9] you'll see that it always contains the address of the page requested, which in this case is `http://localhost:3000/site/about`. If you look closely at the request environment information (Figure 6.8), you can see that `REQUEST_URI` is actually a hash key inside of an instance variable called `@env_table`. Rails lets you access this through the attribute `request.env_table`, so that

```
request.env_table["REQUEST_URI"]
```

is the request URL. In practice, you will usually use the interface provided by the `request` variable (see below), but we mention how to get to the request URL using the raw environment table in case you ever have to puncture the abstraction layer to get at a variable not exposed by `request`. Because the environment variables are so useful, our debug JavaScript also includes a way to show just the environment information, as shown in Figure 6.9.

While grabbing the request this way will usually work, idiomatically correct Rails uses instead `request.request_uri`,[10] which is a function provided by the class for request objects, AbstractRequest.[11] It's not identical to `request.env_`

---

[9] URI is pretentious-talk for URL. Well, actually, a Uniform Resource Identifier is more general than a Uniform Resource Locator, but when it comes to URL terminology we are decidedly old-school.

[10] Using `request.env_table["REQUEST_URI"]` breaks on Microsoft's IIS web server (it's just a blank), but `request.request_uri` works fine.

[11] It's worth going to the Rails API entry for AbstractRequest to see what other request variables and functions the request object has; see `http://api.rubyonrails.org/classes/ActionController/AbstractRequest.html`

Figure 6.7   The full request dump with `REQUEST_URI` highlighted.

`table["REQUEST_URI"]`, but it's close: Rails is smart enough to strip off the opening `http://localhost:3000` from the URL, since on the local site that information is superfluous. In our example, `request.request_uri` is simply `/site/about`, which you can find out by putting

```
raise request.request_uri.inspect
```

in the `about` action.

6.5.2   Friendly login forwarding

Now that we know how to get the request URL, let's update the `protect` function to capture it in a session variable so that we can forward the user there after successfully

Figure 6.8 The full request dump with `env_table` highlighted.

logging in. We'll put the request URL for the protected page in the session under the symbol `:protected_page`:

Listing 6.26 app/controllers/user_controller.rb

```ruby
def protect
  unless session[:user_id]
    session[:protected_page] = request.request_uri
    flash[:notice] = "Please log in first"
    redirect_to :action => "login"
    return false
  end
end
```

Figure 6.9   The environment hash displayed separate from the request.

Then, in the login action, instead of redirecting blindly to the index page, we'll redirect to the forwarding URL:

Listing 6.27   app/controllers/user_controller.rb

```
def login
  @title = "Log in to RailsSpace"
  if request.post? and params[:user]
    @user = User.new(params[:user])
    user = User.find_by_screen_name_and_password(@user.screen_name,
                                                  @user.password)
```

```
    if user
      session[:user_id] = user.id
      flash[:notice] = "User #{user.screen_name} logged in!"
      if (redirect_url = session[:protected_page])
        session[:protected_page] = nil
        redirect_to redirect_url
      else
        redirect_to :action => "index"
      end
    else
      # Don't show the password again in the view.
      @user.password = nil
      flash[:notice] = "Invalid screen name/password combination"
    end
  end
end
```

The line

```
if (redirect_url = session[:protected_page])
```

may look a bit confusing. It simultaneously makes an assignment to the `redirect_url` and tests to see if it's `nil`. Even though a simultaneous assignment/test saves a line of code, we don't particularly like this style of coding, which is easily confused with the boolean comparison `==` and feels way too much like C for our taste.[12] It's relatively common, though, so we thought it would be a good idea to introduce it in case you encounter it in other people's code.

We'd also like to note how smart `redirect_to` is. Up till now, we've always redirected using an options hash with an action and possibly a controller, like so:

```
redirect_to :action => "login", :controller => "user"
```

As we saw in Section 6.5.1, `request.request_uri` is of the form `/site/about`, which is quite different. Happily, `redirect_to` can also accept a literal URL:

```
redirect_to "/site/about"
```

does just what you'd expect.

6.5.3   Friendly register forwarding

Friendly forwarding from the login action is an obvious step, but we can add a nice detail by implementing the same forwarding machinery in the register action. This way, if the

---

[12] Another reason is that we're both retreaded Python programmers, and Python doesn't allow this construction.

user hits a protected page but isn't already a RailsSpace member, after registering he will automatically be forwarded to the place he was trying to go:

Listing 6.28 app/controllers/user_controller.rb

```
def register
  @title = "Register"
  if request.post? and params[:user]
    @user = User.new(params[:user])
    if @user.save
      session[:user_id] = @user.id
      flash[:notice] = "User #{@user.screen_name} created!"
      if (redirect_url = session[:protected_page])
        session[:protected_page] = nil
        redirect_to redirect_url
      else
        redirect_to :action => "index"
      end
    end
  end
end
```

Of course, the friendly forwarding code in `register` is identical to the code in `login`, which we achieved by using the ability of our editor to copy text. This programming technique, known as the *cut-and-paste abstraction*, is an egregious violation of the DRY principle. We'll take care of this problem shortly (Section 6.6). But first, let's test our newly amiable forwarding code.

6.5.4 Friendly testing

The sequence for testing friendly forwarding is simple: Get a protected page, make sure we're forwarded to login, log in, make sure we're forwarded to the protected page:

Listing 6.29 test/functional/user_controller_test.rb

```
# Test forward back to protected page after login.
def test_login_friendly_url_forwarding
  # Get a protected page.
  get :index
  assert_response :redirect
  assert_redirected_to :action => "login"
  try_to_login @valid_user
  assert_response :redirect
  assert_redirected_to :action => "index"
```

```
  # Make sure the forwarding url has been cleared.
  assert_nil session[:protected_page]
end
```

This gives

```
> ruby test/functional/user_controller_test.rb \
      -n test_login_friendly_url_forwarding
Loaded suite test/functional/user_controller_test
Started
.
Finished in 0.112218 seconds.

1 tests, 5 assertions, 0 failures, 0 errors
```

The URL forwarding test for the `register` action is virtually identical to the one for the login test:

Listing 6.30   test/functional/user_controller_test.rb

```
# Test forward back to protected page after register.
def test_register_friendly_url_forwarding
  # Get a protected page.
  get :index
  assert_response :redirect
  assert_redirected_to :action => "login"
  post :register, :user  => { :screen_name => "new_screen_name",
                              :email       => "valid@example.com",
                              :password    => "long_enough_password" }
  assert_response :redirect
  assert_redirected_to :action => "index"
  # Make sure the forwarding url has been cleared.
  assert_nil session[:protected_page]
end
```

Running this gives

```
> ruby test/functional/user_controller_test.rb \
      -n test_register_friendly_url_forwarding
Loaded suite test/functional/user_controller_test
Started
.
Finished in 0.13922 seconds.

1 tests, 5 assertions, 0 failures, 0 errors
```

Though this second test works fine, it uses the cut-and-paste abstraction again—part of a disturbing trend this entire chapter. It's time to fix this; it's time to roll up our sleeves and *refactor*.

6.6 Refactoring basic login

During the process of writing the actions in the User controller, we've accumulated quite a bit of cruft: We've exposed in several places our implementation of user login status, and we've also cluttered both our actions and our tests with duplicated code. In this section, we'll make our code beautiful again by *refactoring* it—that is, we'll change the appearance of the code without altering what it does. If you haven't experienced the joys of refactoring, this may seem pointless; after all, what could possibly matter other than the behavior of our application? The answer, of course, is that the guts of the application might not matter to our users, or to our computers, but they matter a lot to the programmers.[13] Well-organized, beautiful code is easier to maintain and easier to extend, and it tends to have fewer bugs as well.

In many cases, refactoring involves eliminating duplication of code by capturing the patterns in some abstraction (such as a new object or function), but that's not necessarily the case. In refactoring the login function, we'll mainly be defining auxiliary functions, not to remove duplication, but rather to allow us to write a shorter main function while moving code around so that its location better reflects the logical structure of our application. In our case, this will eliminate duplication, but improving the readability of the code is an end in itself.

Of course, refactoring can be dangerous business. How can we be confident that we're not altering what our code does? How can we be sure that we're not introducing bugs? There's no way to be sure, of course, but we do have one huge factor in our favor: by diligently writing tests for our model, our controllers, and our views, we have accumulated a comprehensive suite of tests. Tests let you refactor mercilessly; as long as the new code passes our test suite, we can be confident that its essential behavior is unchanged.

6.6.1 Logged in?

One theme of good programming practice, for which refactoring is especially useful, is building *abstraction layers*. This technique involves erecting barriers between different parts of the system in order to hide irrelevant details and allow the programmer to deal with higher-level constructs. We've already seen several examples of this design principle in Rails, most prominently in Active Record, which is an abstraction layer for SQL databases.

---

[13] That would be us.

In our present case, we have unnecessarily exposed the implementation details of user login status in several places. In particular, when checking to see if the user is logged in, we have been using the session variable explicitly. What we really want to ask, though, is whether the user is logged in, which has nothing necessarily to do with the session.

Let's build a (very small) abstraction layer by defining a function called `logged_in?` in the test to see if the user id session variable is `nil`. The only question is, where should we put it? If we put `logged_in?` in the User controller, we can use it in the `protect` function, but we won't be able to use it in the layout. If we put it in the Application helper file `app/helpers/application_helper.rb` (the same place we put `nav_link` in Section 4.4.1), we can use it in the layout but not in the controller.

The tension here is a product of the MVC achitecture that Rails uses: We can nicely partition our application into distinct pieces, but what if we need a function (such as `logged_in?`) in more than one place? The solution is to pick one place to put the function and then *include* it into the other parts of the application that need it.

The Ruby way to make a function available to multiple classes is to define that function in a *module* and then include the module into any classes that need it, producing a so-called *mixin* (because the functions in the module are mixed into the class). If you look at `app/helpers/application_helper.rb`, you'll see that it defines the `ApplicationHelper` module, whereas the User controller defines a class, not a module. What this means is that if we put our utility function in the Application helper, we can mix it into our User controller, thereby having it in both places. So, first we define the function as follows:

Listing 6.31 app/helpers/application_helper.rb

```
# Return true if some user is logged in, false otherwise.
def logged_in?
  not session[:user_id].nil?
end
```

Then we mix it in:

Listing 6.32 app/controllers/user_controller.rb

```
class UserController < ApplicationController
  include ApplicationHelper
  .
  .
  .
end
```

Note that, in contrast to our previous use, the `logged_in?` function explicitly tests to see if `session[:user_id]` is `nil` by calling the `nil?` method. If we had followed our previous practice, we would have left the comparison implicit and written

```ruby
def logged_in?
  session[:user_id]
end
```

As long as we always used `logged_in?` in a boolean context, this code would work fine, but we think it's downright confusing—providing further evidence that explicitly testing for `nil` is a good idea.

As mentioned above, there are several places where we can use our new `logged_in?` function. The most obvious use is in our protection filter, `protect`:

Listing 6.33 app/controllers/user_controller.rb

```ruby
def protect
  unless session[:user_id]
    session[:protected_page] = request.request_uri
    flash[:notice] = "Please log in first"
    redirect_to :action => "login"
    return false
  end
end
```

becomes

Listing 6.34 app/controllers/user_controller.rb

```ruby
def protect
  unless logged_in?
    session[:protected_page] = request.request_uri
    flash[:notice] = "Please log in first"
    redirect_to :action => "login"
    return false
  end
end
```

The navigation in our layout is another place:

Listing 6.35 app/views/layouts/application.rhtml

```
<% if session[:user_id] -%>
  <%= nav_link "Hub", "user", "index" %> |
  <%= nav_link "Logout", "user", "logout" %>
<% else -%>
  <%= nav_link "Register", "user", "register" %> |
  <%= nav_link "Login", "user", "login" %>
<% end -%>
```

becomes

Listing 6.36 app/views/layouts/application.rhtml

```
<% if logged_in? -%>
  <%= nav_link "Hub", "user", "index" %> |
  <%= nav_link "Logout", "user", "logout" %>
<% else -%>
  <%= nav_link "Register", "user", "register" %> |
  <%= nav_link "Login", "user", "login" %>
<% end -%>
```

Finally, we can even use `logged_in?` in our tests, as long as we include `Application-Helper` at the beginning of the test class:

Listing 6.37 test/functional/user_controllor_test.rb

```
class UserControllerTest < Test::Unit::TestCase
  include ApplicationHelper
  fixtures :users
  .
  .
  .
  # Test a valid registration.
  def test_registration_success
    post :register, :user  => { :screen_name => "new_screen_name",
                                :email       => "valid@example.com",
                                :password    => "long_enough_password" }
    # Test assignment of user.
    user = assigns(:user)
    .
    .
    .
    # Make sure user is logged in properly.
```

Continues

```
    assert logged_in?
    assert_equal user.id, session[:user_id]
  end
  .
  .
  .

  # Test a valid login.
  def test_login_success
    try_to_login @valid_user
    assert logged_in?
    assert_equal @valid_user.id, session[:user_id]
    assert_equal "User #{@valid_user.screen_name} logged in!", flash[:notice]
    assert_response :redirect
    assert_redirected_to :action => "index"
  end
  .
  .
  .

  # Test the logout function.
  def test_logout
    try_to_login @valid_user
    assert logged_in?
    get :logout
    assert_response :redirect
    assert_redirected_to :action => "index", :controller => "site"
    assert_equal "Logged out", flash[:notice]
    assert !logged_in?
  end
```

Note that, as in Section 5.6.1, we use the negation operator ! (pronounced "bang"), in this case to assert that the user is not logged in (`assert !logged_in?`); using the `not` keyword instead would require a profusion of parentheses: `assert((not logged_in?))`.

6.6.2 Log in!

There's a second place where we've exposed the session machinery behind login status, namely, in the `login` action:

Listing 6.38 app/controllers/user_controller.rb

```
  def login
    .
    .
    .
```

```
if user
   session[:user_id] = user.id
```

Our current login action reduces our flexibility if we decide to change something about the way we implement user login. In addition, as it stands our code requires the reader to infer that `session[:user_id]` will be used to determine login status. We really want the code to tell the reader what it does, namely, log the user in:

Listing 6.39   app/controllers/user_controller.rb

```
def login
   .
   .
   .
   if user
      user.login!(session)
```

Note that we've ended our new user login method with an exclamation point (see the sidebar "If yes then `change!`").

If yes? then change!

By now, we've seen many examples of how boolean functions in Ruby usually end with question marks. Ruby follows a second useful punctuation convention: Functions that change the state of the variable—an operation called *mutation*—typically end in an exclamation point. Among other things, mutation can result in all sorts of subtle bugs, so Ruby considers it good form to warn the reader when it occurs.

We've chosen to call our user login function `login!` to indicate that something (in this case, the session) is being mutated. A second example appears in the `logout!` function in Section 6.6.3. (These examples aren't as "pure" as most native Ruby examples; for example, `user.login!` mutates the session, not the user. But that's the nature of web programming—because HTTP is a stateless protocol, we have to maintain some sort of information about the user outside of the User model.)

A simple `irb` example should make clear the distinction between mutating and nonmutating actions. If `a` is an array, `a.reverse` returns the reversed array but leaves `a` alone, while `a.reverse!` mutates `a` by reversing it in place:

```
irb(main):001:0> a = [1, 2, 3, 4, 5]
=> [1, 2, 3, 4, 5]
irb(main):002:0> a.reverse
=> [5, 4, 3, 2, 1]
irb(main):003:0> a
```

```
=> [1, 2, 3, 4, 5]
irb(main):004:0> a.reverse!
=> [5, 4, 3, 2, 1]
irb(main):005:0> a
=> [5, 4, 3, 2, 1]
```

As far as we can tell, Ruby borrowed both the `boolean?` and `mutation!` conventions from Scheme, a dialect of Lisp invented by Guy Steele and Gerry Sussman.[14]

To get this code to work, we need to implement `login!` in the User model:

Listing 6.40 app/models/user.rb
_____

```
# Log a user in.
def login!(session)
  session[:user_id] = self.id
end
```
_____

Though we've encountered it before briefly in migrations, this is the first time we've written our own code using the `self` keyword. Inside of a class, all of the class attributes are available using `self`; that is, instead of writing `user.id`, inside the User class we write `self.id` instead. In fact, we can go one better: When accessing a class attribute inside of the class, we can even omit `self`:

Listing 6.41 app/models/user.rb
_____

```
# Log a user in.
def login!(session)
  session[:user_id] = id
end
```
_____

Notice that we've simply passed the session as an argument to our `login!` method. Even though the session is a fairly complicated object, implemented using either a filesystem or a database (if you followed our suggestion in Section 6.1.1), Rails allows us to treat it just like a hash, which includes the ability to pass it as a parameter to a function.[15]

_____

[14] For a challenging introduction to computer programming using Scheme, we warmly recommend *Structure and Interpretation of Computer Programs* by Abelson and Sussman (known as SICP—"sick-pee"—to the cognoscenti). The entire text of SICP is available online through `http://mitpress.mit.edu/sicp/`, but you may find that investing in a hard copy is worthwhile nevertheless.

[15] In other words, `session` is an abstraction layer for the underlying session mechanism (whatever it may be).

There are two actions that log the user in—`register` and `login`—so we should update both of them to use the new `login!` method:

Listing 6.42   app/controllers/user_controller.rb

```
class UserController < ApplicationController
  .
  .
  .

  def register
    @title = "Register"
    if request.post? and params[:user]
      @user = User.new(params[:user])
      if @user.save
        @user.login!(session)
        flash[:notice] = "User #{@user.screen_name} created!"
        if (redirect_url = session[:protected_page])
          session[:protected_page] = nil
          redirect_to redirect_url
        else
          redirect_to :action => "index"
        end
      end
    end
  end

  def login
    @title = "Log in to RailsSpace"
    if request.post? and params[:user]
      @user = User.new(params[:user])
      user = User.find_by_screen_name_and_password(@user.screen_name,
                                                   @user.password)
      if user
        user.login!(session)
        flash[:notice] = "User #{user.screen_name} logged in!"
        if (redirect_url = session[:protected_page])
          session[:protected_page] = nil
          redirect_to redirect_url
        else
          redirect_to :action => "index"
        end
      else
        # Don't show the password again in the view.
        @user.password = nil
        flash[:notice] = "Invalid screen name/password combination"
      end
```

Continues

```
      end
    end
      .
      .
      .
  end
```

6.6.3 Log out!

Since we've hidden the login machinery behind the `login!` function, it makes sense to have a complementary `logout!` function as well. Unfortunately, while the user login function can be attached to a user object, we can't easily do the same for the `logout!` function. When the user clicks the Logout button, we really aren't doing anything to the user; instead, we are breaking the association between the current browser session and the user. In our original `logout` action, we acted directly on the session, setting the session's `user_id` to `nil`. But if we wanted to have the `logout!` function be a normal (instance) method attached to an object, we would first have to create a user object, which we would then use to call the `logout!` method. Creating a User object just to call `logout!` seems a bit wasteful; fortunately, we have another option. We can create a *class function*—a function that is attached to the entire class, not just to specific instances of the class. We have already used some class fuctions, including `User.new` and `User.find_by_screen_name_and_password`; now we'll create one of our own:

Listing 6.43 app/models/user.rb

```
# Log a user out.
def self.logout!(session)
  session[:user_id] = nil
end
```

Note that we define a class method with the `self` keyword. Just as `self.id` is the user id in the context of a user method that would typically be written `user.id` elsewhere, `self.logout!` is used inside the User class to define a method that is written as `User.logout!` outside of the class. (We can't omit `self` in this case because that would create a normal method attached to user objects.)

Of course, the purpose of this new method is to be used in our `logout` action:

Listing 6.44 app/controllers/user_controller.rb

```
def logout
  User.logout!(session)
  flash[:notice] = "Logged out"
  redirect_to :action => "index", :controller => "site"
end
```

This makes it clear to the reader that the method logs the user out, without the ugliness of creating a superfluous user instance.

Is creating a `User.logout!` method for just one line of code a bit of overkill? Perhaps. But then, practical experience shows that improving readability is useful by itself; moreover, having a separate method just to perform the user logout (as opposed to filling the flash and performing the redirect) puts that one line of code in a useful context, and introduces a nice symmetry with the `login!` method. Finally, making abstraction layers is a good habit of mind to cultivate; a useful rule of thumb is: When in doubt, build an abstraction layer. (We will, in fact, see our `User.logout!` pay off a bit in Section 7.2.3.)

6.6.4   Clear password!

There's another one-line function we can use to improve the readability of one of our actions, in this case `login`:

Listing 6.45 app/controllers/user_controller.rb

```
def login
  .
  .
  .
    else
      # Don't show the password again in the view.
      @user.password = nil
      flash[:notice] = "Invalid screen name/password combination"
    end
  end
end
```

The line

```
@user.password = nil
```

doesn't describe what it does, namely, clear the password so it won't be shown again in the view. In fact, its meaning is obscure enough that we felt compelled to write a clarifying comment. We believe in writing self-documenting code whenever possible, which means defining functions to describe what a block of code is doing (even if it's only one line); often, apart from documentation comments (Section 4.4.1), we find that explanatory comments are a sign of a missing function. In this spirit, let's define a function called `clear_password!` in the User model:

Listing 6.46 app/models/user.rb

```
# Clear the password (typically to suppress its display in a view).
def clear_password!
  self.password = nil
end
```

Since this function mutates a user, we've chosen to end the function name with an exclamation point.

There is an important subtlety in this function as well: notice that we've left the `self` keyword in front of `password`. This is because Ruby lets us define local variables that override the class attributes. The line

```
password = nil
```

would create a *local* variable called `password` with value `nil`. In order to assign to a user object's attribute, we have to keep the `self` keyword.

With our new function in hand, our login function appears as follows:

Listing 6.47 app/controllers/user_controller.rb

```
def login
  @title = "Log in to RailsSpace"
  if request.post? and params[:user]
    @user = User.new(params[:user])
    user = User.find_by_screen_name_and_password(@user.screen_name,
                                                 @user.password)
    if user
      user.login!(session)
      flash[:notice] = "User #{user.screen_name} logged in!"
      if (redirect_url = session[:protected_page])
        session[:protected_page] = nil
        redirect_to redirect_url
      else
        redirect_to :action => "index"
      end
    else
```

```
      @user.clear_password!
      flash[:notice] = "Invalid screen name/password combination"
    end
  end
end
```

Let's take this opportunity to incorporate our newly paranoid attitude toward passwords by clearing the password in the register action in the same way that we do in login:

```
def register
  @title = "Register"
  if request.post? and params[:user]
    @user = User.new(params[:user])
    if @user.save
      @user.login!(session)
      flash[:notice] = "User #{@user.screen_name} created!"
      if (redirect_url = session[:protected_page])
        session[:protected_page] = nil
        redirect_to redirect_url
      else
        redirect_to :action => "index"
      end
    else
      @user.clear_password!
    end
  end
end
```

If you run the functional tests at this point, you'll realize that this change necessitates a corresponding change in the registration failure test. Where before we had `:value =>` `"sun"`, we now use `:value => nil`:[16]

Listing 6.48   test/functional/user_controller_test.rb

```
# Test an invalid registration
def test_registration_failure
  post :register, :user  => { :screen_name => "aa/noyes",
                              :email       => "anoyes@example,com",
                              :password    => "sun" }
  .
  .
  .
```

Continues

---

[16] In this context, using `:value =>` `" "` also works, but using the empty string doesn't work if the input tag is missing the `value` attribute altogether. In contrast, `:value => nil` works in both cases.

```
    assert_tag "input",
              :attributes => { :name => "user[password]",
                               :value => nil },
              :parent => error_div
end
```

6.6.5 Unduplicated form handling

So far, our refactoring has focused on improving the readability and logical structure
of our application. Now we come to the second major purpose of refactoring, the
elimination of code duplication. You may have noticed that both the login and register
actions use the same code to test for a valid form submission:

```
if request.post? and params[:user]
```

We expect that this kind of test will be common in RailsSpace, so it makes sense to
eliminate this duplication and capture the common pattern in a function, which we'll
call `param_posted?` and put in the User controller:

Listing 6.49 app/controllers/user_controller.rb

```
    private
    .
    .
    .
    # Return true if a parameter corresponding to the given symbol was posted.
    def param_posted?(symbol)
      request.post? and params[symbol]
    end
```

Note that we've designed `param_posted?` to take a symbol as an argument so that it
can be used for more than just the `:user` symbol. Note also that we didn't have to pass
`params` as an argument, since it's a global variable inside of any controller.

With this new function in hand, both the login and register actions are cleaned
up nicely:

Listing 6.50 app/controllers/user_controller.rb

```
    def register
      @title = "Register"
      if param_posted?(:user)
        .
        .
        .
```

```
      end
    end

  def login
    @title = "Log in to RailsSpace"
    if param_posted?(:user)
      .
      .
      .
    end
  end
```

6.6.6 Unduplicated friendly forwarding

The last bit of refactoring packages the friendly forwarding machinery from Section 6.5 into a function:

Listing 6.51 app/controllers/user_controller.rb

```
  private
  .
  .
  .

  # Redirect to the previously requested URL (if present).
  def redirect_to_forwarding_url
    if (redirect_url = session[:protected_page])
      session[:protected_page] = nil
      redirect_to redirect_url
    else
      redirect_to :action => "index"
    end
  end
```

Then we simply use the function in both actions where it's needed:

Listing 6.52 app/controllers/user_controller.rb

```
def register
  @title = "Register"
  if param_posted?(:user)
    @user = User.new(params[:user])
    if @user.save
      @user.login!(session)
```

Continues

```
      flash[:notice] = "User #{@user.screen_name} created!"
      redirect_to_forwarding_url
    else
      @user.clear_password!
    end
  end
end

def login
  @title = "Log in to RailsSpace"
  if param_posted?(:user)
    @user = User.new(params[:user])
    user = User.find_by_screen_name_and_password(@user.screen_name,
                                                 @user.password)
    if user
      user.login!(session)
      flash[:notice] = "User #{user.screen_name} logged in!"
      redirect_to_forwarding_url
    else
      @user.clear_password!
      flash[:notice] = "Invalid screen name/password combination"
    end
  end
end
```

Finally, we can remove the side effects of the cut-and-paste abstraction in our tests by defining an auxiliary function for testing friendly URL forwarding, and then use it in each of the relevant tests:

Listing 6.53 test/functional/user_controller_test.rb

```
# Test forward back to protected page after login.
def test_login_friendly_url_forwarding
  user = { :screen_name => @valid_user.screen_name,
           :password    => @valid_user.password }
  friendly_url_forwarding_aux(:login, :index, user)
end

# Test forward back to protected page after register.
def test_register_friendly_url_forwarding
  user = { :screen_name => "new_screen_name",
           :email       => "valid@example.com",
           :password    => "long_enough_password" }
  friendly_url_forwarding_aux(:register, :index, user)
end
```

```
private
.
.
.

def friendly_url_forwarding_aux(test_page, protected_page, user)
  get protected_page
  assert_response :redirect
  assert_redirected_to :action => "login"
  post test_page, :user  => user
  assert_response :redirect
  assert_redirected_to :action => protected_page
  # Make sure the forwarding url has been cleared.
  assert_nil session[:protected_page]
end
```

6.6.7 Sanity check

With all that refactoring finished, let's run our tests to show that everything still works:

```
> rake
.
.
.
  12 tests, 53 assertions, 0 failures, 0 errors
.
.
.
  17 tests, 78 assertions, 0 failures, 0 errors
```

Phew!

CHAPTER 7

Advanced login

Although the basic login functions in Chapter 6 are probably already good enough for government work, there's one feature we'd like to add that turns out to be both challenging and instructive: a "remember me" box that, when checked, allows RailsSpace to remember the login status of its users. Like basic login, this involves using the session to maintain user state, but it also requires using browser *cookies* (and the methods Rails has for manipulating them). Cookies represent a more permanent way of maintaining state than the session, allowing us to remember users even after they've closed their browsers.

Implementing the "remember me" feature is surprisingly complicated, producing rather bloated and ugly code. Before tackling this code bloat, we'll dig even deeper into Rails tests, including extensive testing of our cookie functions and an example of integration testing (mentioned briefly in Chapter 5). Once our test suite is complete, we'll refactor the authentication functions with a vengeance, producing a surprisingly compact and elegant login action.

7.1 So you say you want to be remembered?

As the login code stands now (as of the end of Chapter 6), users are automatically logged out if they close their browsers. It's a bit inconvenient to have to log in to a site every time you relaunch your browser, though, so let's create a way for users to avoid logging in repeatedly. To do this, we'll need a way of maintaining user state that goes beyond a disk- (or database-) based session; we'll need to use a cookie, which is a small piece of text placed on the user's computer that can persist even if the user shuts down his browser.[1]

---

[1] Rails actually maintains its sessions using a cookie, but that cookie expires automatically upon closing the browser. Making that cookie more permanent would not only involve mucking around with the Rails internals, it would also present a security risk if the user happened to visit RailsSpace from a public computer.

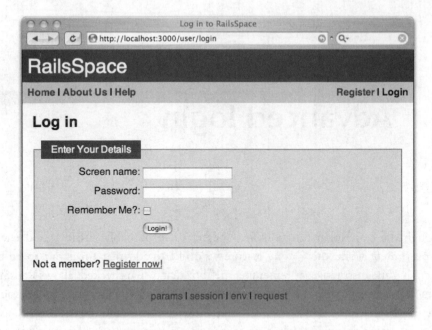

Figure 7.1 The "remember me?" checkbox.

7.1.1 A "remember me" box

We're sure our readers have seen a "remember me" checkbox on the login page of many sites. Unless you have a really good reason to violate them, it's best to conform to web conventions, so we'll implement the "remember me" feature using a checkbox as well. Let's add the following code to login.rhtml after the password field, resulting in a login page as shown in Figure 7.1:

Listing 7.1 app/views/user/login.rhtml

```
    .
    .
    .
<div class="form_row">
  <label for="password">Password:</label>
  <%= form.password_field :password,
                          :size => User::PASSWORD_SIZE,
                          :maxlength => User::PASSWORD_MAX_LENGTH %>
</div>

<div class="form_row">
  <label for="remember_me">Remember Me?:</label>
```

```
  <%= form.check_box :remember_me %>
</div>

<div class="form_row">
  <%= submit_tag "Login!", :class => "submit" %>
</div>
.
.
.
```

Before submitting this form, let's take a look at where we ended in Chapter 6:

Listing 7.2 app/controllers/user_controller.rb

```
def login
  @title = "Log in to RailsSpace"
  if param_posted?(:user)
    @user = User.new(params[:user])
    user = User.find_by_screen_name_and_password(@user.screen_name,
                                                 @user.password)
    if user
      user.login!(session)
      flash[:notice] = "User #{user.screen_name} logged in!"
      redirect_to_forwarding_url
    else
      @user.clear_password!
      flash[:notice] = "Invalid screen name/password combination"
    end
  end
end
```

There's nothing suspicious looking in this code, so let's enter Foo Bar's screen name (`foobar`) and password (`bazquux`) and click submit.

Alas, the page breaks (Figure 7.2). For a hint about why, take another look at `login.rhtml`. There are fields corresponding to two attributes of a user: the screen name and password. On submission, these fields get passed to the controller via `params` under the key `:user`, which we turn into a user instance variable using the line

```
@user = User.new(params[:user])
```

The problem is that, with the added `remember_me` field, `params` also contains a reference to `:remember_me`, so `User.new` gamely tries to create an `@user.remember_me` attribute—which doesn't, in fact, exist.

Let's open a console session to see just what went wrong.

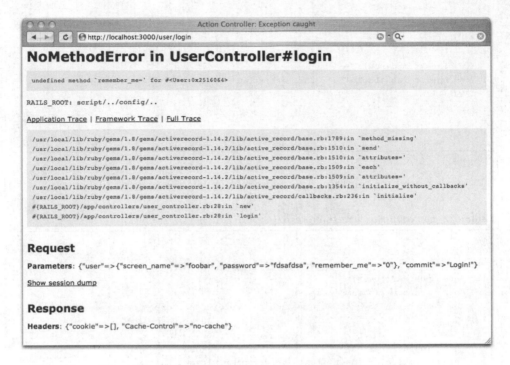

Figure 7.2   The error Rails displays when trying to log in `foobar`.

```
> ruby script/console
>> @user = User.new(:screen_name => "foobar", :password => "bazquux")
=> #<User:0xb7638438 @attributes={"screen_name"=>"foobar",
"password"=>"bazquux", "email"=>""}, @new_record=true>
>> @user = User.new(:screen_name => "foobar", :password => "bazquux",
?>                  :remember_me => "1")
NoMethodError: undefined method `remember_me=' for #<User:0xb76877e0>
```

So, if we pass in a hash with just a screen name and password, the user works fine, but if we give it a "remember me" key-value pair as well, we get a NoMethodError exception. Somehow, we have to add a method that responds to a call like `@user.remember_me`.

7.1.2   A "remember me" attribute

We could fix the problem of the missing user `remember_me` attribute by adding a column to the User model using a migration. That would cause Active Record to create a `remember_me` attribute in just the same way it created the `screen_name` and `password` attributes. There's absolutely no reason to do this, though, since there are only two uses for the `remember_me` parameter:

1. To provide the value for a `remember_me` cookie on the user's browser and
2. To create an `@user` instance variable for use in the login action and view.[2]

In neither case do we need to use the database.

What we need is a way to create a `remember_me` attribute in the User class without introducing a new column name in the database. Unsurprisingly, Ruby provides a convenient construct to do exactly this, called `attr_accessor` ("attribute accessor"):

Listing 7.3 app/models/user.rb

```
class User < ActiveRecord::Base
  attr_accessor :remember_me
  .

  .

  .
end
```

Let's take a look at the console again and see if we've made an improvement:

```
>> reload!
>> @user = User.new(:screen_name => "foobar", :password => "bazquux",
?>                   :remember_me => "1")
=> #<User:0xb76115e0 @attributes={"screen_name"=>"foobar",
"password"=>"bazquux", "email"=>""}, @new_record=true, @remember_me="1">
>> @user.remember_me
=> "1"
```

Now our user has no trouble handling a "remember me" attribute.

We can get an even better hint about what's going on by looking at the result

```
=> #<User:0xb76115e0 @attributes={"screen_name"=>"foobar",
"password"=>"bazquux", "email"=>""}, @new_record=true, @remember_me="1">
```

Note that the user instance has an `@attributes` variable containing the user attributes from the columns in our User model, while "remember me" has its own instance variable `@remember_me`.[3] Through the magic of Active Record, we can access both the elements of `@attributes` and normal class attributes like `remember_me` using the same uniform dot syntax.

---

[2] Just as `@user.screen_name` determines the text appearing in the screen name text box, the value of `@user.remember_me` determines whether or not the checkbox is checked.

[3] In fact, inside of the User class, the "remember me" attribute is an instance variable, available in any of the functions in the class in much the same way that controller instance variables are available in the views. Creating an instance variable using `attr_accessor :remember_me` exposes it to the user, granting both read and write access on `remember_me`.

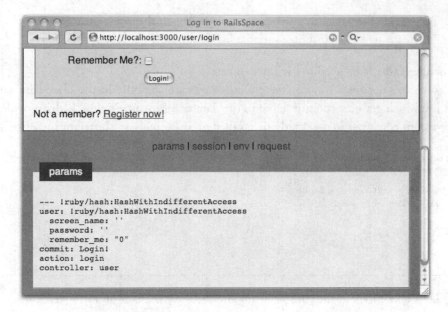

Figure 7.3 Debug information shown when blank form is submitted with checkbox unchecked.

7.1.3 The "remember me" cookie

We're now at the point where submitting the page won't cause it to break, but it still doesn't do anything. What we need to do is set a cookie indicating that the user wants to be remembered if he checks the box. By reading the Rails API—or, more conveniently, by submitting the login page and looking at the debug information—we can figure out that the `check_box` function uses the string `"0"` for "unchecked" (Figure 7.3) and `"1"` for "checked" (Figure 7.4).

Now, `@user = User.new(params[:user])` takes all of the user attributes from the request and sets them as attributes of the instance variable `@user`. This means that we can just look at the `remember_me` attribute of `@user` to find out if the box is checked:

Listing 7.4 app/controllers/user_controller.rb

```
def login
  @title = "Log in to RailsSpace"
  if param_posted?(:user)
    @user = User.new(params[:user])
    user = User.find_by_screen_name_and_password(@user.screen_name,
                                                 @user.password)
```

```
if user
  user.login!(session)
  if @user.remember_me == "1"
    # The box is checked, so set the remember_me cookie.
  end

  .
  .
  .
```

Now we come to the matter of setting the cookie. Rails provides a hash-like `cookies` variable (similar to the `session` variable) for storing and retrieving values from the browser's cookies. (Each cookie is simply a key-value pair stored as text on the browser, so they map naturally to hashes.) To set a cookie, we simply assign a value for a particular key; for example, to set the "remember me" cookie to `"1"`, we could use this:

Listing 7.5 app/controllers/user_controller.rb

```
if @user.remember_me == "1"
  cookies[:remember_me] = "1"
end
```

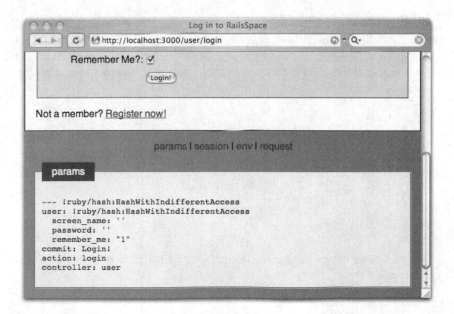

Figure 7.4 Debug information shown when a blank form is submitted with the checkbox checked.

(Before being sent to the browser, the symbol `:remember_me` is converted to the string `"remember_me"`.)

This would appear to work at first, but cookies set in this manner have the default behavior for cookies: They disappear after the browser is closed—hardly the behavior we want for the "remember me" cookie! To get the behavior we want, we can pass `cookies` a hash, giving the cookie both a value and an expiration:

Listing 7.6   app/controllers/user_controller.rb

```
if @user.remember_me == "1"
  cookies[:remember_me] = { :value   => "1",
                            :expires => 10.years.from_now }

end
```

This code will set a cookie with value `"1"` that expires ten years from now (a time chosen simply to be "a long time"). The expiration code—which might look a bit mysterious—is an example of the remarkable ability of Ruby to add methods onto virtually anything, even numbers (see the sidebar "`1.language.to_rule_them_all`").

1.language.to_rule_them_all

Ruby grants a lot of power to its users and, in a frantic act of desperation to gain market share, actually trusts them to be sensible about using it. There is perhaps no better example of this than Ruby's policy of allowing programmers to add methods to any Ruby class, even built-in ones such as `Fixnum`:[4]

```
> irb
irb(main):001:0> class Fixnum
irb(main):002:1>   def foo
irb(main):003:2>     "bar"
irb(main):004:2>   end
irb(main):005:1> end
=> nil
irb(main):006:0> 2.foo
=> "bar"
```

You can even, if you're drunk enough, override a default method, such as exponentiation (`**`):

---

[4] A *fixnum* is a particular machine's definition of a "small" integer. On a typical 32-bit machine, the biggest fixnum is $2^{30}-1$, which is a little over a billion.

```
> irb
irb(main):001:0> 2**3
=> 8
irb(main):002:0> class Fixnum
irb(main):003:1>   def **(other)
irb(main):004:2>     0
irb(main):005:2>   end
irb(main):006:1> end
=> nil
irb(main):007:0> 2**3
=> 0
```

Rails takes advantage of this freedom to add a bunch of extraordinary methods to the `Numeric` class, the fundamental base class for numbers in Ruby.[5] The most useful in the context of a typical application has to do with time, as in the `10.years.from_now` we used to set the "remember me" cookie's expiration date. Here are a few more examples:[6]

```
> ruby script/console
Loading development environment.
>> 2.seconds
=> 2
>> 2.minutes
=> 120
>> 2.days
=> 172800
>> 2.days.ago
=> Mon Aug 14 08:49:42 PDT 2006
>> 2.days.from_now
=> Fri Aug 18 08:49:55 PDT 2006
>> 2.months.from_now
=> Sun Oct 15 08:50:14 PDT 2006
```

Sweet!

With our cookie-setting code inserted, our login function appears as follows:

Listing 7.7   app/controllers/user_controller.rb

```
def login
  @title = "Log in to RailsSpace"
```

Continues

---

[5] As a result, these methods work with "big" integers (class `Bignum`) and floating-point numbers (class `Float`) as well as with fixnums.

[6] Since these are Rails additions to Ruby, they won't work in `irb`.

```
  if param_posted?(:user)
    @user = User.new(params[:user])
    user = User.find_by_screen_name_and_password(@user.screen_name,
                                                  @user.password)

    if user
      user.login!(session)
      if @user.remember_me == "1"
        cookies[:remember_me] = { :value   => "1",
                                  :expires => 10.years.from_now }
      end
      flash[:notice] = "User #{user.screen_name} logged in!"
      redirect_to_forwarding_url
    else
      @user.clear_password!
      flash[:notice] = "Invalid screen name/password combination"
    end
  end
end
```

We're almost done, but not quite. Suppose that we log in as Foo Bar with the "remember me" box checked, log out, and then revisit the login page. Conventional web usage dictates that the checkbox should still be checked, but that's not what happens now. We can get the behavior we want by setting the "remember me" attribute of a user instance variable for a GET request, since that's the kind of request for a normal (unsubmitted) hit:

Listing 7.8 app/controllers/user_controller.rb

```
def login
  @title = "Log in to RailsSpace"
  if request.get?
    @user = User.new(:remember_me => cookies[:remember_me] || "0")
  elsif param_posted?(:user)
    @user = User.new(params[:user])
    .
    .
    .
end
```

(We should note briefly the use of the elsif keyword, which is Rubyspeak for else if. Where the middle "e" went, we'll never know.)

To make sure that the user instance variable has the right value for its remember_me attribute, we use the code snippet cookies[:remember_me] || "0". If that looks confusing, a quick irb session should make things a bit clearer:

```
> irb
irb(main):001:0> "1" || "0"
=> "1"
irb(main):002:0> nil || "0"
=> "0"
```

The reason this works is that the || operator uses *short-circuit evaluation*: It returns the first true value it encounters. In other words, if the value is "1", return it; if it's nil (i.e., if the cookie hasn't been set or has been deleted[7]), return "0". We should note that using or in place of || won't work because the two operators have different precedence (see the sidebar "or or ||?").

---

or or ||?

Like most modern computer languages, Ruby has a rich set of operators whose order of execution depends on their relative *precedence*. For example, as in the rules of arithmetic, in Ruby 2 + 3 * 4 is 14 instead of 20 because multiplication (*) has a higher precedence than addition (+). (See http://phrogz.net/ ProgrammingRuby/language.html#table_18.4 for a complete operator precedence table.)

The rules of precedence in Ruby are mostly obvious, but an important exception concerns the "word" boolean operators not, or, and and, together with their corresponding "symbolic" versions !, ||, and &&. They are the same except for their precedence, and this is the source of a couple of common gotchas.

In the case of assigning a hash value, as in the login action's User.new (:remember_me => cookies[:remember_me] || "0"), the lower precedence of or results in an error:

```
> irb
irb(main):001:0> foo = nil
=> nil
irb(main):002:0> bar = "not nil"
=> "not nil"
irb(main):003:0> h = { :baz => foo or bar }
SyntaxError: compile error
(irb):3: parse error, unexpected kOR, expecting '}'
h = { :baz => foo or bar}
                  ^
        from (irb):3
        from :0
irb(main):004:0> h = { :baz => foo || bar }
=> {:baz=>"not nil"}
```

---

[7] When we add the code to forget the user at the end of Section 7.2, we plan to delete the "remember me" cookie.

The error saves us in this case, but we can see an even more pernicious pitfall by continuing the `irb` session and alternately using `or` and `||` in an assignment:

```
irb(main):005:0> baz = foo or bar
=> "not nil"
irb(main):006:0> baz
=> nil
irb(main):007:0> baz = foo || bar
=> "not nil"
irb(main):008:0> baz
=> "not nil"
```

Because `or` has a lower precedence than the assignment operator `=`, a construction such as `baz = foo or bar` *always* assigns `foo` to `baz`, even when `foo` is `nil`. In contrast, the symbolic version `||` has a higher precedence than `=`, so `baz = foo || bar` assigns `foo` to `baz` *unless* `foo` is `nil` (or `false`), in which case `baz` is assigned the value of `bar`.

Our practice is to use the word versions for readability in boolean tests; for example,

```
if one_thing or another
```

We reserve use of the symbolic versions for when they are necessary because of their higher precedence.

With that last bit of cookie manipulation in place, our "remember me" checkbox feature is complete: The box will be checked or not depending on the user's choice. There's only one problem: At no point do we actually remember the user!

7.2 Actually remembering the user

To remember the user, the plan is to place a second cookie on his browser to identify him[8] on subsequent visits. To this end, we'll create an authorization token—which can be any sequence of characters that identifies the user uniquely—and then store it both in the database and on the user's browser. Then we'll implement a function to check for an authorization cookie when a user visits our site; if it matches the authorization cookie for a valid user, the user will automatically be logged in.

---

[8] We welcome female members of RailsSpace, but we have to choose either *him* or *her* in order to avoid the ungrammatical *them*, and we've gone with the traditional (male) choice. Also, we are realistic about our site's demographics.

In contrast to the "remember me" cookie, we want to associate the authorization token with a particular user, so it should be part of the User model. Let's add a column to the users table:

```
> ruby script/generate migration AddAuthorizationToken
      exists  db/migrate
      create  db/migrate/004_add_authorization_token.rb
```

Listing 7.9 db/migrate/004_add_authorization_token.rb

```
class AddAuthorizationToken < ActiveRecord::Migration
  def self.up
    add_column :users, :authorization_token, :string
  end

  def self.down
    remove_column :users, :authorization_token
  end
end
```

As usual, we update the database using `rake`:

```
> rake db:migrate
(in /rails/rails_space)
== AddAuthorizationToken: migrating ==========================================
-- add_column(:users, :authorization_token, :string)
   -> 0.3528s
== AddAuthorizationToken: migrated (0.3531s) =================================
```

7.2.1 An authorization cookie

Now that we've created a place in the User model for an authorization token, it's time to set the token and put it in a cookie for future retrieval. It's tempting to use the obvious unique value for the user, namely, his id. Let's do that now for simplicity (but be sure to see Section 7.2.4 to find out why this is actually a terrible solution):

Listing 7.10 app/controllers/user_controller.rb

```
def login
  .
  .
  .
  if @user.remember_me == "1"
    cookies[:remember_me] = { :value   => "1",
                              :expires => 10.years.from_now }
```

Continues

```
      user.authorization_token = user.id
      user.save!
      cookies[:authorization_token] = {
        :value   => user.authorization_token,
        :expires => 10.years.from_now }
    end
      .
      .
      .
end
```

Note that we've used the `save!` function in place of `save` (see the sidebar "Another use!"). The difference between the two is that `save!` results in an error (by raising an `ActiveRecord::RecordInvalid` exception) if the save fails rather than returning `nil` as `save` does. Previously, in the context of saving an Active Record object back to the database, we've always had some sort of test to make sure that the save actually worked (i.e., `if @user.save...`). We have elected to use `save!` when remembering the user because we want to make sure that the function successfully updates the user object with a new authorization token. If we were to use `save` instead, then any problems would cause a silent failure—`save` would simply return `nil`, and that would have no effect whatsoever. We would be none the wiser that our "remember me" functionality had failed. (Of course, a good test suite would catch any consistent problem, but a transient failure on the production machine would go undetected; moreover, assuming that we don't run our test suite every few minutes, the immediate failure would alert us sooner rather than later.)

Another use!

We've mentioned the philosophy of using an exclamation point to indicate mutation (Section 6.6.2). We've now seen a second, closely related use: If we have a user object, we distinguish between two distinct kinds of saving by using either `user.save` or `user.save!`.

Invoking `user.save` *might* mutate the user object in the database, but it might not; if it doesn't, it just returns `nil`, which we can include in an `if` clause to take appropriate action depending on the outcome. We might call this case *weak mutation*, since no mutation necessarily takes place. In contrast, `user.save!` *must* successfully mutate the user object in the database, or else it raises an exception. We can call this case *strong mutation*, since a failure to mutate is an error. The exclamation point is a reminder that a mutation must occur.

As a last step in the "remember me" section of the login action, we should forget the user by deleting the cookies if the remember me box is unchecked:

Listing 7.11 app/controllers/user_controller.rb

```
if @user.remember_me == "1"
  cookies[:remember_me] = { :value   => "1",
                            :expires => 10.years.from_now }
  user.authorization_token = user.id
  user.save!
  cookies[:authorization_token] = {
    :value   => user.authorization_token,
    :expires => 10.years.from_now }
else
  cookies.delete(:remember_me)
  cookies.delete(:authorization_token)
end
```

Here we use the `cookies.delete` function, which simply deletes the cookie corresponding to the given symbol.[9]

7.2.2 Remembering that we remembered

Now that we've placed a unique authorization cookie on the user's browser, all we need to do is find that user when he returns to the site (in case he closed his browser in the interim). The function to check for proper authorization should be run on every page on the site, since every page is potentially affected by the user login status. The proper home for such a site-wide function is in the Application controller, `application.rb` (which we met briefly when discussing the controller inheritance hierarchy in Section 2.4.1). We'll define an authorization function to check for the cookie on the browser, look for the corresponding user in the database, and log the user in if such a user exists:

Listing 7.12 app/controllers/application.rb

```
# Filters added to this controller will be run for all controllers in the^
application.
# Likewise, all the methods added will be available for all controllers.
class ApplicationController < ActionController::Base
```

Continues

---

[9] In case you're not in the habit yet, this would be a good time to look up `cookies` in the Rails API.

```
  # Pick a unique cookie name to distinguish our session data from others'
  session :session_key => '_rails_space_session_id'

  # Check for a valid authorization cookie, possibly logging the user in.
  def check_authorization
    if cookies[:authorization_token] and not session[:user_id]
      user = User.find_by_authorization_token(cookies[:authorization_token])
      if user
        session[:user_id] = user.id
      end
    end
  end
end
```

Since `authorization_token` is a column in the User model, you might already have guessed that Rails automagically creates a `find_by_authorization_token` for us, which we have used to good effect. Note also that, in case the authorization token is invalid for some reason, we only log the user in if we find a user corresponding to that token using `if user`.

The only necessary step left is to run `check_authorization` before every action in every controller on the entire site. We learned in Section 6.4.2 that we could run a function before any action in the User controller by placing a `before_filter` in that controller (though in that case it turned out we wanted to restrict the before filter to certain pages only). Since the Application controller lies at the base of all our controller classes, all we need to do is set up a `before_filter` inside the `Application-Controller` class to run it on every action in RailsSpace:

Listing 7.13 app/controllers/application.rb

```
class ApplicationController < ActionController::Base

  before_filter :check_authorization

  # Pick a unique cookie name to distinguish our session data from others'
  session :session_key => '_rails_space_session_id'

  # Check for a valid authorization cookie, possibly logging the user in.
  def check_authorization
    if cookies[:authorization_token] and not session[:user_id]
      user = User.find_by_authorization_token(cookies[:authorization_token])
      if user
        session[:user_id] = user.id
      end
```

```
      end
    end
end
```

This `check_authorization` function will work fine, but it may leave you with a slightly unclean feeling: What about all the nice utility functions we defined when refactoring the login function in Section 6.6? It would be great to use them again here. We'll include the `ApplicationHelper` module as in Section 6.6.1 to get the `logged_in?` function; meanwhile, we get the `login!` function for free since it's a method on the user object. Finally, we have one more piece of (minor) duplication—we access the authorization token cookie twice, so let's create a local variable to hold its value. With these bits of polish, `check_authorization` appears as follows:[10]

Listing 7.14 app/controllers/application.rb

```
class ApplicationController < ActionController::Base
  include ApplicationHelper

  before_filter :check_authorization

  # Pick a unique cookie name to distinguish our session data from others'
  session :session_key => '_rails_space_session_id'

  def check_authorization
    authorization_token = cookies[:authorization_token]
    if authorization_token and not logged_in?
      user = User.find_by_authorization_token(authorization_token)
      user.login!(session) if user
    end
  end
end
```

And that's it!

7.2.3 Updating `logout`

Unsurprisingly, since we're now storing authentication information in a cookie, we need to delete that cookie when the user logs out. Let's put the relevant code in the `logout!` function we defined when refactoring the logout action in Chapter 6:

---

[10] Since `UserController` inherits from `ApplicationController`, you can now remove the line `include ApplicationHelper` from `app/controllers/user_controller.rb`, though it does no harm if you leave it in.

Listing 7.15 app/models/user.rb

```
# Log a user out.
def self.logout!(session, cookies)
  session[:user_id] = nil
  cookies.delete(:authorization_token)
end
```

Note that we haven't deleted the "remember me" cookie. This is just a convention, but it's a common one on the web: Just because a user has logged out doesn't mean that he doesn't want his screen name remembered the next time he logs in. This way, that "remember me" box will still be checked the next time he visits the login page.

Because logging out now requires a cookie deletion, we've added the cookies as an argument to `logout!`. That means we need to update the call to `User.logout!` in the User controller by including `cookies`. It's incredibly easy to forget to update the argument list in this manner; suppose that we did forget but were in the habit of running our test suite regularly:

```
> rake
.
.
.
Started
..........E.....
Finished in 0.545465 seconds.

  1) Error:
test_logout(UserControllerTest):
ArgumentError: wrong number of arguments (1 for 2)
  /rails/rails_space/config/../app/controllers/user_controller. rb:58:in 'logout!'
.
.
.
```

You can see how a test suite can really save you a lot of pain.

Now that we've caught the mistake, we'll correct it by adding `cookies` to `User.logout!`:

Listing 7.16 app/controllers/user_controller.rb

```
def logout
  User.logout!(session, cookies)
  flash[:notice] = "Logged out"
  redirect_to :action => "index", :controller => "site"
end
```

You should be sufficiently paranoid by now to run the tests again, just to make sure:

```
> rake
(in /rails/rails_space)
/usr/local/bin/ruby -Ilib:test "/usr/local/lib/ruby/gems/1.8/gems/rake-
0.7.1/lib/rake/rake_test_loader.rb" "test/unit/user_test.rb"
Loaded suite /usr/local/lib/ruby/gems/1.8/gems/rake-0.7.1/lib/rake/rake_test_loader
Started
...........
Finished in 0.352008 seconds.

12 tests, 51 assertions, 0 failures, 0 errors
/usr/local/bin/ruby -Ilib:test "/usr/local/lib/ruby/gems/1.8/gems/rake-
0.7.1/lib/rake/rake_test_loader.rb" "test/functional/site_controller_test.rb"
"test/functional/user_controller_test.rb"
Loaded suite /usr/local/lib/ruby/gems/1.8/gems/rake-0.7.1/lib/rake/rake_test_loader
Started
................
Finished in 0.599558 seconds.

17 tests, 86 assertions, 0 failures, 0 errors
```

Whew!

7.2.4   A more secure cookie

Using the user id as the authentication token works fine, but only in the sense that it will take an enterprising black hat about 30 seconds[11] to figure out how to log in as virtually any user on the site. The reason is that anyone who looks at his browser cookies will see that the authorization token is just an integer. If a malicious cracker were user number 145, for example, he would see 145 in his browser cookies, and he could easily guess that setting the cookie to 146 would let him log in as the user who registered immediately after him. He would then go on to realize that he could compromise other accounts using virtually any integer (up to the total number of RailsSpace users).

To plug this terrible hole, we should use an authorization token that is both unique and hard to guess. We'll use a standard approach to this problem and run a string identifying the user through a secure *hashing algorithm*. A hashing algorithm converts some piece of data into a kind of digital "fingerprint" (called a *message digest*) identifying that data. One common use of hashing algorithms is, appropriately enough, in hash tables, which are essentially arrays of values indexed by the corresponding key digests.

---

[11] Only 20 seconds if he also has a mustache.

Secure hash functions are designed so that it's difficult to figure out anything about the data using just the digest.

At first glance, it seems that hashing the user's screen name will identify him uniquely. That's true, but screen names are easy to guess, so anybody using the same hashing algorithm could impersonate our user by hashing his username. Hashing just the password doesn't work, either; although that piece of data is presumably harder to guess, two different users could easily have the same password. But, taken together, the screen name and password do constitute a unique string identifying the user—as long as they are separated by a character that's not allowed in a screen name. Otherwise, there would be no way to tell the difference between screen name `foobar`/password `bazquux` and screen name `foobarb`/password `azquux`, since both would have the same combination `foobarbazquux`. Any invalid screen name character will do as a separator; we'll use a colon (`:`), yielding a combination like `foobar:bazquux`. (For a slightly more involved solution to the same basic problem, do a web search on *salted hash*.)

Ruby comes equipped with SHA1, a commonly used secure hashing algorithm, which we'll use to make the authorization token. To see how it works, let's use the console:[12]

```
> ruby script/console
Loading development environment.
>> require 'digest/sha1'
=>[]
>> user = User.find_by_screen_name("foobar"); 0
=> 0
>> "#{user.screen_name}:#{user.password}"
=> "foobar:bazquux"
>> Digest::SHA1.hexdigest("#{user.screen_name}:#{user.password}")
=> "599d203b3ac93126851f5566c3bf059d07e47183"
```

That digest looks pretty hard to guess. The only way to generate it would be to know both the screen name and password, but of course in that case you wouldn't have any trouble logging in as the user anyway. (By the way, don't worry if the expression `Digest::SHA1.hexdigest` looks intimidating or confusing; we stole this code from Dave Thomas and used it long before we understood it. Never let a little mysterious syntax get in the way of stealing some good code.)

To use SHA1 on RailsSpace, all we need to do is require it at the top of our User model (just as we did in the console session):

---

[12] Note that we're suppressing the display of the user object using the `; 0` trick from Section 5.6.3.

Listing 7.17 app/controllers/user_controller.rb

```ruby
require 'digest/sha1'
class UserController < ApplicationController
  .
  .
  .
  def login
    .
    .
    .
      if @user.remember_me == "1"
        cookies[:remember_me] = {:value   => "1",
                                 :expires => 10.years.from_now}
        user.authorization_token = Digest::SHA1.hexdigest(
                                  "#{user.screen_name}:
                                  #{user.password}")
        user.save!
        cookies[:authorization_token] = {
          :value   => user.authorization_token,
          :expires => 10.years.from_now }
      else
        cookies.delete(:remember_me)
        cookies.delete(:authorization_token)
      end
    .
    .
    .
  end
  .
  .
  .
end
```

Now, upon logging in with the "remember me" box checked, the `authorization_token` cookie will be placed on the user's browser, as shown in Figure 7.5.

7.2.5 The finished (?) functions

With the cookie authorization feature added, our complete login function looks like this:

Listing 7.18 app/controllers/user_controller.rb

```ruby
def login
  @title = "Log in to RailsSpace"
  if request.get?
```

Continues

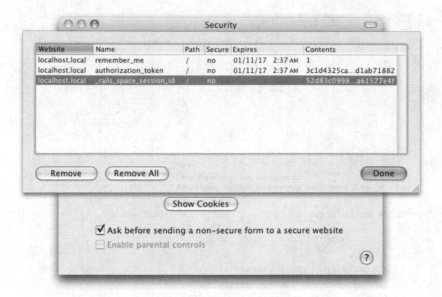

Figure 7.5 Viewing cookies on the Safari browser.

```ruby
    @user = User.new(:remember_me => cookies[:remember_me] || "0")
  elsif param_posted?(:user)
    @user = User.new(params[:user])
    user = User.find_by_screen_name_and_password(@user.screen_name,
                                                 @user.password)
    if user
      user.login!(session)
      if @user.remember_me == "1"
        cookies[:remember_me] = { :value   => "1",
                                  :expires => 10.years.from_now }
        user.authorization_token = Digest::SHA1.hexdigest(
                                  "#{user.screen_name}:#{user.password}")
        user.save!
        cookies[:authorization_token] = {
          :value   => user.authorization_token,
          :expires => 10.years.from_now }
      else
        cookies.delete(:remember_me)
        cookies.delete(:authorization_token)
      end
      flash[:notice] = "User #{user.screen_name} logged in!"
      redirect_to_forwarding_url
    else
      @user.clear_password!
      flash[:notice] = "Invalid screen name/password combination"
```

```
      end
   end
end
```

We hope you agree that the login function has gotten rather unwieldy, and we're just itching to refactor it. But don't forget the cardinal rule: first test, then refactor. Once we've updated our test suite to verify the correctness of our "remember me" machinery, we'll refactor with gusto.

7.3 "Remember me" tests

We've added quite a lot of functionality with the "remember me" feature, so there are several tests to update and a couple of new tests to write. First, we'll update the login tests and add a new one. Then we'll update the logout function. Finally, we'll test the check_authorization filter to make sure that users who log out, close their browsers, and return to the site are automatically logged back in. This final test will use the amazing integration testing mentioned briefly in the introduction to this chapter. In the process of writing all these tests, we'll discover several subtleties to Rails testing, including an important cautionary tale.

By the way, if you want to run the tests as we go along, you will need to prepare the test database, since we've added some migrations since our last test:

```
> rake db:test:prepare
  (in /rails/rails_space)
```

7.3.1 Updated login tests

The first test update is test_login_page, just to make sure that the checkbox is actually there:

Listing 7.19 test/functional/user_controller_test.rb

```
# Make sure the login page works and has the right fields.
def test_login_page
  .
  .
  .
  assert_tag "input", :attributes => { :name => "user[remember_me]",
                                       :type => "checkbox" }
  assert_tag "input", :attributes => { :type => "submit",
                                       :value => "Login!" }
end
```

That was easy; the first real challenge is the update to `test_login_success`. We'll use this test to verify that the right things happen when the checkbox is unchecked. This means posting a `remember_me` variable with value `"0"`. We expect that the user's "remember me" attribute won't be `"1"`,[13] and we expect both the "remember me" and authorization cookies to be `nil`:

Listing 7.20 test/functional/user_controller_test.rb

```ruby
# Test a valid login.
def test_login_success
  try_to_login @valid_user, :remember_me => "0"
  assert logged_in?
  assert_equal @valid_user.id, session[:user_id]
  assert_equal "User #{@valid_user.screen_name} logged in!", flash[:notice]
  assert_response :redirect
  assert_redirected_to :action => "index"

  # Verify that we're not remembering the user.
  user = assigns(:user)
  assert user.remember_me != "1"
  # There should be no cookies set.
  assert_nil cookies[:remember_me]
  assert_nil cookies[:authorization_token]
end
.
.
.
private

# Try to log a user in using the login action.
# Pass :remember_me => "0" or :remember_me => "1" in options
# to invoke the remember me machinery.
def try_to_login(user, options = {})
  user_hash = { :screen_name => user.screen_name,
                :password    => user.password }

  user_hash.merge!(options)
  post :login, :user => user_hash
end
```

Note that we've updated the `try_to_login` function to take an options hash, which is empty by default; if `options` is `:remember_me => "0"`, then the user hash gains

---

[13] We could check to see if it's `"0"`, but in the production code what we actually check is whether it's `"1"` or not, so we've decided to test that behavior directly.

that key-value pair through the `merge!` method, which combines the attributed of two hashes.[14] A quick `irb` session shows how it works:

```
> irb
irb(main):001:0> user_hash = { :screen_name => "foo", :password => "barbaz" }
=> {:screen_name=>"foo", :password=>"barbaz"}
irb(main):002:0> options = { :remember_me => "0" }
=> {:remember_me=>"0"}
irb(main):003:0> user_hash.merge!(options)
=> {:screen_name=>"foo", :password=>"barbaz", :remember_me=>"0"}
```

Apart from the updated `try_to_login` function, our test seems fairly straightforward, but unfortunately it doesn't work. Or rather, it works, but for the wrong reason: it turns out that, inside of tests, Rails (as of version 1.2) always returns `nil` when cookies are accessed using symbols (as you would have discovered to your consternation in the next test, when the "remember me" box is checked, and we expect that the corresponding cookie is not `nil`).

Instead of using symbols, in tests you have to use strings as hash keys and extract the cookie value explicitly; in other words, `cookies["remember_me"].value`, in the context of tests, lets you access the value given by `cookies[:remember_me]` in a controller. Unfortunately, it's still not quite the same thing: In a test, an empty cookie is not `nil`, but is rather the empty array `[]`. In addition, for a nonempty cookie, the value is returned inside of an array; for example, when the "remember me" box is checked, the corresponding cookie value `cookies["remember_me"].value` is `["1"]` inside the test rather than just `"1"`. What a pain in the neck.[15]

Those are a lot of annoyances, and we expect that they will be fixed in future versions of Rails; in the meantime, there are several ways around these problems. Our solution is to write a couple of auxiliary functions to help us look at cookie values (and expirations, which we'll need momentarily) using a more convenient notation:

Listing 7.21 test/functional/user_controller_test.rb

```
private
  .
  .
  .
```

Continues

---

[14] See `http://www.ruby-doc.org/core/classes/Hash.html`.

[15] By the way, we figured all these things out by interrupting our tests using the `raise object.inspect` trick from Section 4.3—using, for example, `raise cookies["remember_me"].inspect` to look at the "remember me" cookie.

```
# Return the cookie value given a symbol.
def cookie_value(symbol)
  cookies[symbol.to_s].value.first
end

# Return the cookie expiration given a symbol.
def cookie_expires(symbol)
  cookies[symbol.to_s].expires
end
```

These functions use the `to_s` ("to string") method (which exists for all Ruby objects) and the `first` method on arrays:

```
> irb
irb(main):001:0> :remember_me.to_s
=> "remember_me"
irb(main):002:0> ["1", "2"].first
=> "1"
irb(main):003:0> ["1"].first
=> "1"
irb(main):004:0> [].first
=> nil
```

With these utility functions on hand, we can rewrite our test as follows:

Listing 7.22   test/functional/user_controller_test.rb

```
# Test a valid login.
def test_login_success
  try_to_login @valid_user, :remember_me => "0"
  assert logged_in?
  assert_equal @valid_user.id, session[:user_id]
  assert_equal "User #{@valid_user.screen_name} logged in!", flash[:notice]
  assert_response :redirect
  assert_redirected_to :action => "index"

  # Verify that we're not remembering the user.
  user = assigns(:user)
  assert user.remember_me != "1"
  # There should be no cookies set.
  assert_nil cookie_value(:remember_me)
  assert_nil cookie_value(:authorization_token)
end
```

Let's run it to make sure it works:

```
> ruby test/functional/user_controller_test.rb -n test_login_success
Loaded suite test/functional/user_controller_test
```

```
Started
.
Finished in 0.160388 seconds.

1 tests, 8 assertions, 0 failures, 0 errors
```

The test of a checked "remember me" box now seems relatively straightforward:

Listing 7.23   tests/functional/user_controller_test.rb

```
def test_login_success_with_remember_me
  try_to_login @valid_user, :remember_me => "1"
  test_time = Time.now
  assert logged_in?
  assert_equal @valid_user.id, session[:user_id]
  assert_equal "User #{@valid_user.screen_name} logged in!", flash[:notice]
  assert_response :redirect
  assert_redirected_to :action => "index"

  # Check cookies and expiration dates.
  user = User.find(@valid_user.id)

  # Remember me cookie
  assert_equal "1", cookie_value(:remember_me)
  assert_equal 10.years.from_now(test_time),
               cookie_expires(:remember_me)

  # Authorization cookie
  cookie_token = cookies["authorization_token"].value.to_s
  assert_equal user.authorization_token, cookie_value(:authorization_token)
  assert_equal 10.years.from_now(test_time),
               cookie_expires(:authorization_token)
end
```

There are two subtleties in this test. First, the login function sets a cookie based on the timestamp `10.years.from_now` as calculated *within* the login function itself. There's no simple way to get access to that timestamp, so we do the next best thing by recording the time immediately after posting the login information. We then feed that test time to `10.years.from_now`, which takes an optional timestamp to use as the start time for its calculation.[16]

The second subtlety involves a difficulty in comparing timestamps, and in fact our test doesn't work as currently written:

```
> ruby test/functional/user_controller_test.rb \
      -n test_login_success_with_remember_me
```

---

[16] The default is just `Time.now`.

```
Started
F
Finished in 0.424256 seconds.

  1) Failure:
test_login_success_with_remember_me(UserControllerTest) [./test/
functional/user_controller_test.rb:145]:
<Thu Sep 08 08:33:23 PDT 2016> expected but was
<Thu Sep 08 08:33:23 PDT 2016>.
```

That doesn't make any sense, since the two expirations appear to be identical. What's going on is that internally Ruby stores timestamps as microseconds since the *epoch* (January 1, 1970 00:00 UTC), and the two timestamps we're comparing don't agree to the microsecond. The solution is to use the Ruby assertion `assert_in_delta`, which asserts that the difference between two floating point numbers is less than some error tolerance (delta). On any modern computer, the timestamps should agree to within 100 microseconds, but any disagreement much bigger than that indicates a problem, so the test should fail in that case. Modifying the cookie expiration assertions to use `assert_in_delta` completes our test:

Listing 7.24 tests/functional/user_controller_test.rb

```
# Test a valid login with the remember box checked.
def test_login_success_with_remember_me
  try_to_login @valid_user, :remember_me => "1"
  test_time = Time.now
  assert logged_in?
  assert_equal @valid_user.id, session[:user_id]
  assert_equal "User #{@valid_user.screen_name} logged in!", flash[:notice]
  assert_response :redirect
  assert_redirected_to :action => "index"

  # Check cookies and expiration dates.
  user = User.find(@valid_user.id)
  time_range = 100 # microseconds range for time agreement

  # Remember me cookie
  assert_equal "1", cookie_value(:remember_me)
  assert_in_delta 10.years.from_now(test_time),
                  cookie_expires(:remember_me),
                  time_range

  # Authorization cookie
  assert_equal user.authorization_token, cookie_value(:authorization_token)
  assert_in_delta 10.years.from_now(test_time),
                  cookie_expires(:authorization_token),
                  time_range
end
```

Finally, we have working tests for the "remember me" function:

```
> ruby test/functional/user_controller_test.rb -n /test_login_success/
Loaded suite test/functional/user_controller_test
Started
..
Finished in 0.282308 seconds.

2 tests, 17 assertions, 0 failures, 0 errors
```

7.3.2   Updated logout test

There's just one more function in the User controller to test: the logout function. We just need to make sure that the authorization token cookie is deleted:

Listing 7.25   tests/functional/user_controller_test.rb

```ruby
# Test the logout function.
def test_logout
  try_to_login @valid_user, :remember_me => "1"
  assert logged_in?
  assert_not_nil cookie_value(:authorization_token)
  get :logout
  assert_response :redirect
  assert_redirected_to :action => "index", :controller => "site"
  assert_equal "Logged out", flash[:notice]
  assert !logged_in?
  assert_nil cookie_value(:authorization_token)
end
```

We put in a lot of effort in this section, but finally all the User controller tests should work:

```
> ruby test/functional/user_controller_test.rb
Loaded suite test/functional/user_controller_test
Started
............
Finished in 0.93413 seconds.

14 tests, 81 assertions, 0 failures, 0 errors
```

Hallelujah!

7.4   Advanced tests: Integration testing

The last aspect of the "remember me" functionality that we have to test is remembering that we remembered. Our plan will be to log in with the "remember me" box checked, then clear the session (thereby simulating the user closing his browser), and

finally visit some arbitrary page of our site to verify that the user has automatically
been logged in. This is quite a complicated test, requiring multiple page views on more
than one controller—just the situation handled by integration testing, which essentially
simulates a user clicking through the pages on our site.

7.4.1   Testing cookie remembering: The first cut

Since integration tests typically span more than one controller, they haven't been
automatically created by any of our previous `generate` commands, which have been
restricted to single controllers or models. Unsurprisingly, though, there is a way to generate them; since we're testing our "remember me" machinery, let's create an integration
test for `remember_me`:

```
> ruby script/generate integration_test remember_me
      exists  test/integration
      create  test/integration/remember_me_test.rb
```

Note that the generate script automatically knows to create a test called
`remember_me_test.rb` based on the argument `remember_me`.

Let's take a look at our shiny new integration test:

Listing 7.26   test/integration/remember_me_test.rb

```
require "#{File.dirname(__FILE__)}/../test_helper"

class RememberMeTest < ActionController::IntegrationTest
  # fixtures :your, :models

  # Replace this with your real tests.
  def test_truth
    assert true
  end
end
```

As with our previous tests, the default test is trivial; let's run it with the `rake` task
specialized for integration tests, `rake test:integration`:

```
> rake test:integration
(in /rails/rails_space)
.
Finished in 0.105 seconds.

1 tests, 1 assertions, 0 failures, 0 errors
```

For the real test, we'll need to load a valid user, so let's include our users fixture with
`fixtures :users`, together with a setup function defining a user instance variable

@user. We'll also include the `ApplicationHelper` module so that we have access to our login utility function `logged_in?`. With these changes, our "remember me" test looks like this:

Listing 7.27   test/integration/remember_me_test.rb

```ruby
require "#{File.dirname(__FILE__)}/../test_helper"

class RememberMeTest < ActionController::IntegrationTest
  include ApplicationHelper

  fixtures :users

  def setup
    @user = users(:valid_user)
  end

  # Replace this with your real tests.
  def test_truth
    assert true
  end
end
```

Now that those steps are done, let's write a test for the "remember me" feature:

Listing 7.28   test/integration/remember_me_test.rb

```ruby
require "#{File.dirname(__FILE__)}/../test_helper"

class RememberMeTest < ActionController::IntegrationTest
  include ApplicationHelper

  fixtures :users

  def setup
    @user = users(:valid_user)
  end

  def test_remember_me
    # Log in with "remember me" enabled.
    post "user/login", :user => { :screen_name => @user.screen_name,
                                  :password    => @user.password,
                                  :remember_me => "1" }
    # Simulate "closing the browser" by clearing the user id from the session.
    @request.session[:user_id] = nil
    # Now access an arbitrary page.
```

Continues

```
    get "site/index"
    # The check_authorization before_filter should have logged us in.
    assert logged_in?
    assert_equal @user.id, session[:user_id]
  end
end
```

We'll take this step by step. The initial login step should look familiar from the User controller test `test_login_with_remember_me`, except for the argument to `post`. Before, we supplied `post` with a symbol corresponding to the relevant action (i.e., `post:login`), which was unambiguous because the test was specific to the User controller; the test knows to use the User controller automatically. Since integration tests can access multiple controllers, though, we need to post a string specifying both the action and the controller.

After logging in with "remember me" enabled, we simulate closing the browser with the line[17]

```
@request.session[:user_id] = nil
```

Once we've cleared the user id from the session, we hit an arbitrary page on the site using `get` (which we choose to be the site index without loss of generality) and then make sure that the `before_filter` logged the user in.

Run the test, and you'll see that it passes:

```
> rake test:integration
(in /rails/rails_space)
.
Finished in 0.185 seconds.

1 tests, 2 assertions, 0 failures, 0 errors
```

7.4.2   Testing the test: A cautionary tale

The test in the previous section sure does look good, and it is. But beware: Looks can be deceiving. Consider, for example, this virtually identical test:

Listing 7.29 test/integration/remember_me_test.rb

```
  def test_remember_me
    # Log in with remember me enabled.
    post "user/login", :user => { :screen_name => @user.screen_name,
```

---

[17] Recall from Section 6.3.2 that we must use `@request.session` when assigning to the session in a test.

```
                                     :password    => @user.password,
                                     :remember_me => "1" }
     # Simulate "closing the browser" by clearing the user id from the session.
     session[:user_id] = nil
     # Now access an arbitrary page.
     get "site/index"
     # The check_authorization before_filter should have logged us in.
     assert logged_in?
     assert_equal @user.id, session[:user_id]
   end
```

The only difference between this test and the previous one is the line

```
session[:user_id] = nil
```

instead of

```
@request.session[:user_id] = nil
```

Why is this such a big problem? As we saw starting in Section 6.2.2, in tests we can *access* the session variable using `session` (without the `@request`), so that `session[:user_id]` returns the correct value (1 in this case). Unfortunately, in integration tests you can seemingly assign to it the same way. Unfortunately, such manipulations don't actually do anything, even though the test appears to work:[18]

Listing 7.30   test/integration/remember_me_test.rb

```
   def test_remember_me
     # Log in with remember me enabled.
     post "user/login", :user => { :screen_name => @user.screen_name,
                                    :password    => @user.password,
                                    :remember_me => "1" }
     puts session[:user_id]     # Prints "1", the string for @user.id.
     session[:user_id] = 42     # some bogus value
     puts session[:user_id]     # Prints "42".
     # Now access an arbitrary page.
     get "site/index"
     # The session has reverted to its previous value!
     puts session[:user_id]     # Prints "1"!
     # The check_authorization before_filter should have logged us in.
     assert logged_in?
     assert_equal @user.id, session[:user_id]
   end
```

---

[18] Thankfully, a similar assignment to `session` in a functional test raises an error.

We discovered this problem accidentally. We forgot to use `@request.session`, using plain `session` instead; meanwhile, it turned out there was actually a typo in our `check_authorization` function: we had written `log_in!` (with an underscore) instead of `login!`:

Listing 7.31   app/controllers/application.rb

```
class ApplicationController < ActionController::Base
  include ApplicationHelper

  before_filter :check_authorization

  # Log a user in by authorization cookie if necessary.
  def check_authorization
    authorization_token = cookies[:authorization_token]
    if authorization_token and not logged_in?
      user = User.find_by_authorization_token(authorization_token)
      user.log_in!(session) if user
    end
  end
end
```

Despite (apparently) giving the user id in the session a completely bogus value, while simultaneously having a broken authorization check, this test passes easily. The problem is that the assignment to the session variable is a fraud. There is, in fact, a global variable called `session`, but assigning to it in an integration test doesn't actually change that variable; instead, it creates a new *local* variable, also called `session`—which promptly gets overwritten (and restored back to the global `session` variable) when we get a new page.

The solution is simple: In tests, always use `@request.session` when accessing or assigning to the session variable.

7.4.3   Some reflections on Rails testing

It should be clear from all our "remember me" testing that the Rails testing facilities have several pitfalls waiting to trap the unwary. In particular, we've seen that the handling of cookies in functional tests is distinctly suboptimal, and there's a big gotcha associated with using the session in integration tests. It's a good idea when using the less mature aspects of Rails testing to "test the tests" by occasionally breaking parts of the site by hand (with typos, for example) just to make sure that the relevant tests fail.

Despite these issues, it's important that the larger points don't get lost. First, the vast majority of Rails testing facilities are rock solid. The things that broke (cookie symbol access, integration testing session assignment) are on the bleeding edge of testing, and aren't even attempted by most other frameworks. Rails testing is clearly pushing the envelope, so it's hard to fault it for having a few rough edges. In addition, Rails continues to evolve and improve rapidly, and we expect that as it matures further, its testing facilities will rapidly converge on perfect. Finally, we *were* able to hack around the problems. Rails and Ruby give us enough power to overcome even enormous obstacles.

7.5   Refactoring redux

When last we left the login action, it had become bloated and ugly—nothing like the svelte login function we knew and loved at the end of Chapter 6. Here is where we stand:

Listing 7.32   app/controllers/user_controller.rb

```
def login
  @title = "Log in to RailsSpace"
  if request.get?
    @user = User.new(:remember_me => cookies[:remember_me] || "0")
  elsif param_posted?(:user)
    @user = User.new(params[:user])
    user = User.find_by_screen_name_and_password(@user.screen_name,
                                                  @user.password)
    if user
      user.login!(session)
      if @user.remember_me == "1"
        cookies[:remember_me] = { :value   => "1",
                                  :expires => 10.years.from_now }
        user.authorization_token = Digest::SHA1.hexdigest(
                                     "#{user.screen_name}:#{user.password}")
        user.save!
        cookies[:authorization_token] = {
          :value   => user.authorization_token,
          :expires => 10.years.from_now }
      else
        cookies.delete(:remember_me)
        cookies.delete(:authorization_token)
      end
      flash[:notice] = "User #{user.screen_name} logged in!"
      redirect_to_forwarding_url
    else
      @user.clear_password!
      flash[:notice] = "Invalid screen name/password combination"
    end
  end
end
```

Now that we've updated our test suite to exercise all of the "remember me" machinery, it's time to refactor this puppy. Let's start by changing the code we use to remember the user.

7.5.1   Refactoring remember

If you look at the code between `if @user.remember_me == "1"` and `else`, you'll see that it's basically all concerned with remembering the user. This is similar in many ways to recording the user's login status with `login!`, so let's go with that analogy and define a user method called `remember!`. In order to get it to work, we only have to do two things: change `user` to `self`, and move the line requiring the SHA1 library from the User controller to the User model:

Listing 7.33   app/models/user.rb

```
require 'digest/sha1'
class User < ActiveRecord::Base
  .
  .
  .
  # Remember a user for future login.
  def remember!(cookies)
    cookies[:remember_me] = { :value   => "1",
                              :expires => 10.years.from_now }
    self.authorization_token = Digest::SHA1.hexdigest(
                                "#{self.screen_name}:#{self.password}")
    self.save!
    cookies[:authorization_token] = {
      :value   => self.authorization_token,
      :expires => 10.years.from_now }
  end
end
```

The login action is already cleaned up considerably:

Listing 7.34   app/controllers/user_controller.rb

```
def login
  .
  .
  .
  if user
    user.login!(session)
```

```
    if @user.remember_me == "1"
      user.remember!(cookies)
    else
      cookies.delete(:remember_me)
      cookies.delete(:authorization_token)
    end
      .
      .
      .
end
```

Let's turn now to beautifying the `remember!` function. We learned in Section 6.6.2 that we can omit the `self` keyword when accessing functions or attributes that are part of the class, so that (for example) `id` is the same as `self.id`. There's a bit of a subtlety, though; we can eliminate most of the `self`s, but we have to keep the `self` in front of `authorization_token`. As we noted in Section 6.6.4, in order to assign to an object's attribute, we have to prefix the variable name with `self`; otherwise, Ruby would simply create a local variable called `authorization_token`.

With this one caveat, we can rewrite `remember!` as follows:

Listing 7.35 app/models/user.rb

```
# Remember a user for future login.
def remember!(cookies)
  cookie_expiration = 10.years.from_now
  cookies[:remember_me] = { :value   => "1",
                            :expires => cookie_expiration }
  self.authorization_token = Digest::SHA1.hexdigest(
                              "#{screen_name}:#{password}")
  save!
  cookies[:authorization_token] = { :value   => authorization_token,
                                    :expires => cookie_expiration }
end
```

Note that we've taken this opportunity to bind the cookie expiration date to the variable `cookie_expiration`, both for readability and because we use it twice in this function.

We're pretty sure that we want to use SHA1 to make the user authorization token, at least for now, but in the future we might want to change to a different hashing algorithm. We can make the `remember!` function a little more flexible by building an abstraction layer between the unique identifier used to remember the user and the algorithm used to generate it:

Listing 7.36 app/models/user.rb

```
# Remember a user for future login.
def remember!(cookies)
  cookie_expiration = 10.years.from_now
  cookies[:remember_me] = { :value   => "1",
                            :expires =>  cookie_expiration }
  self.authorization_token =  unique_identifier
  save!
  cookies[:authorization_token] = { :value   => authorization_token,
                                    :expires => cookie_expiration }
end

private

# Generate a unique identifier for a user.
def unique_identifier
  Digest::SHA1.hexdigest("#{screen_name}:#{password}")
end
```

7.5.2 Refactoring forget

In addition to a bunch of code to remember the user, there's a second (two-line) block of code that simply forgets the user by deleting the cookies. Let's reorganize that code into its own function, called (naturally enough) `forget!`. While we're at it, we'll make a utility function to hide the ugly explicit comparison in `@user.remember_me == "1"` by defining a `remember_me?` function in the User model. With these enhancements, the relevant chunk of the login action appears as follows:

Listing 7.37 app/controllers/user_controller.rb

```
def login
  .
  .
  .
  if user
    user.login!(session)
    if @user.remember_me?
      user.remember!(cookies)
    else
      user.forget!(cookies)
    end
```

```
     .
     .
     .
end
```

And here are the new functions in the model:

Listing 7.38 app/models/user.rb

```
# Remember a user for future login.
def remember!(cookies)
  .
  .
  .
end

# Forget a user's login status.
def forget!(cookies)
  cookies.delete(:remember_me)
  cookies.delete(:authorization_token)
end

# Return true if the user wants the login status remembered.
def remember_me?
  remember_me == "1"
end
  .
  .
  .
```

Note that we've omitted the explicit `self` keyword inside the `remember_me?`
function.

7.5.3   Just two more bits of polish

We've already come a long way with the login action, but there are a couple more
refinements we just can't resist. The first is to replace `cookies[:remember_me] ||`
`"0"` with a short function explicitly indicating its purpose, namely, a string indicating
the status of the "remember me" checkbox:

Listing 7.39 app/controllers/user_controller.rb

```
def login
  @title = "Log in to RailsSpace"
```

Continues

```
  if request.get?
    @user = User.new(:remember_me => remember_me_string)
    .
    .
    .
end
.
.
.
private
.
.
.
# Return a string with the status of the remember me checkbox.
def remember_me_string
  cookies[:remember_me] || "0"
end
```

That's a distinctly minor improvement, and we couldn't really fault you for not making it. The final refinement, though, is one of our favorites, and we really hope you'll come to like it as much as we do. Let's take another look at the "remember me" control flow:

```
if @user.remember_me?
  user.remember!(cookies)
else
  user.forget!(cookies)
end
```

This five-line pattern is extraordinarily common and a bit cumbersome. It can be replaced by an equivalent but pithier construction using the wonderful *ternary operator* (see the sidebar "10 types of people"). With that replacement made, our login action finally assumes its fully refactored form:

Listing 7.40   app/controllers/user_controller.rb

```
def login
  @title = "Log in to RailsSpace"
  if request.get?
    @user = User.new(:remember_me => remember_me_string)
  elsif param_posted?(:user)
    @user = User.new(params[:user])
    user = User.find_by_screen_name_and_password(@user.screen_name,
                                                 @user.password)
```

```
    if user
      user.login!(session)
      @user.remember_me? ? user.remember!(cookies) : user.forget! (cookies)
      flash[:notice] = "User #{user.screen_name} logged in!"
      redirect_to_forwarding_url
    else
      @user.clear_password!
      flash[:notice] = "Invalid screen name/password combination"
    end
  end
end
```

10 types of people

There are 10 kinds of people in the world: Those who like the ternary operator, those who don't, and those who don't know about it. (If you happen to be in the third category, soon you won't be any longer.)

When you do a lot of coding, you quickly learn that one of the most common bits of control flow goes something like this:

```
if boolean?
  do_one_thing
else
  do_something_else
end
```

Ruby, like many other languages (including C, Perl, PHP, and Java), allows you to replace this with a much more compact expression using the little-used but oh-so-useful ternary operator (so-called because it consists of three parts):

```
boolean? ? do_one_thing : do_something_else
```

You can even use the ternary operator to replace assignment:

```
if boolean?
  var = foo
else
  var = bar
end
```

becomes

```
var = boolean? ? foo : bar
```

Even though the ternary operator may look a little obscure, the 5:1 line compression is (in our estimation) well worth the potential confusion. We'll always be on the lookout for a chance to shrink our code using the ternary operator.

7.5.4   The fully refactored login function

We're now done with our refactoring. Let's take a look at where we started and where we ended up. Expanding all of the refactored components (including those from Chapter 6), we effectively began with this ugly monstrosity:

Listing 7.41   app/controllers/user_controller.rb

```ruby
def login
  @title = "Log in to RailsSpace"
  if request.get?
    @user = User.new(:remember_me => cookies[:remember_me] || "0")
  elsif request.post? and params[:user]
    @user = User.new(params[:user])
    user = User.find_by_screen_name_and_password(@user.screen_name,
                                                  @user.password)
    if user
      session[:user_id] = user.id
      if @user.remember_me == "1"
        cookies[:remember_me] = { :value   => "1",
                                  :expires => 10.years.from_now }
        user.authorization_token = Digest::SHA1.hexdigest(
                         "#{user.screen_name}:#{user.password}")
        user.save!
        cookies[:authorization_token] = {
          :value   => user.authorization_token,
          :expires => 10.years.from_now }
      else
        cookies.delete(:remember_me)
        cookies.delete(:authorization_token)
      end
      flash[:notice] = "User #{user.screen_name} logged in!"
      if (redirect_url = session[:protected_page])
        session[:protected_page] = nil
        redirect_to redirect_url
      else
        redirect_to :action => "index"
      end
    else
      # Don't show the password again in the view.
      @user.password = nil
      flash[:notice] = "Invalid screen name/password combination"
    end
  end
end
```

We ended up with a much more compact and readable login function:

Listing 7.42   app/controllers/user_controller.rb

```
def login
  @title = "Log in to RailsSpace"
  if request.get?
    @user = User.new(:remember_me => remember_me_string)
  elsif param_posted?(:user)
    @user = User.new(params[:user])
    user = User.find_by_screen_name_and_password(@user.screen_name,
                                                 @user.password)
    if user
      user.login!(session)
      @user.remember_me? ? user.remember!(cookies) : user.forget!(cookies)
      flash[:notice] = "User #{user.screen_name} logged in!"
      redirect_to_forwarding_url
    else
      @user.clear_password!
      flash[:notice] = "Invalid screen name/password combination"
    end
  end
end
```

It may seem like we're cheating a bit here; after all, the refactored function is so much more compact only because we brushed the code complexity dust under an abstraction layer rug. This practice doesn't necessarily result in less total code, so does it really do us any good? Absolutely—even when they don't save us any lines of code, abstraction layers reduce the mental overhead of programming by allowing us to ignore irrelevant details and focus on higher-level constructs. Of course, by eliminating or preventing code duplication, abstraction layers nearly always result in fewer lines of code as well.

7.5.5   Some parting thoughts

So far in *RailsSpace* we've focused on writing (possibly ugly) working functions, testing them, and then refactoring if necessary. This has allowed us to focus on the many new ideas we have introduced rather than getting caught up in premature refinement. Because we've now laid a foundation for understanding the basics of Rails, throughout the rest of this book we'll usually build abstraction layers preemptively, before our code gets ugly. Bear in mind, though, that even when you aggressively capture patterns in abstractions, code has a way of getting crufty nonetheless. When that happens, we hope that the refactoring lessons from Chapters 6 and 7 prove valuable.

Finally, it's always nice to take a look at our stats:

```
> rake stats
(in /rails/rails_space)
+----------------------+-------+-------+---------+---------+-----+-------+
| Name                 | Lines |  LOC  | Classes | Methods | M/C | LOC/M |
+----------------------+-------+-------+---------+---------+-----+-------+
| Controllers          |   123 |    97 |       3 |      12 |   4 |     6 |
| Helpers              |    17 |    13 |       0 |       2 |   0 |     4 |
| Models               |    74 |    54 |       1 |       7 |   7 |     5 |
| Libraries            |     0 |     0 |       0 |       0 |   0 |     0 |
| Components           |     0 |     0 |       0 |       0 |   0 |     0 |
| Integration tests    |    25 |    17 |       1 |       2 |   2 |     6 |
| Functional tests     |   347 |   263 |       4 |      28 |   7 |     7 |
| Unit tests           |   161 |   113 |       1 |      13 |  13 |     6 |
+----------------------+-------+-------+---------+---------+-----+-------+
| Total                |   747 |   557 |      10 |      64 |   6 |     6 |
+----------------------+-------+-------+---------+---------+-----+-------+
  Code LOC: 164    Test LOC: 393    Code to Test Ratio: 1:2.4
```

CHAPTER 8

Updating user information

We're nearly ready to start building the social networking aspects of RailsSpace, but there are a couple of loose ends to tie off before we leave the User model. In Chapter 4, we developed a registration page to create users for RailsSpace, each with a screen name, email address, and password. It's time to give our users the ability to edit (some of) these attributes.

We'll start by fleshing out the user hub (introduced in Section 4.3.4) with the basic user information. Then we'll set up a form to edit the email address and password, and write the edit action to handle the input from the form. Finally, we'll write tests for the new user information update functionality.

It's important to note that we will *not* allow users to change their screen names. The reason is that we would like to incorporate screen names into URLs. For example, it would be nice for the address of each RailsSpace profile to be something like

```
http://RailsSpace.com/profile/<screen_name>
```

(We'll achieve this goal in Chapter 9.) We also plan to use the screen name in the URLs for email messages (Chapter 13) and the friendship request system (Chapter 14)). Allowing users to change their screen names would break these URLs, so we've decided not to allow it.

We'll see that in the process of making the edit form and writing the new tests, we will generate a lot of duplicated code. We've already seen some of the ways Rails makes it possible to eliminate duplication; in this chapter, we'll introduce two new methods: Rails *partials* and the Rails test helper.

8.1 A non-stub hub

As a first step toward building up the RailsSpace user hub, let's add the user's basic information. To get this to work, we first need to find the user:

Listing 8.1 app/controllers/user_controller.rb

```
def index
  @title = "RailsSpace User Hub"
  @user = User.find(session[:user_id])
end
```

Note that, instead of a fancy function like `find_by_screen_name_and_password`, we simply use `User.find` to find the user by id. Since accessing the hub requires a logged-in user (as enforced by our before filter from Chapter 6), we can just use the user id from the session.

The view is simple:

Listing 8.2 app/views/user/index.rhtml

```
<h2>Your basic information</h2>
<ul>
  <li>Screen name: <%= @user.screen_name %></li>
  <li>Email: <%= @user.email %></li>
  <li>Password: *******</li>
</ul>
<ul>
  <li><%= link_to "Edit my info", :action => "edit" %></li>
</ul>
```

Note that we've hard-coded the password for security purposes. We've also taken this opportunity to add a link to the user's edit action. The result is shown in Figure 8.1.

8.2 Updating the email address

Updating the email address is easy with Rails. We start with a basic edit form, which is similar to those we have seen before:

Listing 8.3 app/views/user/edit.rhtml

```
<h2><%= @title %></h2>
<%= error_messages_for 'user' %>
<% form_for :user do |form| %>
```

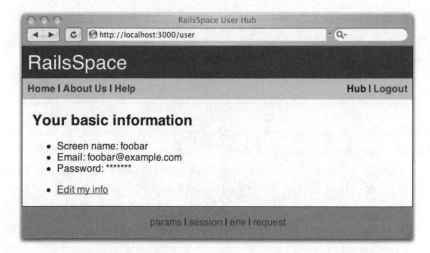

Figure 8.1 The logged-in user experience begins to take form.

```
<fieldset>
  <legend>Email</legend>
  <div class="form_row">
    <label for="email">Email:</label>
    <%= form.text_field :email,
                        :size => User::EMAIL_SIZE,
                        :maxlength => User::EMAIL_MAX_LENGTH %>
  </div>
  <div class="form_row">
    <%= submit_tag "Update", :class => "submit" %>
  </div>
</fieldset>
<% end %>
```

Note that we have once again made use of the User model constants.

The action is also similar to the register and login actions we've seen, with one main difference: Instead of creating a new user instance, as in the case of the register action, we update a *current* user using the Active Record `update_attributes` function:

Listing 8.4 app/controllers/user_controller.rb

```
# Edit the user's basic info.
def edit
  @title = "Edit basic info"
  @user = User.find(session[:user_id])
  if param_posted?(:user)
```

Continues

```
      if @user.update_attributes(params[:user])
        flash[:notice] = "Email updated."
        redirect_to :action => "index"
      end
    end
  end
```

In this function, `@user.update_attributes(params[:user])` updates the attributes of `@user` corresponding to the hash in `params[:user]`. In other words, if `params[:user]` is `:email => "new_email@example.com"`, `update_attributes` changes the user's email address in the database. Moreover, it performs all the same validations as `@user.save`, so invalid email addresses will automatically be caught; since we put

```
<%= error_messages_for 'user' %>
```

in the view, this will result in an appropriate error message being displayed back to the user (Figure 8.2).

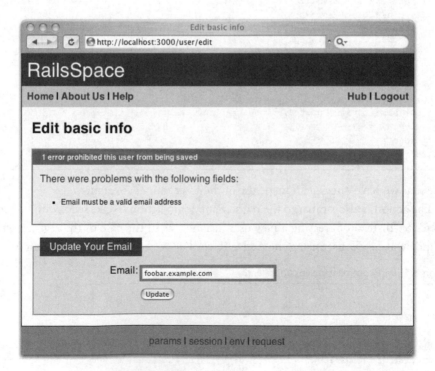

Figure 8.2   Editing the email address (with error).

Figure 8.3 Changing the email address to `bazquux@example.com`.

There's one final touch before we move on to password editing. Since only logged-in users of RailsSpace can edit their information, we need to add our new edit action to the page protection `before_filter`:

Listing 8.5 app/controllers/user_controller.rb

```
class UserController < ApplicationController

  before_filter :protect, :only => [:index, :edit]
    .
    .
    .
```

With this, a logged-in user (and only a logged-in user) can update his email address (Figure 8.3).

8.3 Updating password

In contrast to the email update, the password update machinery is surprisingly challenging, but it's made much easier by some clever Rails magic. Most of the complexity comes from including a confirmation box in the password edit form. As before, we use the form_for function to build up our form, this time with three fields, one each for the current password, the new password, and the password confirmation:

Listing 8.6 app/views/user/edit.rhtml

```
<h2><%= @title %></h2>
<%= error_messages_for 'user' %>
<% form_for :user do |form| %>
<fieldset>
  <legend>Email</legend>
  .
  .
  .
</fieldset>
<% end %>

<% form_for :user do |form| %>
<fieldset>
  <legend>Password</legend>
  <div class="form_row">
    <label for="current_password">Current password:</label>
    <%= form.password_field :current_password,
                            :size =>       User::PASSWORD_SIZE,
                            :maxlength => User::PASSWORD_MAX_LENGTH %>
  </div>

  <div class="form_row">
    <label for="password">New password:</label>
    <%= form.password_field :password,
                            :size =>       User::PASSWORD_SIZE,
                            :maxlength => User::PASSWORD_MAX_LENGTH %>
  </div>

  <div class="form_row">
    <label for="password_confirmation">Confirm:</label>
    <%= form.password_field :password_confirmation,
                            :size =>       User::PASSWORD_SIZE,
                            :maxlength => User::PASSWORD_MAX_LENGTH %>
  </div>

  <%= submit_tag "Update", :class => "submit" %>
</fieldset>
<% end %>
```

That's a lot of new code, but the structure is simple: We just have form rows for the current password, the new password, and the password confirmation, with each field being generated using `form.password_field`. (If this password code looks awfully repetitive, you're ahead of the game; see Section 8.5 below.) Note that the argument to `form.password_field` for the new password field is `password` rather than `new_password`; this is simply because otherwise we would have to add a `new_password` attribute to the User model.

Unlike the new password field, in order to handle the current password field we do have to add a new attribute, since the User model doesn't have a current password attribute. We'll use the same `attr_accessor` technique we use for the "remember me" attribute (Section 7.1.2); at the same time, we'll add a validation enforcing the proper password confirmation:

Listing 8.7 app/models/user.rb

```
class User < ActiveRecord::Base
  attr_accessor :remember_me
  attr_accessor :current_password
  .
  .
  .
  validates_uniqueness_of :screen_name, :email
  validates_confirmation_of :password
  .
  .
  .
end
```

But wait—the form has a field for `password_confirmation`. Why don't we have to add a `password_confirmation` attribute the way we did for `current_password`? Since text and password field confirmations are so common, Rails makes it easy to make them simply by appending `_confirmation` to the attribute name; Rails then creates a confirmation attribute on the fly and compares it to the original field. In other words, when trying to save or update a user, `validates_confirmation_of :password` automatically looks for a `password_confirmation` attribute and compares it to the `password` attribute, yielding an error if they don't match.

With this new code in place, the edit page is poised to edit passwords as well as email (Figure 8.4). Unfortunately, the new password field is prefilled with the (cleartext) value of `@user.password`, a problem we encountered before in Section 6.6.4. The solution is to use the `clear_password!` method from that section (updated to clear all the different passwords):

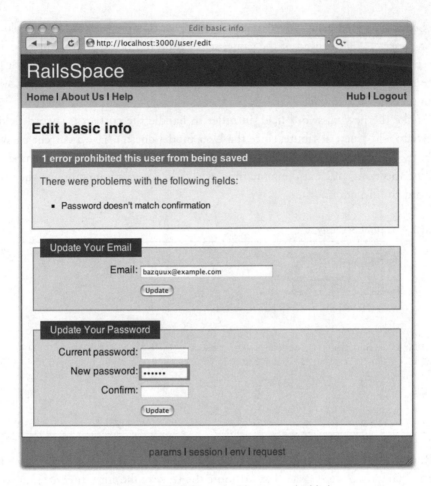

Figure 8.4   The edit page with password added.

Listing 8.8 app/models/user.rb

```
# Clear the password (typically to suppress its display in a view).
def clear_password!
  self.password = nil
  self.password_confirmation = nil
  self.current_password = nil
end
```

Then we simply add a line to the end of the edit action:

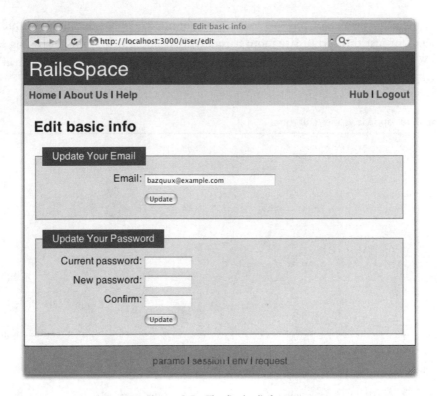

Figure 8.5 The final edit form.

Listing 8.9 app/controllers/user_controller.rb

```
# Edit the user's basic info.
def edit
  .
  .
  .
  # For security purposes, never fill in password fields.
  @user.clear_password!
end
```

With that, our edit form—or at least its appearance—is complete (Figure 8.5).

8.3.1 Handling password submissions

As we hinted at the end of the last section, we're not quite done with the edit form yet. In order to handle both email and password editing from the same form, we need to tell the action which of the two forms was submitted. HTML has a tag for hidden elements for just this sort of situation; naturally, Rails has a helper for generating such tags. We'll make a hidden field called "attribute" whose value will be either "email" or "password":

Listing 8.10 app/views/user/edit.rhtml

```
.
.
.
<legend>Update Your Email</legend>
<%= hidden_field_tag "attribute", "email", :id => nil%>
.
.
.
<legend>Update Your Password</legend>
<%= hidden_field_tag "attribute", "password", :id => nil %>
.
.
.
```

The embedded Ruby

```
<%= hidden_field_tag "attribute", "password", :id => nil %>
```

generates the HTML

```
<input name="attribute" type="hidden" value="email" />
```

(We include :id => nil because otherwise hidden_field_tag gives both hidden attributes the same id, which is not valid XHTML.)

With the edit form thus updated, the attribute to be edited will show up in params[:attribute], which will be either "email" or "password". In the edit action, for convenience we'll first assign this value to the variable attribute, and then use the Ruby case statement to determine the proper course of action:[1]

```
# Edit the user's basic info.
def edit
  @title = "Edit basic info"
  @user = User.find(session[:user_id])
```

---

[1] By restricting valid attributes to "email" and "password", this version of edit is actually superior to the previous one. The action in Section 8.2 technically allowed a user to change his screen name by posting the appropriate parameters from an external form.

```
   if param_posted?(:user)
     attribute = params[:attribute]
     case attribute
     when "email"
       try_to_update @user, attribute
     when "password"
       # Handle password submission.
     end
   end
   # For security purposes, never fill in password fields.
   @user.clear_password!
 end

 private

 .
 .
 .
 # Try to update the user, redirecting if successful.
 def try_to_update(user, attribute)
   if user.update_attributes(params[:user])
     flash[:notice] = "User #{attribute} updated."
     redirect_to :action => "index"
   end
 end
end
```

Here we've packaged the update attempt in the `try_to_update` in anticipation of using that code again when trying to update the password attribute.

The case expression is simple to use, and is essentially a more convenient way of switching on the values of the variable than `if...elsif`; the code

```
case foo
when "bar"
  puts "It's a bar!"
when "baz"
  puts "It's a baz!"
end
```

is equivalent to

```
if foo == "bar"
  puts "It's a bar!"
elsif foo == "baz"
  puts "It's a baz!"
end
```

This doesn't necessarily save any code—in fact, in this example it's actually longer— but sometimes it just feels more natural to use a case statement. (This is one of those times.)

Of course, we punted on the actual password handling above, mainly because it relies on two utility functions, one of which is rather sophisticated. Once we've defined those helpers, which are User model methods called `correct_password?` and `password_errors`, the final form of the added action is as follows:

Listing 8.11   app/controllers/user_controller.rb

```
# Edit the user's basic info.
def edit
  @title = "Edit basic info"
  @user = User.find(session[:user_id])
  if param_posted?(:user)
    attribute = params[:attribute]
    case attribute
    when "email"
      try_to_update @user, attribute
    when "password"
      if @user.correct_password?(params)
        try_to_update @user, attribute
      else
        @user.password_errors(params)
      end
    end
  end
  # For security purposes, never fill in password fields.
  @user.clear_password!
end
```

The utility functions for the password edit action are alternately simple and complex. The `correct_password?` function is extremely simple, to the point of perhaps being unnecessary:

Listing 8.12   app/models/user.rb

```
# Return true if the password from params is correct.
def correct_password?(params)
  current_password = params[:user][:current_password]
  password == current_password
end
```

The `password_errors` function, on the other hand, is significantly more difficult. If we fall through to that part of the `edit` function, we need to test to see if the new password and its confirmation match. The most robust way to do this is to assign the values from `params` to our User object and then call `valid?`, which creates the proper error messages as a side effect:

Listing 8.13 app/models/user.rb

```
# Generate messages for password errors.
def password_errors(params)
  # Use User model's valid? method to generate error messages
  # for a password mismatch (if any).
  self.password = params[:user][:password]
  self.password_confirmation = params[:user][:password_confirmation]
  valid?
  # The current password is incorrect, so add an error message.
  errors.add(:current_password, "is incorrect")
end
```

As you may recall from the discussion of validations starting in Section 3.2.3, validations add error messages to an internal Rails object called `errors`. In our case, if we reach the `else` branch under `when "password"`, it must be that the current (submitted) password doesn't match the user's actual password, so the last line of the function adds an error message to that effect (Figure 8.6). (This doesn't happen automatically since `current_password` is not a column in the User model.)

That was quite a bit of effort, but our reward is the ability to update user passwords and email addresses from the same form, with validations and password confirmation to boot.

8.4 Testing user edits

Even though we've only added two new actions, there are a lot of new things to test: the HTML structure of each form; successful edits for email address and password; and failures for all of the main failure modes. Since we've already covered testing in such detail, we aren't going to put the full text of all of the tests in this chapter. On the other hand, testing is an essential part of Rails, so we will summarize what some of the tests look like.

Writing tests is good practice in any case, of course, but we have a second motivation: The views for editing user attributes share a lot of HTML structure in common with the register and login views (`register.rhtml` and `login.rhtml`). In Section 8.5, we'll eliminate this unnecessary duplication, and (as usual) having tests working beforehand will give us confidence that the updated code works correctly.

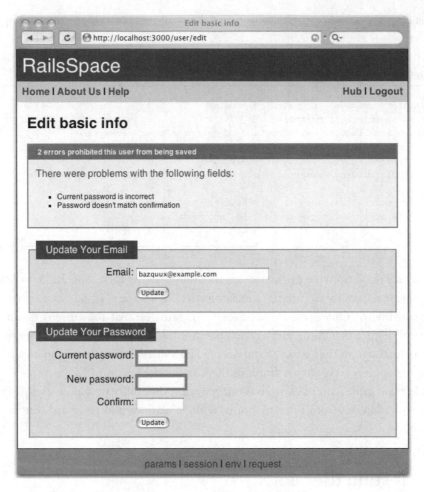

Figure 8.6   Errors generated manually and using the `valid?` function.

8.4.1   Test helpers

The tests for editing users are similar to those for user registration and login; as a result, they are easy to write, but they also potentially produce a lot of duplicate code. To prevent such duplication, before writing any new tests we'll first define some helper functions. We'll put some of these functions in `user_controller_test.rb`, as we have with functions such as `try_to_login`, `authorize`, and `friendly_URL_forwarding_aux`. Some of the helper functions, though, are likely to be useful across different controller tests, and Rails provides a special file called `test_helper.rb` for such general-use functions, which are available to any functional, unit, or integration test.[2]

Here are a couple of simple examples of functions we expect to be used by multiple controller tests:

Listing 8.14   test/test_helper.rb

```
ENV["RAILS_ENV"] = "test"
require File.expand_path(File.dirname(__FILE__) + "/../config/environment")
require 'test_help'

class Test::Unit::TestCase

  .
  .
  .

  # Add more helper methods to be used by all tests here...

  # Assert the form tag.
  def assert_form_tag(action)
    assert_tag "form", :attributes => { :action => action,
                                        :method => "post" }
  end

  # Assert submit button with optional label.
  def assert_submit_button(button_label = nil)
    if button_label
      assert_tag "input", :attributes => { :type => "submit",
                                           :value => button_label}
    else
      assert_tag "input", :attributes => { :type => "submit" }
    end
  end
end
```

Even though these assertions are very simple, we expect that asserting the presence of form tags and submit buttons will be common to views from other controllers, so we have placed them in the file `test/test_helper.rb`.

Take a moment now to look over the User controller tests in `user_controller_test.rb`. Notice the common pattern of asserting the presence of an input field with a particular name, type (such as text or password), size, and maximum length. We can capture this pattern in a second helper function called `assert_input_field`:

---

[2] If `authorize` seems like just such a general-use function, you're exactly right; we'll promote it to `test_helper.rb` in Section 9.3.5 when we begin testing the controllers for RailsSpace user profiles.

Listing 8.15 test/test_helper.rb

```
        .
        .
        .


# Add more helper methods to be used by all tests here...


        .
        .
        .


# Assert existence of form input field with attributes.
def assert_input_field(name, value, field_type, size, maxlength, options = {})
  attributes = { :name  => name,
                 :type  => field_type,
                 :size  => size,
                 :maxlength => maxlength }
  # Surprisingly, attributes[:value] == nil is different from attributes
  # not having a :value key at all.
  attributes[:value] = value unless value.nil?
  tag = { :tag => "input", :attributes => attributes }
  # Merge tag hash with options, especially to handle :parent => error_div
  # option in error tests.
  tag.merge!(options)
  assert_tag tag
end
```

Note the use of the `merge!` function (which we first met in Section 7.3.1) to add options to the tag hash.

With `assert_input_field`, we can write compact HTML assertions as follows:

Listing 8.16 test/functional/user_controller_test.rb

```
private
  .
  .
  .
# Some utility assertions for testing HTML.

# Assert that the email field has the correct HTML.
def assert_email_field(email = nil, options = {})
  assert_input_field("user[email]", email, "text",
                     User::EMAIL_SIZE, User::EMAIL_MAX_LENGTH,
                     options)
end

# Assert that the password field has the correct HTML.
def assert_password_field(password_field_name = "password", options = {})
  # We never want a password to appear pre-filled into a form.
```

```
   blank = nil
   assert_input_field("user[#{password_field_name}]", blank, "password",
                      User::PASSWORD_SIZE, User::PASSWORD_MAX_LENGTH,
                      options)
end

# Assert that the screen name field has the correct HTML.
def assert_screen_name_field(screen_name = nil, options = {})
   assert_input_field("user[screen_name]", screen_name, "text",
                      User::SCREEN_NAME_SIZE, User::SCREEN_NAME_MAX_LENGTH,
                      options)
end
```

Since we expect these assertions to be of more restricted use, we've placed them in `user_controller_test.rb`.

With our judiciously chosen test utility functions, some rather verbose tests can be simplified considerably. In Section 5.4.2, for example, we wrote the following:

Listing 8.17 test/functional/user_controller_test.rb

```
# Make sure the registration page responds with the proper form.
def test_registration_page
   get :register
   title = assigns(:title)
   assert_equal "Register", title
   assert_response :success
   assert_template "register"
   # Test the form and all its tags.
   assert_tag "form", :attributes => { :action => "/user/register",
                                       :method => "post" }
   assert_tag "input",
              :attributes => { :name => "user[screen_name]",
                               :type => "text",
                               :size => User::SCREEN_NAME_SIZE,
                               :maxlength => User::SCREEN_NAME_MAX_LENGTH }
   assert_tag "input",
              :attributes => { :name => "user[email]",
                               :type => "text",
                               :size => User::EMAIL_SIZE,
                               :maxlength => User::EMAIL_MAX_LENGTH }
   assert_tag "input",
              :attributes => { :name => "user[password]",
                               :type => "password",
                               :size => User::PASSWORD_SIZE,
                               :maxlength => User::PASSWORD_MAX_LENGTH }
   assert_tag "input", :attributes => { :type => "submit",
                                        :value => "Login!" }
end
```

With the helper functions as defined above, the test is both shorter and easier to understand:

Listing 8.18 test/functional/user_controller_test.rb

```
# Make sure the registration page responds with the proper form.
def test_registration_page
  get :register
  title = assigns(:title)
  assert_equal "Register", title
  assert_response :success
  assert_template "register"
  # Test the form and all its tags.
  assert_form_tag "/user/register"
  assert_screen_name_field
  assert_email_field
  assert_password_field
  assert_submit_button "Register!"
end
```

8.4.2 Testing the edit page

In this section, we'll test the edit page for the email and password fields. As with the tests of the login and register pages, to test the edit page we first verify the basic properties (title, HTTP response, and rhtml template), followed by tests of the form HTML— in this case, fields for the email address and passwords. Since we're editing attributes that already exist, these fields should be prefilled with the user's current information; not coincidentally, we designed both `assert_email_field` and `assert_password_field` to take optional arguments for the values of their respective fields.

With the helper functions from Section 8.4.1 in hand, the test for the edit page is nicely succinct:

Listing 8.19 test/functional/user_controller_test.rb

```
# Test the edit page.
def test_edit_page
  authorize @valid_user
  get :edit
  title = assigns(:title)
  assert_equal "Edit basic info", title
  assert_response :success
  assert_template "edit"
  # Test the form and all its tags.
```

```
    assert_form_tag "/user/edit"
    assert_email_field @valid_user.email
    assert_password_field "current_password"
    assert_password_field
    assert_password_field "password_confirmation"
    assert_submit_button "Update"
  end
```

Running this gives

```
> ruby test/functional/user_controller_test.rb -n test_edit_page
Loaded suite test/functional/user_controller_test
Started
.
Finished in 0.172981 seconds.

1 tests, 9 assertions, 0 failures, 0 errors
```

8.4.3 An advanced test

Before leaving the subject of testing, we'd like to mention another use of test helpers. When writing tests for the User model in Section 5.5, we tested the minimum and maximum lengths for the various user attributes. One test, for example, verified the validation for the minimum length of the screen name:

Listing 8.20 test/unit/user_test.rb

```
def test_screen_name_minimum_length
  user = @valid_user
  min_length = User::SCREEN_NAME_MIN_LENGTH

  # Screen name is too short.
  user.screen_name = "a" * (min_length - 1)
  assert !user.valid?, "#{user.screen_name} should raise a minimum length error"
  # Format the error message based on minimum length.
  correct_error_message = sprintf(@error_messages[:too_short], min_length)
  assert_equal correct_error_message, user.errors.on(:screen_name)

  # Screen name is minimum length.
  user.screen_name = "a" * min_length
  assert user.valid?, "#{user.screen_name} should be just long enough to pass"
end
```

There are several similar functions for the maximum length of the screen name, the minimum and maximum length of the password, and the maximum length of the email address.

We encountered these tests in the first chapter to include any tests, so it didn't make sense to get too fancy at the time. Now that we have more experience with Ruby and Rails, the time has come for a test helper to capture the common pattern represented by these functions. The resulting `assert_length` function is fairly advanced (requiring, among other things, two additional helpers, `barely_invalid_string` and `correct_error_message`), and we present it without detailed explanation, but you are probably in a position by now either to understand it or to figure it out:[3]

Listing 8.21   test/test_helper.rb

```ruby
# Test the minimum or maximum length of an attribute.
def assert_length(boundary, object, attribute, length options = {})
  valid_char = options[:valid_char] || "a"
  barely_invalid = barely_invalid_string(boundary, length, valid_char)
  # Test one over the boundary.
  object[attribute] = barely_invalid
  assert !object.valid?,
         "#{object[attribute]} (length #{object[attribute].length}) " +
         "should raise a length error"
  assert_equal correct_error_message(boundary, length),
               object.errors.on(attribute)

  # Test the boundary itself.
  barely_valid = valid_char * length
  object[attribute] = barely_valid
  assert object.valid?,
         "#{object[attribute]} (length #{object[attribute].length}) " +
         "should be on the boundary of validity"
end

# Create an attribute that is just barely invalid.
def barely_invalid_string(boundary, length, valid_char)
  if boundary == :max
    invalid_length = length + 1
  elsif boundary == :min
    invalid_length = length - 1
  else
    raise ArgumentError, "boundary must be :max or :min"
  end
  valid_char * invalid_length
end

# Return the correct error message for the length test.
```

---

[3] Note in particular the `var = foo || bar` construction (first encountered in the sidebar "or or ||" in Section 7.13), which assigns `foo` to `var` unless `foo` is `nil` (or `false`), in which case `var` is `bar`. We will see many examples of this idea throughout the rest of the book.

```
def correct_error_message(boundary, length)
  error_messages = ActiveRecord::Errors.default_error_messages
  if boundary == :max
    sprintf(error_messages[:too_long], length)
  elsif boundary == :min
    sprintf(error_messages[:too_short], length)
  else
    raise ArgumentError, "boundary must be :max or :min"
  end
end
```

With this one utility function, we can collapse our length tests down to just a few lines; four moderately long tests become two two-line tests:

Listing 8.22 test/unit/user_test.rb

```
def test_screen_name_length_boundaries
  assert_length :min, @valid_user, :screen_name, User::SCREEN_NAME_MIN_LENGTH
  assert_length :max, @valid_user, :screen_name, User::SCREEN_NAME_MAX_LENGTH
end

def test_password_length_boundaries
  assert_length :min, @valid_user, :password, User::PASSWORD_MIN_LENGTH
  assert_length :max, @valid_user, :password, User::PASSWORD_MAX_LENGTH
end
```

Since `assert_length` contains multiple assertions, the tests give 12 assertions instead of just 4:

```
> ruby test/unit/user_test.rb -n /length_boundaries/
Loaded suite test/unit/user_test
Started
..
Finished in 0.181779 seconds.

2 tests, 12 assertions, 0 failures, 0 errors
```

Building such a general utility function can be a lot of work, but you'll have to admit that the results are pretty sweet.

8.5 Partials

As per usual, now that we have our tests we can feel free to move things around and try to eliminate duplication. In previous chapters, we've always eliminated duplication in models or actions, but Rails gives us a way to do the same thing in views using *partials*.

8.5.1   Two simple partials

Considering RailsSpace as it currently stands, you may have noticed that the register, login, and edit forms contain a lot of HTML in common. For example, register and edit forms both contain this code snippet:

Listing 8.23   app/views/user/_email_field_row.rhtml

```
<div class="form_row">
  <label for="email">Email:</label>
  <%= form.text_field :email, :size => User::EMAIL_SIZE,
                              :maxlength => User::EMAIL_MAX_LENGTH %>
</div>
```

As you can tell from the filename above, we've extracted this common code into a file called `_email_field_row.rhtml`. Note the leading underscore in the filename—it identifies the file as a partial; that is to say, it's a partial rhtml file intended for use in the view. Among other things, this underscore convention is useful for lumping all the partials together in a directory listing.

Wherever the code in the partial appears, replace it with a command to render the partial:

```
<%= render :partial => "email_field_row", :locals  => { :form => form } %>
```

Since we've given `render` the option `:partial =>"email_field_row"` (without the leading underscore), Rails knows to look for a partial file called`_email_field_row.rhtml`, which, according to the Rails convention, is just the partial name preceded by an underscore.

Since the email partial references the `form` variable generated by the `form_for` function in each corresponding rhtml file, we need to send it a local variable called `form`, which we do using the `locals` option. (Be careful not to get confused by the variable names; if the register action used `form_for :dude` to generate the registration form, thereby creating the `dude` variable, then we would write `:locals => { :form => dude }` when rendering the partial. By using the symbol `:form`, we tell Rails to associate the variable `dude` in the view with the local variable `form` in the partial.)

Now that we have the basic idea of partials, we can replace more repeated code. The screen name form code, for example, is also repeated across multiple forms:

Listing 8.24   app/views/user/_screen_name_field_row.rhtml

```
<div class="form_row">
  <label for="screen_name">Screen name:</label>
```

```
    <%= form.text_field :screen_name,
                        :size => User::SCREEN_NAME_SIZE,
                        :maxlength => User::SCREEN_NAME_MAX_LENGTH %>
</div>
```

This partial is then invoked using

```
<%= render :partial => "screen_name_field_row", :locals  => { :form => form } %>
```

8.5.2 A more advanced partial

Having captured the common form field pattern for screen name and email, it is natural to do the same for the password field, which appears in `register.rhtml`, `login.rhtml`, and `edit.rhtml`. There's a subtle difference compared to our previous cases, though: There are several slight variations in the password name, both in the `input` tag itself and in the text label for the field. For example, the password section on the login page looks like this:

Listing 8.25 app/views/user/login.rhtml

```
    <div class="form_row">
      <label for="password">Password:</label>
      <%= form.password_field :password,
                              :size => User::PASSWORD_SIZE,
                              :maxlength => User::PASSWORD_MAX_LENGTH %>
    </div>
```

In contrast, the edit view has a section that looks like this, with `for="current_password"` and `:current_password` in place of `for="password"` and `:password`:

Listing 8.26 app/views/user/edit.rhtml

```
    <div class="form_row">
      <label for="current_password">Current password:</label>
      <%= form.password_field :current_password,
                              :size =>        User::PASSWORD_SIZE,
                              :maxlength => User::PASSWORD_MAX_LENGTH %>
    </div>
```

In order to make a partial for the password HTML, we need to do more than create a local variable for `form`; we also need a local variable, which we will call `field`,

that contains the name of the label; for the examples above `field` will be alternately
`"password"` and `"current_password"`. We therefore expect the partial to have a
line like

```
<label for="<%= field %>">Password:</label>
```

Since we've adopted the convention that the label name is always the same as the
argument to the `form.password_field` function, `field` can actually do double duty:
It's valid Ruby to write

```
<%= form.password_field "current_password", ...
```

thereby using a string instead of a symbol. We will therefore be able to write

```
<%= form.password_field field, ...
```

in the partial.

Finally, the field title labeling the box changes depending on context; it's either
`"Password"` or `"New password"` in our example. In general, we'll associate that title
with a local variable called `form_title`. We don't always have to define this variable,
though, since `field` sometimes has the information we need. For example, when `field`
= `"current_password"`, we can generate the title `"Current password"` using the
convenient `humanize` function:

```
> ruby script/console
Loading development environment.
>> field = "current_password"
=> "current_password"
>> field.humanize
=> "Current password"
```

Putting all of this together leads to the following partial:

Listing 8.27 app/views/user/_password_field_row.rhtml

```
<div class="form_row">
  <label for="<%= field %>">
    <%= field_title || field.humanize %>:
  </label>
  <%= form.password_field field,
                          :size =>       User::PASSWORD_SIZE,
                          :maxlength => User::PASSWORD_MAX_LENGTH %>
</div>
```

This partial requires the `form` and `field` variables, and takes an optional field title
variable which gets used to label the row if present; otherwise, we use `field.humanize`.

With the partial defined as above, the edit view looks like this:

Listing 8.28 app/views/user/edit.rhtml

```
<h2><%= @title %></h2>
<%= error_messages_for 'user' %>
<% form_for :user do |form| %>
<fieldset>
  <legend>Email</legend>
  <%= render :partial => "email_field_row", :locals => { :form => form } %>
  <%= hidden_field_tag "attribute", "email", :id => nil%>
  <%= submit_tag "Update", :class => "submit" %>
</fieldset>
<% end %>

<% form_for :user do |form| %>
<fieldset>
  <legend>Password</legend>
  <%= render :partial => "password_field_row",
             :locals  => { :form => form,
                           :field => "current_password" } %>
  <%= render :partial => "password_field_row",
             :locals  => { :form => form,
                           :field => "password",
                           :field_title => "New password" } %>
  <%= render :partial => "password_field_row",
             :locals  => { :form => form,
                           :field => "password_confirmation",
                           :field_title => "Confirm" } %>
  <%= hidden_field_tag "attribute", "password", :id => nil %>
  <%= submit_tag "Update", :class => "submit" %>
</fieldset>
<% end %>
```

Note that the new password and password confirmation both get `field_title` variables, but the current password doesn't need one since `field.humanize` does the job for us.

8.5.3 A wrinkle, then done

The password partial as written above works fine if you go to the /user/edit page, but there's one small wrinkle—if you run the test suite (which you should be in the habit of doing frequently by now), you get a bunch of errors in the User controller test:

```
> ruby test/functional/user_controller_test.rb
.
.
.
...undefined local variable or method 'field_title'
```

where the dots represent a big chunk of omitted text.

The problem lies in how the tests handle local variable scope, which differs from the main application in some subtle way (and which, frankly, we don't understand). The bottom line is that the application knows to assign `field_title` the value `nil` if it's not set by the code invoking the partial, but the test isn't quite that smart, and `field_title` isn't even defined unless set explicitly.

Luckily, there's an easy fix using the Ruby `defined?` function, which returns `true` if the variable is defined and `false` otherwise. Our strategy is to check to see if there's a variable called `field_title`; if not (as will be the case in the test), we'll create one and set it to `nil`. This leads to the final form of our password partial:

Listing 8.29 app/views/user/_password_field_row.rhtml

```
<% field_title = nil if not defined?(field_title) -%>
<div class="form_row">
  <label for="<%= field %>">
   <%= field_title || field.humanize %>:
  </label>
  <%= form.password_field field,
                          :size =>       User::PASSWORD_SIZE,
                          :maxlength => User::PASSWORD_MAX_LENGTH %>
</div>
```

Embedded Ruby saves the day again!

8.5.4 Updating login and register

The whole point of creating the partials was to eliminate duplicated rhtml, so as a final step we'll update the register and login views. The new login view is simpler, so we'll start with that:

Listing 8.30 app/views/user/login.rhtml

```
<% form_for :user do |form| %>
<fieldset>
  <legend><%= @title %></legend>

  <%= render :partial => "screen_name_field_row",
             :locals  => { :form => form } %>
  <%= render :partial => "password_field_row",
             :locals  => { :form => form, :field => "password" } %>
  .
  .
  .
```

The update to the register view is similar, and we even get a bonus: With our new password partial, adding password confirmation to the registration page is a snap. We've already done the heavy lifting by adding the proper validation to the User model, and we can render the confirmation partial using the same code that we used in the edit view:

Listing 8.31 app/views/user/register.rhtml

```
<% form_for :user do |form| %>
<fieldset>
  <legend>Enter Your Details</legend>

  <%= error_messages_for 'user' %>

  <%= render :partial => "screen_name_field_row",
            :locals  => { :form => form } %>
  <%= render :partial => "email_field_row",
            :locals  => { :form => form } %>
  <%= render :partial => "password_field_row",
            :locals  => { :form => form, :field => "password" } %>
  <%= render :partial => "password_field_row",
            :locals  => { :form => form,
                          :field => "password_confirmation",
                          :field_title => "Confirm" } %>
  <div class="form_row">
    <%= submit_tag "Register!", :class => "submit" %>
  </div>
</fieldset>
<% end %>
```

This adds a nice refinement to RailsSpace registration (Figure 8.7); before, an errant keystroke in the password box during registration would leave our intrepid user unable to log in. Now, it would take two identical errant keystrokes in two different boxes to achieve the same lamentable result —a much less likely occurrence.

While we're at it, it's probably a good idea to add a password confirmation assertion to the registration page test:

Listing 8.32 test/functional/user_controller_test.rb

```
# Make sure the registration page responds with the proper form.
def test_registration_page
  .
  .
  .
```

Continues

Figure 8.7 The registration page now handles password confirmation automatically.

```
    assert_password_field "password_confirmation"
    assert_submit_button "Register!"
  end
```

This gives

```
> ruby test/functional/user_controller_test.rb -n test_registration_page
Loaded suite test/functional/user_controller_test
Started
.
Finished in 0.14769 seconds.

1 tests, 9 assertions, 0 failures, 0 errors
```

PART II

Building a social network

CHAPTER 9

Personal profiles

In the first part of this book, we gave RailsSpace users the ability to register, login, and edit their basic information. The rest of the book will be dedicated to building a social network on this foundation. We'll start off in this chapter by creating a basic profile page consisting of a user "specification" (or *spec*) and a personalized list of answers to Frequently Asked Questions (the user FAQ). Future chapters will add search capabilities, a simple email interface, a friendship system, and several upgrades to the user profile.

In the process of building the machinery to create, edit, and display user profiles, a lot of our previous work will come together. We'll have occasion to make several new controllers, which should help to clarify exactly what a controller is (or should be) (see the sidebar "Controlling our controllers"). We'll also finally create a second model (and a third), which will give us the opportunity to show how to use Rails to stitch data models together into one coherent whole. This chapter will also deepen our understanding of partials, especially when used for presenting collections of data.

Controlling our controllers

Of the three parts of the MVC architecture, controllers are perhaps the most confusing. What exactly is a controller, and how do we know when to create a new one? A useful first step is to follow a simple convention:

1. Use nouns for controller names
2. Use verbs for action names

It's impossible to adhere strictly to these rules (index actions violate number 2, for example), but together they form a good rule of thumb. As a concrete example, consider our only nontrivial controller so far, the User controller, which has (among others) `login`, `logout`, `register`, and `edit` actions.

In the process of developing RailsSpace, it might seem natural to use the User controller for virtually everything, since everything has to do with users. If you follow the noun/verb convention for controller/action, you'll find that using a single controller quickly leads to lots of URLs of the form `/user/edit_spec` and `/user/show_profile`. This is a strong linguistic hint that we've outgrown our single controller.

If you find yourself starting to define actions with underscores—especially if they follow the template `<verb>_<noun>`—consider making a new controller corresponding to the noun, and then define an action corresponding to the verb. For example, instead of using `/user/edit_spec` to edit the user specification, instead create a Spec controller and use `/spec/edit`.

You'll find that the resulting site structure consists of many short, digestible controllers, rather than one monolithic controller in charge of everything. As your site grows, and as you add additional features, you will find that each controller can grow with it, becoming larger but never unwieldy. Each controller will then fulfill the promise made in Chapter 2 by serving as "a container for a group of related pages."

9.1 A user profile stub

Although we don't yet have anything to put on the user profile page, when developing websites we find that even having a (nearly) blank page has great psychological value, since once it's created "all we need to do is fill it in with stuff." In this section we'll create a stub for the user profile, which will involve creating a Profile controller together with a few actions and views. We'll also use Rails routes to make a pretty profile URL.

9.1.1 Profile URLs

For our example user Foo Bar, whose screen name is `foobar`, it would be natural to display the profile at the URL

`http://www.RailsSpace.com/profile/foobar`

(and similarly for other screen names). This suggests creating a Profile controller, which we'll make using the `generate` script. Before we do, though, we have to address a subtlety: According to the default Rails convention for URLs,

`http://www.RailsSpace.com/profile/foobar`

will look for an *action* called `foobar`, which isn't what we want at all. We can solve this using essentially the same method that we used in Section 2.2.3 to get `http://localhost:3000` to point to the site index. We'll make an action to display user profiles, and then use `routes.rb` to remap the URL to the one we want. That is, the URL

```
http://www.RailsSpace.com/profile/foobar
```

will get mapped by `routes.rb` to the appropriate controller/action pair:

```
http://www.RailsSpace.com/profile/show/foobar
```

Note that, in the example above, we defined an action called `show` to display profiles rather than `display`; we learned the hard way that `display` is not a valid action name (see the sidebar "`display`ing your ignorance"). Together with the ever-present default `index` action, this suggests generating the Profile controller as follows:

```
> ruby script/generate controller Profile index show
      exists   app/controllers/
      exists   app/helpers/
      exists   app/views/profile
      exists   test/functional/
      create   app/controllers/profile_controller.rb
      create   test/functional/profile_controller_test.rb
      create   app/helpers/profile_helper.rb
      create   app/views/profile/index.rhtml
      create   app/views/profile/show.rhtml
```

displaying your ignorance

If you were to be so foolish as to create an action called `display`, you would find that, no matter what you do, all instance variables in the corresponding view are `nil`. As a result, such an action is virtually useless.

What's the problem? The answer is that `display` is already a Ruby function, a method attached to the `Object` class. We're not sure exactly what goes wrong, but unintentionally overriding an `Object` method is evidently a Bad Thing. If you find yourself wrestling with a problematic view, all of whose instance variables are mysteriously `nil`, check out the Ruby documentation to make sure that you're not accidentally clashing with a predefined method.

Post-generate, a URL of the form `/profile/show/foobar` will already work (though it will be blank). In order to get `/profile/foobar` to work, add the following line to the routes file, somewhere above the default route:

Listing 9.1 config/routes.rb
_____

```
map.connect 'profile/:screen_name', :controller => 'profile', :action => 'show'
  .
  .
  .
```

Continues

```
# Install the default route as the lowest priority.
map.connect ':controller/:action/:id'
```

Since this rule maps anything of the form `/profile/foobar` to `/profile/show/`
`foobar`, any other actions in the Profile controller would get mapped to `/profile/`
`show/<action>` and would therefore lead to an error—unless by chance some RailsSpace
user happened to choose that action as a screen name, and even in that case the result
would be to display that user's profile instead of executing the action. What this means
is that we can't add any more actions to the Profile controller. This would be a crippling
restriction in general, which is one of the reasons we elected to make a dedicated Profile
controller to show user profiles. Any other actions associated with user profiles will go
in other controllers.

9.1.2 Profile controller and actions

Since it only has one nontrivial action, the Profile controller itself is very simple:

Listing 9.2 app/controllers/profile_controller.rb

```ruby
class ProfileController < ApplicationController

  def index
    @title = "RailsSpace Profiles"
  end

  def show
    screen_name = params[:screen_name]
    @user = User.find_by_screen_name(screen_name)
    if @user
      @title = "My RailsSpace Profile for #{screen_name}"
    else
      flash[:notice] = "No user #{screen_name} at RailsSpace!"
      redirect_to :action => "index"
    end
  end
end
```

You can see that we've decided to forward requests for invalid users to the Profile
controller index, along with a helpful flash error message.

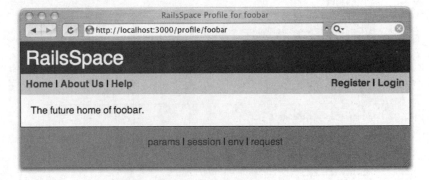

Figure 9.1   The basic stub for Foo Bar's RailsSpace profile.

Eventually, the view to show a user profile will be quite sophisticated (Section 9.6), but for now we'll make it dirt simple:

Listing 9.3   app/views/profile/show.rhtml

```
<p>
  The future home of <%= @user.screen_name %>.
</p>
```

This way, /profile/foobar exists (Figure 9.1) and serves as a starting place for a real profile later on.

The index action will always be simple, and will just be a reminder of the proper form for RailsSpace profile URLs:

Listing 9.4   app/views/profile/index.rhtml

```
<p>
  RailsSpace profile URLs are of the form
</p>
<blockquote>
  http://www.RailsSpace.com/profile/<i>screen_name</i>
</blockquote>
```

When trying to access an invalid profile, a visitor to RailsSpace now gets a helpful error message, as shown in Figure 9.2.

Figure 9.2   The result of visiting `http://localhost:3000/profile/foobar2`
for nonexistent user "foobar2."

9.2 User specs

The most basic element of a RailsSpace user profile is the spec. A user spec contains simple
facts about each user, including name and A/S/L (age/sex/location for all you non-stalker
types). Since RailsSpace is designed to be more about meeting people to work or share
ideas with than about hooking up,[1] we'll also include a space for the user's occupation.

In principle, we could pack all of the spec information into the User model, but the
same could be said for virtually any information connected to a user. The result would
be a giant User model, with virtually no other models in our application. Instead, we'll
create a new model just for specs. Still, we need some way of indicating that specs and
users are associated with each other, and we'll see in this section how Rails (through its
use of Active Record) handles relationships between different models.

9.2.1 Generating the Spec model

We've gotten pretty far with only one model, and the time has finally come to make a
second one. Recall from Section 3.1.2 that we can use `generate` to create the model
and its associated files:

```
> ruby script/generate model Spec
     exists  app/models/
```

---

[1] Not that this describes any social networking sites we know of.

```
exists   test/unit/
exists   test/fixtures/
create   app/models/spec.rb
create   test/unit/spec_test.rb
create   test/fixtures/specs.yml
create   db/migrate
create   db/migrate/005_create_specs.rb
```

As in the case of the User model, the last act of `generate` is to create a migration file, which we will use to construct the specs table in the database. We can create any kinds of columns we want; we can always modify the Spec model by making another migration. The only column we really have to create is `user_id`, which will identify the user corresponding to a given spec. For now, we'll also include the user's first name, last name, gender, birthdate, occupation, city, state, and zip code. With these choices for our initial columns, the migration appears as follows:

Listing 9.5 db/migrate/005_create_specs.rb

```
class CreateSpecs < ActiveRecord::Migration
  def self.up
    create_table :specs do |t|
      t.column :user_id,    :integer, :null => false
      t.column :first_name, :string, :default => ""
      t.column :last_name,  :string, :default => ""
      t.column :gender,     :string
      t.column :birthdate,  :date
      t.column :occupation, :string, :default => ""
      t.column :city,       :string, :default => ""
      t.column :state,      :string, :default => ""
      t.column :zip_code,   :string, :default => ""
    end
  end

  def self.down
    drop_table :specs
  end
end
```

Note that the `user_id` cannot be null (which in the database is the special value NULL) since every spec must be associated with some user. We've also given a default value of `""` to most of the columns; otherwise, these attributes are `nil` by default, which would leave us unable to validate their lengths, as we'll discuss further in Section 9.3.5.

As usual, we use Rake to run the migration:

```
> rake db:migrate
  (in /rails/rails_space)
```

```
== CreateSpecs: migrating ===================================================
-- create_table(:specs)
   -> 0.1225s
== CreateSpecs: migrated (0.1227s) =========================================
```

9.2.2 The Spec model

The Spec model is fairly simple. It needs just a few model constants and a handful of validations. After filling in the blank template created by `generate`, the Spec model looks like this:

Listing 9.6 app/models/spec.rb

```
class Spec < ActiveRecord::Base

  ALL_FIELDS = %w(first_name last_name occupation gender birthdate
                  city state zip_code)
  STRING_FIELDS = %w(first_name last_name occupation city state)
  VALID_GENDERS = ["Male", "Female"]
  START_YEAR = 1900
  VALID_DATES = DateTime.new(START_YEAR)..DateTime.now
  ZIP_CODE_LENGTH = 5

  validates_length_of STRING_FIELDS,
                      :maximum => DB_STRING_MAX_LENGTH

  validates_inclusion_of :gender,
                         :in => VALID_GENDERS,
                         :allow_nil => true,
                         :message => "must be male or female"

  validates_inclusion_of :birthdate,
                         :in => VALID_DATES,
                         :allow_nil => true,
                         :message => "is invalid"

  validates_format_of :zip_code, :with => /(^$|^[0-9]{#{ZIP_CODE_LENGTH}}$)/,
                      :message => "must be a five digit number"
end
```

As with the User model, the Spec model contains several constants associated with the attributes of the model, together with validations for those attributes. The first constant, `ALL_FIELDS`, is a list of all the attributes that we will allow the user to edit. The next constant is an array of strings specifying which fields are strings whose length should be validated. We then have a constant for all of the valid genders; we use the strings

"Male" and "Female" to indicate the user's gender. We then define a couple of constants for validating birthdates; the second, VALID_DATES, creates a range of DateTime objects defining valid birthdates. Finally, we bind a name to the number of digits in a zip code.[2]

We should note that we didn't put all these constants in right away; we discovered the need for them as we wrote our views and tests, adding them one by one. As we discovered in the case of the User model, class constants are a convenient way to collect information specific to the model for use elsewhere in the application. It's not a bad idea to include some class constants preemptively, which we will probably do for future models, or you can rely on adding them as the need arises, but in any case we warmly recommend their use.

Although we have some experience with models and validations through the User model, several aspects of the Spec model deserve some amplification. Note first that validates_length_of can take an array of strings as its first argument, validating the length of each one in turn. Since we don't have any particular reason to restrict the length of the first name, last name, or occupation, we've simply used the maximum length allowed by the database string type. This, in turn, uses the constant DB_STRING_MAX_LENGTH, which we could define in the Spec model, but since we know it will be useful to other models, we'll put it in config/environment.rb where it will be globally accessible:

Listing 9.7 config/environment.rb

```
.
.
.

# Include your application configuration below

DB_STRING_MAX_LENGTH = 255
```

The Spec model uses a new validation, validates_inclusion_of, which simply verifies that the given field is in a particular list or range of valid options. Note in particular how smart Ruby is in comparing different kinds of objects; even though our birthdate is a string, Ruby knows how to make sure that it's in a valid range of DateTimes. Both

---

[2] This may seem like overkill, but the descriptive model constant will look good in the tests and views, and it gives us the flexibility to add, for example, a four-digit extension at some point.

genders and birthdates can be blank, which we indicate in `validates_inclusion_of` by using the option `:allows_nil`.

The final validation uses `validates_format_of` to check the zip code format (which we saw for the first time in Section 3.2.5 in the context of screen name and email format validations). The only tricky thing here is the regular expression used for zip code validation; it matches either an empty zip code or a sequence of digits of length `ZIP_CODE_LENGTH`. Let's open up an `irb` session to see how it works:

```
> irb
irb(main):001:0> ZIP_CODE_LENGTH = 5
=> 5
irb(main):002:0> pattern = /(^$|^[0-9]{#{ZIP_CODE_LENGTH}}$)/
=> /(^$|^[0-9]{5}$)/
irb(main):003:0> "" =~ pattern
=> 0
irb(main):004:0> "91125" =~ pattern
=> 0
irb(main):005:0> "911250" =~ pattern
=> nil
irb(main):006:0> "fubar" =~ pattern
=> nil
```

After defining the relevant zip code constant, first we replicate the pattern used in the validation; notice in particular that variable interpolation works in regular expressions. Then we use the `=~` syntax (borrowed from Perl) to test for a regular expression match, showing a few examples of successful and unsuccessful matches. (By now, you've no doubt gotten used to `nil` being `false`; it's essential in this context also to recall that 0 is `true`, since that's what `irb` returns for a successful match.)

9.2.3 Tying models together

With the class constants and validations from the previous section, we are very nearly done with our new Spec model. We've encountered class constants and validations before in the context of the User model, of course, but for the purposes of registration and authentication, the User model could stand on its own. In contrast, now we have two models that are related in a specific way: Each user has one spec, and each spec belongs to a user. Let's tell that to Rails.

If you've done much web programming before, it's likely you've tied databases together either by the get-id-write-SQL-to-get-user-related-table-row idiom or by joining one or more tables by common id. Rails uses the first approach, but it's completely hidden behind the scenes. In Rails, all we do is use the normal "dot syntax" for accessing object attributes:

```
@user.spec
```

references the spec for a particular User. Active Record lets us do this as long as three conditions are met.

1. The specs table has a column identifying its corresponding user.
2. The User class declares that each user has one spec.
3. The Spec class declares that each spec belongs to a user.

We've already met the first of these requirements by including a `user_id` column in the `specs` table (Section 9.2.1). The second and third requirements simply involve adding a couple of lines to our models. First, we tell Rails that each user has one spec:

Listing 9.8 app/models/user.rb

```
class User < ActiveRecord::Base
  has_one :spec
  .
  .
  .
end
```

Next, we tell Rails that each spec belongs to a user:

Listing 9.9 app/models/spec.rb

```
class Spec < ActiveRecord::Base
  belongs_to :user
  .
  .
  .
end
```

By implementing these three simple steps, we allow Rails to perform all kinds of wonderful magic. For example, if a user already has a spec, we can use

```
@user.spec
```

to gain access to it. If there is no spec, we can write something like

```
@user.spec = Spec.new
# some manipulations creating a valid spec
@user.save
```

and automatically create an entry in the `specs` table corresponding to the proper user (as identified by the user id).

This is all a bit abstract, so let's move on to editing user specs for some concrete examples of data model associations.

9.3 Editing the user specs

Our method for editing user specs parallels the screen name, email, and password edit-ing forms and actions from Chapter 8. As before, we'll use the standard Rails way of manipulating a model using a form, as well as some fairly slick embedded Ruby.

As with previous forms, the view for editing specs uses `form_for` to build up a form for editing a Spec model object. It introduces a couple of new helper functions, as well as a custom-built helper to capture a recurring pattern in our forms.

9.3.1 Spec controller

Since we'll be handling requests from the browser in order to edit the spec, naturally enough we need a Spec controller:

```
> ruby script/generate controller Spec index edit
      exists   app/controllers/
      exists   app/helpers/
      create   app/views/spec
      exists   test/functional/
      create   app/controllers/spec_controller.rb
      create   test/functional/spec_controller_test.rb
      create   app/helpers/spec_helper.rb
      create   app/views/spec/index.rhtml
      create   app/views/spec/edit.rhtml
```

Although the index action isn't strictly necessary (in fact, we will just forward it to the user index), we like the idea that every controller has some default action.

In addition to the rather trivial index action, we'll also include the slightly less trivial edit action. Like many of the actions in the User controller, `edit` uses the `param_posted?` function to test for the proper posted parameter, but first we have to make this function available to the Spec controller. Since `param_posted?` is gener-ally useful, we'll put it in the Application controller so that it will be available to all our controllers:

Listing 9.10 app/controllers/application.rb
_____

```
class ApplicationController < ActionController::Base
  .
  .
  .
  # Return true if a parameter corresponding to the given symbol was posted.
  def param_posted?(sym)
    request.post? and params[sym]
```

```
  end
end
```

For the most part, the spec `edit` action parallels the edit action in the User controller from Section 8.2:

Listing 9.11 app/controllers/spec_controller.rb

```
class SpecController < ApplicationController

  def index
    redirect_to :controller => "user", :action => "index"
  end

  # Edit the user's spec.
  def edit
    @title = "Edit Spec"
    @user = User.find(session[:user_id])
    @user.spec ||= Spec.new
    @spec = @user.spec
    if param_posted?(:spec)
      if @user.spec.update_attributes(params[:spec])
        flash[:notice] = "Changes saved."
        redirect_to :controller => "user", :action => "index"
      end
    end
  end
end
```

The first two lines are familiar: We give the spec edit page a title and then find the user in the database using the user id in the session (using the same `User.find` method that we first encountered in Section 8.2).[3] The third line is the key piece of new material: It assigns a new spec object to `@user.spec` unless the user already has a spec, in which case it does nothing. It uses the rather obscure yet entirely logical operator `||=` to accomplish this task (see the sidebar "What the &*!@ is `||=`?").

> **What the &*!@ is `||=` ?**
>
> The first time I (Michael) saw `||=` (read "or-equals"), I said "Huh?" The second time I saw it, I'd forgotten that I'd seen it once before, and I said " *<head explodes>*". But, upon further reflection, I realized that it actually makes a lot of sense.

---

[3] If you're worried about what happens if no user is logged in, you're ahead of the game; see Section 9.3.4.

A common operation when programming is incrementing a variable by a particular quantity, as in

```
foo = foo + bar
```

Many languages (including Ruby) provide a syntactic shortcut for this:

```
foo += bar
```

Sometimes, we want a variable to keep its current value, unless it's nil, in which case we want to give it some other value. For example, we might want to assign to a user spec either the current spec (if there is one) or a new one. Using the short-circuit property of the || operator, we might write this as follows:

```
@user.spec = @user.spec || Spec.new
```

But this is just the foo = foo + bar pattern with || in place of +. By analogy with the += construction, we can therefore write

```
@user.spec ||= Spec.new
```

Voilà!

The rest of the function is also important. The edit view needs an @spec variable since it contains the same kind of form_for that we've used before to manipulate the User model. Then, if the form is posted with a :spec element in params, we update the user spec attributes with the parameters from the form:

```
@user.spec.update_attributes(params[:spec])
```

This line contains some magic made possible by our efforts in Section 9.2.3 to tie the Spec and User models together. Based on the id of the user, Active Record knows to update the corresponding row in the specs table. We never have to worry about the association between the two tables explicitly; Active Record does the hard work for us.

9.3.2 An HTML utility

In order to simplify the spec edit view, we'll define a custom function called text_field_for, which makes a text field based on the form object and the name of the field. Its purpose is to generate HTML of the form

```
<div class="form_row">
  <label for="last_name">Last name</label>
  <input id="spec_last_name" maxlength="255" name="spec[last_name]" size="15"
         type="text" value="Bar" />
</div>
```

using code like

```
<%= text_field_for form, "Last name" %>
```

This effectively captures the pattern that we've used previously where the content of the `label` is the humanized version of the field name and the input tag is generated by `form.text_field`.

The `text_field_for` could be defined in the Spec helper, but we expect that it will be useful in many different views, so we'll define it in the Application helper, where it will be available to our entire application:

Listing 9.12   app/helpers/application_helper.rb

```
.
.
.
def text_field_for(form, field,
                   size=HTML_TEXT_FIELD_SIZE,
                   maxlength=DB_STRING_MAX_LENGTH)
  label = content_tag("label", "#{field.humanize}:", :for => field)
  form_field = form.text_field field, :size => size, :maxlength => maxlength
  content_tag("div", "#{label} #{form_field}", :class => "form_row")
end
.
.
.
```

This uses the Rails `content_tag` function to form the relevant tags, rather than explicitly using strings such as `"<label>"`. This way, we never have to worry about closing our tags, since `content_tag` does it for us. We're not naming names, but we've seen quite a lot of Ruby-generated HTML with hard-coded tag names out there that is ugly and error-prone; we suggest always using `content_tag` or the related `tag` function rather than explicit tag strings when using Ruby to make HTML.[4]

To get `text_field_for` to work, we have to define `HTML_TEXT_FIELD_SIZE`, which is a global constant for the default size of an HTML text field. As with `DB_STRING_MAX_LENGTH` (Section 9.2.2), we define `HTML_TEXT_FIELD_SIZE` in `environment.rb`:

Listing 9.13   config/environment.rb

```
.
.
.
# Include your application configuration below
```

Continues

---

[4] See also `Builder::XmlMarkup` in the Rails API for a general approach that works for arbitrary XML structures.

```
DB_STRING_MAX_LENGTH = 255
HTML_TEXT_FIELD_SIZE = 15
```

(The value 15 is somewhat arbitrary, and you're free to choose a different value; its arbitrariness is all the more reason to have a global constant, since we may very well decide that, say, 25 is a more reasonable default value for text fields.)

Before moving on, be sure to restart the development server to load the new environment settings.

The `text_field_for` helper function is like a partial, but unlike a partial it is defined entirely in Ruby instead of rhtml. This allows us to use default arguments and to handle multiple arguments more elegantly than partials, which have a somewhat cumbersome mechanism for passing local variables. Choosing between a partial or a Ruby function to eliminate duplicate HTML is a matter of judgment; in this case using Ruby seems more natural.

9.3.3 The spec edit view

With the `text_field_for` function in hand, the spec edit form is relatively straightforward, apart from a couple of new Rails helpers:

Listing 9.14 app/views/spec/edit.rhtml

```
<% form_for :spec do |form| %>
<fieldset>
  <legend><%= @title %></legend>

  <%= error_messages_for 'spec' %>
  <%= text_field_for form, "first_name" %>
  <%= text_field_for form, "last_name"  %>
  <div class="form_row">
    <label for="gender">Gender:</label>
    <%= radio_button :spec, :gender, "Male"   %> Male
    <%= radio_button :spec, :gender, "Female" %> Female
  </div>
  <div class="form_row">
    <label for="birthdate">Birthdate:</label>
    <%= date_select :spec, :birthdate,
                          :start_year => Spec::START_YEAR,
                          :end_year => Time.now.year,
                          :include_blank => true,
                          :order => [:month, :day, :year] %>
  </div>
  <%= text_field_for form, "occupation" %>
```

```
    <%= text_field_for form, "city" %>
    <%= text_field_for form, "state" %>
    <%= text_field_for form, "zip_code", Spec::ZIP_CODE_LENGTH %>

    <%= submit_tag "Update", :class => "submit" %>
</fieldset>
<% end %>
```

The page resulting from this view shown in Figure 9.3.

The spec edit introduces a couple of new Rails form helpers, the `radio_button` and `date_select` functions. Like the other form helpers, these functions both take symbols representing the type of object to be manipulated (in this case, a spec) and the attribute to be modified (either the gender or the birthdate). The `date_select` function is particularly clever; enter an invalid birthdate and take a look at the `params` variable if you're curious about the implementation (Figure 9.4).

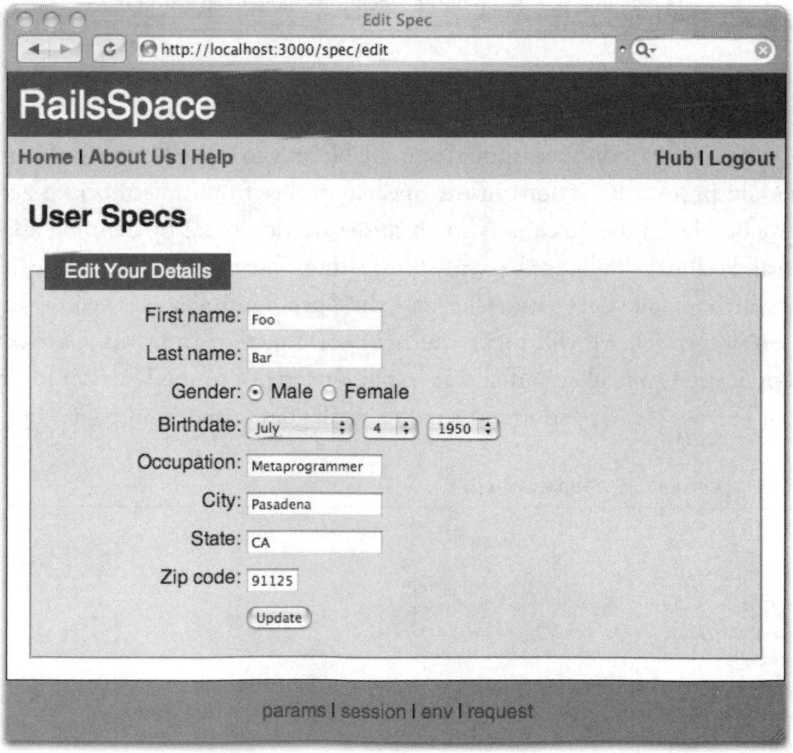

Figure 9.3   Editing Foo Bar's spec.

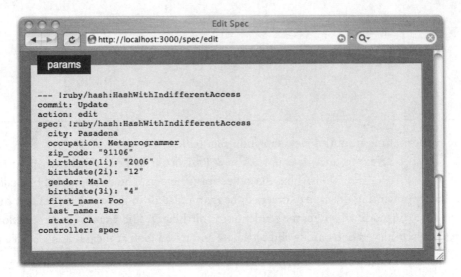

Figure 9.4 Exposing the date select implementation by way of posting an invalid date
(a date that was in the future when this chapter was written).

9.3.4 Protecting specs

The ability to view and edit specs should be available only to logged-in users of RailsSpace, so we should protect the actions in the Spec controller from unauthorized access. Of course, we developed the machinery to do this in Section 6.4.2 by defining a `protect` function and using the Rails `before_filter` feature. Since we want to be able to protect functions in both the User controller and the Spec controller (as well as any other controllers we create), we will move the `protect` function from the User controller to the Application controller and add an explicit reference to the User controller using `:controller => "user"` so that the redirect still goes to the login page:

Listing 9.15 app/controllers/application.rb

```
    .
    .
    .
# Protect a page from unauthorized access.
def protect
  unless logged_in?
    session[:protected_page] = request.request_uri
    flash[:notice] = "Please log in first"
    redirect_to :controller => "user", :action => "login"
    return false
```

```
     end
  end
   .
   .
   .
```

Then, add a before filter to the Spec controller:

Listing 9.16 app/controllers/spec_controller.rb

```
class SpecController < ApplicationController
  before_filter :protect
   .
   .
   .
end
```

Now, all of the actions in the Spec controller require a user login.

9.3.5 Testing specs

Of course, we would be remiss not to test our spec functionality. The full listing for both the spec functional and unit tests can be downloaded at `http://RailsSpace.com/book`; we list below a couple of the tests and comment on some of their novel features.

Perhaps the most important thing to test is a successful edit. As in our previous test for login and register, we `post` information to the `edit` action and then check to see that the appropriate steps were taken:

Listing 9.17 test/functional/spec_controller_test.rb

```
require File.dirname(__FILE__) + '/../test_helper'
require 'spec_controller'

# Re-raise errors caught by the controller.
class SpecController; def rescue_action(e) raise e end; end

class SpecControllerTest < Test::Unit::TestCase
  fixtures :users
  fixtures :specs

  def setup
    @controller = SpecController.new
    @request    = ActionController::TestRequest.new
```

Continues

```
  @response    = ActionController::TestResponse.new
  @user        = users(:valid_user)
  @spec        = specs(:valid_spec)
end

.

.

.

def test_edit_success
  authorize @user
  post :edit,
      :spec  => { :first_name => "new first name",
                  :last_name  => "new last name",
                  :gender     => "Male",
                  :occupation => "new job",
                  :zip_code   => "91125" }
  spec = assigns(:spec)
  new_user = User.find(spec.user.id)
  assert_equal new_user.spec, spec
  assert_equal "Changes saved.", flash[:notice]
  assert_response :redirect
  assert_redirected_to :controller => "user", :action => "index"
end

.

.

.


end
```

Don't try to run this test just yet; first we need to explain what's going on here. The main novelty is the use of the `@spec` variable defined by the action to access the user id:[5]

```
spec = assigns(:spec)
new_user = User.find(spec.user.id)
```

We've seen before how we can access a spec through a user using an expression such as `user.spec`; here we see the complementary ability to access a user through a spec with `spec.user.id`.[6] One other aspect of `test_edit_success` deserves note: The `authorize` function, which previously lived in the User controller test (Section 6.3.2), has been moved to the test helper so that it can be used by multiple controllers:

---

[5] Recall that `assigns` looks for an *instance* variable in the corresponding action, so `assigns(:spec)` looks for `@spec` in the action.

[6] Of course, in this case we could also use `spec.user_id`.

Listing 9.18   test/test_helper.rb

```
# Authorize a user.
def authorize(user)
  @request.session[:user_id] = user.id
end
```

We're now in a position to appreciate the necessity of the `authorize` function, in addition to the `try_to_login` function. Since functional tests can only call actions in the controller they test, we need an authorization function that works independently of the `login` action (which is only accessible when testing the User controller).

Now, to run the test, you'll need to edit the Spec YAML file:

Listing 9.19   test/fixtures/specs.yml

```
# Read about fixtures at http://ar.rubyonrails.org/classes/Fixtures.html
valid_spec:
  id: 1
  user_id: 1
  first_name: Kip
  last_name: Thorne
  gender: Male
  birthdate: 1940-06-01
  occupation: Feynman Professor of Theoretical Physics
  city: Pasadena
  state: CA
  zip_code: 91125

blank_spec:
  id: 2
  user_id: 2
```

Once you prepare the test database, you'll be good to go:

```
> rake db:test:prepare
(in /rails/rails_space)
> ruby test/functional/spec_controller_test.rb -n test_edit_success
Loaded suite test/functional/spec_controller_test
Started
.
Finished in 0.288183 seconds.

1 tests, 4 assertions, 0 failures, 0 errors
```

As with the Spec controller tests, the full Spec model tests can be downloaded from the RailsSpace website, but one test in particular deserves to be highlighted:

Listing 9.20 test/unit/spec_test.rb

```
# Test saving blank spec.
def test_blank
  blank = Spec.new
  assert blank.save, blank.errors.full_messages.join("\n")
end
```

This effectively tests the attributes whose default values are supposed to be the empty
string `" "` (Section 9.2.1). The reason we mention this test specifically is because the error
messages are very confusing if you forget to put the default value of `" "` in the migration.
In that case, the attributes for a new spec object would be `nil` rather than blank. Our
test would then fail as follows:

```
> ruby test/unit/spec_test.rb -n test_blank
Loaded suite test/unit/spec_test
Started
F
Finished in 0.48 seconds.

  1) Failure:
test_blank(SpecTest) [test/unit/spec_test.rb:19]:
City is too long (maximum is 255 characters)
State is too long (maximum is 255 characters)
Occupation is too long (maximum is 255 characters)
First name is too long (maximum is 255 characters)
Last name is too long (maximum is 255 characters).
<false> is not true.

1 tests, 1 assertions, 1 failures, 0 errors
```

If these error messages seem confusing in a test result, imagine how perplexing they
would be coming back to a user on the RailsSpace site. How can a blank (that is to say,
`nil`) first name possibly be too long? The answer is, it isn't too long, but our validation
requires finding, for example, `first_name.length`, which raises an exception when
`first_name` is `nil`. Unfortunately, Rails interprets this exception as a validation failure
and reports that the corresponding attribute is too long. Since that is confusing, it's
important to have a test for it.

Of course, since our migration includes the proper default value, the test passes:

```
> ruby test/unit/spec_test.rb -n test_blank
Loaded suite test/unit/spec_test
Started
.
Finished in 0.57 seconds.

1 tests, 1 assertions, 0 failures, 0 errors
```

9.4 Updating the user hub

Now that we have an editable Spec model, it's time to update the user hub with information from the spec. Recall that the user hub lives at the `index` action of the User controller (Section 4.3.3). All we need to do in the action is to create a user spec using the same `||=` construction that we used in Section 9.3.1:

Listing 9.21 app/controllers/user_controller.rb

```ruby
def index
  @title = "RailsSpace User Hub"
  @user = User.find(session[:user_id])
  @user.spec ||= Spec.new
  @spec = @user.spec
end
```

We've also created a spec instance variable for use in the hub view.

In preparation for displaying the user's full name and location, we'll add a couple of functions to the Spec model:

Listing 9.22 app/models/spec.rb

```ruby
class Spec < ActiveRecord::Base
  .
  .
  .
  # Return the full name (first plus last).
  def full_name
    [first_name, last_name].join(" ")
  end

  # Return a sensibly formatted location string.
  def location
    [city, state, zip_code].join(" ")
  end
end
```

Both the full name and the location use the `join` method to join array elements together, separated by a particular string (in this case, a space).

9.4.1 The new hub view

We're now ready to make the updated user hub. First we have to make a couple of minor changes to the global layout file `application.rhtml` by including the profile stylesheet and adding a `<br clear="all" />` to reset any float alignments defined in the page content:

Listing 9.23   app/views/layouts/application.rhtml

```
    .
    .
    .
<title><%= @title %></title>
<%= stylesheet_link_tag "site" %>
<%= stylesheet_link_tag "profile" %>
    .
    .
    .
<%= yield %>
<br clear="all" />
    .
    .
    .
```

Then add the following styles to the profile stylesheet:

Listing 9.24   public/stylesheets/profile.css

```
/* Profile Styles */

td.label {
  text-align: right;
  font-weight:  bold;
  white-space: nowrap;
}

input {
  font-family: Arial, Helvetica, sans-serif;
}

.edit_link a {
  text-decoration: none;
  color: blue;
}

#left_column {
  float:  left;
  width: 300px;
}

#main_content {
```

```
  margin-left:  320px;
}

.sidebar_box {
  background-color: #ddd;
  border: 1px solid #aaa;
  font-size: 12px;
  margin-bottom:  10px;
}

.sidebar_box h2 {
  margin-top:  0px;
  padding: 6px;
  background-color: #ccc;
  font-size: 13px;
  color: maroon;
  font-weight:bold;
}
.sidebar_box p {
  padding-left:  6px;
  padding-right: 6px;
}

.sidebar_box .header  {
  float: left;
}

.sidebar_box .edit_link {
  float: right;
}
```

With these changes, the updated hub view appears as follows:

Listing 9.25   app/views/user/index.rhtml

```
<h1>User Hub</h1>

<div id="left_column">
  <div class="sidebar_box">
    <h2>
      <span class="header">Basic User Info</span>
      <span class="edit_link"><%= link_to "(edit)", :action => "edit" %></span>
      <br clear="all" />
    </h2>
    <div class="sidebar_box_contents">
      <table>
        <tr>
```

Continues

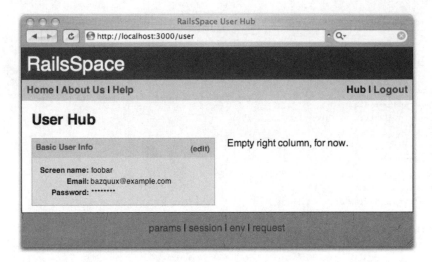

Figure 9.5   The updated user hub with user info moved into a sidebar.

```
      <td class="label">Screen name:</td>
      <td><%= @user.screen_name %></td>
    </tr>
    <tr>
      <td class="label">Email:</td>
      <td><%= @user.email %></td>
    </tr>
    <tr>
      <td class="label">Password:</td>
      <td>********</td>
    </tr>
    </table>
  </div>
  </div>
</div>
<div id="main_content">
  Empty right column, for now.
</div>
```

Here we've introduced a two-column format, with the left column starting off with the basic user information. The result appears in Figure 9.5.

9.4.2 A Spec box

The user info part of the left columns is completely straightforward, but the next section, user spec, is a little bit trickier:

Listing 9.26   app/views/user/index.rhtml

```
  .
  .
  .

  <div class="sidebar_box">
    <h2>
      <span class="header">Spec</span>
      <span class="edit_link">
        <%= link_to "(edit)", :controller => "spec", :action => "edit" %>
      </span>
      <br clear="all" />
    </h2>
    <div class="sidebar_box_contents">
      <table>
        <%= render :partial    => "spec/field_row",
                   :collection => Spec::ALL_FIELDS %>
      </table>
    </div>
  </div>
</div>
<div id="main_content">
  .
  .
  .
```

This view uses a partial to render the spec fields:

Listing 9.27   app/views/spec/_field_row.rhtml

```
<tr>
  <td class="label"><%= field_row.humanize %>:</td>
  <td><%= h @user.spec[field_row] %></td>
</tr>
```

Note that we use the humanize function (which we first met in Section 8.5.2) to label each field.

Since the Spec model has a constant ALL_FIELDS containing the names of all the attributes we want to list, you might have expected code such as

```
<% Spec::ALL_FIELDS.each do |field| %>
  <%= render :partial    => "spec/field_row"
             :locals     => { :field_row => field } %>
<% end %>
```

Rails partials are clever enough to anticipate this situation through the `:collection` option, which allows this pithier code:

```
<%= render :partial    => "spec/field_row",
           :collection => Spec::ALL_FIELDS %>
```

If you're wondering how the `_field_row.rhtml` partial knows how to assign the proper value to `field_row`, the answer is that it gets it from the filename. In other words, passing a collection to a file called `_field_row.rhtml` automatically invokes that partial with a local variable called `field_row` for each element in the collection.

The partial itself contains a couple of tricks. First, Active Record allows us to access an attribute using a hash-like notation as well as the traditional Ruby dot syntax; for example,

```
@user.spec["first_name"]
```

is the same as

```
@user.spec.first_name
```

This is particularly convenient when we have a variable (such as `field_row`) that contains a string with the attribute name; instead of having to hard-code each object attribute, we can use a variable instead.[7]

The second trick is the letter `h`. This is the minimalist Rails function for *HTML escape*, which replaces HTML tags with their escaped versions (e.g., `&lt;` for <). Though there would be little harm in allowing our users to put their names in boldface or make their occupations italicized, displaying arbitrary text on a web page is a Bad Thing, and would open up RailsSpace to a *cross-site scripting* (XSS) attack through the inclusion of malicious tags, forms, or JavaScript. (Of course, escaping text in this way also prevents the use of any HTML tags, which is fine for short fields such as those in the spec, but it might be a little heavy-handed for the text fields we'll find in other parts of the profile. To allow some HTML tags while disabling the most dangerous elements, use the *sanitize* function in place of `h`; see Section 9.5.4.)

Figure 9.6 shows the user hub after adding the spec sidebar.

9.4.3 Named routes and the profile URL

One important element on the user hub will be a link to the user's public profile, as identified by screen name. We could code this directly using something like

```
<%= link_to "http://RailsSpace.com/profile/#{@user.screen_name}",
            "/profile/#{@user.screen_name}" %>
```

---

[7] We could achieve this same result with pure Ruby using the more general but somewhat less clear syntax `@user.spec.send(field_row)`.

Figure 9.6   The updated user hub with spec sidebar.

This would work, but it feels like we're repeating ourselves a bit, and it's not robust to changes in the URL routing rules. The preferred Rails way to handle this is to use a technique called *named routes*.

Recall from Section 9.1.1 that we created a special routing rule for user profiles:

Listing 9.28   config/routes.rb

```
map.connect 'profile/:screen_name', :controller => 'profile', :action => 'show'
```

To take advantage of named routes, all we need to do is change `map.connect` to `map.profile`:

```
map.profile 'profile/:screen_name', :controller => 'profile', :action => 'show'
```

This change automatically creates a function called `profile_url`, which in our case takes the screen name as an argument. In other words,

```
profile_url(:screen_name => 'foobar')
```

automatically connects to

```
/profile/foobar
```

With our newly rerouted profile, we can link to the profile URL with `profile_url`:

```
<%= link_to profile_url(:screen_name => @user.screen_name),
            profile_url(:screen_name => @user.screen_name) %>
```

This is still a bit verbose for our taste, so we'll make a helper function for it:

Listing 9.29   app/helpers/profile_helper.rb

```
module ProfileHelper

  # Return the user's profile URL.
  def profile_for(user)
    profile_url(:screen_name => user.screen_name)
  end

end
```

This will allow us to write the user's profile URL as

```
<%= link_to profile_for(@user), profile_for(@user) %>
```

We'll make good use of this in the next section.

Note that we've put `profile_for` in the Profile helper file. So far in RailsSpace, we've put all helpers functions in the global Application helper file, which is convenient but can become rather cumbersome. Given the large number of helpers that we'll be adding throughout the rest of this book, we'll mainly put helper functions in the controller-specific helper files (such as `profile_helper.rb`). The cost of this is having to include the helper in every controller that uses any of the functions. In this case, we'll be putting the profile URL on the user hub, so we have to tell the User controller to include the Profile helper file:

```
class UserController < ApplicationController
  include ApplicationHelper
  helper :profile
  before_filter :protect, :only => [ :index, :edit, :edit_password ]
  .
  .
  .
end
```

Here we've used the `helper` function, which takes in a symbol corresponding to the name of the helper file. We could have written `include ProfileHelper` instead, but the effect is slightly different;

```
helper :profile
```

makes the Profile helper functions available only in the *views* of the User controller. In contrast,

```
include ProfileHelper
```

includes the helper functions into both the views and the controller itself. This distinction will be important when we want to use helper functions in controllers.

9.4.4 The hub main content

Now that we've finished the machinery needed to display the RailsSpace profile URL, we need to decide what to do with the user's name, occupation, and location. Since these attributes are optional aspects of the user spec, we should have sensible defaults in case the user leaves them blank. For example, we would like to display `Your Name` if the user decides not to fill in the first or last name fields. We'll accomplish this using the `or_else` function, which we will discuss momentarily:

Listing 9.30 app/views/user/index.rhtml

```
.
.
.
<div id="main_content">
  <div id="full_name">
    <%= h @spec.full_name.or_else("Your Name") %>
  </div>
  <div id="occupation">
    <%= h @spec.occupation.or_else("Your Occupation") %>
  </div>
  <div id="location">
    <%= h @spec.location.or_else("Your Location") %>
  </div>
  <span class="edit_link">
    <%= link_to "(edit)", :controller => "spec", :action => "edit" %>
  </span>

  <hr noshade />
  Profile URL: <%= link_to profile_for(@user), profile_for(@user) %>
  <hr noshade />
```

Continues

```
  My Bio:

</div>
```

Note that we've left space for the bio, which we'll fill in starting in Section 9.5. We've also linked in the profile URL, as promised in the previous section.

This needs just a few more styles:

Listing 9.31 public/stylesheets/profile.css

```
  .
  .
  .

/* Spec Style */

#full_name  {
  font-size: xx-large;
}

#occupation{
  font-size: x-large;
}

#location {
  font-size: large;
}
```

The rhtml for the main content is straightforward except for the or_else function, which returns an alternate value if the string it's called on is blank. This allows us to accomplish our goal of having placeholders for the user information (e.g., Your Name if @spec.full_name is blank).

We've seen something similar to this several times before, most recently in Section 8.5.2 (the password field partial), where we used the construction

```
field_title || field.humanize
```

to display the field title if field_title is not nil, or else display the humanized version of the field. In the case of a blank string, this won't work, though, since a blank string such as " " evaluates to true in a boolean context. What we want is a function, which we call or_else, that enables the following syntax:

```
first_name.or_else("Your Name")
```

We'll follow the Ruby Way by writing the or_else function as a String method. Recall from the sidebar in Section 7.1 that Ruby lets us open the String class itself to add such a method. The traditional Rails location for such a generic library function is in the `lib` directory, so we'll put our new string method there:

Listing 9.32 lib/string.rb

```
class String
  # Return an alternate string if blank.
  def or_else(alternate)
    blank? ? alternate : self
  end
end
```

Note that `or_else` uses the `blank?` method, which returns `true` for any string that is empty (so that the String method `empty?` returns `true`) or consists only of whitespace. `blank?` is not part of Ruby, but rather is added to the `String` class by Rails in much the same way that we have added `or_else`.

To use the `or_else` method with the strings in our application, we have to require the string class in one of our helpers;[8] we'll use the Application helper:

Listing 9.33 app/helpers/application_helper.rb

```
module ApplicationHelper
  require 'string'
    .
    .
    .
end
```

It's important to note that files located in the `lib/` directory are only loaded once, when you start your server. In order to get the updated user hub to work, you will therefore have to restart your local webserver.

Once you've added the `or_else` function to the `String` class and restarted the server, the user hub appears as in Figure 9.7.

---

[8] The `blank?` method is apparently undocumented (at least, we couldn't find it in the API), and before discovering this we actually added our own `blank?` function with exactly the same behavior as the one used by Rails; we then forgot to require the updated string class in any of our helpers. You can imagine our confusion when Rails was unable to locate the `or_else` function—after all, the `blank?` function worked fine!

Figure 9.7   The user hub with the right column starting to fill in.

9.5 Personal FAQ: Interests and personality

In the spirit of a technical specification, the user spec contains only a minimal amount of information. In this section we'll implicitly ask (and explicitly answer) Frequently Asked Questions for our users. These will simply be categories such as the user bio, computer (and other) skills, and favorite movies, music, television shows, etc. The FAQ will be freer-form than the spec; the answer for each category will simply be a block of text that the user is free to edit.

9.5.1 The FAQ model

By now you should be expecting the first step, which is to generate a model for the FAQ:

```
> ruby script/generate model Faq
      exists  app/models/
```

```
exists   test/unit/
exists   test/fixtures/
create   app/models/faq.rb
create   test/unit/faq_test.rb
create   test/fixtures/faqs.yml
exists   db/migrate
create   db/migrate/006_create_faqs.rb
```

Note that we use a model called `Faq` since Rails converts `FAQ` to `Faq` anyway, which is a minor limitation of the `CamelCase-camel_case` convention used by Rails. We're not going to swim upstream against the Rails convention, so we'll keep `Faq`, but we will continue to use FAQ in our discussion.

The next step is to edit the migration file and add some FAQ categories as text fields:

Listing 9.34 db/migrate/006_create_specs.rb

```
class CreateFaqs < ActiveRecord::Migration
  def self.up
    create_table :faqs do |t|
      t.column :user_id,     :integer, :null => false
      t.column :bio,         :text
      t.column :skillz,      :text
      t.column :schools,     :text
      t.column :companies,   :text
      t.column :music,       :text
      t.column :movies,      :text
      t.column :television,  :text
      t.column :magazines,   :text
      t.column :books,       :text
    end
  end

  def self.down
    drop_table :faqs
  end
end
```

Run migrate (which should be starting to become second nature). In the case of the spec, we supplied the default of `""` for several of the fields, but that doesn't work here: MySQL doesn't allow default values for columns of type TEXT.[9] We still want the default values for these fields to be blank, of course; that's no problem, since we can use Ruby to do it in the FAQ model.

---

[9] See `http://dev.mysql.com/doc/refman/5.0/en/blob.html`.

The FAQ model itself is quite short, but it nevertheless has a couple of things we haven't seen before. We'll start with the familiar territory: Like a spec, a FAQ belongs to a user, so we use the `belongs_to :user` declaration to tell that to Rails. We also define a few model constants and add a single, simple validation, which just makes sure that the submitted text isn't too absurdly huge:

Listing 9.35 app/models/faq.rb

```
class Faq < ActiveRecord::Base
  belongs_to :user

  QUESTIONS = %w(bio skillz schools companies
                 music movies television books magazines)
  # A constant for everything except the bio
  FAVORITES = QUESTIONS - %w(bio)
  TEXT_ROWS = 10
  TEXT_COLS = 40

  validates_length_of QUESTIONS,
                      :maximum => DB_TEXT_MAX_LENGTH

  def initialize
    super
    QUESTIONS.each do |question|
      self[question] = ""
    end
  end
end
```

Here the second model constant called FAVORITES indicates the parts of the FAQ that are likely to be simple lists so that they can be displayed differently from the bio. (We call it "favorites" since most of them are lists of favorite things.) The final two constants get used in the view to format the text area where users fill in their answers for the FAQ. The validation uses a constant defined in the environment file:

Listing 9.36 config/environment.rb

```
# Include your application configuration below

DB_STRING_MAX_LENGTH = 255
DB_TEXT_MAX_LENGTH = 40000
HTML_TEXT_FIELD_SIZE = 15
```

As usual, restart the development server to load the new environment settings.

The most significant new material in the FAQ model is the `initialize` function, which is the general Ruby class initialization function. If a class has an `initialize` function, it will automatically be called every time we create a new instance of the class. If a class inherits from another class, there is no need to define an `initialize` function since the parents class's `initialize` function will be called automatically. Since all our models inherit from `ActiveRecord::Base`, so far we have always relied on the initialization function in the parent class (also called the *superclass*). In the present case, though, we need to define our own `initialize`, since we want to set the default text for each question to `""`.

Looking at the text of `initialize`, we see that there are essentially two actions taken. The second is the initialization we need, which uses the hash-style access to Active Record attributes that we first met in Section 9.4:

```
def initialize
  super
  QUESTIONS.each do |question|
    self[question] = ""
  end
end
```

But what about the first line, `super`? Since we want the FAQ model to be a proper Active Record class, we need to call the initialize function of the superclass first; the command to do this is simply `super`. (See `before_validation` in the Rails API for an alternate method.)

The second new piece of syntax is the definition of `FAVORITES`, which uses the `Array` subtraction operator (in conjunction with the `%w` shortcut for creating string arrays):

```
> irb
irb(main):001:0> a = %w(foo bar bar baz quux)
=> ["foo", "bar", "bar", "baz", "quux"]
irb(main):002:0> b = %w(bar quux)
=> ["bar", "quux"]
irb(main):003:0> a - b
=> ["foo", "baz"]
```

As you can see, the operation `a - b` removes from `a` any element appearing in `b`.

Before moving on to the FAQ controller, there's just one change we need to make: we need to tell Rails that a `User` has one FAQ:

Listing 9.37   app/models/user.rb

```
class User < ActiveRecord::Base
  has_one :spec
  has_one :faq
```

Continues

```
attr_accessor :remember_me
  .
  .
  .
end
```

9.5.2 The FAQ controller

So far, each of our models has gotten its own controller, and FAQ is no exception:

```
> ruby script/generate controller Faq index edit
        exists   app/controllers/
        exists   app/helpers/
        create   app/views/spec
        exists   test/functional/
        create   app/controllers/faq_controller.rb
        create   test/functional/faq_controller_test.rb
        create   app/helpers/faq_helper.rb
        create   app/views/faq/index.rhtml
        create   app/views/faq/edit.rhtml
```

We'll fill in the edit method shortly, but for now we'll put in a before filter to protect the FAQ pages, and redirect the FAQ index to the user hub:

Listing 9.38 app/controllers/faq_controller.rb

```
class FaqController < ApplicationController
  before_filter :protect

  def index
    redirect_to hub_url
  end

  def edit
  end
end
```

Here we redirect to hub_url, which requires that we create a named route (Section 9.4.3) for the hub using map.hub:

Listing 9.39 config/routes.rb

```
map.hub 'user', :controller => 'user', :action => 'index'
```

For most pages on RailsSpace, making a named route isn't worth the trouble, but in this case it's a good idea since we expect to redirect frequently to the user hub.

9.5.3   Editing the FAQ

Editing the user FAQ is scandalously easy with the use of Rails partials. The added function is virtually identical to the form for the spec:

Listing 9.40 app/controllers/faq_controller.rb

```
# Edit the user's FAQ.
def edit
  @title = "Edit FAQ"
  @user = User.find(session[:user_id])
  @user.faq ||= Faq.new
  @faq = @user.faq
  if param_posted?(:faq)
    if @user.faq.update_attributes(params[:faq])
      flash[:notice] = "FAQ saved."
      redirect_to hub_url
    end
  end
end
```

As before, we use `form_for` to build up the FAQ form:

Listing 9.41 app/views/faq/edit.rhtml

```
<h1>Frequently Asked Questions</h1>
<p>
  Please answer some basic questions about yourself.
</p>
<% form_for :faq do |form| %>
<fieldset>
  <legend>Update Your FAQ</legend>
  <%= error_messages_for 'faq' %>
  <%= render :partial => "answer_text_area", :collection => Faq::QUESTIONS,
             :locals => { :form => form } %>
  <br clear="all" />
  <%= submit_tag "Update All", :class => "submit" %>
</fieldset>
<% end %>
```

With the form `text_area` helper function, the partial is a snap:

Listing 9.42 app/views/faq/_answer_text_area.rhtml

```
<div class="faq">
  <%= answer_text_area.humanize %>:
  <%= submit_tag "Update", :align => "right" %>
  <br />
  <%= form.text_area answer_text_area, :rows => Faq::TEXT_ROWS,
                                       :cols => Faq::TEXT_COLS %>
</div>
```

Finally, add the FAQ styles to the profile stylesheet:

Listing 9.43 public/stylesheets/profile.css

```
.
.
.
/* FAQ Style */

.faq {
  float: left;
  padding: 20px;
}

#bio {
  padding: 10px;
}
.sidebar_box_contents, .faq_answer {
  padding:  0 10px 10px 10px;
}

.faq_answer textarea {
  width:  280px;
  background: #ff9;
}
```

(Not all of these are needed now, but we'll use them all shortly.) The result appears in Figure 9.8.

9.5.4 Adding the FAQ to the hub

Since we're using the user hub to display the editable profile, we should add the FAQ as well. The first step is to add FAQ instance variables to the user index action:

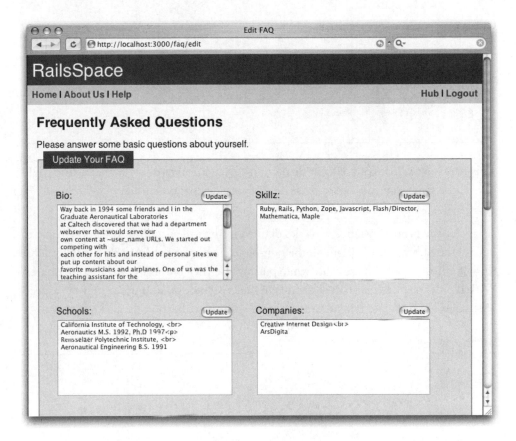

Figure 9.8 The FAQ edit page. Feel free to change the rows/cols to suit your style!

Listing 9.44 app/controllers/user_controller.rb

```
def index
  @title = "RailsSpace User Hub"
  @user = User.find(session[:user_id])
  @user.spec ||= Spec.new
  @spec = @user.spec
  @user.faq ||= Faq.new
  @faq = @user.faq
end
```

The two-variable definition pattern evident in this action is quite common, and each one can be condensed into one line as follows:

Listing 9.45 app/controllers/user_controller.rb

```
def index
  @title = "RailsSpace User Hub"
  @user = User.find(session[:user_id])
  @spec = @user.spec ||= Spec.new
  @faq = @user.faq ||= Faq.new
end
```

This may look a little confusing at first, but it's straightforward if you read it from right to left, the same way you would parse a multivariable assignment like

```
a = b = c = 0
```

With the proper instance variables defined in the index action, we're now ready to update the hub view. We'll put all the non-bio elements of the FAQ on the left sidebar along with the spec (Figure 9.9), while putting the user bio in the main content area. With the FAVORITES constant as defined in the FAQ model, adding the non-bio aspects of the FAQ is as simple as rendering a partial with the collection Faq::FAVORITES:

Listing 9.46 app/views/user/index.rhtml

```
<div id="left_column">
  <div class="sidebar_box">
  .
  .
  .
  </div>

  <div class="sidebar_box">
  .
  .
  .
  </div>
  <%= render :partial => 'faq/sidebar_box', :collection => Faq::FAVORITES %>
</div>
<div id="main_content">
  .
  .
  .
  <hr noshade />
  <%= link_to profile_for(@user), profile_for(@user) %>
  <hr noshade />

  My Bio:
  <span class="edit_link">
    <%= link_to "(edit)", :controller => "faq", :action => "edit" %>
```

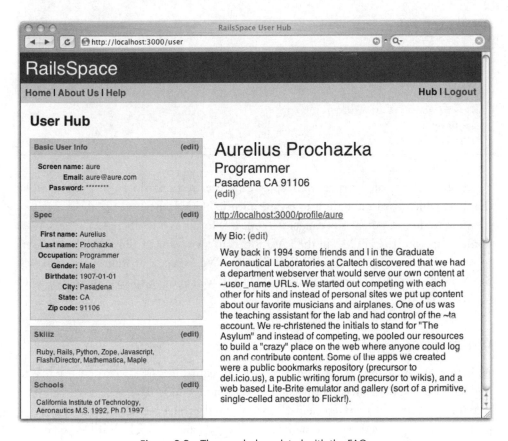

Figure 9.9   The user hub updated with the FAQ.

```
  </span>
  <div id="bio" class="faq_answer">
    <%= sanitize @faq.bio %>
  </div>
</div>
```

The FAQ sidebar partial is relatively straightforward; the only new material is the use of the `sanitize` function (which we also used in the bio section above):

Listing 9.47   app/views/faq/_sidebar_box.rhtml

```
<div class="sidebar_box">
  <h2>
    <span class="edit_link">
```

Continues

```
      <%= link_to "(edit)", :controller => "faq", :action => "edit" %>
    </span>
    <span class="header"><%= sidebar_box.humanize %></span>
    <br clear="all" />
  </h2>
  <div class="faq_answer">
    <%= sanitize @faq[sidebar_box] %>
  </div>
</div>
```

As in the case of the spec, we display each user response in its own `div`; unlike the spec, which used the Rails `h` to escape out the HTML, here we use the `sanitize` function to disable potentially dangerous code like forms and JavaScript. The reason we don't escape out the HTML in the FAQ is because we want to allow RailsSpace users to style their responses using HTML if desired. (We expect that RailsSpace users will be among the most likely people to know HTML well enough to style their own FAQ responses.)

9.5.5 FAQ tests

As before, we have tests for the FAQ model and controller. We'd particularly like to highlight the test of the maximum length validation for FAQs. The `test_max_lengths` is a good example of how test helper functions and model constants can combine to pack a ton of productivity into a tiny test. First, make a simple FAQ entry in the fixture file:

Listing 9.48   test/fixtures/faqs.yml

```
valid_faq:
  id: 1
  user_id: 1
  bio: bio
  skillz: skillz
  schools: schools
  companies: companies
  music: music
  movies: movies
  television: tv
  books: books
  magazines: magazine
```

Now we can test the maximum length of each of the FAQ fields in one fell swoop using the `assert_length` test helper from Section 8.4.3 and the model constant `Faq::QUESTIONS` (together with the `DB_TEXT_MAX_LENGTH` constant from `config/environment.rb`):

Listing 9.49 test/unit/faq_test.rb

```
require File.dirname(__FILE__) + '/../test_helper'

class FaqTest < Test::Unit::TestCase
  fixtures :faqs

  def setup
    @valid_faq = faqs(:valid_faq)
  end

  def test_max_lengths
    Faq::QUESTIONS.each do |question|
      assert_length :max, @valid_faq, question, DB_TEXT_MAX_LENGTH
    end
  end
end
```

Running this gives

```
> rake db:test:prepare
(in /rails/rails_space)
> ruby test/unit/faq_test.rb
Loaded suite test/unit/faq_test
Started
.
Finished in 8.753472 seconds.

1 tests, 27 assertions, 0 failures, 0 errors
```

9.6 Public-facing profile

We've now given each user the ability to create a serviceable (if minimal) profile, so it's time to fill in the `show` action and view (first defined in Section 9.1) to make the first cut of the public-facing profile.

Since we already have ways to display the user's information, it would be wasted effort to code everything from scratch. If you look at the user hub (see Figure 9.9), you'll see that, apart from the edit links, most of the display is suitable for use on the profile. This suggests defining a boolean instance variable called @hide_edit_links in the show action to indicate that those links should be suppressed:

Listing 9.50 app/controllers/profile_controller.rb

```
def show
  @hide_edit_links = true
  screen_name = params[:screen_name]
  @user = User.find_by_screen_name(screen_name)
  if @user
    @title = "My RailsSpace Profile for #{screen_name}"
    @spec = @user.spec ||= Spec.new
    @faq = @user.faq ||= Faq.new
  else
    flash[:notice] = "No user #{screen_name} at RailsSpace!"
    redirect_to :action => "index"
  end
end
```

Lamentably, although Ruby allows function names to end in a question mark, the same is not true for variable names, so we'll define a simple function in the Profile helper so that we can continue the convention of ending all boolean things with ?:

Listing 9.51 app/helpers/profile_helper.rb

```
module ProfileHelper
  .
  .
  .
  # Return true if hiding the edit links for spec, FAQ, etc.
  def hide_edit_links?
    not @hide_edit_links.nil?
  end
end
```

By the way, the reason hide_edit_links? works in general is that instance variables are nil if not defined, so the function returns false unless @hide_edit_links is set explicitly.

Since it reuses the HTML layout and partial code from the user hub, the profile view is simple:

Listing 9.52 app/view/profile/show.rhtml

```
<div id="left_column">
  <%= render :partial => 'faq/sidebar_box', :collection => Faq::FAVORITES %>
</div>

<div id="main_content">
  <div id="full_name">
    <%= h @spec.full_name.or_else(@user.screen_name) %>
  </div>
  <div id="occupation">
    <%= h @spec.occupation %>
  </div>
  <div id="location">
    <%= h @spec.location %>
  </div>


  <hr noshade />

  Bio:
  <div id="bio">
    <%= sanitize @faq.bio %>
  </div>


</div>
```

The only trick is the use of `hide_edit_links?` to hide the edit links on the FAQ sidebar:

Listing 9.53 app/views/faq/_sidebar_box.rhtml

```
<div class="sidebar_box">
  <h2>
    <% unless hide_edit_links? %>
      <span class="edit_link">
        <%= link_to "(edit)", :controller => "faq", :action => "edit" %>
      </span>
    <% end %>
    <span class="header"><%= sidebar_box.humanize %></span>
    <br clear="all">
  </h2>
  <div class="faq_answer">
    <%= sanitize @faq[sidebar_box] %>
  </div>
</div>
```

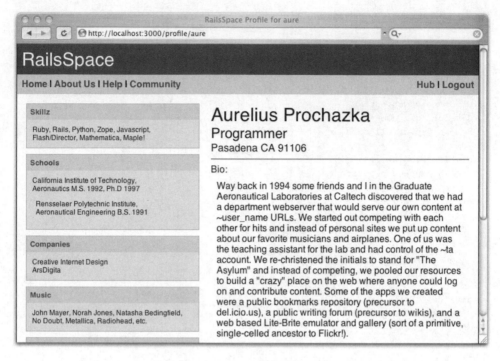

Figure 9.10   A public-facing profile.

With this, the basic user profile is complete (Figure 9.10).

CHAPTER 10

Community

Giving users the ability to create and edit profiles is a good start, but for RailsSpace to be useful to its members, we need to have ways for them to find each other. In this chapter and the next, we develop three methods for finding users.

1. A simple index by name.
2. Browsing by age, sex, and location.
3. Full-text searches through all user information, including specs and FAQs.

In this chapter, we'll populate the RailsSpace development database with sample users so that our various attempts to find users will not be in vain. Then we'll develop an alphabetical community index to list RailsSpace members in the simplest way possible. Though straightforward, the community index will introduce several new aspects of Rails, including results pagination and a demonstration of the `find` function's remarkable versatility.

10.1 Building a community (controller)

Finding users will involve a community index, as well as the capability to browse and search for users. "Browse" and "search" are verbs, which suggests that they should be actions inside of a controller. We'd like to continue the convention of using nouns for controller names, so we need an appropriate collective noun to describe the set of users that can be browsed and searched. Since our search functions take place within the context of a community of users, let's create a Community controller:

```
> ruby script/generate controller Community index browse search
    exists  app/controllers/
    exists  app/helpers/
```

```
create  app/views/community
exists  test/functional/
create  app/controllers/community_controller.rb
create  test/functional/community_controller_test.rb
create  app/helpers/community_helper.rb
create  app/views/community/index.rhtml
create  app/views/community/browse.rhtml
create  app/views/community/search.rhtml
```

This way, users will (for example) be able to search for other users through the URL

```
http://localhost:3000/community/search
```

and similarly for browse. Let's update the site navigation now:

Listing 10.1 app/views/layouts/application.rhtml

```
.
.
.
<%= nav_link "Help",       "site", "help" %> |
<%= nav_link "Community", "community", "index" %>
.
.
.
```

We'll spend the rest of this chapter and the next filling in the Community controller. First, though, we need to address a fundamental problem: As the site now stands, essentially all efforts to find RailsSpace users will return nothing.

10.2 Setting up sample users

Since a niche social networking site like RailsSpace might have hundreds or possibly thousands of users, we should develop it in the context of a database that contains many sample users. That way, the various browses and searches will return a realistic number of results. Alas, currently we have only one user, our old friend Foo Bar, and adding users by hand (as we did for Foo) would be incredibly cumbersome and time-consuming. Moreover, our development database is subject to obliteration through migrations and other catastrophes; even if we did enter a bunch of users by hand, we would risk losing that data.

Our solution is to use the computer to do the hard work for us. We'll create YAML files containing a sample database of users (as well as their corresponding specs and FAQs). Then we'll automate the loading of that data using a custom Rake task.

10.2.1 Collecting the data

In this section we'll construct sample users, specs, and FAQs in YAML format. Our source of data will be the information for Caltech's Distinguished Alumni, available publicly at

```
http://alumni.caltech.edu/distinguished_alumni
```

If you'd prefer to fill your files with data some other way—even writing them by hand— you're welcome to do so. The key is to have the data in a format that can be conveniently loaded on demand, so that if the database gets clobbered, we can restore its previous state easily.

   If you were an ordinary mortal, you could screen-scrape the Distinguished Alumni information yourself, but since Aure built the Caltech Alumni website, the sample data is available for download in YAML format:

```
http://alumni.caltech.edu/distinguished_alumni/users.yml
http://alumni.caltech.edu/distinguished_alumni/specs.yml
http://alumni.caltech.edu/distinguished_alumni/faqs.yml
```

The same data files are available at

```
http://RailsSpace.com/book
```

In order to get the results we show in this chapter, you should download these YAML files and put them in the following directory:

```
lib/tasks/sample_data
```

(This will require creating the `sample_data` directory.)

   By the way, the Distinguished Alumni data is a mix of real and fake information. We use their real names and official Distinguished Alumni biographies (which we used for the FAQ bio field), but we made up their birthdates, locations, and ages. For locations, we spread out their zip codes within the range 92101 (San Diego) to 98687 (Vancouver). For their birthdates, we pretended that they were 50 years old when they got their Distinguished Alumnus award and gave them a birthdate of January 1, 50 years before the award.

10.2.2 Loading the data

With the sample user data in hand, we next need to copy it from the YAML files to the development database. In principle, any technique would do; we could parse the file using Ruby (or even, say, Perl or Python), establish some sort of database connection, and do all the inserts explicitly. If you think about it, though, Rails must already have a way to do this, since Rails tests populate a test database with data from YAML files using fixtures. Our strategy is to piggyback on this machinery to put our sample data into the development database.

We could write a plain Ruby script to do the data insertion, but it's more in the spirit of the Rails way of doing things to make a custom Rake task to do the job. This involves writing our own Rakefile. Unsurprisingly, there's a standard location in the Rails directory tree for such Rakefiles, `lib/tasks` (so now you see why we put the data in `lib/tasks/sample_data`).

Since our Rake tasks involve loading sample data, we'll call our file `sample_data.rake`. Rakefiles consist of a series of *tasks* written in Ruby; in our case, we define the tasks `load` and `delete`:

Listing 10.2   lib/tasks/sample_data.rake

```
# Provide tasks to load and delete sample user data.
require 'active_record'
require 'active_record/fixtures'

namespace :db do
  DATA_DIRECTORY = "#{RAILS_ROOT}/lib/tasks/sample_data"
  namespace :sample_data do
    TABLES = %w(users specs faqs)
    MIN_USER_ID = 1000     # Starting user id for the sample data

    desc "Load sample data"
    task :load => :environment do |t|
      class_name = nil     # Use nil to get Rails to figure out the class.
      TABLES.each do |table_name|
        fixture = Fixtures.new(ActiveRecord::Base.connection,
                               table_name, class_name,
                               File.join(DATA_DIRECTORY, table_name.to_s))
        fixture.insert_fixtures
        puts "Loaded data from #{table_name}.yml"
      end
    end

    desc "Remove sample data"
    task :delete => :environment do |t|
      User.delete_all("id      >= #{MIN_USER_ID}")
      Spec.delete_all("user_id >= #{MIN_USER_ID}")
      Faq.delete_all( "user_id >= #{MIN_USER_ID}")
    end
  end
end
```

Our method for loading data involves fixtures, so we require the Active Record fixtures library at the top of the Rakefile. We also follow standard Rakefile practice by preceding each task with a description (`desc`). This way, if we ask Rake for all the available tasks, the descriptions for `load` and `delete` appear on the list:

```
> rake --tasks
.
.
.
rake db:sample_data:delete        # Delete sample data
rake db:sample_data:load          # Load sample data
.
.
.
```

Note that by wrapping the task definitions in `namespace` blocks we've ensured that the Rake tasks can be invoked using a syntax that is consistent with the other tasks we've seen, such as

```
> rake db:test:prepare
```

The `load` task uses `Fixtures.new` to create a fixture, taking in the database connection, table name, class name, and full path to the fixture data:

```
Fixtures.new(connection, table_name, class_name, fixture_path)
```

By setting `class_name` to `nil`, we arrange for Rails to figure out the class name based on the table name. We also build up the various paths using `File.join`, which constructs a file path appropriate for the given platform. Once we've created a fixture, we use the `inserts_fixtures` method to insert the data into the database. We can reverse `load` using the `delete` task, which uses the Active Record `delete_all` function to delete all the data corresponding to users with ids greater than 1,000 (thereby preserving users such as Foo Bar who have lower ids).

But wait—how did the fixture know about (for example) the User class? And how did it know how to connect to the database? The answer is the magical line

```
task :load => :environment do |t|
```

(and similarly for the `delete` task). This tells Rake that the `load` task depends on the Rails environment. Rake responds by loading the local Rails (development) environment, including the models and the database connection (which it gets from `database.yml`). By using Rails to handle all those details, Rake reduces the system to a previously solved problem.

If you want your results to match ours, before moving on you should run the Rake task to load the sample data:

```
> rake db:sample_data:load
(in /rails/rails_space)
Loaded data from users.yml
Loaded data from specs.yml
Loaded data from faqs.yml
```

10.3 The community index

As in the case of all our other controllers, we've created an `index` action for the Community controller—but, for the first time we can recall, the name "index" actually makes sense, since we can use the index page as an alphabetical index of the RailsSpace community members. The design we have in mind is simple: Just link each letter to the RailsSpace users whose last names start with that letter.

The implementation of this design requires several different layers, including a couple of partials and some new Active Record trickery. While implementing the various steps, it might be helpful to bear in mind where we're headed (Figure 10.1). Note that the URL

```
http://localhost:3000/community/index/H
```

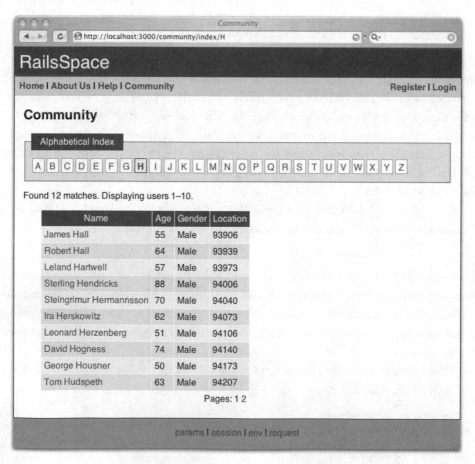

Figure 10.1   The finished community index (shown for the letter H).

has the full complement of parameters—controller, action, and id—handled by the
default route in `routes.rb` (Section 2.2.4):

Listing 10.3 config/routes.rb

```
ActionController::Routing::Routes.draw do |map|
  .
  .
  .
  # Install the default route as the lowest priority.
  map.connect ':controller/:action/:id'
end
```

It's worth mentioning that each of the three elements is available in the `params` variable;
for example, `params[:id]` is H in this case.

10.3.1 `find`'s new trick

The Community controller index action will need to find all the users with a particular
last initial. Recall from Section 9.2 that this name information is in the user spec.
Somehow we have to search through the specs to find the relevant names.

You could accomplish such a search in raw SQL using the wildcard symbol % to find
all names starting with (for example) the letter N, in alphabetical order by name:[1]

```
SELECT * FROM specs WHERE last_name LIKE 'N%'
ORDER BY last_name, first_name
```

Unsurprisingly, Active Record provides an abstraction layer for a query like this. It's
more surprising that the solution is to use the `find` method, which we've seen before in
the context of finding elements by id:

```
User.find(session[:user_id])
```

This is not the extent of `find`'s abilities; `find` is actually quite versatile, able to execute
a variety of different queries. In particular, we can find all the users whose last names
start with the letter N by giving `find` the options `:all`, `:conditions`, and `:order`:

```
> ruby script/console
Loading development environment.
>> initial = "N"
>> Spec.find(:all, :conditions => "last_name LIKE '#{initial}%'",
```

---

[1] In general, ordering names by `last_name`, `first_name` sorts the results first by last name and then by first
name; this ensures that, for example, `Michelle Feynman` would come before `Richard Feynman`, and they
would both come before `Murray Gell-Mann`.

```
?>              :order => "last_name, first_name")
=> [#<Spec:0x36390a4 @attributes={"city"=>"", "occupation"=>"", "birthdate"=>"19
36-01-01", "zip_code"=>"96012", "gender"=>"Male", "id"=>"731", "first_name"=>"Ro
ddam", "user_id"=>"1117", "last_name"=>"Narasimha", "state"=>""}>, #<Spec:0x3638
f3c @attributes={"city"=>"", "occupation"=>"", "birthdate"=>"1945-01-01", "zip_c
ode"=>"96045", "gender"=>"Male", "id"=>"655", "first_name"=>"Jerry", "user_id"=>
"1118", "last_name"=>"Nelson", "state"=>""}>, #<Spec:0x3638dac @attributes={"cit
y"=>"", "occupation"=>"", "birthdate"=>"1941-01-01", "zip_code"=>"96079", "gende
r"=>"Male", "id"=>"713", "first_name"=>"Navin", "user_id"=>"1119", "last_name"=>
"Nigam", "state"=>""}>, #<Spec:0x3638ba4 @attributes={"city"=>"", "occupation"=>
"", "birthdate"=>"1939-01-01", "zip_code"=>"96112", "gender"=>"Male", "id"=>"723
", "first_name"=>"Robert", "user_id"=>"1120", "last_name"=>"Noland", "state"=>""
}
```

This replicates the raw SQL given above, and it works fine as it is, but we expect that on RailsSpace the initial will come from the web through `params[:id]`. Since a user can type in any "initial" he wants, a malicious cracker could fill `params[:id]` with a string capable of executing arbitrary SQL statements—including (but not limited to) deleting our database.[2] In order to prevent such an attack—called *SQL injection*—we need to escape any strings inserted into SQL statements. Active Record accomplishes this by using ? as a place-holder:

```
Spec.find(:all, :conditions => ["last_name LIKE ?", initial+"%"],
          :order => "last_name, first_name")
```

This way, if a user types in

```
http://RailsSpace.com/community/index/<dangerous string>
```

in an effort to execute some sort of dangerous query, that dangerous string will be converted to something benign before being inserted into the conditions clause. Incidentally, we can't write

```
:conditions => ["last_name LIKE ?%", initial]
```

since Rails would then try to execute a query containing

```
last_name LIKE 'N'%
```

which is invalid.

Note that, for the escaped version, the value for `:conditions` is an array rather than a string, whose first element is the string containing the conditions and whose subsequent elements are the strings to be escaped and inserted. We can enforce multiple conditions by using multiple question marks:[3]

---

[2] Even if we arrange for Rails to access the database as a MySQL user with limited privileges (as should certainly be the case in a production environment), allowing arbitrary queries is still a Bad Thing.

[3] See Section 11.3.2 for a second way to insert multiple conditions.

```
Spec.find(:all, :conditions => ["first_name = ? AND last_name = ?", "Foo", "Bar"])
```

Of course, in this case we could also use

```
Spec.find_by_first_name_and_last_name("Foo", "Bar")
```

which does the escaping for us. This is an example of how Active Record allows us to move between different levels of abstraction when executing SQL queries, thus giving the user the best of both worlds: convenience by default but maximum power if needed (see the sidebar "Puncturing the tire of abstraction").

Puncturing the tire of abstraction

One of the design principles of Rails is to provide a layer of nice high-level functions for many common tasks, while still leaving open a window to the layers underneath. For example, in order to find a user by screen name and password, we've seen that Rails creates a function called

```
User.find_by_screen_name_and_password(screen_name,password)
```

We've also seen how to push down to a lower level using `find`:

```
spec = Spec.find(:all, :conditions => "last_name LIKE 'N%'",
            :order => "last_name, first_name")
```

If you want to, you can drop down another layer deeper and use raw SQL:

```
spec = Spec.find_by_sql("SELECT * FROM specs
                    WHERE last_name LIKE 'N%'
                    ORDER BY last_name, first_name")
```

This happens to be essentially the same query as the one above, but since `find_by_sql` executes plain SQL, we can perform arbitrary selects this way.[4] So, for example, if the bottleneck in your application is some very hairy query—for which raw SQL can sometimes be an excellent solution—you can always drop down to the lowest layer and construct an optimized solution.

10.3.2 The `index` action

As mentioned above, the community index will serve as a directory of RailsSpace users. With our newfound Active Record expertise, we're ready to grab the users whose last names begin with a particular letter. All we need to do in addition to this is create a few instance variables for use in the views:

---

[4] For truly arbitrary queries, you can even use `ActiveRecord::Base.connection.execute(query)`, where `query` is a raw SQL command such as `"DROP TABLE users"`.

Listing 10.4 app/views/controllers/community_controller.rb

```ruby
class CommunityController < ApplicationController
  helper :profile

  def index
    @title = "Community"
    @letters = "ABCDEFGHIJKLMNOPQRSTUVWXYZ".split("")
    if params[:id]
      @initial = params[:id]
      specs = Spec.find(:all,
                        :conditions => ["last_name like ?", @initial+'%'],
                        :order => "last_name, first_name")
      @users = specs.collect { |spec| spec.user }
    end
  end

  def browse
  end

  def search
  end
end
```

Note that we've included the Profile helper (using `helper :profile`) since the community index will use `profile_for` to link to user profiles.

There are a couple of new pieces of Ruby syntax in this action. The first and easier one is

```ruby
"ABCDEFGHIJKLMNOPQRSTUVWXYZ".split("")
```

This creates an array of strings, one for each letter of the alphabet. It uses the `split` method, which may be familiar from Perl, Python, or any of a number of other languages that have a similar function. Most commonly, `split` is used to split a string into an array based on whitespace, but it can split on other strings as well, as shown in this `irb` example:

```
> irb
irb(main):001:0> "foo bar   baz".split
=> ["foo", "bar", "baz"]
irb(main):002:0> "1foo2fooredfoobluefoo".split("foo")
=> ["1", "2", "red", "blue"]
```

In the case of the `index` action, using the blank string `""` splits the given string into its component characters:

```
irb(main):003:0> "ABCDEFGHIJKLMNOPQRSTUVWXYZ".split("")
=> ["A", "B", "C", "D", "E", "F", "G", "H", "I", "J", "K", "L", "M", "N", "O", "
P", "Q", "R", "S", "T", "U", "V", "W", "X", "Y", "Z"]
```

(Of course, we could also have used

```
%w(A B C D E F G H I J K L M N O P Q R S T U V W X Y Z)
```

but that's more typing than we wanted to do; plus, it's high time we introduced the important `split` function.)

The second and more important new Ruby syntax shows up in our method for building up the `@users` instance variable. In the community index action, the line

```
users = specs.collect { |spec| spec.user }
```

marches through `specs` and collects an array of the corresponding users.[5] As you might guess from context, the curly braces { . . . } are an alternate syntax for Ruby blocks; the effect of the code shown is essentially identical[6] to the syntax we've seen before using `do . . . end`:

```
users = specs.collect do |spec|
        spec.user
      end
```

In fact, you can use the brace syntax across multiple lines if you want, as follows:

```
users = specs.collect { |spec|
        spec.user
      }
```

Which version to use is purely a matter of convention. We follow the convention used by our two favorite Ruby books, *Programming Ruby* and *The Ruby Way*: Use the brace syntax for one-line blocks and the `do . . . end` syntax for multiline blocks.

10.3.3 The alphabetical index

It's time now to put our instance variables to work in the community index view. We'll start with a display of the index itself, which starts out simply as a list of letters:

Listing 10.5 app/views/community/index.rhtml

```
<h2><%= @title %></h2>
<fieldset>
  <legend>Alphabetical Index</legend>
  <% @letters.each do |letter| %>
    <% letter_class = (letter == @initial) ? "letter_current" : "letter" %>
```

Continues

---

[5] We first encountered `collect` in Section 5.6.5 when we built up a list of valid email addresses for testing validations.

[6] The only difference is that braces have a higher precedence than `do . . . end`; this rarely matters.

```
      <%= link_to letter, { :action => "index", :id => letter },
                  :class => letter_class %>
  <% end %>
  <br clear="all" />
</fieldset>
```

We iterate over all the letters in the alphabet using the `each` method (see the sidebar "`for letter in @letters?`" for an alternate method), and for each letter we define a CSS class (using the ternary operator) to indicate whether a particular letter is currently selected. Then we link back to the index page with the current letter as the id.

It's important to emphasize that the curly braces around { `:action => "index"`, `:id => letter` } are necessary in the call to `link_to`. The arguments to `link_to` take the form

```
link_to(name, options = {}, html_options = nil)
```

We need the curly braces to tell Rails when the options hash ends and the HTML options hash begins; if we wrote

```
<%= link_to letter, :action => "index", :id => letter,
            :class => letter_class %>
```

the entire hash

```
:action => "index", :id => letter, :class => letter_class
```

would end up in `options`. As a result, instead of links like

```
<a href="/community/index/A" class="letter">A</a>
```

we would get links of the form

```
<a href="/community/index/A?class=letter">A</a>
```

which isn't what we want at all.

---

for letter in @letters?

To construct the alphabetical list for the community index, we use the syntax

```
<% @letters.each do |letter| %>
  .
  .
  .
<% end %>
```

This is the canonical Ruby way to iterate through an array, but you should be aware that, inside views, some Rails programmers use the alternate syntax

```
<% for letter in @letters %>
```

```
    .
    .
    .
<% end %>
```

This is possibly because they think this syntax will be less confusing to any nonprogrammers—web designers come to mind—who might chance upon it.

We have no problem with the alternate syntax—it's identical to Python's main looping construct, which we love—but using each is definitely more Rubyish: Ruby typically uses methods to send instructions to objects,[7] in this case using each to tell an array to return each of its elements in turn. Because we see no compelling reason for a style bifurcation, we'll stick with each, even in views.

To get the look we want for the community index, we will take advantage of the great power CSS provides to style anchor (a) tags. Just add the following rules to site.css:

Listing 10.6 public/stylesheets/site.css

```
/* Community Styles */

a, a#visited {
  color: maroon;
  text-decoration: none;
}

.letter, .letter_current {
  width: 1em;
  text-align: center;
  border: 1px solid gray;
  background: #fff;
  padding: 5px 2px 1px 2px;
  float: left;
  margin: 2px
}

.letter:hover {
  background: #fe4;
}

.letter_current {
  background: #fe4;
  font-weight: bold;
  border: 1px solid black;
}
```

---

[7] This design philosophy, called "message passing" is inspired principally by Smalltalk.

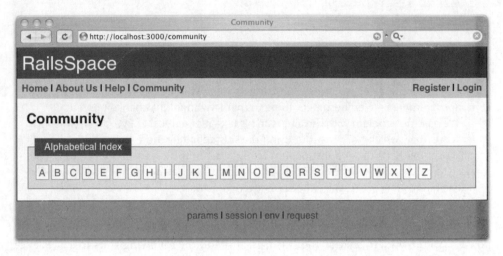

Figure 10.2   The RailsSpace community page with a nicely styled alphabetical index.

Now the community index page is already looking fairly good (Figure 10.2), even though it doesn't really do anything yet. Let's take care of that second part now.

10.3.4   Displaying index results

In Section 10.3.2, the community index action created an instance variable @users containing the users for display in the view. We'll put that variable to good use in a user results table, which we'll put in a partial called `app/views/community/_user_table.rhtml`. First, we need to invoke the partial from `index.rhtml`:

Listing 10.7   app/views/community/index.rhtml

```
.
.
.
<%= render :partial => "user_table" %>
```

The user table partial then creates a results table (if there are any results to show), iterating through the users to create a table row for each one:

Listing 10.8   app/views/community/_user_table.rhtml

```
<% if @users and not @users.empty? %>
<table class="users" border="0" cellpadding="5" cellspacing="1">
```

```
<tr class="header">
  <th>Name</th> <th>Age</th> <th>Gender</th> <th>Location</th>
</tr>
<% @users.each do |user| %>
<tr class="<%= cycle('odd', 'even') %>">
  <td><%= link_to user.name, profile_for(user) %>
  </td>
  <td><%= user.spec.age %></td>
  <td><%= user.spec.gender  %></td>
  <td><%= user.spec.location %></td>
</tr>
<% end %>
</table>
<% end %>
```

Note the use of the Rails helper function `cycle`, which (by default) cycles back and forth between its two arguments,[8] making the assignment of alternating CSS classes a snap. Notice also that in the call to `link_to`, we used the `profile_url` function generated by the routing rule introduced in Section 9.1.1:

Listing 10.9   config/routes.rb

```
map.connect 'profile/:screen_name', :controller => 'profile', :action => 'show'
```

We also used the new `name` method in the User model, which returns the user's full name if available and otherwise returns the screen name:

Listing 10.10   app/models/user.rb

```
# Return a sensible name for the user.
def name
  spec.full_name.or_else(screen_name)
end
```

This function could also be used in `app/views/user/index.rhtml` from Section 9.4.4 and `app/view/profile/show.rhtml` from Section 9.6; go ahead and use it in those places if you like.

To get the partial to work, we need to do one more thing: add an `age` method to the Spec model so that `@user.spec.age` exists:

---

[8] See the Rails API entry on `cycle` for some fancier examples.

Listing 10.11 app/models/spec.rb

```
# Return the age using the birthdate.
def age
  return if birthdate.nil?
  today = Date.today
  if today.month >= birthdate.month and today.day >= birthdate.day
    # Birthday has happened already this year.
    today.year - birthdate.year
  else
    today.year - birthdate.year - 1
  end
end
```

That essentially completes the functionality, as shown in Figure 10.3, but it doesn't look good yet. To add some style to the user results, including the alternating table row styles from `cycle`, add the following rules to the Community Styles section of `site.css`:

Listing 10.12 public/stylesheets/site.css

```
/* Community Styles */
.
.
.

table.users {
  background: #fff;
  margin-left: 2em;
}

table.users td.bottom {
  border-top: 1px solid #999;
  padding-top: 10px;
}

table.users th {
  color: white;
  background: maroon;
  font-weight: normal;
}

table.users th a {
  color: white;
  text-decoration: underline;
}
```

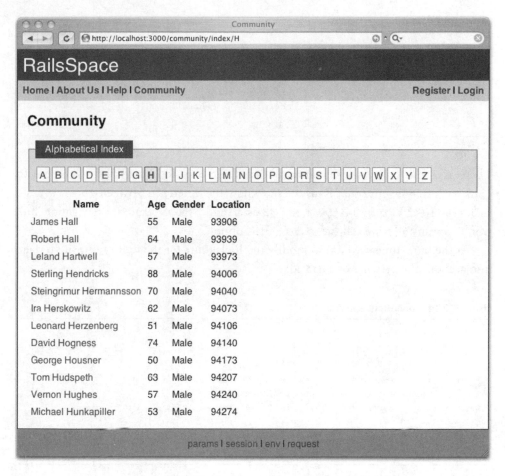

Figure 10.3   The final form of the community index.

```
table.users tr.even {
  background: #ddd;
}

table.users tr.odd {
  background: #eee;
}
```

There's one small change left to get everything to work right; we have to change our navigation link function in the Application helper:

Listing 10.13 app/helpers/application_helper.rb

```
# Return a link for use in site navigation.
def nav_link(text, controller, action="index")
  link_to_unless_current text, :id => nil,
                               :action => action,
                               :controller => controller
end
```

The reason this is necessary is quite subtle: Without an id of any kind in the call to `link_to_unless_current`, Rails doesn't know the difference between `/community/index` and (say) `/community/index/A`; as a result, the `Community` navigation link won't appear unless we add the `:id => nil` option.

At the same time, we have to modify the Rails route for the root of our site to take into account the presence of a `nil` id:

Listing 10.14 config/routes.rb

```
  .
  .
  .
  # You can have the root of your site routed by hooking up ''
  # -- just remember to delete public/index.html.
  map.connect '', :controller => 'site', :action => 'index', :id => nil
  .
  .
  .
```

This way, `/` will still automatically go to `/site/index`.

With that one niggling detail taken care of, we're finally done with the community index (Figure 10.4).

10.4 Polishing results

As it stands, our user table is a perfectly serviceable way to display results. There are a couple of common refinements, though, that lead to better displays when there are a relatively large number of users. In this section, we show how Rails makes it easy to *paginate* results, so that links to the list of users will be conveniently partitioned into smaller pieces. We'll also add a helpful result summary indicating how many results

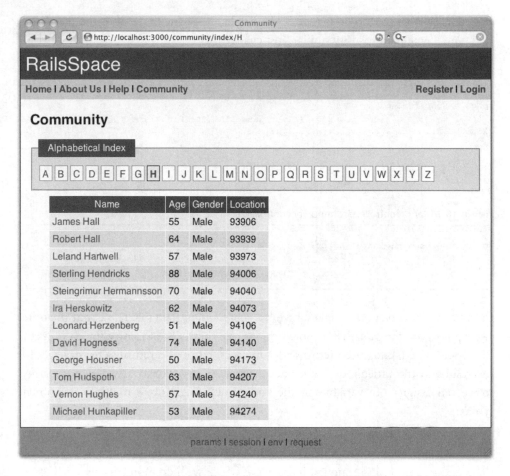

Figure 10.4   Page after adding style to the results table.

were found. As you might suspect, we'll put the code we develop in this section to good use later on when we implement searching and browsing.

10.4.1   Adding pagination

Our community index should be able to handle multiple pages of results, so that as RailsSpace grows the display stays manageable. We'll plan to display one page of results at a time, while providing links to the other pages. This is a common pattern for displaying information on the web, so Rails has a couple of helper functions to make it easy. In the controller, all we need to do is replace the database `find` with a call to the `paginate` function. Their syntax is very similar; just change this:

Listing 10.15 app/controllers/community_controller.rb

```
specs = Spec.find(:all,
                  :conditions => ["last_name LIKE ?", @initial+'%'],
                  :order => "last_name")
```

to this:

Listing 10.16 app/controllers/community_controller.rb

```
@pages, specs = paginate(:specs,
                         :conditions => ["last_name LIKE ?", @initial+"%"],
                         :order => "last_name, first_name")
```

In place of `:all`, `paginate` takes a symbol representing the table name, but the other two options are the same. (For more options, see the Rails API entry for `paginate`.) Like `Spec.find`, `paginate` returns a list of specs, but it also returns a list of pages for the results in the variable `@pages`; note that `paginate` returns a two-element array, so we can assign both variables at the same time using Ruby's multiple assignment syntax:

```
a, b = [1, 2]  # a is 1, b is 2
```

Don't worry too much about what `@pages` is exactly; its main purpose is to be fed to the `pagination_links` function in the view, which we'll do momentarily.

We'll be paginating results only if the `@pages` variable exists and has a length greater than one, so we'll make a short helper function to test for that:

Listing 10.17 app/helpers/application_helper.rb

```
module ApplicationHelper
  .
  .
  .
  # Return true if results should be paginated.
  def paginated?
    @pages and @pages.length > 1
  end
end
```

Since we can expect to use `paginated?` in more than one place, we put it in the main Application helper file.

All we have left is to put the paginated results at the end of the user table if necessary, using the `pagination_links` helper function mentioned above:

Listing 10.18 app/views/community/_user_table.rhtml

```
<% if @users and not @users.empty? %>
<table class="users" border="0" cellpadding="5" cellspacing="1">
  .
  .
  .
  <% end %>
  <% if paginated? %>
  <tr>
    <td colspan="4" align="right">
    Pages: <%= pagination_links(@pages, :params => params) %>
    </td>
  </tr>
  <% end %>
</table>
<% end %>
```

Here we use the function `pagination_links`, which takes the pages variable generated by `paginate` and produces links for multiple pages as shown in Figure 10.5.

By the way, we've told `pagination_links` about the `params` variable using `:params => params` so that it can incorporate submitted parameters into the URLs of the links it creates. We don't actually need that right now, but we will in Chapter 11, and it does no harm now.

10.4.2 A results summary

It's common when returning search results to indicate the total number of results and, if the results are paginated, which items are being displayed. In other words, we want to say something like "Found 15 matches. Displaying users 1–10." Let's add a partial to implement this result summary feature:

Listing 10.19 app/views/community/_result_summary.rhtml

```
<% if @pages %>
<p>
Found <%= pluralize(@pages.item_count, "match") %>.
```

Continues

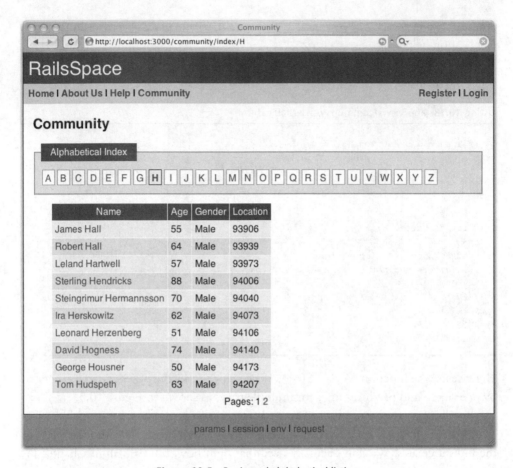

Figure 10.5   Paginated alphabetical listing.

```
    <% if paginated? %>
      <% first = @pages.current_page.first_item %>
      <% last  = @pages.current_page.last_item %>
      Displaying users <%= first %>&ndash;<%= last %>.
    <% end %>
  </p>
<% end %>
```

Then render the partial in the index:

Listing 10.20 app/views/community/index.rhtml

```
    .
    .
    .

<%= render :partial => "result_summary" %>
<%= render :partial => "user_table" %>
```

You can see from this that the `@pages` variable returned by `paginate` has several attributes making just such a result summary easier: `item_count`, which has the total number of results, and `current_page.first_item` and `current_page.last_item` which have the number of the first and last items on the page. The results are now what we advertised—that is, what we promised to achieve way back in Figure 10.1.

We should note that the result summary partial also uses a convenient Rails helper function, `pluralize`:[9]

```
> ruby script/console
Loading development environment.
>> include ActionView::Helpers::TextHelper
=> Object
>> pluralize(0, "box")
=> "0 boxes"
>> pluralize(1, "box")
=> "1 box"
>> pluralize(2, "box")
=> "2 boxes"
>> pluralize(2, "box", "boxen")
=> "2 boxen"
```

`pluralize` uses the Rails *inflector* (mentioned briefly in Section 3.1.3) to determine the appropriate plural of the given string based on the first argument, which indicates how many objects there are. If you want to override the inflector, you can give a third argument with your preferred pluralization. All of this is to say, there's no excuse for having "1 result(s) found"—or, God forbid, "1 results found"—in a Rails app.[10]

---

[9] `pluralize` is not included by default in a console session, so we have to include it explicitly; we figured out which module to load by looking in the Rails API.

[10] The `1 tests, 1 assertions` nonsense you may have noticed in the test output is the fault of Ruby's `Test::Unit` framework, not Rails.

CHAPTER 11

Searching and browsing

In principle, our alphabetical community index lets any user find any other user, but using it in this way would be terribly cumbersome. In this chapter, we add more convenient and powerful ways to find users. We begin by adding full-text search to RailsSpace by making use of an open-source project called *Ferret*. We then stalker-enable our site with browsing by age, sex, and location.

Adding search and browse capability to RailsSpace will involve the creation of custom pagination and validations, which means that we will start to rely less on the built-in Rails functions. This chapter also contains a surprising amount of geography, some fairly fancy `finds`, and even a little math.

11.1 Searching

Though it was quite a lot of work to get the community index to look and behave just how we wanted, the idea behind it is very simple. In contrast, full-text search—for user information, specs, and FAQs—is a difficult problem, and yet most users probably expect a site such as RailsSpace to provide it. Luckily, the hardest part has already been done for us by the Ferret project,[1] a full-text search engine written in Ruby. Ferret makes adding full-text search to Rails applications a piece of cake through the `acts_as_ferret` plugin.

In this section, we'll make a simple search form (adding it to the main community page in the process) and then construct an action that uses Ferret to search RailsSpace based on a query submitted by the user.

---

[1] `http://ferret.davebalmain.com/trac/`

11.1.1 Search views

Since there's some fairly hairy code on the back-end, it will be nice to have a working search form that we can use to play with as we build up the search action incrementally. Since we'll want to use the search form in a couple of places, let's make it a partial:

Listing 11.1 app/views/community/_search_form.rthml

```
<% form_tag({ :action => "search" }, :method => "get") do %>
<fieldset>
  <legend>Search</legend>
    <div class="form_row">
      <label for="q">Search for:</label>
      <%= text_field_tag "q", params[:q] %>
      <input type="submit" value="Search" />
    </div>
</fieldset>
<% end %>
```

This is the first time we've constructed a form without using the `form_for` function, which is optimized for interacting with models. For search, we're not constructing a model at any point; we just need a simple form to pass a query string to the search action. Rails makes this easy with the `form_tag` helper, which has the prototype

```
form_tag(url_for_options = {}, options = {})
```

The `form_tag` function takes in a block for the form; when the block ends, it automatically produces the `</form>` tag to end the form. This means that the rhtml

```
<% form_tag({ :action => "search" }, :method => "get") do %>
.
.
.
<% end %>
```

produces the HTML

```
<form action="/community/search" method="get">
.
.
.
</form>
```

Note that in this case we've chosen to have the search form submit using a GET request, which is conventional for search engines (and allows, among other things, direct linking to search results since the search terms appear in URL).

As in the case of the `link_to` in the community index (Section 10.3.3), the curly braces around `{ :action => "search" }` are necessary. If we left them off and wrote instead

```
<% form_tag(:action => "search", :method => "get") %>
  .
  .
  .
<% end %>
```

then Rails would generate

```
<form action="/community/search?method=get" method="post">
  .
  .
  .
</form>
```

instead of

```
<form action="/community/search" method="get">
  .
  .
  .
</form>
```

The other Rails helper we use is `text_field_tag`, which makes a text field filled with the value of `params[:q]`. That is, if `params[:q]` is `"foobar"`, then

```
<%= text_field_tag "q", params[:q] %>
```

produces the HTML

```
<input id="q" name="q" type="text" value="foobar" />
```

We've done a lot of work making useful partials, so the search view itself is beautifully simple:

Listing 11.2 app/views/community/search.rthml

```
<%= render :partial => "search_form" %>
<%= render :partial => "result_summary" %>
<%= render :partial => "user_table" %>
```

We'll also put the search form on the community index page (but only if there is no `@initial` variable, since when the initial exists we want to display only the users whose last names begin with that letter):

Listing 11.3 app/views/community/index.rhtml

```
  .
  .
  .
<% if @initial.nil? %>
  <%= render :partial => "search_form" %>
<% end %>
```

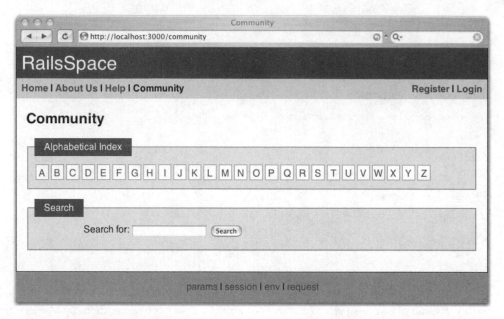

Figure 11.1 The evolving community index page now includes a search form.

You can submit queries to the resulting search page (Figure 11.1) to your heart's content, but of course there's a hitch: It doesn't do anything yet. Let's see if we can ferret out a solution to that problem.

11.1.2 Ferret

As its web page says, "Ferret is a high-performance, full-featured text search engine library written for Ruby." Ferret, in combination with `acts_as_ferret`, builds up an index of the information in any data model or combination of models. In practice, what this means is that we can search through (say) the user specs by associating the special `acts_as_ferret` attribute with the Spec model and then using the method `Spec.find_by_contents`, which is added by the `acts_as_ferret` plugin. (If this all seems overly abstract, don't worry; there will be several concrete examples momentarily.)

Ferret is relatively easy to install, but it's not entirely trouble-free. On OS X it looks something like this:[2]

```
> sudo gem install ferret
Attempting local installation of 'ferret'
```

---

[2] As with the installation steps in Chapter 2, if you don't have `sudo` enabled for your user, you will have to log in as root to install the ferret gem.

```
Local gem file not found: ferret*.gem
Attempting remote installation of 'ferret'
Updating Gem source index for: http://gems.rubyforge.org
Select which gem to install for your platform (powerpc-darwin7.8.0)
 1. ferret 0.10.11 (ruby)
 2. ferret 0.10.10 (ruby)
 3. ferret 0.10.9 (mswin32)
 .
 .
 .
39. Cancel installation
> 1
Building native extensions.  This could take a while...
 .
 .
 .
Successfully installed ferret, version 0.10.11
```

The process is virtually identical for Linux; in both Mac and Linux cases, you should choose the most recent version of Ferret labeled "(ruby)", which should be #1. If, on the other hand, you're using Windows, run

```
> gem install ferret
```

and be sure to choose the most recent version of Ferret labeled "mswin32", which probably won't be the first choice.

The second step is to install the Ferret plugin:[3]

```
> ruby script/plugin install svn://projects.jkraemer.net/acts_as_ferret/tags/
stable/acts_as_ferret
A    /rails/rails_space/vendor/plugins/acts_as_ferret
A    /rails/rails_space/vendor/plugins/acts_as_ferret/LICENSE
A    /rails/rails_space/vendor/plugins/acts_as_ferret/rakefile
A    /rails/rails_space/vendor/plugins/acts_as_ferret/init.rb
A    /rails/rails_space/vendor/plugins/acts_as_ferret/lib
A    /rails/rails_space/vendor/plugins/acts_as_ferret/lib/more_like_this.rb
A    /rails/rails_space/vendor/plugins/acts_as_ferret/lib/multi_index.rb
A    /rails/rails_space/vendor/plugins/acts_as_ferret/lib/acts_as_ferret.rb
A    /rails/rails_space/vendor/plugins/acts_as_ferret/lib/instance_methods.rb
A    /rails/rails_space/vendor/plugins/acts_as_ferret/lib/class_methods.rb
A    /rails/rails_space/vendor/plugins/acts_as_ferret/README
```

---

[3] If you don't have the version control system Subversion installed on your system, you should download and install it at this time (http://subversion.tigris.org/). If you have experience compiling programs from source, you should have no trouble, but if you are more comfortable with Windows installations, then you should skip right to http://subversion.tigris.org/servlets/ProjectDocumentList?folderID=91 and download the svn-<version>-setup.exe with the highest version number. Double-clicking on the resulting executable file will then install Subversion.

That may look intimidating, but the good news is that you don't have to touch any of these files. All you have to do is restart the development webserver to activate Ferret and then indicate that the models are searchable using the (admittedly somewhat magical) `acts_as_ferret` function:

Listing 11.4 app/models/spec.rb

```
class Spec < ActiveRecord::Base
  belongs_to :user
  acts_as_ferret
  .
  .
  .
```

Listing 11.5 app/models/faq.rb

```
class Faq < ActiveRecord::Base
  belongs_to :user
  acts_as_ferret
  .
  .
  .
```

Listing 11.6 app/models/user.rb

```
class User < ActiveRecord::Base
  has_one :spec
  has_one :faq
  acts_as_ferret :fields => ['screen_name', 'email'] # but NOT password
  .
  .
  .
```

Notice in the case of the User model that we used the `:fields` options to indicate which fields to make searchable. In particular, we made sure not to include the password field!

11.1.3 Searching with `find_by_contents`

Apart from implying that he occasionally chases prairie dogs from their burrows, what does it mean when we say that a user `acts_as_ferret`? For the purposes of RailsSpace search, the answer is that `acts_as_ferret` adds a function called `find_by_contents` that uses Ferret to search through the model, returning results corresponding to a given query string (which, in our case, comes from the user-submitted search form). The structure of our search action builds on `find_by_contents` to create a list of matches for the query string:

Listing 11.7 app/controllers/community_controller.rb

```
def search
  @title = "Search RailsSpace"
  if params[:q]
    query = params[:q]
    # First find the user hits...
    @users = User.find_by_contents(query, :limit => :all)
    # ...then the subhits.
    specs = Spec.find_by_contents(query, :limit => :all)
    faqs  = Faq.find_by_contents(query, :limit => :all)
    .
    .
    .
```

Here we've told Ferret to find all the search hits in each of the User, Spec, and FAQ models.

Amazingly, that's all there is to it, as far as search goes: Just those three lines are sufficient to accomplish the desired search. In fact, if you submit a query string from the search form at this point, the results should be successfully returned—though you will probably find that your system takes a moment to respond, since the first time Ferret searches the models it takes a bit of time while it builds an index of search results. This index, which Ferret stores in a directory called `index` in the Rails root directory, is what makes the magic happen—but it is also the source of some problems (see the sidebar "A dead Ferret").

A dead Ferret[4]

Occasionally, when developing with Ferret, the search results will mysteriously disappear. This is usually associated with changes in the database schema (from a migration, for example). When Ferret randomly croaks in this manner, the solution is simple:

---

[4] "He's not dead—he's resting!"

1. Shut down the webserver.
2. Delete Ferret's `index` directory.
3. Restart the webserver.

At this point, Ferret will rebuild the index the next time you try a search, and everything should work fine.

Now that we've got the search results from Ferret, we have to collect the users for display; this requires a little Ruby array manipulation trickery:

Listing 11.8 app/controllers/community_controller.rb

```
def search
  if params[:q]
    query = params[:q]
    # First find the user hits...
    @users = User.find_by_contents(query, :limit => :all)
    # ...then the subhits.
    specs = Spec.find_by_contents(query, :limit => :all)
    faqs  = Faq.find_by_contents(query, :limit => :all)

    # Now combine into one list of distinct users sorted by last name.
    hits = specs + faqs
    @users.concat(hits.collect { |hit| hit.user }).uniq!
    # Sort by last name (requires a spec for each user).
    @users.each { |user| user.spec ||= Spec.new }
    @users = @users.sort_by { |user| user.spec.last_name }
  end
```

This introduces the `concat` and `uniq!` functions, which work like this:

```
> irb
irb(main):001:0> a = [1, 2, 2, 3]
=> [1, 2, 2, 3]
irb(main):002:0> b = [4, 5, 5, 5, 6]
=> [4, 5, 5, 5, 6]
irb(main):003:0> a.concat(b)
=> [1, 2, 2, 3, 4, 5, 5, 5, 6]
irb(main):004:0> a
=> [1, 2, 2, 3, 4, 5, 5, 5, 6]
irb(main):005:0> a.uniq!
=> [1, 2, 3, 4, 5, 6]
irb(main):006:0> a
=> [1, 2, 3, 4, 5, 6]
```

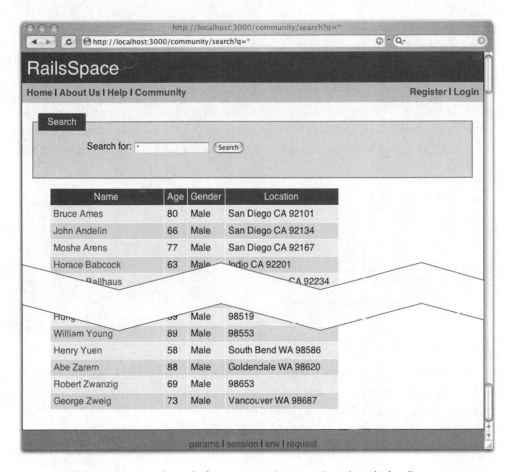

Figure 11.2   Search results for q=*, returning unpaginated results for all users.

You can see that `concat` concatenates two arrays—a and b—by appending b to a, while `a.uniq!` modifies a[5] by removing duplicate values (thereby ensuring that each element is unique).

We should note that the line

```
@users = @users.sort_by { |user| user.spec.last_name }
```

also introduces a new Ruby function, used here to sort the users by last name; it's so beautifully clear that we'll let it pass without further comment.

At this stage, the search page actually works, as you can see from Figure 11.2. But, like the first cut of the RailsSpace community index, it lacks a result summary and

---

[5] Recall from Section 6.6.2 that the exclamation point is a hint that an operation mutates the object in question.

pagination. Let's make use of all the work we did in Section 10.4 and add those features to the search results.

11.1.4 Adding pagination to search

Now that we've collected the users for all of the search hits, we're tantalizingly close to being done with search. All we have to do is paginate the results and add the result summary. In analogy with the pagination from Section 10.4.1, what we'd really like to do is this:

Listing 11.9 app/controllers/community_controller.rb

```
def search
  if params[:q]
    .
    .
    .
    @pages, @users = paginate(@users)
  end
end
```

Unfortunately, the built-in `paginate` function only works when the results come from a single model. It's not too hard, though, to extend `paginate` to handle the more general case of paginating an arbitrary list—we'll just use the `Paginator` class (on which `paginate` relies) directly. Since we'd like the option to paginate results in multiple controllers, we'll put the `paginate` function in the Application controller:

Listing 11.10 app/controllers/application.rb

```
class ApplicationController < ActionController::Base
  .
  .
  .
  # Paginate item list if present, else call default paginate method.
  def paginate(arg, options = {})
    if arg.instance_of?(Symbol) or arg.instance_of?(String)
      # Use default paginate function.
      collection_id = arg  # arg is, e.g., :specs or "specs"
      super(collection_id, options)
    else
      # Paginate by hand.
      items = arg  # arg is a list of items, e.g., users
      items_per_page = options[:per_page] || 10
      page = (params[:page] || 1).to_i
```

```
      result_pages = Paginator.new(self, items.length, items_per_page, page)
      offset = (page - 1) * items_per_page
      [result_pages, items[offset..(offset + items_per_page - 1)]]
    end
  end
end
```

There is some moderately advanced Ruby here, but we'll go through it step by step. In order to retain compatibility with the original `paginate` function, the first part of our `paginate` checks to see if the given argument is a symbol or string (such as, for example, `:specs` as in Section 10.4.1), in which case it calls the original `paginate` function using `super` (a usage we saw before in Section 9.5).

If the first argument is not a symbol or string, we assume that it's an array of items to be paginated. Using this array, we create the result pages using a `Paginator` object, which is initialized as follows:

```
Paginator.new(controller, item_count, items_per_page, current_page=1)
```

In the context of the Application controller, the first argument to `new` is just `self`, while the item count is just the length of `items` and the items per page is either the value of `options[:per_page]` or 10 (the default). We get the number of the current page by using

```
page = (params[:page] || 1).to_i
```

which uses the `to_i` function to convert the result to an integer, since `params [:page]` will be a string if it's not `nil`.[6]

Once we've created the results pages using the Paginator, we calculate the array indices needed to extract the page from `items`, taking care to avoid off-by-one errors. For example, when selecting the third page (`page = 3`) with the default pagination of 10,

```
offset = (page - 1) * items_per_page
```

yields

```
offset = (3 - 1) * 10 = 20
```

This means that

```
items[offset..(offset + items_per_page - 1)]
```

is equivalent to

```
items[20..39]
```

which is indeed the third page.

---

[6] Calling `to_i` on 1 does no harm since it's already an integer.

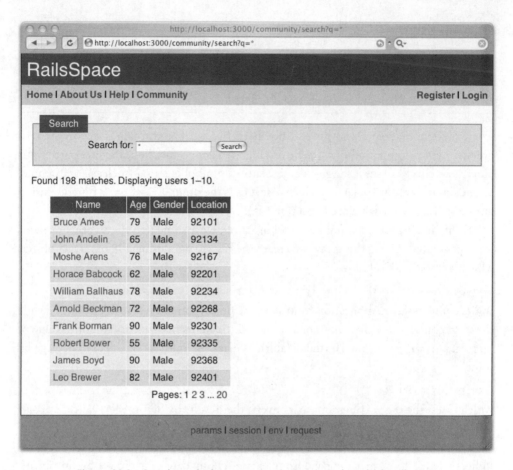

Figure 11.3   Search results for `q=*`, returning paginated results for all users.

Finally, at the end of `paginate`, we return the two-element array

```
[result_pages, items[offset..(offset + items_per_page - 1)]]
```

so that the object returned by our `paginate` function matches the one from the original `paginate`.

That's a lot of work, but it's worth it; the hard-earned results appear in Figure 11.3. Note that if you follow the link for (say) page 2, you get the URL of the form

```
http://localhost:3000/community/search?page=2&q=*
```

which contains the query string as a parameter. This works because back in Section 10.4.1 we told `pagination_links` about the `params` variable:

Listing 11.11 app/views/community/_user_table.rhtml

```
    .
    .
    .

    Pages: <%= pagination_links(@pages, :params => params) %>

    .
    .
    .
```

Rails knows to include the contents of params in the URL.

11.1.5 An exception to the rule

We're not quite done with search; there's one more thing that can go wrong. Alas, some search strings cause Ferret to croak. In this case, as seen in Figure 11.4, Ferret raises the exception

```
Ferret::QueryParser::QueryParseException
```

indicating its displeasure with the query string "--".[7]

The way to handle this in Ruby is to wrap the offending code in a begin...rescue block to catch and handle the exception:

Listing 11.12 app/controllers/community_controller.rb

```ruby
def search
  if params[:q]
    query = params[:q]
    begin
      # First find the user hits...
      @users = User.find_by_contents(query, :limit => :all)
      # ...then the subhits.
      specs = Spec.find_by_contents(query, :limit => :all)
      faqs = Faq.find_by_contents(query, :limit => :all)
      # Now combine into one list of distinct users sorted by last name.
      hits = specs + faqs
      @users.concat(hits.collect { |hit| hit.user }).uniq!
      # Sort by last name (requires a spec for each user).
      @users.each { |user| user.spec ||= Spec.new }
      @users = @users.sort_by { |user| user.spec.last_name }

      @pages, @users = paginate(@users)
    rescue Ferret::QueryParser::QueryParseException
```

Continues

---

[7] This appears to be fixed as of Ferret 0.11.0.

Figure 11.4   Ferret throws an exception when given an invalid search string.

```
      @invalid = true
    end
  end
end
```

Here we tell `rescue` to catch the specific exception raised by Ferret parsing errors, and then set the `@invalid` instance variable so that we can put an appropriate message in the view (Figure 11.5):

Listing 11.13   app/views/community/search.rhtml

```
<%= render :partial => "search_form" %>
<% if @invalid %>
<p>Invalid character in search.</p>
```

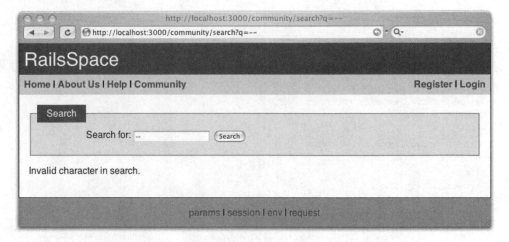

Figure 11.5   The ferret query parse exception caught and handled.

```
<% end %>
<%= render :partial => "result_summary" %>
<%= render :partial => "user_table" %>
```

And with that, we're finally done with search!

11.2 Testing search

Testing the search page is easy in principle: Just hit `/community/search` with an appropriate query string and make sure the results are what we expect. But a key part of testing search should be to test the (currently untested) pagination. Since we're using the default pagination value of 10, that means creating at least eight more users to add to the three currently in our users fixture:[8]

Listing 11.14   test/fixtures/users.yml

```
# Read about fixtures at http://ar.rubyonrails.org/classes/Fixtures.html
valid_user:
  id: 1
  screen_name: millikan
```

Continues

---

[8] Even though one of these users is invalid, it still exists in the test database when the Rails test framework loads the fixtures; Ferret doesn't know anything about validations, so it gamely finds all three users.

```
    email: ram@example.com
    password: electron

invalid_user:
  id: 2
  screen_name: aa/noyes
  email: anoyes@example,com
  password: sun

# Create a user with a blank spec.
specless:
  id: 3
  screen_name: linusp
  email: lpauling@example.com
  password: 2nobels
```

Of course, we could hand-code eight more users, but that's a pain in the neck. Fortunately, Rails has anticipated our situation by enabling embedded Ruby in YAML files, which works the same way that it does in views. This means we can generate our extra users automatically by adding a little ERb to `users.yml`:

Listing 11.15 test/fixtures/users.yml

```
   .
   .
   .
# Create 10 users so that searches can invoke pagination.
<% (1..10).each do |i| %>
user_<%= i %>:
  id: <%= i + 3 %>
  screen_name: user_<%= i %>
  email: user_<%= i %>@example.com
  password: foobar
<% end %>
```

Note that our generated users have ids given by `<%= i + 3 %>` rather than `<%= i %>` in order to avoid conflicts with the previous users' ids.

With these extra 10 users, a search for all users using the wildcard query string `"*"` should find a total of 13 matches, while displaying matches 1–10:

Listing 11.16 test/functional/community_controller_test

```
   .
   .
   .
class CommunityControllerTest < Test::Unit::TestCase
```

```
  fixtures :users
  fixtures :specs
  fixtures :faqs

    .
    .
    .

  def test_search_success
    get :search, :q => "*"
    assert_response :success
    assert_tag "p", :content => /Found 13 matches./
    assert_tag "p", :content => /Displaying users 1&ndash;10./
  end
end
```

This gives

```
> ruby test/functional/community_controller_test.rb -n test_search_success
Loaded suite test/functional/community_controller_test
Started
.
Finished in 0.849541 seconds.

1 tests, 3 assertions, 0 failures, 0 errors
```

Despite being short, this test catches several common problems, and proved valuable while developing the search action.

11.3   Beginning browsing

Because Ferret does the heavy search lifting, browsing for users—though less general than search—is actually more difficult. In this section and the next (Section 11.4), we'll set out to create pages that allow each user to find others by specifying age (through a birthdate range), sex, and location (within a particular distance of a specified zip code)—the proverbial "A/S/L" from chat rooms. In the process, we'll create a nontrivial custom form (with validations) and also gain some deeper experience with the Active Record `find` function (including some fairly fancy SQL).

11.3.1   The browse page

Let's start by constructing a browse page, which will be a large custom (that is, non-`form_for`) form. On the back-end, the action is trivial for now:

Listing 11.17 app/views/controllers/community_controller.rb

```
def browse
  @title = "Browse"
end
```

The browse view is also trivial, since it just pushes the hard work into a partial:

Listing 11.18 app/views/community/browse.rhtml

```
<%= render :partial => "browse_form" %>
<%= render :partial => "result_summary" %>
<%= render :partial => "user_table" %>
```

This brings us to the browse form itself, which is relatively long but whose structure is simple. Using Rails tag helpers and the params variable, we build up a form with fields for each of the A/S/L attributes:

Listing 11.19 app/views/community/_browse_form.rhtml

```
<% form_tag({ :action => "browse" }, :method => "get") do %>
<fieldset>
  <legend>Browse</legend>
  <div class="form_row">
    <label for="age">Age:</label>
    <%= text_field_tag "min_age", params[:min_age], :size => 2 %>
    &ndash;
    <%= text_field_tag "max_age", params[:max_age], :size => 2 %>
  </div>
  <div class="form_row">
    <label for="gender">Gender:</label>
    <%= radio_button_tag :gender, "Male",
                         params[:gender] == 'Male',
                         :id => "Male" %>Male
    <%= radio_button_tag :gender, "Female",
                         params[:gender] == 'Female',
                         :id => "Female" %>Female
  </div>
  <div class="form_row">
    <label for="location">Location:</label>
    Within
    <%= text_field_tag "miles", params[:miles], :size => 4 %>
    miles from zip code:
    <%= text_field_tag "zip_code", params[:zip_code],
                       :size => Spec::ZIP_CODE_LENGTH %>
  </div>
```

```
  <%= submit_tag "Browse", :class => "submit" %>
</fieldset>
<% end %>
```

As in Section 11.1.1, we use `text_field_tag`, which has the function prototype

```
text_field_tag(name, value = nil, options = {})
```

so that if, for example, `params[:min_age]` is 55, the code

```
<%= text_field_tag "min_age", params[:min_age], :size => 2 %>
```

produces the HTML

```
<input id="min_age" name="min_age" size="2" type="text" value="55" />
```

Similarly, we have the radio button helper,

```
radio_button_tag(name, value, checked = false, options = {})
```

Then if `params[:gender]` is `"Female"`, the code

```
<%= radio_button_tag :gender, "Female",
                     params[:gender] == 'Female',
                     :id => "Female" %>Female
```

produces

```
<input checked="checked" id="Female" name="gender" type="radio" value="Female" />
```

with the `Female` box "checked"[9] since `params[:gender] == 'Female'` is true.

With the browse form partial thus defined, the browse view is already in its final form (Figure 11.6).

11.3.2 Find by A/S/L (hold the L)

The browse form already "works" in the sense that it doesn't break if you submit it, and it even remembers the values you entered (Figure 11.7). Apart from that, though, it doesn't actually do anything. Let's take the first step toward changing that:

Listing 11.20 app/views/controllers/community_controller.rb

```
def browse
  @title = "Browse"
  return if params[:commit].nil?
```

Continues

---

[9] It's actually filled in rather than checked since it's a radio button and not a checkbox, but we can't help the terminology used by the HTML standard.

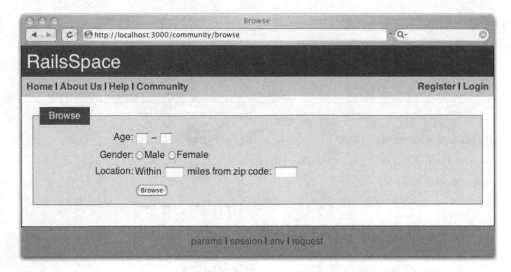

Figure 11.6   The final browse form.

```
  specs = Spec.find_by_asl(params)
  @pages, @users = paginate(specs.collect { |spec| spec.user })
end
```

In keeping with our usual practice, we've hidden as many details as possible beneath an abstraction layer, in this case the function find_by_asl, which we've chosen to be a class method for the Spec model.

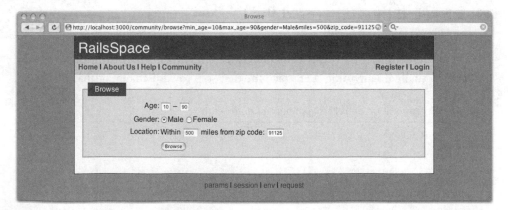

Figure 11.7   The browse form with some values submitted.

We'll implement `find_by_asl` momentarily, but first we need to explain the line

```
return if params[:commit].nil?
```

You may have noticed in Figure 11.7 that the string `browse=commit` appears in the URL;[10] this means that `params[:commit]` tells us if the form has been submitted. As a result,

```
return if params[:commit].nil?
```

returns if the form hasn't been submitted, thereby causing Rails to render the browse form immediately. (In previous chapters, we used the `param_posted?` function defined in Section 6.6.5 to detect form submission via POST requests, but, like the search form, the browse form uses a GET request instead.)

Having addressed the case of hitting the browse page directly, it's now time to handle browse form submission by writing `find_by_asl` for browsing by age and gender. (Though fairly tricky, the age and gender searches are much easier than the search by location, so we defer the latter to Section 11.4.2.) Browsing by age and gender involves the trickiest database query so far, so we'll discuss each piece of the puzzle before assembling them into the final `find_by_asl` method. For concreteness, let's consider the case of searching for all female RailsSpace members between the ages of 55 and 65.[11]

First, let's consider the essential form of the query we need to make. In MySQL, the code to select females with ages between 55 and 65 would look something like this:

```
SELECT * FROM specs WHERE
ADDDATE(birthdate, INTERVAL 55 YEAR) < CURDATE() AND
ADDDATE(birthdate, INTERVAL 66 YEAR) > CURDATE() AND
gender = 'Female'
```

This uses `CURDATE()`, which returns the current date, as well as the MySQL `ADDDATE` function, which is convenient for doing date arithmetic. For example, we use the code

```
ADDDATE(birthdate, INTERVAL 66 YEAR) > CURDATE()
```

to select specs with birthdates that give a date *after* the current date when you add 66 years to them—which will be true for anyone age 65 or younger.

Next, we'll introduce a new aspect of the `:conditions` option in `find`. Recall from Section 10.3.1 that we can ensure safe SQL queries by using question marks as

---

[10] `browse=commit` is inserted automatically by the Rails `submit_tag` helper.

[11] Recall that our sample data is based on Caltech distinguished alumni, with made-up ages starting at 50.

string place-holders; for example, assuming a suitable `params` variable, we could use the following to find all RailsSpace users of a particular gender:

```
Spec.find(:all, :conditions => ["gender = ?", params[:gender]])
```

The new syntax, which we will use in `find_by_asl`, uses a symbol and a full hash instead:

```
Spec.find(:all, :conditions => ["gender = :gender", params])
```

In this case, when building up the SQL query corresponding to this particular `find`, Rails knows to insert an escaped-out version of `params[:gender]` in place of `:gender`.

Finally, the last piece of the puzzle is Ruby's array append syntax `<<`, which we can demonstrate using an `irb` session:

```
> irb
irb(main):001:0> a = []
=> []
irb(main):002:0> a << "foo"
=> ["foo"]
irb(main):003:0> a << "bar" << "baz"
=> ["foo", "bar", "baz"]
irb(main):004:0> a.join(" AND ")
=> "foo AND bar AND baz"
```

Note from line `003` that array appends can be chained together. We've also anticipated a key step in building up the `find` conditions by joining the array elements on `" AND "` in the final line.

Our strategy for `find_by_asl` is to make an array of strings with one element for each potential part of the WHERE clause. We'll then join that array with `" AND "` for use in `:conditions`. A call to `find` will then perform the query using the SQL string we've constructed. Putting everything together leads to the following method:

Listing 11.21 app/models/spec.rb

```
# Find by age, sex, location.
def self.find_by_asl(params)
  where = []
  # Set up the age restrictions as birthdate range limits in SQL.
  unless params[:min_age].blank?
    where << "ADDDATE(birthdate, INTERVAL :min_age YEAR) < CURDATE()"
  end
  unless params[:max_age].blank?
    where << "ADDDATE(birthdate, INTERVAL :max_age+1 YEAR) > CURDATE()"
  end
  # Set up the gender restriction in SQL.
  where << "gender = :gender" unless params[:gender].blank?
```

```
  if where.empty?
    []
  else
    find(:all,
         :conditions => [where.join(" AND "), params],
         :order => "last_name, first_name")
  end
end
```

Note that we've elected to return an empty list if there are no restrictions; another option would be to return *all* users in that case, but we think returning no users makes more sense. We've also added the obligatory ordering by last name, first name in the call to `find`.

By the way, it's worth noting that our method for performing queries in `find_by_sql` violates database independence, which has both advantages and disadvantages (see the sidebar "Getting database religion").

Getting database religion

In building up a `where` string for use in the `:conditions` option, we have used MySQL-specific code such as ADDDATE, thereby violating database agnosticism (and thus becoming *database theists*). This is not such a bad choice, when you consider the alternative. To maintain database independence, we would have to select all of the users and then apply the various conditions to the resulting Ruby array. For a sufficiently small user base, this would be no problem, but it scales horribly with the number of users, since it requires loading a significant part of the database into memory for every call to `find_by_sql`. Building up a query string, on the other hand, allows us to perform the query all at once in the database—thereby making use of exactly what databases are good at.

In the present case, our judgment is that the benefit of breaking database-independence outweighs the cost, but we should be mindful that we would have to rewrite `find_by_sql` if we ever switched to a database other than MySQL.

With `find_by_asl` thus defined, the browse form is live, and searches by age and gender work essentially as advertised (Figure 11.8). What remains is to add location search—a decidedly nontrivial task, but one we will nevertheless rise to accomplish.

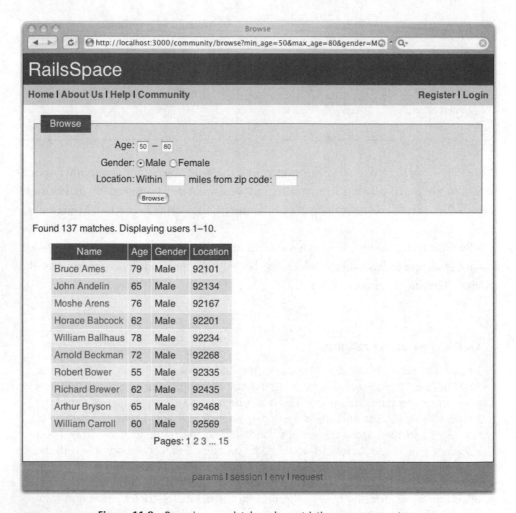

Figure 11.8   Browsing our database by restricting spec parameters.

11.4 Location, location, location

In order to add the "L" in "A/S/L" to our browse feature, we need to include some geographical knowledge in the RailsSpace database. Once we've done that, we'll be in a position to make the distance calculation needed to find all locations within a certain radius of a given zip code. While we're at it, we'll use our newfound geographical prowess to add some polish to the user display tables.

11.4.1   A local database of geographical data

We need to populate our local database with the locations (in latitude and longitude) of various zip codes. We'll use a free zip code database found at

`http://www.populardata.com/`

That data works fine on OS X and Linux, but you need to massage it a little bit to get it to work on Windows; a Windows-friendly version of the data (as well as a copy of the original) can be found at

`http://www.RailsSpace.com/book`

After you download the file (text version), unzip it and rename it to `geo_data.csv`. Since we want all the RailsSpace databases (development, test, and eventually production) to have the geographical information, we'll put the data-loading step in a migration; for convenience, move `geo_data.csv` to the `db/migrate` directory. Then, create the migration, which creates a table called `geo_data` together with the relevant columns:

```
> ruby script/generate migration CreateGeoData
     exists  db/migrate
     create  db/migrate/007_create_geo_data.rb
```

Here is the migration itself:

Listing 11.22 db/migrate/007_create_geo_data.rb

```ruby
class CreateGeoData < ActiveRecord::Migration
  def self.up
    create_table :geo_data do |t|
      t.column :zip_code,  :string
      t.column :latitude,  :float
      t.column :longitude, :float
      t.column :city,      :string
      t.column :state,     :string
      t.column :county,    :string
      t.column :type,      :string
    end
    add_index "geo_data", ["zip_code"], :name => "zip_code_optimization"

    csv_file = "#{RAILS_ROOT}/db/migrate/geo_data.csv"
    fields = '(zip_code, latitude, longitude, city, state, county)'

    execute "LOAD DATA INFILE '#{csv_file}' INTO TABLE geo_data FIELDS " +
            "TERMINATED BY ',' OPTIONALLY ENCLOSED BY \"\"\"\" " +
            "LINES TERMINATED BY '\n' " + fields
  end
```

Continues

```
    def self.down
      drop_table :geo_data
    end
  end
```

```
> rake db:migrate
  (in /rails/rails_space)
  == CreateGeoData: migrating =================================================
  -- create_table("geo_data")
     -> 0.0883s
  -- execute("LOAD DATA INFILE '/rails/rails_space/config/../db/migrate/geo_data."
csv' INTO TABLE
geo_data FIELDS TERMINATED BY ',' OPTIONALLY ENCLOSED BY \"\"\"\" LINES"
TERMINATED BY '\n'(zip_code, latitude, longitude, city, state, county, type)")
     -> 0.9792s
  == CreateGeoData: migrated (1.0684s) ====================================
```

The migration is a bit advanced, and it would take us too far afield to go into all the details,[12] but once you've run it as above, you should be able to see a promising table called geo_data in the database (Figure 11.9). You can see there that the geographical database contains a correspondence between zip codes and latitude/longitude, as well as the city, state, and even county of each location.

Since we will want to manipulate GeoData objects using Active Record—using, in particular, the find_by_zip_code method automatically created due to the zip_code database column—we need to create a (virtually) blank model just to tell Rails that GeoDatum[13] inherits from ActiveRecord::Base:

Listing 11.23 app/models/geo_datum.rb

```
class GeoDatum < ActiveRecord::Base
end
```

With that, we're ready to do the actual distance search.

11.4.2 Using GeoData for location search

When last we left the browse action, we had optimistically called our new find function find_by_asl.

Now that the RailsSpace database is geographically aware, it's time to add the "L."

---

[12] It's worth noting, though, that through the execute command we can execute arbitrary SQL queries in a migration.

[13] Yes, the Rails inflector knows that the singular of GeoData is GeoDatum.

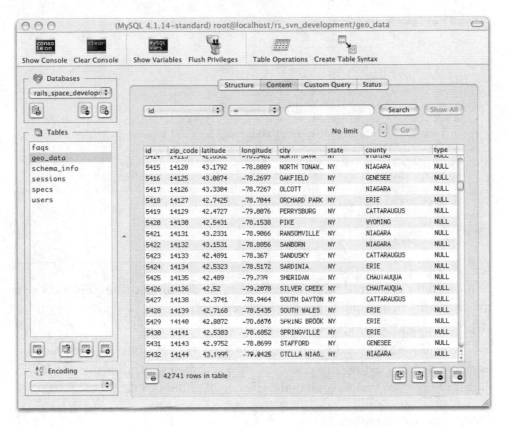

Figure 11.9   The geographical data in the database.

Our strategy will be to take the user-submitted zip code, find the location in the geographical database, and then select every spec whose zip code is within the given number of miles of that location. If this sounds suspiciously like math, you're right: We'll have to use a formula for calculating distances on a sphere as a function of latitude and longitude.[14] We'll start by writing a function in the Spec model that returns a string appropriate for calculating the distance between the given point and an arbitrary location (as identified by longitude and latitude):

---

[14] Seriously, what were the chances that a couple of Caltech Ph.D.'s could write a whole book without using at least a little math?

Listing 11.24 app/models/spec.rb

```
  .
  .
  .
  private

  # Return SQL for the distance between a spec's location and the given point.
  # See http://en.wikipedia.org/wiki/Haversine_formula for more on the formula.
  def self.sql_distance_away(point)
    h = "POWER(SIN((RADIANS(latitude - #{point.latitude}))/2.0),2) + " +
        "COS(RADIANS(#{point.latitude})) * COS(RADIANS(latitude)) * " +
        "POWER(SIN((RADIANS(longitude - #{point.longitude}))/2.0),2)"
    r = 3956 # Earth's radius in miles
    "2 * #{r} * ASIN(SQRT(#{h}))"
  end
end
```

As noted in the comments, this uses the *haversine formula* for calculating distances on a sphere, which can be found (among other places) at

```
http://en.wikipedia.org/wiki/Haversine_formula
```

We're now ready to add distance search to `find_by_asl`. We can get the location using `GeoDatum.find_by_zip_code` and then add the requirement that the (SQL) distance away is less than or equal to the miles supplied through the browse form:

Listing 11.25 app/models/spec.rb

```
  # Find by age, sex, location.
  def self.find_by_asl(params)
    where = []
    .
    .
    .
    where << "gender = :gender" unless params[:gender].blank?

    # Set up the distance restriction in SQL.
    zip_code = params[:zip_code]
    unless zip_code.blank? and params[:miles].blank?
      location = GeoDatum.find_by_zip_code(zip_code)
      distance = sql_distance_away(location)
      where << "#{distance} <= :miles"
    end

    if where.empty?
      []
    else
```

```
    find(:all,
         :joins => "LEFT JOIN geo_data ON geo_data.zip_code = specs.zip_code",
         :conditions => [where.join(" AND "), params],
         :order => "last_name, first_name")
    end
  end
```

By the way, if you were nervous about the appearance of latitude in sql_
distance_away, that's a good sign—after all, the Spec model has no such column,
so there's no way such a query could work. The solution, as you might infer from the
find above, is to *join* the geo_data and specs tables, which effectively endows each
spec with latitude and longitude attributes. So far in this book, we've used lots of joins,
but they've always been implicit, since Active Record handles the details for us; in this
case, we need an explicit join in order to do the age, sex, and location select all in one
step. Moreover, we want to find users by age and gender even if the zip code is blank,
which means we need a specific kind of operation called a *left join*[15]—with an ordinary join, a search for female users, say, would return only those users who specified a
zip code.

With the location query string added in find_by_asl, we can finally bask in the
glory of being able to find all the youngest female RailsSpace users within 250 miles of
Caltech (Figure 11.10). Oops—well, that's pretty much what we expected. Fine—how
about the old men (Figure 11.11)? Yup, that's the Caltech we know and love!

11.4.3 Location names

You may have noticed that in nonempty search results, the location is identified by zip
code alone (Figure 11.11). In real life, we expect that many users would elect to type in
their city and state as well, but—now that we have a geographical database—it would
be nice to fill in those fields automatically based on zip code. That's the aim of this
section.

Our first step is to polish the city name strings, which (as you can see from Figure 11.9) are currently ALL CAPS; we need a way to convert, for example, LOS ANGELES
to Los Angeles. To do this, we'll add a couple of (very closely related) functions to the
String class to capitalize each word in a space-separated string:

---

[15] See, for example, http://www.w3schools.com/sql/sql_join.asp, or do a web search for *SQL join* to
get more information on the different types of joins.

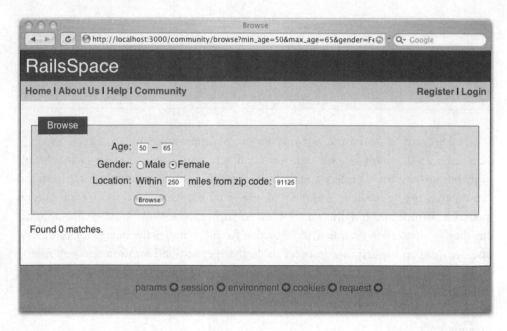

Figure 11.10   All female RailsSpace users between the ages of 50 and 65 within 250 miles of Caltech.

Listing 11.26   lib/string.rb

```
class String
  .
  .
  .
  # Capitalize each word (space separated).
  def capitalize_each
    space = " "
    split(space).each{ |word| word.capitalize! }.join(space)
  end

  # Capitalize each word in place.
  def capitalize_each!
    replace capitalize_each
  end
end
```

Note in the second function `capitalize_each!` that we use the `replace` function, which is a special Ruby function to replace `self` with another object (thereby mutating it); in this case, the given string (`self`) gets replaced by the result of `capitalize_each`.

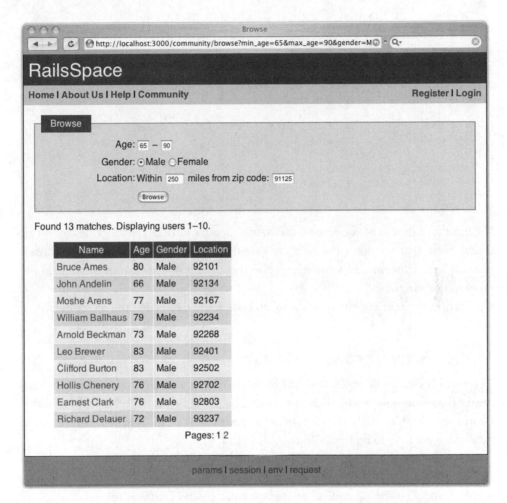

Figure 11.11 All male RailsSpace users between the ages of 65 and 90 within 250 miles of Caltech.

It's important to emphasize that the Ruby `capitalize!` method (on which `capitalize_each` relies) converts both `los` and `LOS` to `Los`, so that the all-caps city names will be properly converted:

```
> ruby script/console
Loading development environment.
>> "LOS ANGELES".capitalize_each
=> "Los Angeles"
```

After restarting the development webserver to load the changes to `string.rb`, we'll be ready to look up the city and state based on zip code and then format the city name appropriately:

Listing 11.27 app/models/spec.rb

```
# Return a sensibly formatted location string.
def location
  if not zip_code.blank? and (city.blank? or state.blank?)
    lookup = GeoDatum.find_by_zip_code(zip_code)
    if lookup
      self.city  = lookup.city.capitalize_each if city.blank?
      self.state = lookup.state if state.blank?
    end
  end
  [city, state, zip_code].join(" ")
end
```

We use the test `if lookup` since our database doesn't have city/state values for all zip codes. Note that we don't override the user-defined city and state if they're already present; we'll trust our users enough to give them the power to trump the data in our geographical database.[16]

Having city and state in addition to zip code really fleshes out the search results, as seen in Figure 11.12.

11.4.4 Adding browse validation

There's only one problem left with the RailsSpace browse page: Putting in invalid data breaks the form rather badly (Figure 11.13). This is the first time we've had to validate a form that wasn't simply the display for a model, so instead of using built-in model validations we have to do things (mostly) by hand.

The validations themselves are fairly simple. We want to verify that the maximum and minimum ages are valid integers, that the number of miles is a valid floating point number, and that the zip code is correctly formatted and exists in our database. We'll create a Spec model object, to which we will attach the errors, so that we can display them using `error_messages_for('spec')`.

It will be helpful when validating the input to have methods to detect invalid integers and floats. We'll add relevant methods to the Object class, taking advantage of Ruby's policy of raising an ArgumentError exception for a failed numerical conversion:

```
> irb
irb(main):001:0> Integer("foo")
ArgumentError: invalid value for Integer: "foo"
        from (irb):1:in 'Integer'
        from (irb):1
```

---

[16] One of the authors once lived in 90048, which shows up as West Hollywood in many databases but is actually located in the city of Los Angeles.

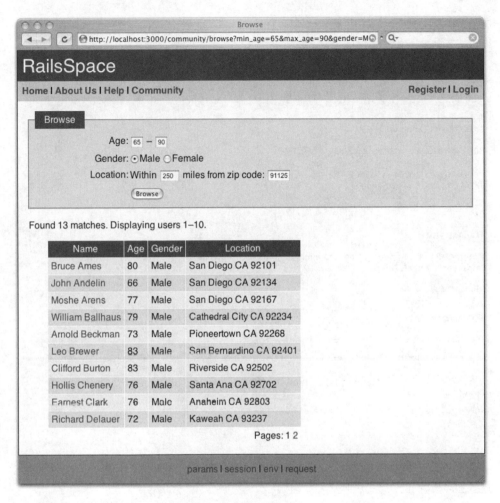

Figure 11.12   Browse results with city and state lookup.

```
irb(main):002:0> Float("bar")
ArgumentError: invalid value for Float(): "bar"
        from (irb):2:in 'Float'
        from (irb):2
```

This behavior suggests the following tests for valid ints and floats, using the same begin...rescue syntax we used in Section 11.1.5 to catch the Ferret exception:

Listing 11.28   lib/object.rb

```
class Object

  # Return true if the object can be converted to a valid integer.
```

Continues

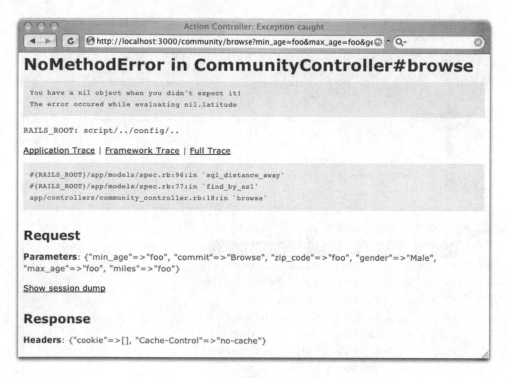

Figure 11.13 Browsing for "foo" instead of integers.

```ruby
def valid_int?
  begin
    Integer(self)
    true
  rescue ArgumentError
    false
  end
end

# Return true if the object can be converted to a valid float.
def valid_float?
  begin
    Float(self)
    true
  rescue ArgumentError
    false
  end
end
end
```

By the way, we put these methods in the Object class (which is the base class for all Ruby objects) rather than in String because we want to be able to test nil; as it turns out, `nil.valid_int?` is true (`Integer(nil) == 0`) while `nil.valid_float?` is false (`Float(nil)` raises an ArgumentError exception).

In order for these new functions to be loaded, we need to add a line to the Application helper:

Listing 11.29   app/helpers/application_helper.rb

```
module ApplicationHelper
  require 'string'
  require 'object'
  .
  .
  .
```

Then, restart the webserver so that the new Object functions will be included.

In order to catch the form entry errors, we'll define a function called `valid_input?` and then wrap `find_by_asl` and pagination inside `if valid_input?`:

Listing 11.30   app/views/controllers/community_controller.rb

```
def browse
  @title = "Browse"
  return if params[:commit].nil?
  if valid_input?
    specs = Spec.find_by_asl(params)
    @pages, @users = paginate(specs.collect { |spec| spec.user })
  end
end
```

Of course, we have to write `valid_input?`, which is reasonably long but is straight-forward. As mentioned above, we'll first create a new spec, on which we will accumulate errors for display in the view. We then march through the different requirements for valid input, adding an error for each one that fails. The only mildly tricky part is the use of `@spec.valid?` to verify the zip code format; this just piggybacks on the zip code validation we already built. The full function appears as follows:

Listing 11.31   app/views/controllers/community_controller.rb

```
  .
  .
  .
private

# Return true if the browse form input is valid, false otherwise.
```

Continues

```
def valid_input?
  @spec = Spec.new
  # Spec validation (with @spec.valid? below) will catch invalid zip codes.
  zip_code = params[:zip_code]
  @spec.zip_code = zip_code
  # There are a good number of zip codes for which we have no information.
  location = GeoDatum.find_by_zip_code(zip_code)
  if @spec.valid? and not zip_code.blank? and location.nil?
    @spec.errors.add(:zip_code, "does not exist in our database")
  end
  # The age strings should convert to valid integers.
  unless params[:min_age].valid_int? and params[:max_age].valid_int?
    @spec.errors.add("Age range")
  end
  # The zip code is necessary if miles are provided.
  miles = params[:miles]
  if miles and not zip_code
    @spec.errors.add(:zip_code, "can't be blank")
  end
  # The number of miles should convert to a valid float.
  unless miles.nil? or miles.valid_float?
    @spec.errors.add("Location radius")
  end
  # The input is valid iff the errors object is empty.
  @spec.errors.empty?
end
```

Note that a line such as `@spec.errors.add("Location radius")` simply leads to an error string of the form `"Location radius is invalid"`, while `@spec.errors.add(:zip_code, "can't be blank")` gives the error string `"Zip code can't be blank"`.

The code as it stands is already sufficient to protect our form from invalid input, but it would be inconsiderate not to tell our users what the problems are. Unfortunately, if we simply use the code

```
<%= error_messages_for('spec') %>
```

as we have in previous chapters, we'll get error messages like "2 errors prohibited this spec from being saved," which would be confusing in the context of our browse form—we're browsing for users, not trying to save a spec. The solution involves using the `sub` string method, which simply substitutes one string for another:[17]

```
> irb
irb(main):001:0> s = "foo bar baz"
```

---

[17] The closely related global substitution method `gsub` is also useful; where `sub` replaces only the first occurrence of a particular string, `gsub` replaces all of them.

```
=> "foo bar baz"
irb(main):002:0> s.sub("baz", "quux")
=> "foo bar quux"
```

Applying this idea to the browse view yields the following:

Listing 11.32 app/views/community/browse.rhtml

```
<%= error_messages_for('spec').sub('prohibited this spec from being saved',
                                    'occurred') %>
<%= render :partial => "browse_form" %>
<%= render :partial => "result_summary" %>
<%= render :partial => "user_table" %>
```

This way, we get errors of the form "3 errors occurred" (Figure 11.14), which makes a lot more sense.

11.4.5 The final community home page

Having built the index, search, and browse pages, we'll end by adding the browse partial to make the RailsSpace community page a one-stop shop for finding RailsSpace users (Figure 11.15):

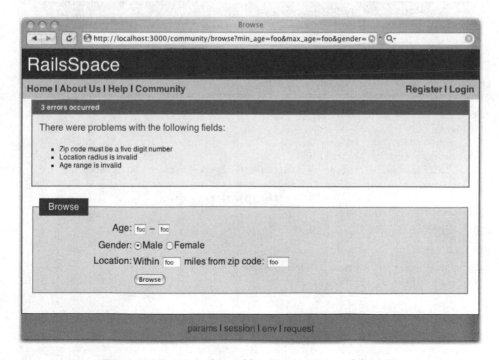

Figure 11.14 Browse form with a nice description of the errors.

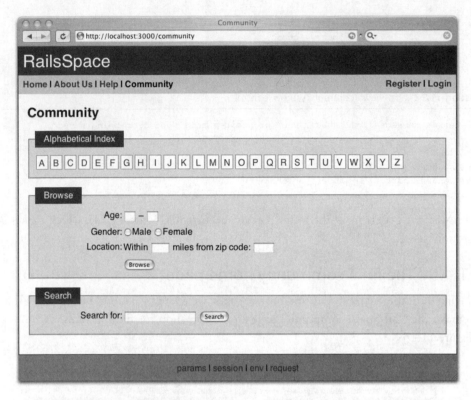

Figure 11.15 The final community page with index, browse, and search.

Listing 11.33 app/views/community/index.rhtml

```
<h2><%= @title %></h2>
<fieldset>
  <legend>Alphabetical Index</legend>
  <% @letters.each do |letter| %>
    <% letter_class = (letter == @initial) ? "letter_current" : "letter" %>
    <%= link_to(letter, { :action => "index", :id => letter },
                         :class => letter_class) %>
  <% end %>
  <br clear="all" />
</fieldset>

 <%= render :partial => "result_summary" %>
 <%= render :partial => "user_table" %>

<% if @initial.nil? %>
  <%= render :partial => "browse_form" %>
  <%= render :partial => "search_form" %>
<% end %>
```

CHAPTER 12

Avatars

Now that we've added a community listing, searching, and browsing, RailsSpace users can find each other, but the profiles they find are rather plain. In this chapter, we take the first step toward improving this situation by adding an avatar image upload so that users have a visual way to represent themselves on their profiles. Future enhancements include a friends listing (Chapter 14) and a blog (Chapters 15 and 16).

In the context of computers, an *avatar* is an image or other graphical representation of a particular person.[1] On RailsSpace, the avatar will simply be an uploaded image. It can be a picture of the user, but it doesn't have to be; any image that expresses the user's personality will do. We'll put the avatar on the user hub and profile, and later we'll use a thumbnail version on the friends list (Chapter 14) and on blog comments (Chapter 16). Accomplishing all this will require understanding image uploads in Rails, as well as learning how to use Ruby to communicate with the underlying filesystem.

12.1 Preparing for avatar upload

We will be storing avatar images as files on the server filesystem (which will be the local machine during development). It is possible to store the images in the database (as BLOBs, or binary large objects), but since it doesn't make much sense to sort a column by images, or to join them to other tables, we don't get much in the process.[2] Moreover, filesystems are highly optimized to deliver static content such as images, while

---

[1] In Hinduism, an avatar is the manifestation of a deity in human or animal form.

[2] We would gain a centralized data store, which we argued in Section 6.1.1 is a Good Thing in the context of sessions, but in the case of images we could simply use NFS (Network File System) to make the image directory network accessible. It would be harder to use the same trick for sessions since we would have to figure out how to tell Rails to use the network drive, whereas with images we have complete control over where the files get written.

database connections are potentially expensive. Finally, we will be using a program called ImageMagick to convert uploaded images to a sensible size, which will involve creating files on the filesystem anyway.

This design decision does involve some extra effort on our part, though, since Rails (through Active Record) is particularly optimized for database-based storage. Our first task, then, is to trick Active Record into using the filesystem. Then we will be in a position to make the Avatar controller and views to handle the image upload itself.

12.1.1 Adapting a model

As with the other models in RailsSpace, we want the Avatar model to be able to create new objects, perform validations on them, and save them if the validations pass. Unlike our other models, though, the Avatar model won't live in the database, so we won't create it using `generate`. Instead, we'll create the avatar files by hand. We'll start by subclassing `ActiveRecord::Base`[3] and making a custom `initialize` function:

Listing 12.1 app/models/avatar.rb

```
class Avatar < ActiveRecord::Base
  # Image directories
  URL_STUB = "/images/avatars"
  DIRECTORY = File.join("public", "images", "avatars")

  def initialize(user, image = nil)
    @user = user
    @image = image
    Dir.mkdir(DIRECTORY) unless File.directory?(DIRECTORY)
  end

  def exists?
    File.exists? (File.join(DIRECTORY, filename))
  end

  alias exist? exists?

  def url
    "#{URL_STUB}/#{filename}"
  end

  def thumbnail_url
    "#{URL_STUB}/#{thumbnail_name}"
  end
```

---

[3] Section 12.2.3 explains exactly what Active Record buys us in the context of the Avatar model.

```
  private

  # Return the filename of the main avatar.
  def filename
    "#{@user.screen_name}.png"
  end

  # Return the filename of the avatar thumbnail.
  def thumbnail_name
    "#{@user.screen_name}_thumbnail.png"
  end
end
```

Here we've used `Dir.mkdir` to make a directory for images unless it already exists, and we've added an `exists?` method to test for avatar existence using `File.exists?`.[4] We've also included some utilities to return the avatar URLs, together with private functions for the avatar filenames (which are based on the user screen names). As in Section 10.2.2, we make use of `File.join` to build up the file paths. (We hard-code forward slashes in the URLs since URLs always use forward slashes.)

Note that we've made the image optional when creating an avatar by using `image - nil` in `initialize`; when saving avatars, we will of course need an image, but when testing for avatar existence using

```
avatar.exists?
```

or returning the avatar URL, there's no need for the avatar to be initialized with an image.[5]

Before moving on to avatar upload, we need to do one more thing: Add an avatar to each user by including one in the User model (just put it anywhere above the `private` keyword):

Listing 12.2 app/models/user.rb

```
  .
  .
  .
  def avatar
```

Continues

---

[4] Ruby provides the synonyms `exist?` and `exists?` for files, so we've done the same for avatars (using the `alias` function). We tend to prefer the plural version, since it sounds more like English.

[5] If you're wondering what an "image" is in this context—is it a file, or maybe some other data structure?—you're ahead of the game. The answer is, it depends; see Section 12.2.2 for more detail.

```
    Avatar.new(self)
  end
 .
 .
 .
```

This construct gives us behavior much like `has_one  :avatar` would if the avatars were stored in the database. For example, we can write things like

```
@user.avatar.exists?
```

to see if a particular user already has an avatar.

There is much to add to this model—we currently have no way of actually saving avatars, for example—but what we have presently is enough to build the pages for uploading and displaying avatars.

12.1.2 Avatar upload page

We'll be giving RailsSpace users the ability to upload and delete avatars, which suggests creating a controller for these actions:

```
> ruby script/generate controller Avatar index upload delete
     exists   app/controllers/
     exists   app/helpers/
     create   app/views/avatar
     exists   test/functional/
     create   app/controllers/avatar_controller.rb
     create   test/functional/avatar_controller_test.rb
     create   app/helpers/avatar_helper.rb
     create   app/views/avatar/index.rhtml
     create   app/views/avatar/upload.rhtml
     create   app/views/avatar/delete.rhtml
```

Following our usual practice, we've included an `index` page, which in this case simply redirects to the user hub.

Initially, the Avatar controller will be simple, with the aforementioned redirect along with a before filter to protect the avatar actions:

Listing 12.3 app/controllers/avatar_controller.rb

```
  class AvatarController < ApplicationController
    before_filter :protect

    def index
      redirect_to hub_url
    end
```

```
  def upload
    @title = "Upload Your Avatar"
    @user = User.find(session[:user_id])
  end

  def delete
  end
end
```

With the Avatar model and controller thus defined, we're now in a position to make the upload page. In order to handle image uploads, the form needs to use a *multipart* encoding[6] and a `file` input field. As a result, the HTML we're aiming for looks something like this:

```
<form action="upload" enctype="multipart/form-data" method="post">
  .
  .
  .
    <input id="avatar_image" name="avatar[image]" size="30" type="file" />
  .
  .
  .
</form>
```

We can arrange for Rails to construct such a form by passing the option `:multipart => true` to `form_tag` and then using the Rails `file_field` tag to generate the file upload field:

Listing 12.4   app/views/avatar/upload.rhtml

```
<h2>Avatar</h2>

<% form_tag("upload", :multipart => true) do %>
<fieldset>
  <legend><%= @title %></legend>

  <% if @user.avatar.exists? %>
  <div class="form_row">
    <label for="current_avatar">Avatar:</label>
    <%= avatar_tag(@user) %>
  </div>
  <% end %>
  <div class="form_row">
```

Continues

---

[6] `multipart/form-data` is the *MIME* type for file uploads. MIME types are general standards for data transmission with origins in email (MIME stands for Multipurpose Internet Mail Extensions).

```
      <label for="new_avatar">New Avatar:</label>
      <%= file_field "avatar", "image" %>
    </div>

      <%= submit_tag "Upload Avatar", :class => "submit" %>
  </fieldset>
  <% end %>
```

The code `<%= file_field "avatar", "image" %>` generates the HTML

`<input id="avatar_image" name="avatar[image]" size="30" type="file" />`

as required.

Note that the upload form uses the avatar object attached to the `@user` instance
variable to see if an avatar exists, displaying it if it does. We've also used the `avatar_tag`
function, defined in `avatar_helper.rb`, which relies on the Rails `image_tag` helper
function:

Listing 12.5 app/helpers/avatar_helper.rb

```
module AvatarHelper

  # Return an image tag for the user avatar.
  def avatar_tag(user)
    image_tag(user.avatar.url, :border => 1)
  end

  # Return an image tag for the user avatar thumbnail.
  def thumbnail_tag(user)
    image_tag(user.avatar.thumbnail_url, :border => 1)
  end
end
```

We've added a `thumbnail_tag` helper function while we were at it. The `avatar_tag`
function won't get called until there's actually an avatar uploaded successfully
(Section 12.2.2), but this way, once there is an avatar, it will show up automatically.

Since we plan to show avatars on profiles and on the user hub, we should include
the Avatar helper in the corresponding controllers:

Listing 12.6 app/controller/profile_controller.rb

```
class ProfileController < ApplicationController
  helper :avatar
```

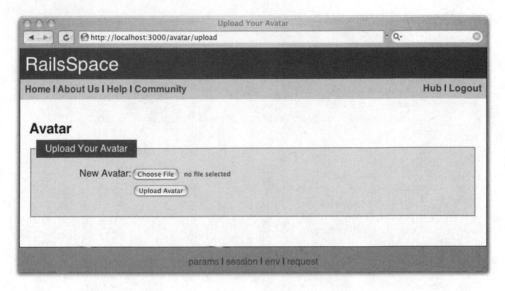

Figure 12.1 The initial avatar upload page.

```
   .
   .
   .
end
```

and

Listing 12.7 app/controllers/user_controller.rb

```
class UserController < ApplicationController
  include ApplicationHelper
  helper :profile, :avatar
   .
   .
   .
end
```

As it currently stands, with no avatar present, the upload view produces the upload form shown in Figure 12.1.

12.1.3 An avatar partial

Since we've anticipated the imminent creation of avatars by including an avatar tag on the upload page, let's put avatar tags on the profile and the hub as well. The two cases are similar enough that (as in the case of the FAQ) we'll define a sidebar box partial:

Listing 12.8 app/views/avatar/_sidebar_box.rhtml

```
<div class="sidebar_box">
  <h2>
    <span class="header">Avatar</span>
    <% unless hide_edit_links? %>
      <span class="edit_link">
        <%= link_to "(edit)", :controller => "avatar", :action => "upload" %>
      </span>
    <% end %>
    <br clear="all" />
  </h2>
  <div class="sidebar_box_contents">
    <% if @user.avatar.exists? %>
      <%= avatar_tag(@user) %>
    <% elsif not hide_edit_links? %>
      No avatar yet?
      <%= link_to "Upload one!", :controller => "avatar",
                                 :action => "upload" %>
    <% end %>
  </div>
</div>
```

As in the case of the FAQ, `hide_edit_links?` handles the differences between the hub and the profile.

On the profile, we'll display the avatar in the upper left:

Listing 12.9 app/views/profile/show.rhtml

```
<div id="left_column">
  <%= render :partial => 'avatar/sidebar_box' %>
  <%= render :partial => 'faq/sidebar_box', :collection => Faq::FAVORITES %>
</div>
.
.
.
```

The addition to the hub is virtually identical:

Listing 12.10 app/views/user/index.rhtml

```
<div id="left_column">
  <div class="sidebar_box">
    ...basic user info...
  </div>
```

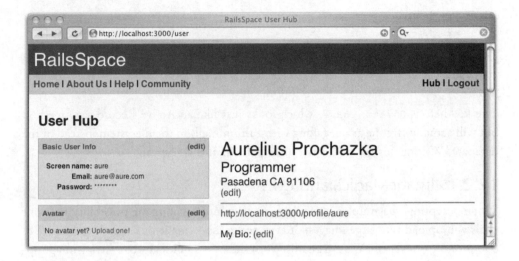

Figure 12.2 The user hub with a link to avatar upload.

```
<%= render :partial => 'avatar/sidebar_box' %>
```

.
.
.

With the partial as presently defined, this leads to a friendly message with a link to the avatar upload page (Figure 12.2).

12.2 Manipulating avatars

We're now ready to complete the avatar upload by writing the `upload` action. Superficially, it looks exactly the same as it would if avatars were stored in the database:

Listing 12.11 app/controllers/avatar_controller.rb

```
def upload
  @title = "Upload Your Avatar"
  @user = User.find(session[:user_id])
  if param_posted?(:avatar)
    image = params[:avatar][:image]
    @avatar = Avatar.new(@user, image)
    if @avatar.save
```

Continues

```
        flash[:notice] = "Your avatar has been uploaded."
        redirect_to hub_url
      end
    end
  end
```

The key here is @avatar.save, which looks just like an Active Record save method but will actually save the avatar (along with a thumbnail) to the filesystem instead of the database. Writing this method is the principal aim of this section.

12.2.1 ImageMagick and `convert`

When accepting image uploads, we have to take into account the possibility that our users will upload very large images, or even try to insert malicious code into the site to compromise our system. We can guard against these possibilities by converting image uploads to a standard size and format. (As implied by the .png filenames in Section 12.1.1, we plan to use PNG [pronounced "ping"], the Portable Network Graphics format.) To that end, we'll use the convert command-line utility provided by ImageMagick (see the sidebar "ImageMagick for your graphick"). Since convert is a regular executable living on the computer, by making a system call from within Rails we can call it in the same way that we would call it from the command line.

> **ImageMagick for your graphick**
>
> ImageMagick is a powerful package for manipulating images that includes (among other things) the remarkable convert command-line utility, which we will use to resize uploaded avatar images and convert them to a standard format. If you're using OS X or Linux, the chances are good that ImageMagick is already installed on your system; you can check by running
>
> ```
> > which convert
> ```
>
> If ImageMagick is not present, or if you're running Windows, download and install it from the ImageMagick website at
>
> ```
> http://www.imagemagick.org/script/binary-releases.php
> ```
>
> You might also like to look into RMagick, a Ruby interface for ImageMagick. The installation and use of RMagick is much more complicated than ImageMagick alone, so we have elected to keep things simple by using convert directly.

We can demonstrate the usage for convert by converting the standard Rails icon rails.png (which comes with every Rails installation). For example, suppose we wanted to enlarge the image so that the longest side is 500 pixels (keeping the same aspect ratio as the original); we could accomplish this with the following command:[7]

```
> convert public/images/rails.png -resize 500x500 tmp/big.png
```

In practice, of course, what we really want to do is keep an image from being too big, so the geometry specification should be less than 500×500:

```
> convert public/images/rails.png -resize 240x300 tmp/normal.png
```

This command will shrink down a large image so that it's at most 240×300, but it will also *enlarge* a small image such as `rails.png`, which probably isn't what we want for avatars. Happily, `convert` comes with many options, including one to handle the case at hand; simply append a right angle bracket (>) at the end of the size specification to prevent enlarging:

```
> convert public/images/rails.png -resize "240x300>" tmp/normal.png
```

(Note that we put the geometry specification in quotes since > is the special "redirect" shell character. For a small file like `rails.png`, this command does nothing, and it resizes larger files as required.)

Our strategy for using `convert` in the context of Rails is to use the Ruby function `system`, which executes commands as if they were typed at a command line. For example, to view the files in a particular directory on a Windows machine, you could call `system` in `irb`:[8]

```
irb(main):001:0> system("dir")
 Volume in drive C has no label.
 Volume Serial Number is D426-147F

 Directory of C:\Documents and Settings\rails\rails_space

12/12/2006  08:30 PM    <DIR>          .
12/12/2006  08:30 PM    <DIR>          ..
09/07/2006  09:47 AM               447 .project
09/07/2006  09:47 AM    <DIR>          app
09/07/2006  09:47 AM    <DIR>          components
12/01/2006  09:09 PM    <DIR>          config
09/07/2006  12:34 PM    <DIR>          db
10/18/2006  08:47 AM               406 demo.rb
09/07/2006  09:47 AM    <DIR>          doc
12/06/2006  09:56 AM    <DIR>          index
```

---

[7] Be warned: If you are using Windows, you'll have to use the full path name to `convert`, such as `"C:\Program Files\ImageMagick-6.3.1-Q16\convert"`. Otherwise, Windows will try to execute an entirely different (and unrelated) `convert` function.

[8] Run `system("ls -l")` on Mac or Linux for a similar result.

```
11/01/2006   09:04 PM    <DIR>              lib
09/07/2006   12:36 PM    <DIR>              log
12/14/2006   04:12 PM    <DIR>              public
09/07/2006   09:47 AM                   307 Rakefile
09/07/2006   09:47 AM    <DIR>              script
12/12/2006   07:18 PM    <DIR>              test
12/15/2006   10:18 AM    <DIR>              tmp
09/07/2006   09:47 AM    <DIR>              vendor
                3 File(s)            1,160 bytes
               15 Dir(s)     1,156,882,432 bytes free
```

This means that inside the Avatar model, we can use a command like

```
system("convert ...")
```

to do our image conversion.

Before we do this, though, we have to take into account that the location of the convert executable is platform-dependent, so before moving on to the save method, we'll make a short (private) utility function to return a string representing the location of convert:

Listing 12.12 app/models/avatar.rb

```
    .
    .
    .
  private
    .
    .
    .
  # Return the (system-dependent) ImageMagick convert executable.
  def convert
    if ENV["OS"] =~ /Windows/
      # Set this to point to the right Windows directory for ImageMagick.
      "C:\\Program Files\\ImageMagick-6.3.1-Q16\\convert"
    else
      "/usr/bin/convert"
    end
  end
    .
    .
    .
```

Note that we've used the OS environment variable and a regular expression match to see if we're on a Windows machine.[9] With our custom convert method, the

---

[9] On Macintosh systems, convert is sometimes located in /usr/local/bin; in this case, the simplest solution is probably to make a symlink by running (as root) ln -s /usr/local/bin/convert/usr/bin. This way, convert will work on, for example, both a Mac development machine and a Linux production server.

eventual system call to the underlying `convert` executable will look something like this:

```
system("#{convert} ...")
```

The appropriate value of `convert` (with full path name) will automatically be interpolated into the string used for the system call.

12.2.2 The `save` method

Now that we know how to convert images, we come finally to the Avatar `save` method. `save` itself is somewhat of an anticlimax, since we push the hard work into an auxiliary function called `successful_conversion?`:

Listing 12.13 app/models/avatar.rb

```ruby
class Avatar < ActiveRecord::Base
  # Image sizes
  IMG_SIZE = '"240x300>"'
  THUMB_SIZE = '"50x64>"'
  .
  .
  .
  # Save the avatar images.
  def save
    successful_conversion?
  end

  private
  .
  .
  .
  # Try to resize image file and convert to PNG.
  # We use ImageMagick's convert command to ensure sensible image sizes.
  def successful_conversion?
    # Prepare the filenames for the conversion.
    source = File.join("tmp", "#{@user.screen_name}_full_size")
    full_size = File.join(DIRECTORY, filename)
    thumbnail = File.join(DIRECTORY, thumbnail_name)
    # Ensure that small and large images both work by writing to a normal file.
    # (Small files show up as StringIO, larger ones as Tempfiles.)
    File.open(source, "wb") { |f| f.write(@image.read) }
    # Convert the files.
    system("#{convert} #{source} -resize #{IMG_SIZE} #{full_size}")
    system("#{convert} #{source} -resize #{THUMB_SIZE} #{thumbnail}")
    File.delete(source) if File.exists?(source)
    # No error-checking yet!
    return true
  end
```

`successful_conversion?` looks rather long, but it's mostly simple. We first define file names for the image source, full-size avatar, and thumbnail, and then we use the `system` command and our `convert` method to create the avatar images. We don't need to create the avatar files explicitly, since `convert` does that for us. At the end of the function, we return `true`, indicating success, thereby following the same convention as Active Record's `save`. This is bogus, of course, since the conversion may very well have failed; in Section 12.2.3 we'll make sure that `successful_conversion?` lives up to its name by returning the failure status of the system command.

The only tricky part of `successful_conversion?` touches on a question we haven't yet answered: What exactly is an "image" in the context of a Rails upload? One might expect that it would be a Ruby `File` object, but it isn't; it turns out that uploaded images are one of two slightly more exotic Ruby types: `StringIO` (string input-output) for images smaller than around 15K and `Tempfile` (temporary file) for larger images. In order to handle both types, we include the line

```
File.open(source, "wb") { |f| f.write(@image.read) }
```

to write out an ordinary file so that `convert` can do its business.[10] `File.open` opens a file in a particular mode—`"wb"` for "write binary" in this case—and takes in a block in which we write the image contents to the file using `@image.read`. (After the conversion, we clean up by deleting the source file with `File.delete`.)

The aim of the next section is to add validations, but `save` already works as long as nothing goes wrong. By browsing over to an image file (Figure 12.3), we can update the hub with an avatar image of our choosing (Figure 12.4).

12.2.3 Adding validations

You may have been wondering why we bothered to make the Avatar model a subclass of `ActiveRecord::Base`. The answer is that we wanted access to the error handling and validation machinery provided by Active Record. There's probably a way to add this functionality without subclassing Active Record's base class, but it would be too clever by half, probably only serving to confuse readers of our code (including ourselves). In any case, we have elected to use Active Record and its associated `error` object to implement validation-style error-checking for the Avatar model.

---

[10] `convert` can actually work with tempfiles, but not with `StringIO` objects. Writing to a file in either case allows us to handle conversion in a unified way.

Figure 12.3   Browsing for an avatar image.

The first step is to add a small error check to the `successful_conversion?` function. By convention, system calls return `false` on failure and `true` on success, so we can test for a failed conversion as follows:

Listing 12.14   app/models/avatar.rb

```
def successful_conversion?
  .
  .
  .
  # Convert the files.
  img   = system("#{convert} #{source} -resize #{IMG_SIZE} #{full_size}")
  thumb = system("#{convert} #{source} -resize #{THUMB_SIZE} #{thumbnail}")
  File.delete(source) if File.exists?(source)
  # Both conversions must succeed, else it's an error.
  unless img and thumb
    errors.add_to_base("File upload failed.  Try a different image?")
    return false
  end
  return true
end
```

Note that we have to use the `return` keyword so that the function returns immediately upon encountering an error. Also note that we've used

```
errors.add_to_base
```

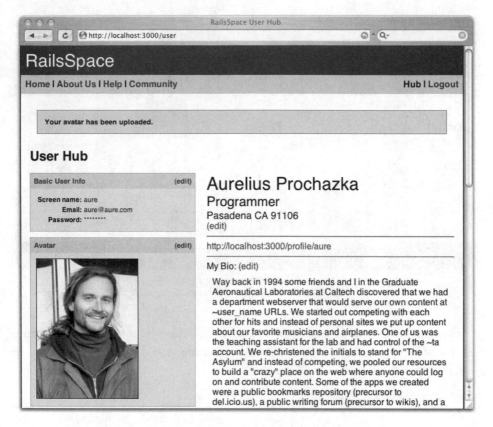

Figure 12.4   The user hub after a successful avatar upload.

rather than simply `errors.add` as we have before, which allows us to add an error message not associated with a particular attribute. In other words,

```
errors.add(:image, "totally doesn't work")
```

gives the error message "Image totally doesn't work", but to get an error message like "There's no freaking way that worked" we'd have to use

```
errors.add_to_base("There's no freaking way that worked")
```

This validation alone is probably sufficient, since any invalid upload would trigger a failed conversion, but the error messages wouldn't be very friendly or specific. Let's explicitly check for an empty upload field (probably a common mistake), and also make sure that the uploaded file is an image that doesn't exceed some maximum threshold (so that we don't try to convert some gargantuan multigigabyte file). We'll put these validations in a new function called `valid_file?`, and then call it from `save`:

Listing 12.15 app/models/avatar.rb

```
  # Save the avatar images.
  def save
    valid_file? and successful_conversion?
  end

  private
  .
  .
  .
  # Return true for a valid, nonempty image file.
  def valid_file?
    # The upload should be nonempty.
    if @image.size.zero?
      errors.add_to_base("Please enter an image filename")
      return false
    end
    unless @image.content_type =~ /^image/
      errors.add(:image, "is not a recognized format")
      return false
    end
    if @image.size > 1.megabyte
      errors.add(:image, "can't be bigger than 1 megabyte")
      return false
    end
    return true
  end
end
```

Here we've made use of the `size` and `content_type` attributes of uploaded images to test for blank or nonimage files.[11] We've also used the remarkable syntax

```
if @image.size > 1.megabyte
```

Does Rails really let you write `1.megabyte` for one megabyte? Rails does.

---

[11] The carat ^ at the beginning of the regular expression means "beginning of line," thus the image content type must begin with the string `"image"`.

Since we've simply reused Active Record's own error-handling machinery, all we need to do to display error messages on the avatar upload page is to use `error_messages_for` as we have everywhere else in RailsSpace:

Listing 12.16 app/views/avatar/upload.rhtml

```
<h2>Avatar</h2>

<% form_tag("upload", :multipart => true) do %>
<fieldset>
  <legend><%= @title %></legend>

  <%= error_messages_for 'avatar' %>
  .
  .
  .
<% end %>
```

Now when we submit (for example) a file with the wrong type, we get a sensible error message (Figure 12.5).

12.2.4 Deleting avatars

The last bit of avatar functionality we want is the ability to delete avatars. We'll start by adding a delete link to the upload page (which is a sensible place to put it since that's where we end up if we click "edit" on the user hub):

Listing 12.17 app/views/avatar/upload.rhtml

```
  .
  .
  .
<%= avatar_tag(@user) %>
[<%= link_to "delete", { :action => "delete" },
                        :confirm => "Are you sure?" %>]
  .
  .
  .
```

We've added a simple confirmation step using the `:confirm` option to `link_to`. With the string argument as shown, Rails inserts the following bit of JavaScript into the link:

```
[<a href="/avatar/delete" onclick="return confirm('Are you sure?');">delete</a>]
```

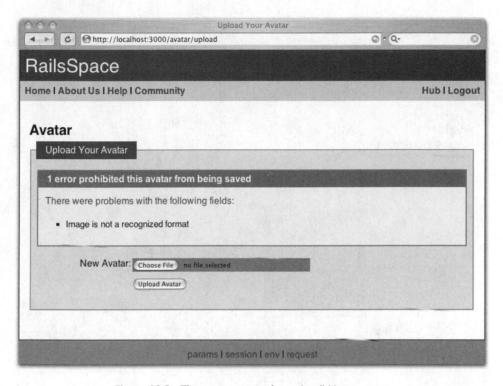

Figure 12.5   The error message for an invalid image type.

This uses the native JavaScript function `confirm` to verify the delete request (Figure 12.6). Of course, this won't work if the user has JavaScript disabled; in that case the request will immediately go through to the `delete` action, thereby destroying the avatar. *C'est la vie.*

As you might expect, the `delete` action is very simple:

Listing 12.18   app/controllers/avatar_controller.rb

```
        .
        .
        .
# Delete the avatar.
def delete
  user = User.find(session[:user_id])
  user.avatar.delete
  flash[:notice] = "Your avatar has been deleted."
```

Continues

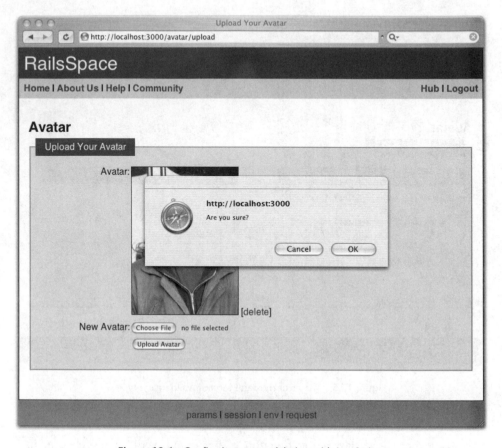

Figure 12.6 Confirming avatar deletion with JavaScript.

```
    redirect_to hub_url
  end
end
```

This just hands the hard work off to the `delete` method, which we have to add to the
Avatar model. The `delete` method simply uses `File.delete` to remove both the main
avatar and the thumbnail from the filesystem:

Listing 12.19 app/models/avatar.rb

```
    .
    .
    .
  # Remove the avatar from the filesystem.
```

```
def delete
  [filename, thumbnail_name].each do |name|
    image = "#{DIRECTORY}/#{name}"
    File.delete(image) if File.exists?(image)
  end
end

private
  .
  .
  .
```

Before deleting each image, we check to make sure that the file exists; we don't want to raise an error by trying to delete a nonexistent file if the user happens to hit the /avatar/delete action before creating an avatar.

12.2.5 Testing Avatars

Writing tests for avatars poses some unique challenges. Following our usual practice post-Chapter 5, we're not going to include a full test suite, but will rather highlight a particularly instructive test—in this case, a test of the avatar upload page (including the delete action).

Before even starting, we have a problem to deal with. All our previous tests have written to a test database, which automatically avoid conflicts with the development and production databases. In contrast, since avatars exist in the filesystem, we have to come up with a way to avoid accidentally overwriting or deleting files in our main avatar directory. Rails comes with a temporary directory called tmp, so let's tell the Avatar model to use that directory when creating avatar objects in test mode:

Listing 12.20 app/models/avatar.rb

```
class Avatar < ActiveRecord::Base
  .
  .
  .
  # Image directories
  if ENV["RAILS_ENV"] == "test"
    URL_STUB = DIRECTORY = "tmp"
  else
    URL_STUB = "/images/avatars"
```

Continues

```
    DIRECTORY = File.join("public", "images", "avatars")
  end
  .
  .
  .
```

This avoids clashes with any files that might exist in `public/images/avatars`.

Our next task, which is considerably more difficult than the previous one, is to simulate uploaded files in the context of a test. Previous tests of forms have involved posting information like this:

```
post :login, :user => { :screen_name => user.screen_name,
                        :password    => user.password }
```

What we want for an avatar test is something like

```
post :upload, :avatar => { :image => image }
```

But how do we make an image suitable for posting?

The answer is, it's difficult, but not impossible. We found an answer on the Rails wiki (`http://wiki.rubyonrails.org/`), and have placed the resulting `uploaded_file` function in the test helper:

Listing 12.21 app/test/test_helper.rb

```
  # Simulate an uploaded file.
  # From http://wiki.rubyonrails.org/rails/pages/HowtoUploadFiles
  def uploaded_file(filename, content_type)
    t = Tempfile.new(filename)
    t.binmode
    path = RAILS_ROOT + "/test/fixtures/" + filename
    FileUtils.copy_file(path, t.path)
    (class << t; self; end).class_eval do
      alias local_path path
      define_method(:original_filename) {filename}
      define_method(:content_type) {content_type}
    end
    return t
  end
```

We are aware that this function may look like deep black magic, but sometimes it's important to be able to use code that you don't necessarily understand—and this is one of those times. The bottom line is that the object returned by `uploaded_file` can be posted inside a test and acts like an uploaded image in that context.

There's only one more minor step: Copy `rails.png` to the fixtures directory so that we have an image to test.

```
> cp public/images/rails.png test/fixtures/
```

Apart from the use of `uploaded_file`, the Avatar controller test is straightforward:

Listing 12.22 test/functional/avatar_controller_test.rb

```ruby
require File.dirname(__FILE__) + '/../test_helper'
require 'avatar_controller'

# Re-raise errors caught by the controller.
class AvatarController; def rescue_action(e) raise e end; end

class AvatarControllerTest < Test::Unit::TestCase
  fixtures :users

  def setup
    @controller = AvatarController.new
    @request    = ActionController::TestRequest.new
    @response   = ActionController::TestResponse.new
    @user = users(:valid_user)
  end

  def test_upload_and_delete
    authorize @user
    image = uploaded_file("rails.png", "image/png")
    post :upload, :avatar => { :image => image }
    assert_response :redirect
    assert_redirected_to hub_url
    assert_equal "Your avatar has been uploaded.", flash[:notice]
    assert @user.avatar.exists?
    post :delete
    assert !@user.avatar.exists?
  end
end
```

Here we've tested both avatar upload and deletion.
Running the test gives

```
> ruby test/functional/avatar_controller_test.rb
Loaded suite test/functional/avatar_controller_test
Started
.
Finished in 1.350276 seconds.

1 tests, 5 assertions, 0 failures, 0 errors
```

CHAPTER 13

Email

In this chapter, we'll learn how to send email using Rails, including configuration, email templates, delivery methods, and tests. In the process, we'll take an opportunity to revisit the user login page in order to add a screen name/password reminder, which will serve as our first concrete example of email. We'll then proceed to develop a simple email system to allow registered RailsSpace users to communicate with each other—an essential component of any social network. We'll see email again in Chapter 14, where it will be a key component in the machinery for establishing friendships between RailsSpace users.

13.1 Action Mailer

Sending email in Rails is easy with the Action Mailer package. Rails applies the MVC architecture to email, with an Action Mailer class playing the part of model. Constructing a message involves defining a method for that message—reminder, for example—that defines variables needed for a valid email message such as sender, recipient, and subject. The text of the message is a view, defined in an rhtml file. Using the method and the view, Action Mailer synthesizes a delivery function corresponding to the name of the method (e.g., `deliver_reminder` for the `reminder` action), which can then be used in a controller to send email based on user input.

The purpose of this section is to turn these abstract ideas into a concrete example by configuring email and then implementing a screen name/password reminder.

13.1.1   Configuration

In order to send email, Action Mailer first has to be configured. The default configuration uses SMTP (Simple Mail Transfer Protocol) to send messages, with customizable `server_settings`:[1]

Listing 13.1   config/environment.rb

```
# Include your application configuration below
.
.
.
ActionMailer::Base.delivery_method = :smtp
ActionMailer::Base.server_settings = {
  :address => "smtp.example.com",
  :port => 25,
  :domain => "your_domain.com",
  :authentication => :login,
  :user_name => "your_user_name",
  :password => "your_password",
}
```

You will need to edit the server settings to match your local environment, which will probably involve using your ISP's SMTP server. For example, to use DSLExtreme (an ISP available in the Pasadena area), we could use the following:

Listing 13.2   config/environment.rb

```
# Include your application configuration below
.
.
.
ActionMailer::Base.delivery_method = :smtp
ActionMailer::Base.server_settings = {
  :address    => "smtp.dslextreme.com",
  :port       => 25,
  :domain     => "railsspace.com"
}
```

We've set up the domain parameter so that our messages will look like they come from `railsspace.com`.

---

[1] This is true in Rails 1.2.1; as of Rails 1.2.2, `server_settings` has been deprecated in favor of `smtp_settings`.

There's one more small change to make: Since we will be sending email in the development environment, we want to see errors if there are any problems with the mail delivery. This involves editing the development-specific environment configuration file:

Listing 13.3 config/environments/development.rb

```
# Raise Errors if the mailer can't send
config.action_mailer.raise_delivery_errors = true
```

Once you make a change in this file, you need to restart your webserver. Your system should then be ready to send email.

13.1.2 Password reminder

Currently, RailsSpace users who forget their screen names or passwords are out of luck. Let's rectify that situation by sending users a helpful reminder when supplied with a valid email address. We'll start by making a mailer for users. Unsurprisingly, Rails comes with a script for generating them:

```
> ruby script/generate mailer UserMailer
      exists  app/models/
      create  app/views/user_mailer
      exists  test/unit/
      create  test/fixtures/user_mailer
      create  app/models/user_mailer.rb
      create  test/unit/user_mailer_test.rb
```

The resulting Action Mailer file, like generated Active Record files, is very simple, with a new class that simply inherits from the relevant base class:

Listing 13.4 app/models/user_mailer.rb

```
class UserMailer < ActionMailer::Base
end
```

Inside this class, we need to create a method for the reminder. As noted briefly above, adding a `reminder` method to the User mailer results in the automatic creation of a `deliver_reminder` function (attached to the UserMailer class). We will use this function in the `remind` action in Section 13.1.3. The `reminder` method itself is simply a series of instance variable definitions:

Listing 13.5 app/models/user_mailer.rb

```
class UserMailer < ActionMailer::Base

  def reminder(user)
    @subject      = 'Your login information at RailsSpace.com'
    @body         = {}
    # Give body access to the user information.
    @body["user"] = user
    @recipients   = user.email
    @from         = 'RailsSpace <do-not-reply@railsspace.com>'
  end
end
```

Action Mailer uses the instance variables inside `reminder` to construct a valid email message. Note in particular that elements in the `@body` hash correspond to instance variables in the corresponding view; in other words,

```
@body["user"] = user
```

gives rise to a variable called `@user` in the reminder view. In the present case, we use the resulting `@user` variable to insert the screen name and password information into the reminder template:

Listing 13.6 app/views/user_mailer/reminder.rhtml

```
Hello,

Your login information is:

  Screen name: <%= @user.screen_name %>
  Password:    <%= @user.password %>

--The RailsSpace team
```

Since this is just an rhtml file, we can use embedded Ruby as usual.

13.1.3 Linking and delivering the reminder

We've now laid the foundation for sending email reminders; we just need the infrastructure to actually send them. We'll start by making a general Email controller to handle the various email actions on RailsSpace, starting with a `remind` action:

```
> ruby script/generate controller Email remind
  exists  app/controllers/
  exists  app/helpers/
```

```
create   app/views/email
exists   test/functional/
create   app/controllers/email_controller.rb
create   test/functional/email_controller_test.rb
create   app/helpers/email_helper.rb
create   app/views/email/remind.rhtml
```

Next, we'll add a reminder link to the login page (Figure 13.1):

Listing 13.7 app/views/user/login.rhtml

```
.
.
.
<p>
  Forgot your screen name or password?
  <%= link_to "Remind Me!", :controller => "email", :action => "remind" %>
</p>

<p>
  Not a member?  <%= link_to "Register now!", :action => "register" %>
</p>
```

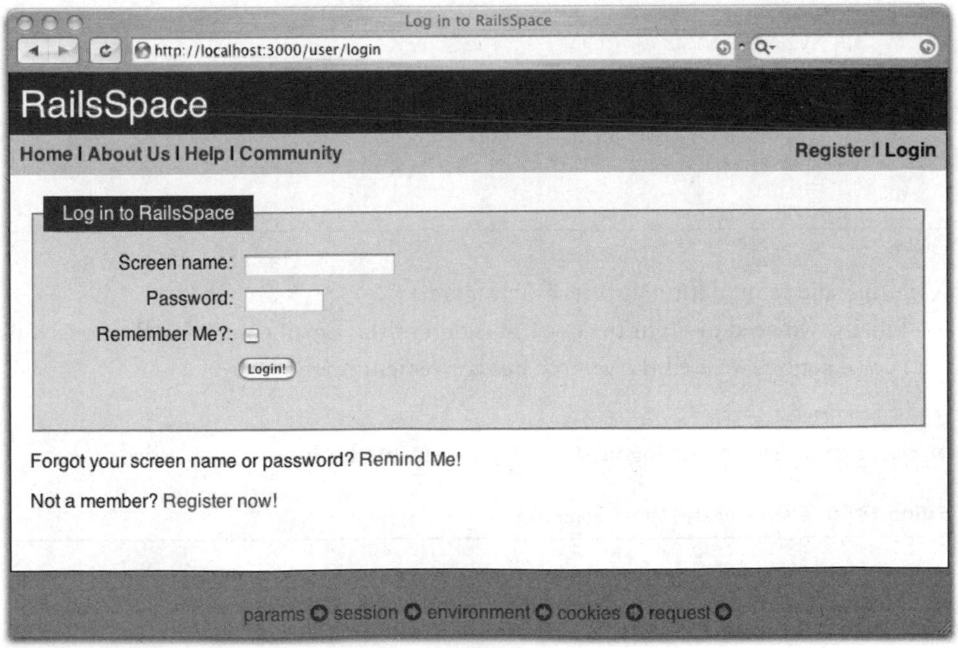

Figure 13.1   The login page with screen name/password reminder.

The remind view is a simple `form_for`:

Listing 13.8 app/views/email/remind.rhtml

```
<% form_for :user do |form| %>
<fieldset>
  <legend><%= @title %></legend>

  <div class="form_row">
    <label for="email">Email:</label>
    <%= form.text_field :email, :size => User::EMAIL_SIZE %>
  </div>

  <div class="form_row">
    <%= submit_tag "Email Me!", :class => "submit" %>
  </div>
</fieldset>
<% end %>
```

Now set `@title` in the Email controller:

Listing 13.9 app/controllers/email_controller.rb

```
class EmailController < ApplicationController

  def remind
    @title = "Mail me my login information"
  end

end
```

With this, the remind form appears as in Figure 13.2.

Finally, we need to fill in the `remind` action in the Email controller. Previously, in the `login` action, we used the verbose but convenient method

`find_by_screen_name_and_password`

In `remind`, we use the analogous `find_by_email` method:

Listing 13.10 app/controllers/email_controller.rb

```
class EmailController < ApplicationController

  def remind
    @title = "Mail me my login information"
    if param_posted?(:user)
```

Figure 13.2   The email reminder form.

```
      email = params[:user][:email]
      user  = User.find_by_email(email)
      if user
        UserMailer.deliver_reminder(user)
        flash[:notice] = "Login information was sent."
        redirect_to :action => "index", :controller => "site"
      else
        flash[:notice] = "There is no user with that email address."
      end
    end
  end
end
```

The key novel feature here is the use of

```
UserMailer.deliver_reminder(user)
```

to send the message. Action Mailer passes the supplied `user` variable to the `reminder` method and uses the result to construct a message, which it sends out using the SMTP server defined in Section 13.1.1.

By default, Rails email messages get sent as plain text; see

```
http://wiki.rubyonrails.org/rails/pages/HowToSendHtmlEmailsWithActionMailer
```

for instructions on how to send HTML mail using Rails.

13.1.4   Testing the reminder

Writing unit and functional tests for mail involves some novel features, but before we get to that, it's a good idea to do a test by hand. Log in as Foo Bar and change the email address to (one of) your own. After logging out, navigate to the password reminder via the login page and fill in your email address. The resulting reminder should show up in your inbox within a few seconds; if it doesn't, double-check the configuration in `config/environment.rb` to make sure that they correspond to your ISP's settings.

Even if you can't get your system to send email, automated testing will still probably work. Unit and functional tests don't depend on the particulars of your configuration, but rather depend on Rails being able to create UserMailer objects and simulate sending mail. The unit test for the User mailer is fairly straightforward; we create (rather than deliver) a UserMailer object and then check several of its attributes:[2]

Listing 13.11   test/unit/user_mailer_test.rb

```
require File.dirname(__FILE__) + '/../test_helper'
require 'user_mailer'

class UserMailerTest < Test::Unit::TestCase
  fixtures :users
  FIXTURES_PATH = File.dirname(__FILE__) + '/../fixtures'
  CHARSET = "utf-8"

  include ActionMailer::Quoting

  def setup
    @user = users(:valid_user)
    @expected = TMail::Mail.new
    @expected.set_content_type "text", "plain", { "charset" => CHARSET }
  end

  def test_reminder
    reminder = UserMailer.create_reminder(@user)
    assert_equal 'do-not-reply@railsspace.com', reminder.from.first
    assert_equal "Your login information at RailsSpace.com", reminder.subject
    assert_equal @user.email, reminder.to.first
    assert_match /Screen name: #{@user.screen_name}/, reminder.body
    assert_match /Password:    #{@user.password}/, reminder.body
  end
```

---

[2] Feel free to ignore the private functions in this test file; they are generated by Rails and are needed for the tests, but you don't have to understand them. Lord knows we don't.

```
  private

  def read_fixture(action)
    IO.readlines("#{FIXTURES_PATH}/user_mailer/#{action}")
  end

  def encode(subject)
    quoted_printable(subject, CHARSET)
  end
end
```

The `UserMailer.create_reminder` method in the first line of `test_reminder`, like the `deliver_reminder` method from Section 13.1.3, is synthesized for us by Rails. The resulting UserMailer object has attributes corresponding to the different fields in an email message, such as `subject`, `to`, and `date`, thereby allowing us to test those attributes. Unfortunately, these are not, in general, the same as the variables created in Section 13.1.2: `from` comes from `@from` and `subject` comes from `@subject`, but `to` comes from `@recipients` and `date` comes from `@sent_on`. These Action Mailer attributes are poorly documented, but luckily you can guess them for the most part.

Let's go through the assertions in `test_reminder`. We use

```
reminder = UserMailer.create_reminder(@user)
```

to create a `reminder` variable whose attributes we can test. The `to` attribute,

```
reminder.to
```

is an array of recipients, so the first element is

```
reminder.to.first
```

which we test against `@user.email`. This test also introduces `assert_match`, which verifies that a string matches a given regular expression—in this case, verifying that the screen name and password lines appear in the reminder message body.

Running the test gives[3]

```
> ruby test/unit/user_mailer_test.rb
Loaded suite test/unit/user_mailer_test
Started
.
Finished in 0.2634 seconds.

1 tests, 5 assertions, 0 failures, 0 errors
```

---

[3] If you are running Rails 1.2.2 or later, you will get a DEPRECATION WARNING when you run the email tests. To get rid of the warning, simply change `server_settings` to `smtp_settings` in `environment.rb`.

The functional test for the password reminder is a little bit more complicated. In particular, the setup requires more care. In test mode, Rails doesn't deliver email messages; instead, it appends the messages to an email delivery object called `@emails`. This list of emails has to be cleared after each test is run, because otherwise messages would accumulate, potentially invalidating other tests.[4] We accomplish this with a call to the `clear` array method in the `setup` function:

Listing 13.12   test/functional/email_controller_test.rb

```
require File.dirname(__FILE__) + '/../test_helper'
require 'email_controller'

# Re-raise errors caught by the controller.
class EmailController; def rescue_action(e) raise e end; end

class EmailControllerTest < Test::Unit::TestCase
  fixtures :users

  def setup
    @controller = EmailController.new
    @request    = ActionController::TestRequest.new
    @response   = ActionController::TestResponse.new
    @emails     = ActionMailer::Base.deliveries
    @emails.clear
    @user = users(:valid_user)
    # Make sure deliveries aren't actually made!
    ActionMailer::Base.delivery_method = :test
  end
    .
    .
    .
```

We've added a line telling Rails that the delivery method is in test mode:

```
ActionMailer::Base.delivery_method = :test
```

This is supposed to happen automatically for tests, but on some systems we've found that setting it explicitly is necessary to avoid actual mail delivery.

Since a successful email reminder should add a single message to `@emails`, the test checks that a message was "sent" by making sure that the length of the `@emails` array is 1:

---

[4] With only one test, it doesn't matter, but presumably we'll be adding more tests later.

Listing 13.13 test/functional/email_controller_test.rb

```
    .
    .
    .
  def test_password_reminder
    post :remind, :user => { :email => @user.email }
    assert_response :redirect
    assert_redirected_to :action => "index", :controller => "site"
    assert_equal "Login information was sent.", flash[:notice]
    assert_equal 1, @emails.length
  end
end
```

Running the test gives

```
> ruby test/functional/email_controller_test.rb
Loaded suite test/functional/email_controller_test
Started
.
Finished in 0.179272 seconds.

1 tests, 4 assertions, 0 failures, 0 errors
```

13.2 Double-blind email system

In this section, we develop a minimalist email system to allow registered RailsSpace users to communicate with each other. The system will be *double-blind*, keeping the email address of both the sender and the recipient private. We'll make an email form that submits to a `correspond` action in the Email controller, which will send the actual message. In the body of the email we'll include a link back to the same email form so that it's easy to reply to the original message.[5]

13.2.1 Email link

We'll get the email system started by putting a link to the soon-to-be-written `correspond` action on each user's profile. Since there is a little bit of logic involved, we'll wrap up the details in a partial:

---

[5] We really ought to allow users to *respond* using their regular email account; unfortunately, this would involve setting up a mail server, which is beyond the scope of this book.

Listing 13.14 app/views/profile/_contact_box.rhtml

```
<% if logged_in? and @user != @logged_in_user %>
<div class="sidebar_box">
  <h2>
    <span class="header">Actions</span>
    <br clear="all" />
  </h2>
  <ul>
    <li><%= link_to "Email this user",
                    :controller => "email", :action => "correspond",
                    :id => @user.screen_name %></li>
  </ul>
</div>
<% end %>
```

We've put the link inside a list element tag in anticipation of having more contact actions later (Section 14.2.1). Since it makes little sense to give users the option to email themselves, we only show the sidebar box if the profile user is different from the logged-in user. To get this to work, we need to define the `@logged_in_user` instance variable in the Profile controller's `show` action:

Listing 13.15 app/controllers/profile_controller.rb

```
def show
  @hide_edit_links = true
  screen_name = params[:screen_name]
  @user = User.find_by_screen_name(screen_name)
  @logged_in_user = User.find(session[:user_id]) if logged_in?
  if @user
    .
    .
    .
end
```

All we have left is to invoke the partial from the profile:

Listing 13.16 app/views/profile/show.rhtml

```
<div id="left_column">
  <%= render :partial => 'avatar/sidebar_box' %>
  <%= render :partial => 'contact_box' %>
  .
  .
  .
```

13.2.2 `correspond` and the email form

The target of the link in the previous section is the `correspond` action, which will also be the target of the email form. The form itself will contain the two necessary aspects of the message, the subject and body. In order to do some minimal error-checking on each message, we'll make a lightweight Message class based on Active Record, which has attributes for the message subject and body:

Listing 13.17 app/models/message.rb

```
class Message < ActiveRecord::Base
  attr_accessor :subject, :body

  validates_presence_of :subject, :body
  validates_length_of :subject, :maximum => DB_STRING_MAX_LENGTH
  validates_length_of :body, :maximum => DB_TEXT_MAX_LENGTH

  def initialize(params)
    @subject = params[:subject]
    @body = params[:body]
  end
end
```

By overriding the `initialize` method, we avoid having to create a stub `messages` table in the database.[6]

Since only registered users can send messages, we first protect the `correspond` action with a before filter. We then use the Message class to create a Message object, which we can then validate by calling the message's `valid?` method:

Listing 13.18 app/controllers/email_controller.rb

```
class EmailController < ApplicationController
  include ProfileHelper
  before_filter :protect, :only => [ "correspond" ]
  .
  .
  .
  def correspond
    user = User.find(session[:user_id])
```

Continues

---

[6] It's annoying that we have to inherit from Active Record just to get validations and error-handling—those functions don't have anything specifically to do with databases. We've heard rumors about a proposed base class called Active Model, which would serve as a parent class for all Active Record-like classes. Someday we hope to be able to use Active Model instead of Active Record in cases such as this one.

```
    recipient = User.find_by_screen_name(params[:id])
    @title = "Email #{recipient.name}"
    if param_posted?(:message)
      @message = Message.new(params[:message])
      if @message.valid?
        UserMailer.deliver_message(
          :user => user,
          :recipient => recipient,
          :message => @message,
          :user_url => profile_for(user),
          :reply_url => url_for(:action => "correspond",
                                :id => user.screen_name)
        )
        flash[:notice] = "Email sent."
        redirect_to profile_for(recipient)
      end
    end
  end
end
```

We've packed a lot of information into the call to `deliver_message`, including a use of our custom `profile_for` function from Section 9.4.3 (included through the line `include ProfileHelper` at the top of the Email controller). We'll deal with the call to `deliver_message` in the next section.

By creating a new Message object in the `correspond` action and including a call to `@message.valid?`, we've arranged for Rails to generate error messages in the usual way, which we can put on the corresponding form:

Listing 13.19 app/views/email/correspond.rhtml

```
<% form_for :message do |form| %>
<fieldset>
  <legend><%= @title %></legend>

  <%= error_messages_for 'message' %>

  <div class="form_row">
    <label for="subject">Subject:</label>
    <%= form.text_field "subject", :size => 60 %>
  </div>
  <div class="form_row">
    <label for="subject">Body:</label>
    <%= form.text_area "body", :rows => 20, :cols => 60 %>
  </div>
  <%= submit_tag "Send", :class => "submit" %>
</fieldset>
<% end %>
```

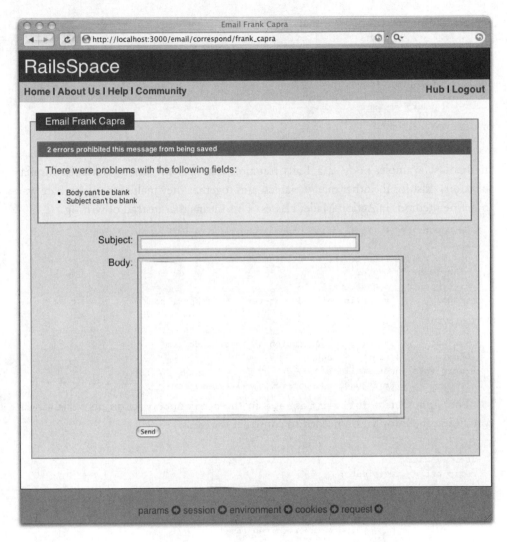

Figure 13.3 The email correspondence page with errors.

This way, if we leave the subject or body blank, we get sensible error messages (Figure 13.3).

13.2.3 Email message

The task remains to complete the `correspond` action by defining a `message` method in the User mailer (so that `UserMailer.deliver_message` exists), along with a `message.rhtml` view for the message itself.

Recall from Section 13.1.2 that

```
@body["user"] = user
```

makes a variable `@user` available in the `reminder.rhtml` view. It turns out that we can also accomplish this by writing

```
@body = {"user" => user}
```

or the even pithier

```
body user
```

In this last example, `body` is a Rails function that sets the `@body` variable. Similar functions exist for the other mail variables, and together they make for an alternate way to define methods in Action Mailer classes. This means that instead of writing

```
@subject      = 'Your login information at RailsSpace.com'
@body         = {}
# Give body access to the user information.
@body["user"] = user
@recipients   = user.email
@from         = 'RailsSpace <do-not-reply@railsspace.com>'
```

we can write

```
subject      'Your login information at RailsSpace.com'
body         {"user" => user}
recipients   user.email
from         'RailsSpace <do-not-reply@railsspace.com>'
```

The argument to `deliver_message` in the `correspond` action above is a hash containing the information needed to construct the message:

```
UserMailer.deliver_message(
  :user => user,
  :recipient => recipient,
  :message => @message,
  :user_url => profile_for(user),
  :reply_url => url_for(:action => "correspond",
                        :id => user.screen_name)
)
```

In the User mailer `message` method, we'll receive this hash as a `mail` variable, which means that we can fill in the message as follows:

Listing 13.20 app/models/user_mailer.rb

```
class UserMailer < ActionMailer::Base
  .
  .
  .
```

```
    def message(mail)
      subject      mail[:message].subject
      from         'RailsSpace <do-not-reply@railsspace.com>'
      recipients   mail[:recipient].email
      body         mail
    end
end
```

By writing

```
body         mail
```

we automatically make everything in the `mail` hash available in the message template, with an instance variable for each key; that is,

```
:user => user,
:recipient => recipient,
:message => @message,
:user_url => profile_for(user),
:reply_url => url_for(:action => "correspond",
                      :id => user.screen_name)
```

gives rise to the instance variables

```
@user, @recipient, @message, @user_url, @reply_url
```

in the message template.

Because all the relevant information is in the instance variables, the message template itself is short. We first include a note at the top indicating the identity of the sender. The text of the message follows, and the message ends with a link to the page needed to respond to the sender:

Listing 13.21 app/views/user_mailer/message.rhtml

```
<%= @user.name %> at RailsSpace (<%= @user_url %>) writes:

<%= @message.body %>

To reply to this message, go to:
<%= @reply_url %>
```

Note from Figure 13.4 that the URL base in a test email is `localhost:3000`, the base for development mode, which happens automatically when we use Rails functions like `url_for` to generate our URLs. This is convenient since test emails link back to the local machine rather than to the actual RailsSpace site.

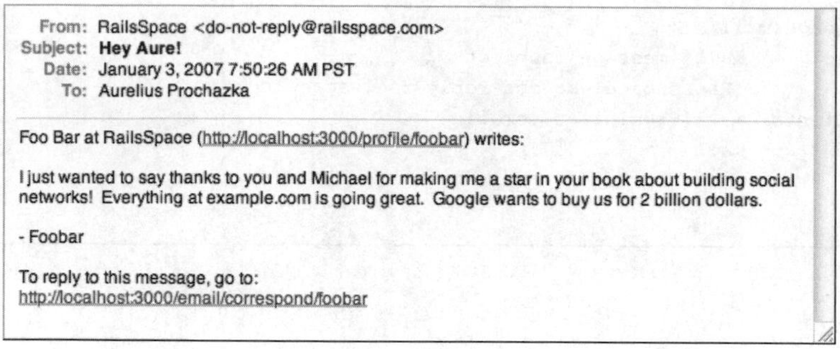

> From: RailsSpace <do-not-reply@railsspace.com>
> Subject: **Hey Aure!**
> Date: January 3, 2007 7:50:26 AM PST
> To: Aurelius Prochazka
>
> ---
>
> Foo Bar at RailsSpace (http://localhost:3000/profile/foobar) writes:
>
> I just wanted to say thanks to you and Michael for making me a star in your book about building social
> networks! Everything at example.com is going great. Google wants to buy us for 2 billion dollars.
>
> - Foobar
>
> To reply to this message, go to:
> http://localhost:3000/email/correspond/foobar

Figure 13.4   A RailsSpace email sent by Foo Bar (in development mode).

With that, the rudimentary RailsSpace email system is complete. At this point, you might want to create a new user and try sending a test message to Foo Bar, which should go to you (assuming that you edited Foo's email address in Section 13.1.4). Of course, that's no substitute for real tests.

13.2.4   Testing double-blind email

In order to test the email interface, we need to create a second user to act as the recipient. In anticipation of the introduction of friends in Chapter 14, we'll call this user `friend` and put his information in the `users.yml` fixture file:[7]

Listing 13.22   test/fixtures/users.yml

```
.
.
.
friend:
  id: 4
  screen_name: amigo
  email: ami@example.com
  password: Freund

# Create 10 users so that searches can invoke pagination.
<% (1..10).each do |i| %>
user_<%= i %>:
  id: <%= i + 4 %>
  screen_name: user_<%= i %>
```

---

[7] Note that this insertion requires renumbering the 10 generated users so that their ids start at 5: `id: <%= i + 3 %>` becomes `id: <%= i + 4 %>`.

```
  email: user_<%= i %>@example.com
  password: foobar
<% end %>
  .
  .
  .
```

We use `recipient.name` in the `correspond` action, which relies on a method in the Spec model, so we also need to create a spec for the friend:

Listing 13.23   test/fixtures/specs.yml

```
  .
  .
  .
friend_spec:
  id: 3
  user_id: 4
  first_name: Dude
  last_name: Dude
  gender: Male
  birthdate: 2000-01-01
  occupation: Dude
  city: Dude
  state: CA
  zip_code: 91125
```

In the User mailer test file, we need to include the fixtures and create the `@user` and `@friend` instance variables. Then we can test the email interface by writing `test_message`:

Listing 13.24   test/unit/user_mailer_test.rb

```
class UserMailerTest < Test::Unit::TestCase
  fixtures :users, :specs
    .
    .
    .
  def setup
    @user = users(:valid_user)
    @friend = users(:friend)
    .
    .
    .
  end
```

Continues

```
  .
  .
  .
def test_message
  user_url = "http://railsspace.com/profile/#{@user.screen_name}"
  reply_url = "http://railsspace.com/email/correspond/#{@user.screen_name}"
  message = Message.new(:subject => "Test message",
                        :body => "Dude, this is totally rad!")
  email = UserMailer.create_message(
            :user => @user,
            :recipient => @friend,
            :message => message,
            :user_url => user_url,
            :reply_url => reply_url
          )
  assert_equal message.subject, email.subject
  assert_equal @friend.email, email.to.first
  assert_equal 'do-not-reply@railsspace.com', email.from.first
  assert_match message.body, email.body
  assert_match user_url, email.body
  assert_match reply_url, email.body
end

private
  .
  .
  .
```

We've used assertions to verify several of the message attributes, including checking the email for the message body, user URL, and reply URL.[8] Now there are two User mailer tests:

```
> ruby test/unit/user_mailer_test.rb
Loaded suite test/unit/user_mailer_test
Started
..
Finished in 0.180634 seconds.

2 tests, 11 assertions, 0 failures, 0 errors
```

In the Email controller functional test, we'll put the new friend to good use again in `test_correspond`, which is similar to `test_remind` from Section 13.1.4:

---

[8] We hard-coded the two test URLs because we were unable to get `profile_for` and `url_for` to work in a unit test. Maybe you can do better.

Listing 13.25 test/functional/email_controller_test.rb

```
class EmailControllerTest < Test::Unit::TestCase
  include ProfileHelper
  fixtures :users, :specs

  def setup
    .
    .
    .
    @user = users(:valid_user)
    @friend = users(:friend)
    # Make sure deliveries aren't actually made!
    ActionMailer::Base.delivery_method = :test
  end
  .
  .
  .
  def test_correspond
    authorize @user
    post :correspond, :id => @friend.screen_name,
                      :message => { :subject => "Test message",
                                    :body => "Dude, this is totally rad!" }
    assert_response :redirect
    assert_redirected_to profile_for(@friend)
    assert_equal "Email sent.", flash[:notice]
    assert_equal 1, @emails.length
  end
end
```

By including `ProfileHelper` in the test class, we've arranged to use `profile_for` in the line

```
assert_redirected_to profile_for(@friend)
```

With `test_correspond` added to our test suite, there are now two Email controller tests:

```
> ruby test/functional/email_controller_test.rb
Loaded suite test/functional/email_controller_test
Started
..
Finished in 0.110034 seconds.

2 tests, 8 assertions, 0 failures, 0 errors
```

CHAPTER 14

Friendships

With the double-blind email system in place, we suppose that RailsSpace is now technically a social network, but most real-world social networks worthy of the name give users a way to select preferred members. Following tradition, we call such distinguished users *friends*. Adding friends to RailsSpace is the goal of this chapter.

Friendships represent the most challenging data modeling problem we've encountered so far. To solve it, we'll have to learn about simulated table names, foreign keys, and the has_many database association. Adding and managing friendships will then take place through both email and web interfaces. By the end of the chapter, we'll be in a position to put a list of friends on the hub and user profile, making use of the avatar thumbnails from Chapter 12.

14.1 Modeling friendships

At first blush, modeling friends looks easy: Just make a friends table for friends. If you start to think about it, though, it's not clear what to put in such a table—would each friend somehow have a list of all the users he's friends with? That would seem to require storing a Ruby list in the database, which seems dubious. Moreover, since friends are just users, a separate friends table would be highly redundant. We could eliminate this redundancy by using the users table itself, but we then have the strange situation of having a table somehow refer to itself.

The way to cut this Gordian knot is to realize that we're missing an underlying abstraction: Fundamentally, what we need to model is not friends, but rather the friendship *relationship* between users. This suggests creating a Friendship model, with each friendship consisting of a *pair* of users.

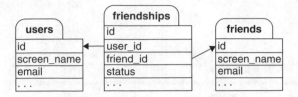

Figure 14.1   A sketch of the database tables needed to model friendships.

14.1.1   Friendships in the abstract

In order to discuss friendships meaningfully, we need a second example in addition to Foo Bar. Let's call the new user Baz Quux (screen name `bazquux`).[1] Creating friendships will involve (say) Foo requesting a friendship with Baz, so that Baz will have a *requested* friendship from Foo, and Foo will have a *pending* friendship with Baz. If Baz accepts Foo's request, the friendship will be *accepted* and they will officially be friends.

In terms of a database table structure, the discussion above suggests something like Figure 14.1. On the left and right, we have `users` and `friends` tables, with a `friendships` table in the middle connecting them. As noted above, having a separate `friends` table would be terribly redundant, but we'd still like to make a distinction between users and friends somehow. Rails lets us have our cake and eat it, too, by allowing us to fake a second table with a name of our choice. In the next section, we'll show how to simulate a table called `friends` while actually using the `users` table behind the scenes.

With the given table structure, each friendship will consist of *two* rows in the `friend-ships` table. For example, a (potential) friendship between Foo (user id 1) and Baz (user id 2) would look like Figure 14.2; as indicated by the `status` column, the first row shows that Foo has a pending friendship with Baz, while the second row shows that Baz has a requested friendship from Foo. When a friendship is accepted, both status columns get set to `'accepted'`.

It might seem wasteful to use two rows per friendship instead of one—we certainly thought so at first—but this way we can use different statuses for each user/friend pair to indicate who made the request and who received it. Even after a friendship is accepted, so that each status is the same, having two rows makes selecting the friends for a particular user much easier (Section 14.3.1).

---

[1] Since friendship requests will happen through email, we suggest that you set the email addresses for both Foo Bar and Baz Quux to accounts you control.

friendships

user_id	friend_id	status
1	2	'pending'
2	1	'requested'

Figure 14.2 The two rows for a (potential) friendship between Foo (1) and Baz (2).

14.1.2 Friendship model

It's time now to take the abstract discussion above and make it concrete in the form of a Friendship model. Figure 14.1 suggests creating a `friendships` table with columns for both user and friend (as identified by their ids), together with a column indicating the status of the friendship. We'll also add a couple of columns to record the time for each friendship request and acceptance. As usual, to get started we generate the Friendship model, but this time with a twist:

```
> ruby script/generate model Friendship user_id:integer friend_id:integer \
      status:string created_at:datetime accepted_at:datetime
    exists  app/models/
    exists  test/unit/
    exists  test/fixtures/
    create  app/models/friendship.rb
    create  test/unit/friendship_test.rb
    create  test/fixtures/friendships.yml
    exists  db/migrate
    create  db/migrate/011_create_friendships.rb
```

Here we've included the data model right on the command line, using the pattern `column:type` to tell `generate` the columns in the `friendships` table. As a result, Rails has generated the proper migration file for us:

Listing 14.1 db/migrate/008_create_friendships.rb

```
class CreateFriendships < ActiveRecord::Migration
  def self.up
    create_table :friendships do |t|
      t.column :user_id, :integer
      t.column :friend_id, :integer
      t.column :status, :string
      t.column :created_at, :datetime
      t.column :accepted_at, :datetime
    end
  end
end
```

Continues

```
    def self.down
      drop_table :friendships
    end
  end
```

Before moving on, run `rake db:migrate` as usual to update the database.

The `status` column is there to keep track of whether a particular friendship is pending, requested, or accepted.[2] As discussed in Section 14.1.1, we'll plan to use the following strings to track the status of user friendships, updating them if the status changes:[3]

```
'pending'
'requested'
'accepted'
```

The only potentially confusing column in the `friendships` table is `friend_id`, and indeed this column is at the heart of the trickery that makes the Friendship model work. The crux of the problem is that the Friendship model naturally `belongs_to` *each* user, one of whom is "the user" and the other of whom is "the friend." Using both `user_id` and `friend_id` in the Friendship data model allows us to distinguish between them as follows:

Listing 14.2 app/models/friendship.rb

```
class Friendship < ActiveRecord::Base
  belongs_to :user
  belongs_to :friend, :class_name => "User", :foreign_key => "friend_id"

  validates_presence_of :user_id, :friend_id
end
```

This says that each friendship belongs to the first user *and* to the second user. By writing

```
belongs_to :friend, :class_name => "User", :foreign_key => "friend_id"
```

we tell Rails that we want to refer to the second user as a "friend" identified by the *foreign key* `friend_id`—that is, as if there were a separate `friends` table. Because of the `:class_name => "User"` option, Rails will actually use the User model (and hence the `users` table) under the hood.

---

[2] We could also keep track of declined friendship requests, but for now we'll just delete them instead.

[3] Those of you familiar with *database normalization* might be cringing at this point. Get over it.

If this all seems too abstract and even a little magical, don't fret. We encountered a similar problem in Chapter 3 when first learning about models. We turn now (as we turned then) to the Rails console, which will allow us to explore the Friendship model with a couple of concrete examples.

14.1.3 Creating pending friendships

As an example of how the Friendship model works, let's fire up the console and play with a couple of concrete objects. For this to work, you'll need to create the user Baz Quux if you haven't already. We'll start by creating a friendship:[4]

```
> ruby script/console
>> user = User.find_by_screen_name("foobar")
>> friend = User.find_by_screen_name("bazquux")
>> Friendship.create(:user => user, :friend => friend, :status => 'pending')
>> Friendship.create(:user => friend, :friend => user, :status => 'requested')
```

Here we've used the Active Record `create` method, which is essentially `new` and `save` rolled into one (although `create` returns the object created rather than a boolean as `save` does). We've also used the compact notation

```
:user => user, :friend => friend
```

instead of

```
:user_id => user.id, :friend_id => friend.id
```

Though they both do the same thing, Rails knows from context to use the object id rather than the object itself, and we prefer the pithier syntax. It's important to emphasize that the only reason the notation works for the friend is that we told Rails that the Friendship model belongs to `friends`, with the foreign key `friend_id`.

Now that we've created them, let's check to see if we can find the friendship rows in the database:

```
>> Friendship.find_by_user_id_and_friend_id(user, friend)
=> #<Friendship:0x2bf74ec @attributes={"status"=>"pending", "accepted_at"=>nil,
"id"=>"1", "user_id"=>"1", "position"=>nil, "created_at"=>"2007-01-03 18:34:09",
"friend_id"=>"1198"}>
>> Friendship.find_by_user_id_and_friend_id(friend, user)
=> #<Friendship:0x490a7a0 @attributes={"status"=>"requested", "accepted_at"=>nil
, "id"=>"2", "user_id"=>"1198", "position"=>nil, "created_at"=>"2007-01-03 18:34
:20", "friend_id"=>"1"}>
```

As in the call to `create`, we've omitted `.id` here, writing

```
Friendship.find_by_user_id_and_friend_id(user, friend)
```

---

[4] In what follows, we'll suppress the console output if it's overly verbose or otherwise unilluminating.

instead of

```
Friendship.find_by_user_id_and_friend_id(user.id, friend.id)
```

In the example above, the friendship is only a potential friendship, as indicated by the `'requested'` and `'pending'` status values; it's also slightly asymmetric since we need to indicate which user made the request. Still, there's an essential symmetry in friendship relationships—when creating friendships we will have to be careful always to create *two* rows: one row indicating that Foo is (possibly potential) friends with Baz, and a second row indicating the converse. We'll have to figure out a way to build this into our model.

14.1.4   Friendship request

Having seen how to create pending friendships in the console, we're now ready to make a Friendship method to do essentially the same thing, again using the `create` method; the result is a class method called `request`.[5] We have to be careful, though, since each friendship request must create two new rows, as noted above; the way to ensure this is to wrap the two calls to `create` inside a *transaction*:

Listing 14.3   app/models/friendship.rb

```
class Friendship < ActiveRecord::Base
  belongs_to :user
  belongs_to :friend, :class_name => "User", :foreign_key => "friend_id"
  validates_presence_of :user_id, :friend_id

  # Return true if the users are (possibly pending) friends.
  def self.exists?(user, friend)
    not find_by_user_id_and_friend_id(user, friend).nil?
  end

  # Record a pending friend request.
  def self.request(user, friend)
    unless user == friend or Friendship.exists?(user, friend)
      transaction do
        create(:user => user, :friend => friend, :status => 'pending')
        create(:user => friend, :friend => user, :status => 'requested')
      end
    end
  end
end
```

---

[5] All the Friendship model functions will be class methods, defined using the `self` keyword. Recall that class methods (such as `User.log_out!` [Section 6.6.3] and `Spec.find_by_asl` [Section 11.3.2]) belong to the class itself, and therefore use the class name when invoked outside the class.

By wrapping the two calls to `create` in a `transaction` block, we ensure that either both succeed or both fail, thereby preventing the creation of a `pending` row without a corresponding `requested` row. This way, if a cosmic ray hits our computer and crashes our system immediately after the first `create`, no rows will be created and the database will be *rolled back* to its previous valid state.[6]

Of course, before creating the friendship we first have to check that the user and the friend aren't the same, since users can't be friends with themselves, and we also need to make sure that no friendship already exists. We've written the auxiliary class method `exists?` function for the latter purpose, but it will prove to be generally useful. Since `exists?` is a class method, inside the class we could omit the class name and write simply `exists?`, but it does no harm to include the class name, and in this case the code is clearer if we write `Friendship.exists?` instead.

14.1.5 Completing the Friendship model

There are just two more methods to add to the Friendship model: one to change a pending friendship into an accepted one, and one to end a friendship. We'll start with the `accept` method, which updates a preexisting pending friendship and turns it into an accepted one, and then add a `breakup` method to remove a friendship from the database:

Listing 14.4 app/models/friendship.rb

```
class Friendship < ActiveRecord::Base
  .
  .
  .
  # Accept a friend request.
  def self.accept(user, friend)
    transaction do
      accepted_at = Time.now
      accept_one_side(user, friend, accepted_at)
      accept_one_side(friend, user, accepted_at)
    end
  end
```

Continues

---

[6] Transactions are a general database concept, and in fact we've used them many times before in this book—or rather, Active Record has used them for us. For example, when saving a user, we simultaneously save the user's spec and FAQ as well; Active Record executes these commands in a transaction to make sure that all the changes happen together.

```
# Delete a friendship or cancel a pending request.
def self.breakup(user, friend)
  transaction do
    destroy(find_by_user_id_and_friend_id(user, friend))
    destroy(find_by_user_id_and_friend_id(friend, user))
  end
end

private

# Update the db with one side of an accepted friendship request.
def self.accept_one_side(user, friend, accepted_at)
  request = find_by_user_id_and_friend_id(user, friend)
  request.status = 'accepted'
  request.accepted_at = accepted_at
  request.save!
end
```

For the `accept` method, we've put the hard work in `accept_one_side`, which finds the pending friendship, changes its status to `'accepted'`, sets the `accepted_at` timestamp, and then saves the result back to the database.

The database manipulations in the `accept` method should all be familiar, but the `destroy` method in `breakup` is new. Its effect is simply to destroy an Active Record object by deleting its corresponding row from the database. In the present case, we've made `breakup` a class method, which means that `destroy` requires an Active Record object as its first argument. `destroy` can also be used as an object method, so that we could destroy a friendship using

```
friendship = find_by_user_id_and_friend_id(user, friend)
friendship.destroy
```

This would be more succinct if we already had a Friendship object, but in our case it's shorter to call `destroy` with an explicit argument instead.

You may wonder why we use `destroy` instead of the possibly more intuitive `delete`. It turns out that there is an Active Record method called `delete` that works in basically the same way as `destroy`, but there's a subtle difference between the two: The `destroy` method invokes the model's validations, as well as certain functions that automatically get called at specific stages during the life of an object.[7] Because it is slightly more powerful than `delete`, `destroy` is the preferred way to eliminate Active Record objects.

---

[7] Yes, this is vague. Do a web search on "ActiveRecord callbacks" to learn more.

14.1.6   Testing the Friendship model

Testing the Friendship model is easy using the friend from the users fixture (defined in Section 13.2.4 for the email tests) and our `Friendship.exists?` utility function:

Listing 14.5   test/units/friendship_test.rb

```
require File.dirname(__FILE__) + '/../test_helper'

class FriendshipTest < Test::Unit::TestCase
  fixtures :users

  def setup
    @user = users(:valid_user)
    @friend = users(:friend)
  end

  def test_request
    Friendship.request(@user, @friend)
    assert Friendship.exists?(@user, @friend)
    assert_status @user, @friend, 'pending'
    assert_status @friend, @user, 'requested'
  end

  def test_accept
    Friendship.request(@user, @friend)
    Friendship.accept(@user, @friend)
    assert Friendship.exists?(@user, @friend)
    assert_status @user, @friend, 'accepted'
    assert_status @friend, @user, 'accepted'
  end

  def test_breakup
    Friendship.request(@user, @friend)
    Friendship.breakup(@user, @friend)
    assert !Friendship.exists?(@user, @friend)
  end

  private

  # Verify the existence of a friendship with the given status.
  def assert_status(user, friend, status)
    friendship = Friendship.find_by_user_id_and_friend_id(user, friend)
    assert_equal status, friendship.status
  end
end
```

Here we've added the private `assert_status` function for convenience.

Preparing the test database and running these tests gives

```
> rake db:test:prepare
(in /rails/rails_space)
> ruby test/unit/friendship_test.rb
Loaded suite test/unit/friendship_test
Started
...
Finished in 0.47111 seconds.

3 tests, 7 assertions, 0 failures, 0 errors
```

14.2 Friendship requests

In this section we'll give RailsSpace users the ability to send friend requests to other users by putting a friendship request link on each user's profile. When a user clicks on such a link, the friendship request action will create a pending/requested friendship using the Friendship model's `request` method and then send a request email using the User mailer introduced in Section 13.1.

The material in this section ties together many different strands from previous parts of the book, with models, views, controllers, partials, helpers, and mailers all well represented.

14.2.1 Friendship request link

To get started with friendship requests, let's first generate a Friendship controller:

```
> ruby script/generate controller Friendship
     exists  app/controllers/
     exists  app/helpers/
     create  app/views/friendship
     exists  test/functional/
     create  app/controllers/friendship_controller.rb
     create  test/functional/friendship_controller_test.rb
     create  app/helpers/friendship_helper.rb
```

We won't actually start filling in the Friendship controller until Section 14.2.2, but we will be using the Friendship helper shortly.

Our first step is to put a friendship request link on each user's profile. We'll place it in the same contact box used in Section 13.2.2 for email:

Listing 14.6 app/views/profile/_contact_box.rhtml

```
<% if logged_in? and @user != @logged_in_user %>
<div class="sidebar_box">
```

```
  <h2>
    <span class="header">Actions</span>
    <br clear="all" />
  </h2>
  <ul>
    <li><%= link_to "Email this user",
                    :controller => "email", :action => "correspond",
                    :id => @user.screen_name %></li>
    <li><%= friendship_status(@logged_in_user, @user) %>
        <% unless Friendship.exists?(@logged_in_user, @user) %>
          <br />
          <%= link_to "Request friendship with #{@user.name}",
                      { :controller => "friendship", :action => "create",
                        :id => @user.screen_name },
                      :confirm =>
                      "Send friend request to #{@user.name}?" %>
        <% end %>
    </li>
  </ul>
</div>
<% end %>
```

Note that we only display the friendship request link if the friendship doesn't exist.
We've also included a brief JavaScript confirmation to help prevent accidental requests.
Above the request link, we've put a short description of the friendship status, using a
helper function defined in the Friendship helper:

Listing 14.7 app/helpers/friendship_helper.rb

```
module FriendshipHelper

  # Return an appropriate friendship status message.
  def friendship_status(user, friend)
    friendship = Friendship.find_by_user_id_and_friend_id(user, friend)
    return "#{friend.name} is not your friend (yet)." if friendship.nil?
    case friendship.status
    when 'requested'
      "#{friend.name} would like to be your friend."
    when 'pending'
      "You have requested friendship from #{friend.name}."
    when 'accepted'
      "#{friend.name} is your friend."
    end
  end

end
```

Figure 14.3   A user's profile with friendship request link and confirmation message.

Since we're using this helper in a profile view, we need to include it in the Profile controller:

Listing 14.8 app/controllers/profile_controller.rb

```
class ProfileController < ApplicationController
  helper :avatar, :friendship
  .
  .
  .
```

The result for users with no friendship relationship appears in Figure 14.3 (together with an example of the confirmation message).

14.2.2 Controlling the request

Now it's time to make the friendship request link actually do something by defining the relevant action in the Friendship controller. The resulting `create` action[8] uses the Friendship model's `request` method to update the database, and then uses the User mailer to send a friendship request email:

Listing 14.9 app/controllers/friendship_controller.rb

```
class FriendshipController < ApplicationController
  include ProfileHelper
  before_filter :protect, :setup_friends

  # Send a friend request.
  # We'd rather call this "request", but that's not allowed by Rails.
  def create
    Friendship.request(@user, @friend)
    UserMailer.deliver_friend_request(
      :user => @user,
      :friend => @friend,
      :user_url => profile_for(@user),
      :accept_url => url_for(:action => "accept",  :id => @user.screen_name),
      :decline_url => url_for(:action => "decline", :id => @user.screen_name)
    )
    flash[:notice] = "Friend request sent."
    redirect_to profile_for(@friend)
  end

  private

  def setup_friends
    @user = User.find(session[:user_id])
    @friend = User.find_by_screen_name(params[:id])
  end
end
```

Using the `@user` and `@friend` variables defined by the `setup_friends` before filter, we first update the `friendships` table with `Friendship.request`, and then call `UserMailer.deliver_friend_request` with the information needed to construct the friend request email; since this uses `profile_for`, we have to include `ProfileHelper`.

---

[8] `request` is reserved by Rails and is not a valid action name.

Of course, we have to make sure that the `deliver_friend_request` method exists. Recall from Section 13.1 that we can do this by defining a `friend_request` method in the UserMailer:

Listing 14.10 app/models/user_mailer.rb

```
class UserMailer < ActionMailer::Base
  .
  .
  .
  def friend_request(mail)
    subject     'New friend request at RailsSpace.com'
    from        'RailsSpace <do-not-reply@railsspace.com>'
    recipients  mail[:friend].email
    body        mail
  end
end
```

As discussed in Section 13.2.3, the hash argument to `deliver_friend_request` means that the `mail` variable has all the relevant user objects and the various URLs. The message therefore appears as follows:

Listing 14.11 app/views/user_mailer/friend_request.rhtml

```
Hello <%= @friend.name %>,

You have a new RailsSpace friend request from <%= @user.name %>.

View <%= @user.name %>'s profile:
<%= @user_url %>

Accept:  <%= @accept_url %>
Decline: <%= @decline_url %>

--The RailsSpace team
```

With that, the request link is live. Clicking on it results in flash and updated status messages (Figure 14.4) and a friendship request email (Figure 14.5).

Figure 14.4   A user's profile immediately after a friendship request.

Figure 14.5   A friendship request email.

14.3 Managing friendships

Now that we've made it possible to send friendship requests, we'll build the core part of friendship management: accepting, declining, and canceling friendship requests, and deleting friendships. We'll build the `accept` and `decline` actions shortly, thereby making the friendship request email links work, but first we'll create a place for viewing and managing friends on the user hub.

14.3.1 `has_many :through`

To display a RailsSpace user's friends on the hub, we'd like to be able to iterate through the friends and make an HTML table row for each one. The rhtml for such a friends listing might look something like this:

```
<table>
<% @user.friends.each do |friend| %>
  <tr>
    <td><%= link_to thumbnail_tag(friend), profile_for(friend) %></td>
    <td><%= link_to friend.name, profile_for(friend) %></td>
  </tr>
<% end %>
</table>
```

We would also want similar listings for requested and pending friends.

Previously in RailsSpace, model associations have been one-to-one, with (for example) each user having one spec—a relationship we encoded using `has_one` and `belongs_to`. In the present case, though, a user potentially has *many* friendships. In keeping with its predilection for natural-language constructs, Rails provides the `has_many` association for exactly this purpose:

```
class User < ActiveRecord::Base
  has_one :spec
  has_one :faq
  has_many :friendships
  .
  .
  .
```

In the same way that `has_one :spec` gives access to the user spec through `user.spec`, `has_many :friendships` gives access to an *array* of the user's friendships through `user.friendships`—that is, each friendship in the array has a different `friend_id`, but they all have a `user_id` equal to that of the given user.

Once we have an array of a particular user's friendships, we could extract the user's current (accepted) friends by marching through `user.friendships`, selecting those with `status` equal to `'accepted'`, and then instantiating an array of users based on the `friend_id` attributes of those accepted users. We could do the same for users whose status is `'requested'` and `'pending'`, thereby assembling arrays of accepted, requested, and pending friends. We might define User model methods to perform these operations, and name them thusly:

```
user.friends
user.requested_friends
user.pending_friends
```

If that sounds like an awful lot of work, we agree—and, happily, so do the Rails designers. We can compress all of the rather confusing steps above into a single command for each type of friend, using the remarkable `has_many :through` construction:

```
class User < ActiveRecord::Base
  .
  .
  .
  has_many :friendships
  has_many :friends,
           :through => :friendships,
           :conditions => "status = 'accepted'"

  has_many :requested_friends,
           :through => :friendships,
           :source => :friend,
           :conditions => "status = 'requested'"

  has_many :pending_friends,
           :through => :friendships,
           :source => :friend,
           :conditions => "status = 'pending'"
  .
  .
  .
```

These give rise to precisely the friends lists we want. By putting conditions on the call to `has_many`, we arrange for Rails to select the friends appropriate to each case based on the value of the `status` column in the `friendships` table. This is even cleverer than it looks at first—there aren't any `requested_friends` or `pending_friends` tables, not even fake ones like the one we have for `friends`. Rails lets us get around this for the requested and pending friends by specifying a *source* for the association, which in our case is the fake `friends` table created by

```
belongs_to :friend, :class_name => "User", :foreign_key => "friend_id"
```

in the Friendship model.

With that, we're finally ready to add the new `has_many` relationships to the User
model. The `has_many` function takes a number of options, including a standard ordering
for results returned from the database; let's add an `:order` option to each `has_many`
`:through` declaration so that the friends in each category come out in a sensible order:

Listing 14.12 app/models/user.rb

```
class User < ActiveRecord::Base
  has_one :spec
  has_one :faq
  has_many :friendships
  has_many :friends,
           :through => :friendships,
           :conditions => "status = 'accepted'",
           :order => :screen_name

  has_many :requested_friends,
           :through => :friendships,
           :source => :friend,
           :conditions => "status = 'requested'",
           :order => :created_at

  has_many :pending_friends,
           :through => :friendships,
           :source => :friend,
           :conditions => "status = 'pending'",
           :order => :created_at
  .
  .
  .
```

14.3.2 Hub friendships

We're now ready to expand on the rhtml stub at the beginning of Section 14.3.1 by
making the `_friends.rhtml` partial. It is a table with rows for accepted, requested, and
pending friends, together with links for deleting friends and accepting, declining, and
canceling friendship requests. In anticipation of using this on both the hub and profile
pages, we've used the `hide_edit_links?` function defined in Section 9.6 to suppress
various parts of the partial depending on context:

Listing 14.13 app/views/friendship/_friends.rhtml

```
<table>
  <tr>
    <th colspan="3" align="left">
```

```
        <%= pluralize(@user.friends.count, "RailsSpace friend") %>
    </th>
</tr>
<% @user.friends.each do |friend| %>
<tr>
  <td width="50">
    <%= link_to thumbnail_tag(friend), profile_for(friend) %>
  </td>
  <td><%= link_to friend.name, profile_for(friend) %></td>
  <td>
    <% unless hide_edit_links? %>
      <%= link_to "Delete",
                  { :controller => "friendship", :action => "delete",
                    :id => friend.screen_name },
                  :confirm =>
                  "Really delete friendship with #{friend.name}?" %>
    <% end %>
  </td>
</tr>
<% end %>
<% unless @user.requested_friends.empty? or hide_edit_links? %>
  <tr>
    <th colspan-"3" align="left">
      <%= pluralize(@user.requested_friends.count, "requested friend") %>
    </th>
  </tr>
  <% @user.requested_friends.each do |requester| %>
  <tr>
    <td><%= link_to thumbnail_tag(requester), profile_for(requester) %></td>
    <td><%= link_to requester.name, profile_for(requester) %></td>
    <td>
        <%= link_to "Accept",
                    :controller => "friendship", :action => "accept",
                    :id => requester.screen_name %> /
        <%= link_to "Decline",
                    { :controller => "friendship", :action => "decline",
                      :id => requester.screen_name },
                    :confirm =>
                    "Really decline friendship with #{requester.name}?" %>
    </td>
  </tr>
  <% end %>
<% end %>
<% unless @user.pending_friends.empty? or hide_edit_links? %>
  <tr>
    <th colspan="3" align="left">
      <%= pluralize(@user.pending_friends.count, "pending friend") %>
    </th>
  </tr>
```

Continues

```
    <% @user.pending_friends.each do |pending_friend| %>
    <tr>
      <td><%= link_to thumbnail_tag(pending_friend),
                      profile_for(pending_friend) %></td>
      <td><%= link_to pending_friend.name,
                      profile_for(pending_friend) %></td>
      <td><%= link_to "Cancel request",
                      { :controller => "friendship", :action => "cancel",
                        :id => pending_friend.screen_name },
                      :confirm =>
                      "Cancel friendship request?" %></td>
    </tr>
    <% end %>
  <% end %>
</table>
```

We should note that there's quite a bit of repeated code here; this is a good example of a situation where each case is *just different enough* that there's no obvious way to make it simpler with helper functions and partials.

There's one more detail to take care of before we can list friends on the hub: We should take into account the possibility that some users won't upload avatar images. We'll do this by editing the `thumbnail_url` method in the Avatar model (Section 12.1.1) so that it returns a default thumbnail if the avatar doesn't exist:

```
class Avatar < ActiveRecord::Base
  .
  .
  .
  def thumbnail_url
    thumb = exists? ? thumbnail_name : "default_thumbnail.png"
    "#{URL_STUB}/#{thumb}"
  end
  .
  .
  .
end
```

A convenient choice for a default thumbnail is `rails.png`, so we'll copy `public/images/rails.png` to `public/images/avatars/default_thumbnail.png`. As a result, even avatar-less users will still be well represented in the friends listing.

The only thing left is to render the partial on the hub:

Listing 14.14 app/views/user/index.rhtml

```
  .
  .
  .
```

Figure 14.6 The user hub with requested and pending friends.

```
My Bio:
<span class="edit_link">
  <%= link_to "(edit)", :controller => "faq", :action => "edit" %>
</span>
<div id="bio" class="faq_answer">
  <%= sanitize @faq.bio %>
</div>


<hr noshade />
<%= render :partial => "friendship/friends" %>
.
.
.
```

There are no accepted friends since we have yet to write the `accept` action, but requested and pending friends already show up on the hub (Figure 14.6).

14.3.3 Friendship actions

In contrast to the hub, the profile listing will only show accepted friends. To get that to work, we first have to write the `accept` action. Adding that—together with `decline`, `cancel`, and `delete` actions—is the goal of this section.

The structure of each action is virtually identical. We include a `setup_friends` before filter to create the instance variables `@user` and `@friend`. Each action checks to make sure that `@friend` is in the relevant friends list (e.g., `requested_friends`).

If so, we use the appropriate method in the Friendship model to accept or delete the friendship:

Listing 14.15 app/controllers/friendship_controller.rb

```
class FriendshipController < ApplicationController
  include ProfileHelper
  before_filter :protect, :setup_friends
  .
  .
  .
  def accept
    if @user.requested_friends.include?(@friend)
      Friendship.accept(@user, @friend)
      flash[:notice] = "Friendship with #{@friend.screen_name} accepted!"
    else
      flash[:notice] = "No friendship request from #{@friend.screen_name}."
    end
    redirect_to hub_url
  end

  def decline
    if @user.requested_friends.include?(@friend)
      Friendship.breakup(@user, @friend)
      flash[:notice] = "Friendship with #{@friend.screen_name} declined"
    else
      flash[:notice] = "No friendship request from #{@friend.screen_name}."
    end
    redirect_to hub_url
  end

  def cancel
    if @user.pending_friends.include?(@friend)
      Friendship.breakup(@user, @friend)
      flash[:notice] = "Friendship request canceled."
    else
      flash[:notice] = "No request for friendship with #{@friend.screen_name}"
    end
    redirect_to hub_url
  end

  def delete
    if @user.friends.include?(@friend)
      Friendship.breakup(@user, @friend)
      flash[:notice] = "Friendship with #{@friend.screen_name} deleted!"
    else
      flash[:notice] = "You aren't friends with #{@friend.screen_name}"
    end
```

```
    redirect_to hub_url
  end

  private

  def setup_friends
    @user = User.find(session[:user_id])
    @friend = User.find_by_screen_name(params[:id])
  end
end
```

Note that the `Friendship.breakup` method does triple duty, since declining, cancel-ing, and deleting friendships are all fundamentally the same database operation.

With these actions defined, the email links from the friendship request message and the links on the hub URL are all live and functional. In particular, we can finally accept friendships. If you want to accept a friend request using the email link, be careful to log out of RailsSpace: If you send a request to Foo Bar from Baz Quux and then click on the accept link, you'll get an error, since you'll still be logged in as Baz. (Of course, such a situation is far less likely to occur in real life than when developing and testing this feature.)

Once a user has accepted a few friends, we can arrange for them to show up on his profile using the `_friends` partial:

Listing 14.16 app/views/profile/show.rhtml

```
    .
    .
    .


<hr noshade />
Friends:
<%= render :partial => "friendship/friends" %>
    .
    .
    .
```

Once you have created a few friendships for Baz (possibly registering a few new users in the process), take a look at his profile. The result should be something like Figure 14.7.

14.3.4 Testing friendship requests

As a final touch, let's write a simple test for friendship requests. The sequence is simple: First, log in as `@user` and `get` the `create` action for `@friend.screen_name`; second,

Figure 14.7   A user profile with friend listing.

log in as @friend and get the accept action for @user.screen_name. The test then
verifies the proper flash message and redirect for each action:

Listing 14.17   test/functional/friendship_controller_test.rb

```
require File.dirname(__FILE__) + '/../test_helper'
require 'friendship_controller'

# Re-raise errors caught by the controller.
class FriendshipController; def rescue_action(e) raise e end; end

class FriendshipControllerTest < Test::Unit::TestCase
  include ProfileHelper
  fixtures :users, :specs

  def setup
    @controller = FriendshipController.new
    @request    = ActionController::TestRequest.new
    @response   = ActionController::TestResponse.new
    @user = users(:valid_user)
    @friend = users(:friend)
    # Make sure deliveries aren't actually made!
    ActionMailer::Base.delivery_method = :test
  end

  def test_create
    # Log in as user and send request.
```

```
    authorize @user
    get :create, :id => @friend.screen_name
    assert_response :redirect
    assert_redirected_to profile_for(@friend)
    assert_equal "Friend request sent.", flash[:notice]
    # Log in as friend and accept request.
    authorize @friend
    get :accept, :id => @user.screen_name
    assert_redirected_to hub_url
    assert_equal "Friendship with #{@user.screen_name} accepted!",
                 flash[:notice]
  end
end
```

Running this gives

```
> ruby test/functional/friendship_controller_test.rb
Loaded suite test/functional/friendship_controller_test
Started
.
Finished in 0.180971 seconds.

1 tests, 5 assertions, 0 failures, 0 errors
```

CHAPTER 15

RESTful blogs

RailsSpace has come a long way since we completed the login and authentication system in Chapter 7. We've added full-text search; browsing by age, sex, and location; a double-blind email interface; and customizable user profiles with avatars and friends lists. In this chapter and the next, we'll add one final feature: a simple weblog, or *blog*,[1] for each of our users. Like its more full-featured cousins (such as the Rails Typo and Mephisto projects[2]), the blog engine developed in this chapter will allow users to create, manage, and publish blog posts. In Chapter 16, we'll extend the blog engine by adding comments (with a healthy dose of Ajax[3]).

We're going to build RailsSpace blogs using a development style called REST, which is a source of considerable excitement in the Rails community. REST support is new as of Rails 1.2, and it represents the cutting edge of Rails development. Since REST represents a marked break from traditional ways of structuring web applications, we begin this chapter with a general introduction to its core principles (Section 15.1).

REST deals with Big Ideas, so discussions about REST are often highly abstract; though we may get a bit theoretical at times, we'll focus on practical examples, with the goal of explaining what REST means for us as Rails programmers. As the chapter unfolds, our examples will become progressively more concrete, leading ultimately to a fully RESTful implementation of blogs and blog posts. (Chapter 16 continues the theme

---

[1] If you didn't know this already, what are you doing reading this book?

[2] `http://typosphere.org/` and `http://mephistoblog.com/`

[3] For "Asynchronous JavaScript and XML"; Jesse James Garrett coined the term in "Ajax: A New Approach to Web Applications," `http://www.adaptivepath.com/publications/essays/archives/000385.php`.

by making the blog comments RESTful as well.) As you gain more experience with the details of REST, we suggest occasionally referring back to Section 15.1 to see how the individual pieces fit into the big picture.

15.1 We deserve a REST today

REST (for Representational State Transfer) is an architectural style for developing distributed, networked systems and software applications—in particular, the World Wide Web and web applications. REST seeks to explain and elucidate how the web works, why it works as well as it does, and how it could work better. According to Roy Fielding, who first identified (and named) REST in his doctoral dissertation,[4]

> REST emphasizes scalability of component interactions, generality of interfaces, independent deployment of components, and intermediary components to reduce interaction latency, enforce security, and encapsulate legacy systems. (Fielding 2000, p. xvii)

That's pretty heady stuff. What are some of the practical implications?

In the context of web applications, REST offers a theoretical foundation for a development style that produces clean and highly structured code while providing a unified interface between applications and clients. RESTful web applications interact through the four fundamental operations supported by the hypertext transfer protocol (HTTP): POST, GET, PUT, and DELETE.[5] Furthermore, because applications based on REST principles usually strive to support both human-machine and machine-machine interactions, a REST interface typically provides data representations specialized for the type of request—for example, returning HTML to a web browser but XML to an RSS feed reader. As a result of these design principles, REST effectively enables web applications to operate together in a distributed fashion through a series of well-defined *resources*—which, in the context of the web, essentially means *URLs*. (An application designed to work with other applications in this manner is often called a *web service*.[6])

---

[4] Fielding, Roy Thomas. *Architectural Styles and the Design of Network-based Software Architectures.* Doctoral dissertation, University of California, Irvine, 2000.

[5] We've met POST and GET already in RailsSpace (Section 4.2.4), but we admit that we didn't know about PUT and DELETE until we started learning about REST—and we suspect that we're not alone.

[6] Many people feel that REST fulfills the promise of other methods (such as RPC and SOAP) designed to solve the same problem.

15.1.1 REST and CRUD

Developing a Rails application using REST principles means exploiting the natural correspondence between the HTTP methods POST, GET, PUT, DELETE and the traditional CRUD (Create, Read, Update, Delete[7]) operations of relational databases. In contrast to the traditional `controller/action/id` approach, REST embraces the radical notion that *there are only four actions*—the four CRUD operations—which, rather than being an explicit part of the URL, are implicit in the HTTP request itself. This has far-reaching implications for the structure of our applications: Thinking always in terms of CRUD operations often leads to deep insights into the data models and associated controllers (a point emphasized by Rails creator David Heinemeier Hansson in his keynote address at RailsConf 2006).

Let's consider these ideas in a more concrete setting by revisiting the Spec controller for user specifications.[8] What would user specs look like if they used the Rails implementation of REST? (Throughout this discussion, we encourage you to refer frequently to Figure 15.1; you can gain much REST wisdom from contemplation of this table.)

Since URLs play such a crucial role in REST, we'll start by taking another look at the URLs in our original, traditional spec. So far in RailsSpace, we have followed the URL construction supported by the default route, namely,

```
/controller/action/id
```

In Chapter 9, we further suggested following the natural convention of using nouns for controllers and verbs for actions. By following these conventions, we arrived at the following URL to edit the user spec:

```
/spec/edit
```

Note that here the spec id doesn't appear in the URL; it is inferred based on the user id in the session. This action actually does four different things, depending on context: invoking the action with a GET request returns a form to create or edit a spec, while hitting it with a POST request actually completes the creation or edit. As far as this URL is concerned, the only kind of requests are GET and POST.

Now imagine implementing specs using REST principles. Since the action is implicit in the HTTP method used to make the request, RESTful URLs don't have actions,

---

[7] or Destroy.

[8] Recall from Section 9.2 that user specs consist of the user's first and last name, gender, birthdate, occupation, city, state, and zip code.

DB	Responder	HTTP method	URL path	Helper function
Actions				
C	create	POST	/specs	specs_path
R	show	GET	/specs/1	spec_path(1)
U	update	PUT	/specs/1	spec_path(1)
D	destroy	DELETE	/specs/1	spec_path(1)
Modifiers				
R	index	GET	/specs	specs_path
R	new	GET	/specs/new	new_spec_path
R	edit	GET	/specs/1;edit	edit_spec_path(1)

spec_path(1) and spec_path(:id => 1) are equivalent.

Each path helper has a corresponding URL helper that returns the full URL.
For example, spec_url(1) gives http://localhost:3000/specs/1.

Figure 15.1   A hypothetical RESTful Specs resource.

but they do always require a controller. In our case, this will be the Specs controller.[9] Performing the basic CRUD operations on specs involves sending the proper HTTP requests to the Specs controller, along with the spec id for the read, update, and delete actions. To create a new spec, we send a POST request to the URL

```
/specs
```

To read (show), update, or delete the spec with id 1, we hit the URL

```
/specs/1
```

with GET, PUT, or DELETE.[10] Getting this to work involves routing the HTTP requests to the `create`, `show`, `update`, and `destroy` actions in the controller (Figure 15.1).

To handle this new routing style, the Rails implementation of REST adds a method called `map.resources` to the `map.connect` and `map.<named_route>` we've encountered previously in RailsSpace. For RESTful specs, this means that our routes file would look like this:

---

[9] Note that REST adds the convention that the controller-nouns should be *plural*.

[10] Web browsers don't actually support PUT or DELETE, so Rails fakes them using a couple of hacks. Most other programs that consume web resources understand all four HTTP methods, and we hope that in the future web browsers will, too.

Listing 15.1 config/routes.rb

```
ActionController::Routing::Routes.draw do |map|
  .
  .
  .
  # Named routes.
  map.hub 'user', :controller => 'user', :action => 'index'
  map.profile 'profile/:screen_name', :controller => 'profile', :action => 'show'

  # REST resources.
  map.resources :specs

  # Install the default route as the lowest priority.
  map.connect ':controller/:action/:id'
end
```

The next section has more details on what exactly `map.resources` buys us.

15.1.2 URL modifiers

We come now to the first minor glitch in our wonderful CRUD-filled REST universe: Though we can GET a page to show specs, we can't GET pages to create or edit them, since if we POST or PUT to a spec URL, it actually performs the action rather than returning a page. The problem here is essentially linguistic in nature. We have a small set of verbs (actions) acting on a potentially large number of nouns (controllers), but we have no way of indicating *in what context* a verb acts on a noun. In the present case, what we want is to tell Rails to GET a page to make a new spec or an edit form to update an existing one.

The solution is to add *modifiers*. To create a new spec, for example, we would GET the Specs controller with the modifier *new*:

`/specs/new`

Similarly, to show an edit form for a preexisting spec, we would GET the Specs controller with the spec id and the modifier *edit*:

`/specs/1;edit`

Since both actions and modifiers respond to HTTP requests, we'll refer to them collectively as *responders*.[11]

---

[11] As we'll see, the actual implementation follows this linguistic hint by introducing a function called `respond_to` that responds to requests.

In addition to `new` and `edit`, it's conventional to provide an `index` modifier, which in this case gives a listing of all specs.[12] Both of the following URLs work in this context

```
/specs/index
```

```
/specs
```

People usually refer to the RESTful `index` as an action, just as it's usually called an action in the context of ordinary URLs, but it isn't really. Logically, such a listing should probably be associated with a modifier such as `all`, but at this point the legacy name `index` is too deeply entrenched to be displaced.

Taken together, the standard CRUD actions and the `index`, `new`, and `edit` modifiers constitute the canonical controller methods for REST applications. For a RESTful spec, we automatically get all seven simply by putting `map.resources :specs` in the routes file (`config/routes.rb`). In addition to routing requests, `map.resources` also gives rise to a variety of URL helpers, much like named routes such as `map.hub` give helpers like `hub_url` (Section 9.5.2). A summary of the Specs resource appears in Figure 15.1.

Since some controllers require modifiers other than the defaults, Rails makes it easy to roll your own. Just define a new controller method for the modifier and tell Rails how to route it. For example, if (as RailsSpace administrators) we wanted a special administrative page for each spec, we could make an `admin` modifier as follows. First, we would add an `admin` method to the Specs controller.[13] Second, we would tell Rails how to route this request properly by adding `admin` as one of the Specs modifiers that responds to GET requests:

```
map.resources :specs, :member => { :admin => :get }
```

Rails automatically gives us helpers to generate the proper URLs, so that

```
admin_spec_path(1)
```

would give

```
/specs/1;admin
```

15.1.3 An elephant;in the room

So far we've managed to walk around the elephant in the room, but now we have to acknowledge its presence: Some of the RESTful URLs contain a semicolon! A semicolon

---

[12] It wouldn't make much sense to expose this to RailsSpace end-users, but in principle such a list might be useful for some sort of administrative back-end.

[13] We'll see what such responder methods look like starting in Section 15.2.3.

is indeed a rather odd character for a URL, but it (or something like it) is necessary to separate the id and the modifier in the URL. At first it might seem like we could just use a slash separator, leading to URLs of the form

```
/specs/1/edit
```

Unfortunately, this would lead to an essential ambiguity by making it impossible to *nest* RESTful resources. For example, we'll see that RESTful RailsSpace blogs will have RESTful posts, leading to URLs of the form

```
/blogs/1/posts
```

If we were to define both a Posts controller *and* a `posts` modifier, there would be no way to tell whether the word `posts` in this URL referred to the controller or to the modifier. Of course, we could only introduce such an ambiguity through sheer stupidity, but we can avoid even the possibility of a clash by using a distinct separator; the Rails designers opted for a semicolon.[14] We admit that this notation is a little funky, and seeing semicolons in URLs takes some getting used to, but we've gotten used to it, and so will you.

As mysterious as the URL semicolons might appear, there is an underlying linguistic reason for their existence: Modifiers are usually *adjectives*, which describe some aspect of a resource (such as a *new* spec or an *edit* form[15]). We can think of some cases where a verb modifier makes more sense—a `cancel` modifier, for example, to cancel an edit form—but there is great conceptual power in maintaining the distinction between adjective modifiers, noun controllers, and verb actions. As argued above, some (nonslash) separator is needed to preserve this distinction in URLs.

Since REST works best when the HTTP methods are the only verbs, defining verb modifiers is often a hint that we should introduce another controller and then use a CRUD action. For instance, if we wanted to allow RailsSpace users to tag the specs of their favorite users, we might be tempted to use a `tag` modifier as if it were an action, so that

```
/specs/1;tag
```

would respond to a PUT request and update the spec with a tag. But look at it another way: Fundamentally, we are *creating* a tag and associating it with a particular spec; the

---

[14] Frameworks differ on this point; for example, the REST support in *Struts* (a Java framework whose name Rails parodies) uses an exclamation point for the same purpose.

[15] Of course, "edit" is also a verb, but in this context it's an adjective.

underlying operation is *create*, which is part of CRUD. This means that we could define a Tags controller (and presumably a Tag model) and then POST to the URL

```
/specs/1/tags
```

to create a tag for spec 1.

We've heard that some people, when they first see the REST implementation in Rails, think that it's sub-moronic, since it seems to trade perfectly sensible URLs of the form

```
/controller/action/id
```

for the seemingly idiotic (and excessively semicoloned)

```
/controller/id;action
```

We agree that this would be crazy if true, but we now know that RESTful URLs don't *have* actions, and (ideally) their modifiers are adjectives, not verbs. The actual prototype for a typical RESTful URL is thus

```
/controller/id;modifier
```

with an implicit (HTTP method) action. It turns out that Rails isn't a sub-moron—it's a super-genius!

15.1.4 Responding to formats and a free API

As noted briefly at the beginning of this section, one aspect of REST involves responding to different requests with different formats, depending on the format expected by the request. In Rails we can accomplish this with a trivial addition to the URL, namely, the filename extension,[16] so that GETting the URL

```
/specs/1.xml
```

would return XML instead of HTML. Using the Rails REST support, we can return other formats as well so that, for example, we could arrange for

```
/specs/1.yml
```

to respond with a YAML version of the spec.

Although we have yet to see the guts of an actual RESTful implementation, just based on the parts of the application exposed to the user—that is, the URLs—we already have a good idea of how the application must behave. The alert reader might notice that this is practically the definition of an Application Programming Interface (API), and

---

[16] More advanced users should note that we can accomplish the same thing by modifying the `Accept` header of the request; for example, setting `Accept` to `text/xml` would cause Rails to return XML.

indeed we can effectively expose an API for our application simply by publishing a list of controllers and modifiers. Moreover, by having a single resource respond differently based on the type of format requested, a REST API can automatically interoperate with applications that understand HTML, XML, or any other format we care to support.

In short, because REST puts such sharp constraints on our URLs—no actions, explicit ids, filename extensions for different formats, and a consistent and structured way to add modifiers—RESTful applications effectively come equipped with a free API.

15.2   Scaffolds for a RESTful blog

In this section we build on the ideas from the simple (and hypothetical) Specs resource to make the more complicated (and real) Blogs and Posts resources. We'll use Rails scaffolding to get us started, and the resulting Posts controller will finally give us a chance to peek behind the REST curtain. Despite the scaffolding head start, bringing the RESTful blog to full fruition will have to wait for the changes made in Section 15.3. Nevertheless, by the end of this section we'll have a good idea of how the different REST pieces fit together.

15.2.1   The first RESTful resource

Our first step will be to generate a resource for blogs. By itself, the Blogs resource won't actually give us much—since each RailsSpace user will have only one blog, we don't plan to update or delete them. Our real goal is the RESTful posts living inside these blogs, but to have fully RESTful URLs this means that blogs have to be RESTful, too.

Based on the scripts used to generate models and controllers, you can probably guess the script to generate a resource:

```
> script/generate resource Blog
     exists  app/models/
     exists  app/controllers/
     exists  app/helpers/
     create  app/views/blogs
     exists  test/functional/
     exists  test/unit/
     create  app/models/blog.rb
     create  app/controllers/blogs_controller.rb
     create  test/functional/blogs_controller_test.rb
     create  app/helpers/blogs_helper.rb
     create  test/unit/blog_test.rb
     create  test/fixtures/blogs.yml
     exists  db/migrate
```

```
create  db/migrate/008_create_blogs.rb
 route  map.resources :blogs
```

This did a ton of work for us by generating both a model and a controller, even using the proper REST-style plural `blogs_controller.rb`.[17] We've seen these before, though, in the context of model and controller generations. The only completely novel effect of generating a resource appears in the final line, which tells us that `generate` added a route to the top of the `routes.rb` file:

Listing 15.2 config/routes.rb

```
ActionController::Routing::Routes.draw do |map|
  map.resources :blogs
  .
  .
  .
```

As mentioned briefly in Section 15.1, REST adds the `resources` aspect of `map` to go along with `connect` and named routes such as `map.hub`. The `map.resources` line doesn't yet do us much good, since it's there mainly as a prerequisite to RESTful post URLs; we'll explain `map.resources` more thoroughly once we make the Posts resource in Section 15.2.2.

Before moving on, we should take care of the Blog model, which corresponds to a simple table whose sole job is to associate users with blogs:

Listing 15.3 db/migrate/008_create_blogs.rb

```
class CreateBlogs < ActiveRecord::Migration
  def self.up
    create_table :blogs do |t|
      t.column :user_id, :integer
    end
  end

  def self.down
    drop_table :blogs
  end
end
```

---

[17] In the present case, the Blogs controller needs no contents, and we will leave it effectively blank—the default content is all we'll ever need. In fact, we actually don't need even that—since we never use CRUD operations on blogs, we could remove the Blogs controller and never notice the difference!

We also need to tie the User model and the Blog model together. Their relationship is the same one we saw in the context of the spec and the FAQ—a user `has_one` blog and a blog `belongs_to` a user:

Listing 15.4 app/models/user.rb

```
class User < ActiveRecord::Base
  has_one :spec
  has_one :faq
  has_one :blog
  .
  .
  .
```

and

Listing 15.5 app/models/blog.rb

```
class Blog < ActiveRecord::Base
  belongs_to :user
end
```

15.2.2 Blog posts

Now we come to the heart of the RESTful blog, a resource for blog posts. Though we won't get there until Section 15.3, a summary of our eventual goal appears in Figure 15.2. It is well worth meditating on.

We'll start by generating a *scaffold resource*, which is like `generate resource` but also gives us rudimentary views and a nearly complete controller. We have avoided scaffolding so far in RailsSpace, but we think it makes a lot of sense in the context of REST (see the sidebar "Rails scaffolding").

Rails scaffolding

Scaffolding, mentioned briefly in Chapter 1, is code generated by Rails for the purposes of interacting with data models, principally through the basic CRUD operations. Some introductions to Rails use scaffolding from the start, but we've avoided scaffolding so far in RailsSpace primarily for two reasons. First, scaffolding can become a crutch, making programmers dependent on autogenerated code. Scaffolding is thus a potential impediment to learning. Second, we find the code generated by the default

DB	Responder	HTTP method	URL path	Helper function
	Actions			
C	create	POST	/blogs/1/posts	posts_path(1)
R	show	GET	/blogs/1/posts/99	post_path(1, 99)
U	update	PUT	/blogs/1/posts/99	post_path(1, 99)
D	destroy	DELETE	/blogs/1/posts/99	post_path(1, 99)
	Modifiers			
R	index	GET	/blogs/1/posts	posts_path(1)
R	new	GET	/blogs/1/posts/new	new_post_path(1)
R	edit	GET	/blogs/1/posts/99;edit	edit_post_path(1, 99)

post_path(1, 99) and post_path(:blog_id => 1, :id => 99) are equivalent.

Inside /blogs/1, the blog id can be omitted in the helper.

In this case, post_path and post_path(:id => 99) (but *not* post_path(99)) all work.

Each path helper has a corresponding URL helper that returns the full URL.

For example, post_url(1, 99) gives http://localhost:3000/blogs/1/posts/99.

Figure 15.2   Nested resources for RESTful blog posts.

scaffold command somewhat cumbersome; it provides a questionable example of Rails programming style. Unfortunately, in a scaffold-first approach it's the first code you see.

Fortunately, RESTful scaffolding code is actually quite nice for the most part.[18] This is mainly because the principal goal of scaffolds—namely, CRUD—maps so nicely to the underlying abstractions of REST. Since it's clean and convenient, and since at this point you're in no danger of becoming overly reliant on generated code, we've elected to use scaffolding in our discussion of REST.

The command to generate REST scaffolding is similar to the command to generate a REST resource, with scaffold_resource in place of resource. To make the scaffolding maximally useful, we'll include the Post data model on the command line (as we did with the Friendship model in Section 14.1.2):

```
> ruby script/generate scaffold_resource Post blog_id:integer title:string \
      body:text created_at:datetime updated_at:datetime
      exists  app/models/
      exists  app/controllers/
```

---

[18] We still don't like the views.

```
exists  app/helpers/
create  app/views/posts
exists  test/functional/
exists  test/unit/
create  app/views/posts/index.rhtml
create  app/views/posts/show.rhtml
create  app/views/posts/new.rhtml
create  app/views/posts/edit.rhtml
create  app/views/layouts/posts.rhtml
create  public/stylesheets/scaffold.css
create  app/models/post.rb
create  app/controllers/posts_controller.rb
create  test/functional/posts_controller_test.rb
create  app/helpers/posts_helper.rb
create  test/unit/post_test.rb
create  test/fixtures/posts.yml
exists  db/migrate
create  db/migrate/009_create_posts.rb
 route  map.resources :posts
```

In the last line we have a second example of a change to the routes file. By default, the generator simply puts the `map.resources` line at the top of `routes.rb`, which gives us this:

Listing 15.6 config/routes.rb

```
ActionController::Routing::Routes.draw do |map|
  map.resources :posts

  map.resources :blogs
  .
  .
  .
```

If posts lived by themselves, this default routing would be fine, but we want posts to live inside blogs. We'll see how to tell this to Rails in Section 15.3.2.

Because of the command-line arguments to `scaffold_resource`, the Post model migration is ready to go:

Listing 15.7 db/migrate/009_create_posts.rb

```
class CreatePosts < ActiveRecord::Migration
  def self.up
    create_table :posts do |t|
      t.column :blog_id, :integer
```

Continues

```
      t.column :title, :string
      t.column :body, :text
      t.column :created_at, :datetime
      t.column :updated_at, :datetime
    end
  end

  def self.down
    drop_table :posts
  end
end
```

Note that we've included a `blog_id` in anticipation of connecting posts to blogs (Section 15.3.1).

All we need to do now is migrate, which (since we haven't migrated since generating the Blogs resource) creates both the `blogs` and `posts` tables:

```
> rake db:migrate
(in /rails/rs_svn)
== CreateBlogs: migrating ============================================
-- create_table(:blogs)
   -> 0.0678s
== CreateBlogs: migrated (0.0681s) ===================================

== CreatePosts: migrating ============================================
-- create_table(:posts)
   -> 0.1386s
== CreatePosts: migrated (0.1389s) ===================================
```

15.2.3 The Posts controller

The actual machinery for handling routed requests lives in the Posts controller, which, thanks to `scaffold_resource`, is already chock full of actions and modifiers. It's important to emphasize that these are the *defaults*, suitable for manipulating a model with the default resources. Since it doesn't take into account the relationship between blogs and posts, this scaffolding won't work out of the box. It's still instructive, though, so let's take a look at it before we modify it for use on RailsSpace.

Inside the Posts controller, the `create`, `show`, `update`, and `destroy` actions correspond to the create, read, update, and delete operations of CRUD, while the `index`, `new`, and `edit` modifiers respond to GET requests with pages for listing posts, creating new ones, and editing existing ones. (It's sometimes hard to keep track of all the different REST responders; we find Figure 15.2 invaluable for this purpose.) Let's take a look at it:

Listing 15.8 app/controllers/posts_controller.rb

```ruby
class PostsController < ApplicationController
  # GET /posts
  # GET /posts.xml
  def index
    @posts = Post.find(:all)

    respond_to do |format|
      format.html # index.rhtml
      format.xml  { render :xml => @posts.to_xml }
    end
  end

  # GET /posts/1
  # GET /posts/1.xml
  def show
    @post = Post.find(params[:id])

    respond_to do |format|
      format.html # show.rhtml
      format.xml  { render :xml => @post.to_xml }
    end
  end

  # GET /posts/new
  def new
    @post = Post.new
  end

  # GET /posts/1;edit
  def edit
    @post = Post.find(params[:id])
  end

  # POST /posts
  # POST /posts.xml
  def create
    @post = Post.new(params[:post])

    respond_to do |format|
      if @post.save
        flash[:notice] = 'Post was successfully created.'
        format.html { redirect_to post_url(@post) }
        format.xml  { head :created, :location => post_url(@post) }
      else
        format.html { render :action => "new" }
        format.xml  { render :xml => @post.errors.to_xml }
```

Continues

```
      end
    end
  end

  # PUT /posts/1
  # PUT /posts/1.xml
  def update
    @post = Post.find(params[:id])

    respond_to do |format|
      if @post.update_attributes(params[:post])
        flash[:notice] = 'Post was successfully updated.'
        format.html { redirect_to post_url(@post) }
        format.xml  { head :ok }
      else
        format.html { render :action => "edit" }
        format.xml  { render :xml => @post.errors.to_xml }
      end
    end
  end

  # DELETE /posts/1
  # DELETE /posts/1.xml
  def destroy
    @post = Post.find(params[:id])
    @post.destroy

    respond_to do |format|
      format.html { redirect_to posts_url }
      format.xml  { head :ok }
    end
  end
end
```

There are some predictable elements here, including familiar Active Record CRUD methods like save, update_attributes, and destroy, together with the flash[:notice] and redirects we've come to know and love. There is one completely novel element, though: the respond_to function.

Together with map.resources, respond_to is the heart of REST: It is respond_to that allows URLs to respond differently to different formats. respond_to takes a block argument, and the block variable (typically called format or wants) then calls methods corresponding to the different formats understood by the responder. If you find yourself a bit confused by respond_to, you're in good company—it is kind of strange, especially because it appears to respond to all requested formats at once. This is not the case, though; for any particular request, only *one* format gets invoked. The lines inside of the `respond_to` block are not executed sequentially, but rather act more like a `case` statement, such as

```
case format
when 'html': # return html
when 'xml':  # return xml
end
```

For our purposes, the most useful line inside each `respond_to` is `format.html`, which by default renders the rhtml template with the same name as the responder. For example, in the `show` action, `format.html` returns the HTML rendered by `show.rhtml`, as indicated by the comment:

```
# GET /posts
# GET /posts.xml
def show
  @post = Post.find(params[:id])

  respond_to do |format|
    format.html # show.rhtml
    format.xml  { render :xml => @post.to_xml }
  end
end
```

Of course, the whole point is to respond to multiple formats, and the second line in the `respond_to` block demonstrates how `show` responds to XML—in this case, rendering the post using the `to_xml` method (which returns a sensible XML string for Active Record objects). We won't be doing anything with the XML response in this book, but by including it we allow other people to use it. For example, since XML is a widely understood machine-readable format, the XML response might be useful to a program seeking to categorize and search blog posts.

In cases where the action needs do something other than render the default template, we simply call `format.html` with a block containing `render` or `redirect_to`. For example, after a successful edit we redirect to the post URL, and after an unsuccessful edit we render the edit form again (presumably with Active Record error messages):[19]

```
# PUT /posts/1
# PUT /posts/1.xml
def update
  @post = Post.find(params[:id])

  respond_to do |format|
    if @post.update_attributes(params[:post])
```

---

[19] Though `edit` is really a modifier, not an action, the Rails internals don't distinguish between the two. We therefore have to use `render :action => "edit"` to render the edit form.

```
      flash[:notice] = 'Post was successfully updated.'
      format.html { redirect_to post_url(@post) }
      format.xml  { head :ok }
    else
      format.html { render :action => "edit" }
      .
      .
      .
```

Here we should note that the call to `post_url(@post)` is the default generated by the scaffolding command, but it won't work in our case since posts are nested inside blogs. We'll see in Section 15.3.3 how to do it for real.

15.3   Building the real blog

Rails scaffolding got us thinking about the REST interface, but so far nothing actually works. It's time to change that by tying blogs and posts together, editing the Posts controller, cleaning up the views, and integrating the blog management machinery into the RailsSpace site. We'll take particular care to establish the proper authorization for the various CRUD actions, as the scaffold-generated code allows any user to edit any other user's blog and posts.

15.3.1   Connecting the models

We'll begin building the working blog by defining the relationship between the Blog model and the Post model. We've laid the foundation for this by including a `blog_id` attribute in the Post model (Section 15.2.2), thus making it easy to tell Rails that a post `belongs_to` a blog:

Listing 15.9   models/post.rb

```
class Post < ActiveRecord::Base
  belongs_to :blog

  validates_presence_of :title, :body, :blog
  validates_length_of :title, :maximum => DB_STRING_MAX_LENGTH
  validates_length_of :body,  :maximum => DB_TEXT_MAX_LENGTH
end
```

While we were at it, we added some basic validations as well.

All we have left is to indicate how blogs are related to posts. Since each blog potentially has many posts, we use the `has_many` database association that we first saw in the context of user friendships in Section 14.3.1:

Listing 15.10 app/models/blog.rb

```
class Blog < ActiveRecord::Base
  belongs_to :user
  has_many :posts, :order => "created_at DESC"
end
```

Since blogs (practically by definition) return posts in reverse chronological order, we've used the :order option to tell Active Record that the order of the posts should be "created_at DESC", where DESC is the SQL keyword for "descending" (which means in this case "most recent first").

Recall from Section 14.3.1 that has_many :friendships in the User model gave us an array of friendships through

```
user.friendships
```

In that section, we used this array only indirectly (with the real work being done by has_many :through), but in this case we will have much use for a list of blog posts. Because of the has_many :posts declaration, when we have a Blog object called blog we get precisely such a list using

```
blog.posts
```

Because of the :order option to has_many in the Blog model, these posts automatically come out in the right order.

15.3.2 Blog and post routing

Having tied blogs and posts together at the database level, we now need to link them at the routing level as well. To tell Rails routes that posts belong to blogs, we *nest* the resources, like so:

Listing 15.11 config/routes.rb

```
ActionController::Routing::Routes.draw do |map|
  map.resources :blogs do |blog|
    blog.resources :posts
  end
  .
  .
  .
```

This is the code that makes possible the URLs and helpers shown in Figure 15.2, such as

```
/blogs/1/posts/99
```

With the routing rules defined above, this URL gets associated with the post with id
99 inside of blog 1. (It's important to realize that this is *not* the 99th post in blog 1;
rather, it's the 99th post *overall*, which in this example happens to belong to blog 1.)
This routing also arranges for the proper correspondence between HTTP methods and
CRUD operations. For example, the nested resources ensure that a POST request to

`/blogs/1/posts`

gets routed to the `create` method inside the Posts controller.

15.3.3 Posts controller, for real

Now that we have arranged for the proper routing of requests, we need to update the controller to respond appropriately. Amazingly, we barely need to change the default Posts
controller (Section 15.2.3); in fact, there are only six changes (and the last two are trivial):

1. **Protect the blog and make @blog.** Add a private `protect_blog` function, and
   invoke `protect` and `protect_blog` in a before filter (creating `@blog` as a side
   effect)

2. **List only the posts for one user, and paginate them.** In `index`, change

   ```
   @post = Post.find(:all)
   ```

   to

   ```
   @pages, @posts = paginate(@blog.posts)
   ```

3. **Create a new post by appending it to the current list of posts.** In `create`, change

   ```
   @post.save
   ```

   to

   ```
   @blog.posts << @post
   ```

4. **Fix the arguments to the post URL helpers.** Globally replace `post_url(@post)`
   with `post_url(:id => @post)`

5. **Add the profile helper.** Put `helper :profile` at the top of the Posts controller
   so that we can use `hide_edit_links?` when displaying posts

6. **Add @title to responders that render templates.**[20]

With these changes, the final Posts controller appears as follows (compare to the
scaffold version from Section 15.2.3):

---

[20] This involves rendering a little unescaped HTML. If you're really paranoid, you can add a call to `h`, the
HTML escape function, in the title section of `application.rhtml`.

```
class PostsController < ApplicationController
  helper :profile
  before_filter :protect, :protect_blog

  # GET /posts
  # GET /posts.xml
  def index
    @pages, @posts = paginate(@blog.posts)
    @title = "Blog Management"

    respond_to do |format|
      format.html # index.rhtml
      format.xml  { render :xml => @posts.to_xml }
    end
  end

  # GET /posts/1
  # GET /posts/1.xml
  def show
    @post = Post.find(params[:id])
    @title = @post.title

    respond_to do |format|
      format.html # show.rhtml
      format.xml  { render :xml => @post.to_xml }
    end
  end

  # GET /posts/new
  def new
    @post = Post.new
    @title = "Add a new post"
  end

  # GET /posts/1;edit
  def edit
    @post = Post.find(params[:id])
    @title = "Edit #{@post.title}"
  end

  # POST /posts
  # POST /posts.xml
  def create
    @post = Post.new(params[:post])

    respond_to do |format|
      if @blog.posts << @post
        flash[:notice] = 'Post was successfully created.'
        format.html { redirect_to post_url(:id => @post) }
```

```ruby
      format.xml  { head :created, :location => post_url(:id => @post) }
    else
      format.html { render :action => "new" }
      format.xml  { render :xml => @post.errors.to_xml }
    end
  end
end


# PUT /posts/1
# PUT /posts/1.xml
def update
  @post = Post.find(params[:id])

  respond_to do |format|
    if @post.update_attributes(params[:post])
      flash[:notice] = 'Post was successfully updated.'
      format.html { redirect_to post_url(:id => @post) }
      format.xml  { head :ok }
    else
      format.html { render :action => "edit" }
      format.xml  { render :xml => @post.errors.to_xml }
    end
  end
end

# DELETE /posts/1
# DELETE /posts/1.xml
def destroy
  @post = Post.find(params[:id])
  @post.destroy

  respond_to do |format|
    format.html { redirect_to posts_url }
    format.xml  { head :ok }
  end
end

private

# Ensure that user is blog owner, and create @blog.
def protect_blog
  @blog = Blog.find(params[:blog_id])
  user = User.find(session[:user_id])
  unless @blog.user == user
    flash[:notice] = "That isn't your blog!"
    redirect_to hub_url
    return false
  end
end
end
```

It's worth noting that the RESTful blog id is available as `params[:blog_id]`, which we use to find `@blog` in the `protect_blog` function. Also note that we write `post_url(:id => @post)` instead of `post_url(:id => @post.id)`; the two give the same result, but it is a common Rails idiom to omit `.id` in cases like this, since Rails can figure out from context that we want the post id and not the whole post. (We saw a similar shortcut in Section 14.1.3 when creating Friendship objects.)

The most novel feature in the Posts controller appears in the `create` action, where we use the array append operator to push a new post onto the current list of blog posts:[21]

```
@blog.posts << @post
```

In this case, `@blog.posts` is not exactly an array—among other things, it interacts with the database in a way that no plain array could—but the "append" operation really does everything that implies: It appends `@post` to the end of `@blog.posts` *and* adds a row to the `posts` table in the database corresponding to the given blog (i.e., with `blog_id` equal to `@blog.id`).[22]

We've replaced the default `find` in the `index` modifier—which finds blog posts for *all* users—with `@blog.posts`, which consists only of the posts owned by the logged-in user (and, thanks to the `:order` option in the Blog model, they're in the right order to boot). Since `@blog.posts` quacks like an array, we can use the `paginate` function from Section 11.1.4 to split the blog posts into pages. We'll put these paginated posts to good use on the blog management page in the next section.

15.3.4   Blog management

Having completed the responders in the Posts controller, all we need to do now is make the necessary views. We'll start with the `index` view, which we'll use as a blog management page. As a first step, let's put a link to the posts `index` on the user hub using the `posts_path` helper (Figure 15.2):

---

[21] Recall from Section 15.3.1 that the existence of `@blog.posts` is a consequence of the `has_many :posts` declaration in the Blog model.

[22] This design principle, where an object's "type" is determined by its behavior with respect to certain operations—such as `@blog.posts` acting like an array—is known to Rubyists as "duck typing," a term presumably derived from the aphorism that if something looks like a duck, walks like a duck, and quacks like a duck, then it's probably a duck.

Listing 15.12 app/views/user/index.rhtml

```
.
.
.
Friends:
<%= render :partial => "friendship/friends" %>
<hr noshade />
Blog:
<span class="edit_link">
  <%= link_to "(manage)", posts_path(@blog) %>
</span>
</div>
```

This requires an `@blog` variable in the User controller index to go along with the spec and FAQ:

Listing 15.13 app/controllers/user_controller.rb

```
def index
  .
  .
  .
  @spec = @user.spec ||= Spec.new
  @faq = @user.faq ||= Faq.new
  @blog = @user.blog ||= Blog.new
end
```

The blog management page itself is simple. We start with a link to create a new post, which uses the `new_post_path` helper created by the nested resources in `routes.rb` (Figure 15.2). We then include pagination links (if necessary) and the posts themselves:

Listing 15.14 app/views/posts/index.rhtml

```
<h2>Your Blog Posts</h2>
<p class="edit_link">
  <%= link_to 'Add a new post', new_post_path %>
  <%= "| Pages: #{pagination_links(@pages)}" if paginated? %>
</p>
<%= render :partial => "post", :collection => @posts %>
```

Here we've reused the `paginated?` function defined in Section 10.4.1. The final line renders a collection of posts using the post partial. Of course, the post partial doesn't

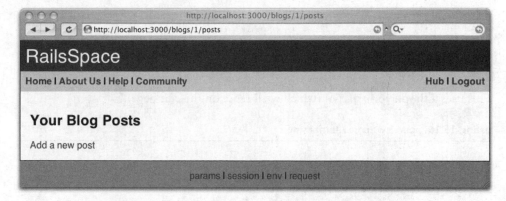

Figure 15.3   Blog post management using the posts index page.

exist yet, but there aren't any posts yet either so it won't be invoked. After we define the post partial in Section 15.3.6, the management page will automatically start working.

By the way, Rails tried to help us by creating a `posts.rhtml` layout file along with the rest of the scaffolding, but it's rather ugly. We'll remove it so that the management pages will use the layout in `application.rhtml` like everything else:

```
> rm app/views/layouts/posts.rhtml
```

This leads us to the spartan yet functional blog post management index page, as shown in Figure 15.3.

15.3.5   Creating posts

Now that we can manage posts, it's probably a good idea to be able to create them. The target of the "Add a new post" link on the blog management page is a URL of the form

```
/blogs/1/posts/new
```

This means that we need to edit the file `new.rhtml` to make a form suitable for creating new posts:

Listing 15.15   app/views/posts/new.rhtml

```
<h2><%= link_to 'Your Blog Posts', posts_path %>: Add a new post</h2>

<% form_for(:post, :url => posts_path) do |form| %>
<fieldset>
  <legend>Blog Post Details</legend>
```

Continues

```
  <%= render :partial => "form", :locals => { :form => form } %>
  <%= submit_tag "Create", :class => "submit" %>
</fieldset>
<% end %>
```

This uses a simple form partial (which we'll reuse on the edit page):[23]

Listing 15.16 app/views/posts/_form.rhtml

```
<%= error_messages_for :post %>

<%= text_field_for form, "title", 60 %>
<div class="form_row">
  <label for="body">Body:</label>
  <%= form.text_area :body, :rows => 20, :cols => 60 %>
</div>
```

We can get to the post creation page by clicking on the "Create a new post" link on the management page, which gives us Figure 15.4. The simple act of clicking on a link might seem trivial, but let's analyze it from a REST perspective. According to Figure 15.2, issuing a GET request to the URL

```
/blogs/1/posts/new
```

yields a page suitable for creating a new post. Since GET is the default HTTP method when following a link, this is precisely the page we get by clicking on "New post."

Now look at the target URL of the form itself. Since the new template uses the helper posts_path to make this URL, the target looks something like

```
/blogs/1/posts
```

If we were to click on a link to this URL (such as the "Manage blog" link on the user hub), the resulting GET request would return the posts index. But the default HTTP method for a form is POST, so clicking on the "create" button issues a POST request to the target URL. According to Figure 15.2, this request gets routed to the create action in the Posts controller, thereby creating the post as required.[24]

---

[23] Elsewhere on RailsSpace, we've always used a string as the argument to error_messages_for, but the scaffolding uses a symbol in this context. This is one of the many cases where either one works fine (as discussed in Section 6.4.2).

[24] Sorry for all the Post post POST verbiage. It's not our fault that the HTTP spec and blogs both use the same word.

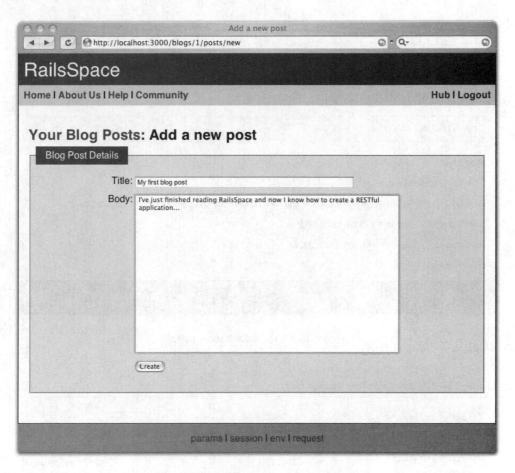

Figure 15.4 The blog post creation page.

Thanks to our efforts in Section 15.3.3, the `create` action is ready to go, so the resulting post creation page is already live on the back-end. Because we generated scaffolding for the Posts resource, the form even works: Upon entering a title and some text and clicking "Create," our new post gets rendered by the `show` scaffold (Figure 15.5).

15.3.6 Showing posts

The scaffold `show` view is better than nothing, but it's certainly not sufficient for use on RailsSpace. Let's fix it up, and in the process define the post partial. We'll start by defining some simple CSS style rules (which we put inside `profile.css` since we think of blogs as part of user profiles):

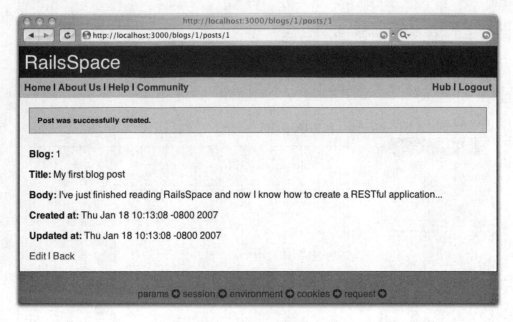

Figure 15.5   The default show page.

Listing 15.17   public/stylesheets/profile.css

```
/* Blog Styles */

.post {
  display: block;
  margin-bottom: 1.5em;
}
.post_title {
  font-weight: bold;
}
.post_body {
  padding: 1em;
}
.post_creation_date, .post_modification_date {
  text-align: right;
}
.post_actions {
  float: right;
}
```

We next replace the scaffolding page with a customized version:

Listing 15.18 app/views/posts/show.rhtml

```
<h2> <%= link_to 'Your Blog Posts', posts_path %>:
Show One Post</h2>

<%= render :partial => "post" %>
```

This renders the post partial:

Listing 15.19 app/views/posts/_post.rhtml

```
<div class="post">
  <div class="post_title">
    <%= sanitize post.title  %>
    <% unless hide_edit_links? %>
      <span style="float:right">
      <%= link_to_unless_current 'Show', post_path(post.blog, post) %> |
      <%= link_to_unless_current 'Edit', edit_post_path(post.blog, post) %> |
      <%= link_to 'Destroy', post_path(post.blog, post),
                  :confirm => 'Are you sure?', :method => :delete %>
      </span>
    <% end %>
  </div>
  <div class="post_body"><%= sanitize post.body %></div>
  <div class="post_creation_date">
    Posted <%= time_ago_in_words post.created_at %> ago
    <% if post.updated_at != post.created_at %>
      <br /> Modified <%= time_ago_in_words post.updated_at %> ago
    <% end %>
  </div>
</div>
```

Here we have used `time_ago_in_words` helper, which converts a Time object to a verbal description such as "about one hour ago," as well as the `sanitize` function from Section 9.5. The result (for a relatively new post) appears in Figure 15.6. Now that the post partial has been defined, the blog management page from Section 15.3.4 works as well (Figure 15.7).

Note that the post partial includes a link to the `destroy` action for the post. So far, we've only hit our RESTful URLs with GET requests (through normal links) and POST requests (through form submission), but according to the principles of REST, we should issue an HTTP DELETE request to destroy a resource. If you look closely at the link to "Destroy," you'll see that we pass `link_to` the option

```
:method => :delete
```

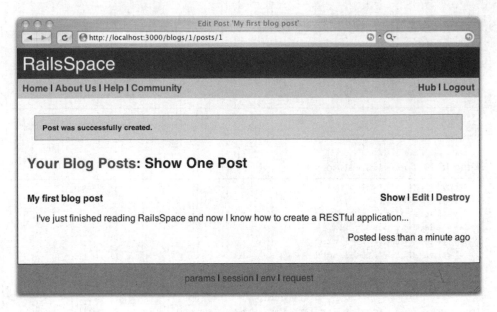

Figure 15.6   Styled show page.

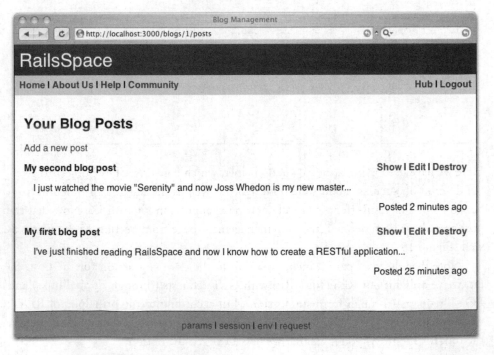

Figure 15.7   Index page with a couple of blog entries added.

This overrides the default GET method, simulating[25] a DELETE request instead, so that clicking on the link destroys the corresponding post.

15.3.7   Editing posts

We can now create, show (read), and delete blog posts, which gives us CRD. To fill in the U, we'll finish by making the post edit page. Because of our efforts on the post creation page, constructing an edit view is simple, apart from one subtlety:

Listing 15.20 app/views/posts/edit.rhtml

```
<h2><%= link_to 'Your Blog Posts', posts_path %>: Edit Post</h2>

<%= render :partial => "post" %>

<% form_for(:post, :url => post_path(:id => @post),
                   :html => { :method => :put }) do |form| %>
<fieldset>
  <legend>Edit Post</legend>
  <%= render :partial => "form", :locals => { :form => form } %>
  <%= submit_tag "Update", :class => "submit" %>
</fieldset>
<% end %>
```

The resulting page (Figure 15.8) is essentially identical to the creation page, but it's worth noting the first appearance of the funky semicolon syntax for the `edit` modifier.

The subtlety alluded to above is the line

```
:html => { :method => :put }
```

This ensures that the form submits using the PUT method instead of the usual POST.[26] In keeping with the correspondence between HTTP methods and CRUD operations, the resulting PUT request gets routed to the `update` action in the Posts controller. Since that action has already been defined—it is, in fact, the default scaffold action—the edit page is good to go. This means that we're done—our RESTful blog is now full of CRUD!

---

[25] As noted briefly in Section 15.1.1, web browsers don't currently support DELETE. Exactly how Rails arranges to simulate DELETE isn't particularly important, though we should mention that it won't work if the user has JavaScript disabled in his browser. If you need to support JavaScript-disabled browsers, you can use a form with the option `:method => :delete`; see Section 15.3.7 for more information.

[26] As noted in Section 15.1.1, browsers don't actually support PUT; Rails fakes it with a hidden input form field. Forms can also send DELETE requests—just replace `:put` with `:delete`. This technique would replace the user-friendly destroy links with more obtrusive destroy buttons, but it has the virtue of working even when JavaScript is disabled.

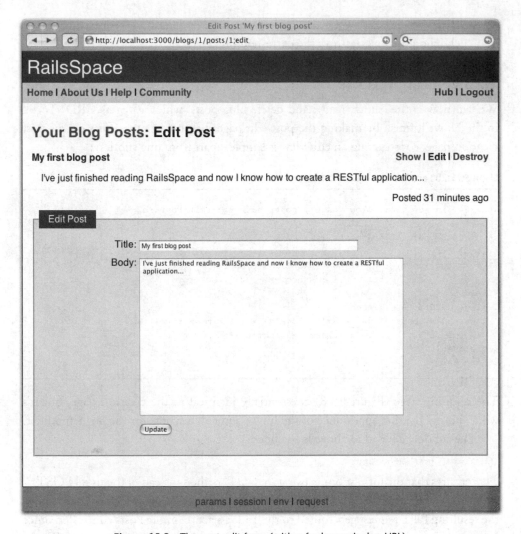

Figure 15.8   The post edit form (with a funky semicolon URL).

15.3.8 Publishing posts

Having a blog doesn't do anyone much good if it never gets published, so to wrap things up we'll put the blog posts on the user profile and the hub. To do this, we need to add @blog instance variables and paginated posts to both the Profile controller's show action and the User controller's index action. Doing this in both places results in uncomfortably redundant code, so we have factored all the shared variable assignments into a common method in the Application controller:

Listing 15.21 app/controllers/application.rb

```
    .
    .
    .
def make_profile_vars
  @spec = @user.spec ||= Spec.new
  @faq = @user.faq ||= Faq.new
  @blog = @user.blog ||= Blog.new
  @pages, @posts = paginate(@blog.posts, :per_page => 3)
end
    .
    .
    .
```

(We've restricted the number of posts per page to 3 since the default of 10 is a bit too many posts for our taste.) A call to `make_profile_vars` then gets added in both places:

Listing 15.22 app/controllers/profile_controller.rb

```
def show
  @hide_edit_links = true
  screen_name = params[:screen_name]
  @user = User.find_by_screen_name(screen_name)
  if @user
    .
    .
    .
    make_profile_vars
  else
    .
    .
    .
  end
end
```

and

Listing 15.23 app/controllers/user_controller.rb

```
def index
  @title = "RailsSpace User Hub"
  @user = User.find(session[:user_id])
  make_profile_vars
end
```

Now that we have the pages of posts stored as instance variables, displaying the blog is a piece of cake since we already have a post partial. There's a little bit of presentation logic to make the language come out right, but otherwise this blog partial is closely related to the display partials from Chapters 10 and 11:

Listing 15.24   app/views/profile/_blog.rhtml

```
<div id="blog">
  <p>
  <% if paginated? %>
    <% first = @pages.current_page.first_item %>
    <% last  = @pages.current_page.last_item %>
    <% if first == last %>
      Post <%= last %> of
    <% else %>
      Posts <%= first %>&ndash;<%= last %> of
    <% end %>
  <% end %>
  <%= pluralize(@blog.posts.count, "blog post") %>
  </p>

  <%= render :partial => "posts/post", :collection => @posts %>
  <%= "Pages: #{pagination_links(@pages)}" if paginated? %>
</div>
```

The embedded Ruby will produce sensible results such as "0 blog posts," "Posts 4–6 of 7 blog posts," and "Post 7 of 7 blog posts" as the number of posts grows.

To complete the blog display, we simply render the blog partial on the profile and the hub:

Listing 15.25   app/views/profile/show.rhtml

```
  .
  .
  .
  Friends:
  <%= render :partial => "friendship/friends" %>
  <% unless @blog.posts.empty? %>
    <hr noshade />
    Blog: <%= render :partial => "blog" %>
  <% end %>
</div>
```

and

Listing 15.26 app/views/user/index.rhtml

```
.
.
.
Friends:
<%= render :partial => "friendship/friends" %>
<hr noshade />
Blog:
<span class="edit_link">
  <%= link_to "(manage)", posts_path(@blog) %>
</span>
<%= render :partial => "profile/blog" %>
</div>
```

The result for the profile page appears in Figure 15.9.

15.3.9 One final niggling detail

Before we leave the RESTful blog, there's one small problem with post creation that we'd like to address. Currently, if you (accidentally) click twice on the "Create" button, it will make two identical posts. In fact, there is probably enough delay in processing the request that you can continue clicking the button to create an arbitrarily large number of posts.[27] Perhaps a user who does this gets what he deserves, but it would be nice to be able to prevent such unfortunate behavior at the application level. (We'll apply these ideas again in Section 16.2.2, where users plagued by duplicate *comments* most assuredly *don't* get what they deserve.)

What we want to do is define a `duplicate?` method in the Post model, so that in the `create` action we can test for a duplicate post before adding it to the blog:

Listing 15.27 app/controllers/posts_controller.rb

```
.
.
.
def create
  @post = Post.new(params[:post])
  @post.blog = @blog

  respond_to do |format|
```

Continues

---

[27] This problem is not particular to our implementation; Rails scaffolding suffers from the same defect.

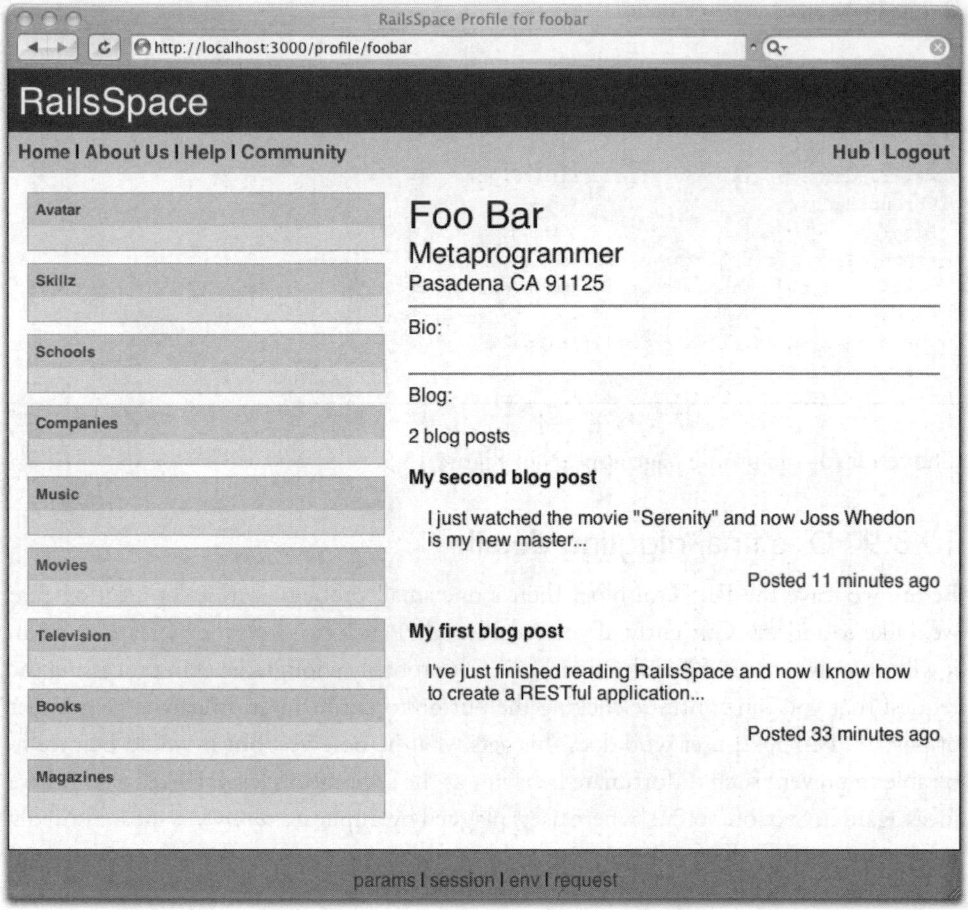

Figure 15.9   The blog on the profile page.

```
if @post.duplicate? or @blog.posts << @post
  flash[:notice] = 'Post was successfully created.'
  format.html { redirect_to post_url(:id => @post) }
  .
  .
  .
```

Here we've arranged for a silent failure for a duplicate post. If the user double-clicks the "Create" button, we assume that it's a mistake, and as far as he's concerned the form will appear to work normally.

The implementation of `duplicate?` uses one of the synthesized `find` methods to see if the current blog already has a post with the same title and body:

Listing 15.28 app/models/post.rb

```
class Post < ActiveRecord::Base
  .
  .
  .
  # Prevent duplicate posts.
  validates_uniqueness_of :body, :scope => [:title, :blog_id]

  # Return true for a duplicate post (same title and body).
  def duplicate?
    post = Post.find_by_blog_id_and_title_and_body(blog_id, title, body)
    # Give self the id for REST routing purposes.
    self.id = post.id unless post.nil?
    not post.nil?
  end
end
```

The call to `find` needs the post's blog id, which is why we added `@post.blog = @blog` at the top of the `create` action. In addition, we set `self.id` to the id of the post (if found); this is because the redirect in `create` needs a post id:

```
format.html { redirect_to post_url(:id => @post) }
```

While we were at it, we included a uniqueness validation, which (through the `:scope` option) ensures that posts with the same body, title, and blog id won't get saved to the database. This way, we are protected against duplicate posts at the model level—even a bug in `duplicate?` or a rogue console session won't spoil our pristine `posts` table. (Experience shows that such a belt-and-suspenders approach prevents all manner of trouble.)

15.4 RESTful testing

The only thing left to do for our RESTful blog is testing. The generated model tests are essentially blank, with only the trivial `assert true` test, but the Posts controller test is full of useful assertions created by `generate scaffold_resource`. Just to get a sense of what the scaffolding gives us, let's take a look at one of the generated tests:

Listing 15.29 test/functional/posts_controller_test.rb

```
class PostsControllerTest < Test::Unit::TestCase
  .
  .
  .
```

Continues

```
def test_should_create_post
  old_count = Post.count
  post :create, :post => { }
  assert_equal old_count+1, Post.count

  assert_redirected_to post_path(assigns(:post))
end
.
.
.

end
```

This uses the Active Record class method `count` to test the post count before and after post creation.

There are two unfortunate things about these tests: First, they all use an utterly superfluous `should_` naming convention; second, and perhaps more seriously, they all break. This is mainly because, as a result of our nested resources, the Posts controller responders need to know which blog the post belongs to. (Since the Post model has some validations, we also have to be careful about making valid posts.) In this section, we'll address both the cosmetic issue and the serious breakage, as well as adding two custom tests of our own.

15.4.1 Default REST functional tests

We'll take a look at the Posts controller functional tests momentarily, but first Rails has a nice surprise in store for us: Because we gave so much information about the data model when we created the scaffold, Rails has generated a totally serviceable `posts.yml` fixture file for us. Let's take a look at it:

Listing 15.30   test/fixtures/posts.yml

```
one:
  id: 1
  blog_id: 1
  title: MyString
  body: MyText
  created_at: 2007-01-16 15:34:32
  updated_at: 2007-01-16 15:34:32
two:
  id: 2
  blog_id: 1
  title: MyString
  body: MyText
  created_at: 2007-01-16 15:34:32
  updated_at: 2007-01-16 15:34:32
```

We then add to this the almost comically simple blogs fixture:

Listing 15.31   test/fixtures/blogs.yml

```
one:
  id: 1
  user_id: 1
two:
  id: 2
  user_id: 1
```

With that, we're ready for the tests. They check for the existence of the pages and for the proper responses to the HTTP methods, and are just slightly fixed-up versions of the scaffold tests. As you might guess, the get and post functions are joined by their RESTful brethren put and delete, and all get put to good use:

Listing 15.32   test/functional/posts_controller_test.rb

```
.
.
.
class PostsControllerTest < Test::Unit::TestCase
  fixtures :posts, :blogs, :users

  def setup
    @controller = PostsController.new
    @request    = ActionController::TestRequest.new
    @response   = ActionController::TestResponse.new
    @user = users(:valid_user)
    authorize @user
    @post = posts(:one)
    @valid_post = { :title => "New title", :body => "New body" }
  end

  def test_get_index
    get :index, :blog_id => @post.blog
    assert_response :success
    assert assigns(:posts)
  end

  def test_get_new
    get :new, :blog_id => @post.blog
    assert_response :success
  end

  def test_create_post
    old_count = Post.count
```

Continues

```
    post :create, :blog_id => @post.blog, :post => @valid_post
    assert_equal old_count+1, Post.count
    assert_redirected_to post_path(:id => assigns(:post))
  end

  def test_show_post
    get :show, :blog_id => @post.blog, :id => @post
    assert_response :success
  end

  def test_get_edit
    get :edit, :blog_id => @post.blog, :id => @post
    assert_response :success
  end

  def test_update_post
    put :update, :blog_id => @post.blog, :id => @post, :post => @valid_post
    assert_redirected_to post_path(:id => assigns(:post))
  end

  def test_destroy_post
    old_count = Post.count
    delete :destroy, :blog_id => @post.blog, :id => @post
    assert_equal old_count-1, Post.count
    assert_redirected_to posts_path
  end
end
```

Note that we've used the trusty search-and-replace function of our text editor to eliminate those annoying `should_`s.

Since we've migrated since the last test, we have to prepare the test database again:

```
> rake db:test:prepare
```

Then we're ready to run the tests:

```
> ruby test/functional/posts_controller_test.rb
Loaded suite test/functional/posts_controller_test
Started
.......
Finished in 1.820859 seconds.

7 tests, 13 assertions, 0 failures, 0 errors
```

15.4.2 Two custom tests

We'll end by adding a couple of tests for the changes we made to the Posts controller. First, we'll test to make sure that the `protect` before filter is in place:

Listing 15.33 test/functional/posts_controller_test.rb

```
    .
    .
    .
def test_unauthorized_redirected
  # Deauthorize user
  @request.session[:user_id] = nil
  [:index, :new, :show, :edit].each do |responder|
    get responder
    assert_response :redirect
    assert_redirected_to :controller => "user", :action => "login"
  end
end
    .
    .
    .
```

Second, we'll test the `protect_blog` before filter:

Listing 15.34 test/functional/posts_controller_test.rb

```
    .
    .
    .
def test_catch_blog_id_mismatch
  # Be some other user.
  authorize users(:friend)
  put :update, :blog_id => @post.blog, :id => @post, :post => @valid_post
  assert_response :redirect
  assert_redirected_to hub_url
  assert_equal "That isn't your blog!", flash[:notice]
end
    .
    .
    .
```

Running the tests gives

```
> ruby test/functional/posts_controller_test.rb
Loaded suite test/functional/posts_controller_test
Started
........
Finished in 1.82027 seconds.

9 tests, 24 assertions, 0 failures, 0 errors
```

That's 24 assertions for relatively little work. There's plenty more to test, but this is a great start.

CHAPTER 16
Blog comments with Ajax

In this chapter, we extend the RailsSpace blog engine by allowing users to comment on blog posts. After all our hard work on RESTful blogs and posts in Chapter 15, comments by themselves are relatively straightforward, so we'll keep things interesting by using Ajax to implement them. Since our comments are RESTful as well, we'll have a chance to see how nicely REST and Ajax play together.

Although there are plenty of useful new techniques in this chapter, including several Rails Ajax helpers and the remarkable *Ruby JavaScript* (RJS), we should note that there is a layer of code that we will not explain. We will peek under the hood to see some of the code that produces the Ajax effects, but ultimately the actual implementation—written in JavaScript using a couple of slick JavaScript libraries—will remain mysterious. Some of the libraries we'll be using are fabulous, miraculous, and, even, ahem, "scriptaculous," and we bow to the JavaScript gods behind these tools.

16.1 RESTful comments

Our first order of business will be to create and configure the Comments resource, which includes defining nested routes and a Comment model. As we'll see, we will only be creating and destroying comments, so we won't be getting quite as much out of the CRUD aspects of REST as we did with posts.[1] On the other hand, being able to respond to multiple formats will be highly useful—one of the formats supported by REST is JavaScript, which we will put to good use when responding to Ajax requests.

---

[1] We will "read" comments by calling a comment partial from the post partial, but we won't be using the RESTful read in the Comments controller.

16.1.1 Comments resource

As in the case of RESTful blogs and posts, our first step is to generate a resource for the comments:

```
> ruby script/generate resource Comment \
        user_id:integer post_id:integer body:text created_at:datetime
  exists  app/models/
  exists  app/controllers/
  exists  app/helpers/
  create  app/views/comments
  exists  test/functional/
  exists  test/unit/
  create  app/models/comment.rb
  create  app/controllers/comments_controller.rb
  create  test/functional/comments_controller_test.rb
  create  app/helpers/comments_helper.rb
  create  test/unit/comment_test.rb
  create  test/fixtures/comments.yml
  create  db/migrate
  create  db/migrate/010_create_comments.rb
   route  map.resources :comments
```

Note that we are not creating scaffolding because comments will be seamlessly integrated with the blog through the magic of Ajax. We won't need any views apart from a few partials, and we'll be making the necessary REST responders by hand.

Since comments naturally belong to both users and posts, we've included an id for each in the data model. Since we included the columns on the command line, our migration is ready to go:

Listing 16.1 db/migrate/010_create_comments.rb

```
class CreateComments < ActiveRecord::Migration
  def self.up
    create_table :comments do |t|
      t.column :user_id,    :integer
      t.column :post_id,    :integer
      t.column :body,       :text
      t.column :created_at, :datetime
    end
  end

  def self.down
    drop_table :comments
  end
end
```

Rake the migration as usual:

```
> rake db:migrate
```

16.1.2 Comment model and associations

Now we're ready to tie the user, post, and comment models together. As indicated above, each comment belongs to both a user and a post:

Listing 16.2 app/models/comment.rb

```
class Comment < ActiveRecord::Base
  belongs_to :user
  belongs_to :post

  validates_presence_of :body, :post, :user
  validates_length_of :body, :maximum => DB_TEXT_MAX_LENGTH
  # Prevent duplicate comments.
  validates_uniqueness_of :body, :scope => [:post_id, :user_id]

  # Return true for a duplicate comment (same user and body).
  def duplicate?
    c = Comment.find_by_post_id_and_user_id_and_body(post, user, body)
    # Give self the id for REST routing purposes.
    self.id = c.id unless c.nil?
    not c.nil?
  end

  # Check authorization for destroying comments.
  def authorized?(user)
    post.blog.user == user
  end
end
```

Here we've included a body uniqueness validation and a `duplicate?` method, which we use in Section 16.2.2 to prevent the creation of duplicate comments in the same way we prevented duplicate posts in Section 15.3.9. We've also added an `authorized?` method, which we'll use in Section 16.2.3 when deleting comments.

Having indicated that a comment `belongs_to` a post, we need to indicate that a post `has_many` comments. There is a slight complication, though: It doesn't make any sense to have a comment without a post. In particular, since we have given users the capability to delete their posts (Section 15.3.7), we need to be sure to delete all of the post's comments when the post itself is deleted. We could do this by hand by iterating through `post.comments` and destroying each one in turn, but we don't have to. Rails lets us build the necessary relationship right into the model by indicating that a post `has_many` *dependent* comments, and that we should `destroy` each of them if the post itself is destroyed:

Listing 16.3 app/models/post.rb

```
class Post < ActiveRecord::Base
  belongs_to :blog
  has_many :comments, :order => "created_at", :dependent => :destroy
  .
  .
  .
```

This is an incredibly compact way to keep our database shiny—when we call `@post.destroy`, all of the corresponding comments will automatically be destroyed as well.[2]

Though we won't need it in this book, it does no harm to tell the User model that it `has_many` comments:

Listing 16.4 app/models/user.rb

```
class User < ActiveRecord::Base
  has_one :spec
  has_one :faq
  has_one :blog
  has_many :comments, :order => "created_at DESC", :dependent => :destroy
  .
  .
  .
```

This would be useful if we ever wanted to list all the comments made by a particular user. Just to be paranoid, we've included the `:dependent => :destroy` in case we ever have occasion to destroy users.

16.1.3 The Comments controller and a preemptive partial

Though we're not yet ready to write its responders, we can already guess some things about the Comments controller. We'll plan to allow only registered users to comment

---

[2] Since it uses `destroy`, this method has the advantage of running the model validations and callbacks (Section 14.1.5), but it is potentially inefficient since it requires a separate SQL call for each object destroyed. In contrast, the option `:dependent => :delete_all` uses a single SQL statement to perform all the deletions at once, which may be preferable if the validations and callbacks don't have to be invoked before object destruction.

on blogs, so we include the `protect` function in a before filter.[3] We also expect to need the comment's parent post, so we'll include a `load_post` function in the before filter:

Listing 16.5 app/controllers/comments_controller.rb

```
class CommentsController < ApplicationController
  helper :profile, :avatar
  include ProfileHelper
  before_filter :protect, :load_post

  private

  def load_post
    @post = Post.find(params[:post_id])
  end
end
```

We plan to redirect back to the blog owner's profile after comment creation using `profile_for`, so we've included `ProfileHelper`. The partial for displaying comments also uses `profile_for`, along with `thumbnail_tag` to display the avatar thumbnail, so we have included the profile and avatar helpers as well.[4]

Though we don't yet have any comments, that doesn't mean we can't define a comment partial preemptively:

Listing 16.6 app/views/comments/_comment.rhtml

```
<div id="comment_<%= comment.id %>" class="comment">
  <hr noshade />

  <span class="thumbnail">
  <%= link_to thumbnail_tag(comment.user), profile_for(comment.user) %>
  </span>
  <%= link_to comment.user.name, profile_for(comment.user) %>
  commented
  <%= time_ago_in_words comment.created_at %> ago:
  <p>
    <%= sanitize comment.body %>
  </p>
</div>
```

---

[3] It would be easy to make this more restrictive by allowing only a user's friends to leave comments, or even make it less restrictive by allowing anyone to comment, but we think that this is a nice middle ground.

[4] Yes, it is annoying that we need both `include ProfileHelper` and `helper :profile`.

We've indicated the author of a comment by displaying the commenter's name linked to the commenter's profile, both of which use the `comment.user` variable produced by `belongs_to :user`. Note that we've arranged for each comment to have a *unique* CSS id by including the comment id in the enclosing div:

```
<div id="comment_<%= comment.id %>" class="comment">
```

This foreshadows the use of Ajax, which finds and manipulates elements of the page using the unique CSS ids.

We'll finish the partial by adding a few CSS rules for the comment partial:

Listing 16.7   public/stylesheets/profile.css

```
.
.
.
/* Comment Styles */

.comment {
  min-height: 90px;
}

.thumbnail {
  display: block;
  float: left;
  margin-right: 1em;
}
```

16.1.4   Routing comments

Before moving on to Ajax, we need to edit the routes file so that RESTful comments get routed correctly. Much like posts were resources of blogs, comments are resources of posts, so they get nested as follows:

Listing 16.8   config/routes.rb

```
ActionController::Routing::Routes.draw do |map|
  map.resources :blogs do |blog|
    blog.resources :posts do |post|
      post.resources :comments
    end
  end
  .
  .
  .
```

Responder	URL path	Helper function
Actions		
create	/blogs/1/posts/99/comments	comments_path(1, 99)
show	/blogs/1/posts/99/comments/1	comment_path(1, 99, 1)
update	/blogs/1/posts/99/comments/1	comment_path(1, 99, 1)
destroy	/blogs/1/posts/99/comments/1	comment_path(1, 99, 1)
Modifiers		
index	/blogs/1/posts/99/comments	comments_path(1, 99)
new	/blogs/1/posts/99/comments/new	new_comment_path(1, 99)
edit	/blogs/1/posts/99/comments/1;edit	edit_comment_path(1, 99, 1)

comment_path(1, 99, 1) and comment_path(:blog_id => 1, :post_id => 99, :id => 1) are equivalent.

Inside /blogs/1/posts/99, the blog and post id can be omitted in the helper. In this case, comment_path and comment_path(:id => 1) (but *not* comment_path(1)) all work.

Each path helper has a corresponding URL helper that returns the full URL. For example, comment_url(1, 99, 1) gives http://localhost:3000/blogs/1/posts/99/comments/1.

Figure 16.1   Nested resources for RESTful blog comments.

This leads to the usual REST responders and helpers (Figure 16.1), though in our case we will be using only a small subset of these.

16.2 Beginning Ajax

Typically, changing the contents of a web page involves the user performing some action (such as clicking a link or submitting a form) and then waiting for a response from the server, which returns a new page to the browser. Ajax refers to the practice of making asynchronous calls to the server to update only *part* of the page, without a full refresh. In contemporary usage, the term *Ajax* is actually more general than this: It is also applied to dynamic HTML effects that don't require asynchronous calls to the server (or indeed any server calls at all). In this more general sense, we can think of Ajax as an umbrella term for making web applications more interactive and responsive.[5]

---

[5] In other words, *making browsers suck less*, as Dave Thomas and Mike Clark are fond of saying.

The actual implementation of Ajax effects—at least, the ones that depend on asynchronous server calls—depends on a JavaScript object called XMLHttpRequest, or XHR. It is XHR that sends requests to the server in response to actions in the browser (such as mouse clicks or mouseovers) and then handles the response. Actually creating and manipulating XHR objects is somewhat complicated, so it's no surprise that we have a choice of several JavaScript frameworks to take care of the details for us. One of the most popular of these projects is Prototype, which (though it can stand alone) integrates seamlessly with Rails. Indeed, Prototype has been developed in parallel with Rails virtually from the start, and a couple of the principal Prototype developers are also on the core team behind Rails. Most of the support Rails provides for Ajax is an abstraction layer on top of Prototype, which in turn is an abstraction layer on top of JavaScript. The result is that we can harness the power of Ajax without ever leaving Ruby.

Of course, somehow we have to include Prototype in our application—but this is, in fact, already done. You may recall that back in Section 6.2.2, while polishing up the debug information at the bottom of each page, we added the following line to the RailsSpace layout:

Listing 16.9 app/views/layouts/application.rhtml

```
.
.
.

    <%= javascript_include_tag :defaults %>
.
.
.
```

This automatically includes Prototype, along with several other useful JavaScript libraries that come bundled with Rails. (If we only wanted Prototype, we could use

```
<%= javascript_include_tag 'prototype' %>
```

instead.) We'll see an example of what a Prototype function looks like in the next section.

16.2.1 New comments

It's time now to dig into the details of creating new comments using Ajax. Our goal in this section is to have a comment creation form appear magically when the user clicks an "Add a comment" link. There are a lot of things going on at once here, but be patient: By the end of the section we will have covered the basics of Ajax.

The structure of a typical Ajax-ready page consists of page elements (most commonly divs) with unique CSS ids, which allow JavaScript to find and manipulate those elements using the Document Object Model (DOM). In our case, we'll add three divs at the end of the post partial defined in Section 15.3.6, one each for the comments themselves, the "Add a comment" link, and a form for creating new comments:

Listing 16.10 app/views/posts/_post.rhtml

```
       .
       .
       .
   <div id="comments_for_post_<%= post.id %>">
     <%= render :partial => "comments/comment", :collection => post.comments %>
   </div>
   <% if logged_in? %>
   <div id="add_comment_link for post_<%= post.id %>">
     <%= link_to_remote "Add a comment",
                          :url => new_comment_path(post.blog, post),
                          :method => :get %>
   </div>
   <div id="new_comment_form_for_post_<%= post.id %>">
   </div>
   <% end %>
</div>
```

Because we've given each of the divs an id based on the Active Record id of the corresponding object, they are guaranteed to be unique.

This addition to the post partial also contains our first Ajax helper function, `link_to_remote`. This works much like the `link_to` function, but instead of linking to a URL, it links to an Ajax call. To better understand this function, let's take a look at the source generated by the post partial:

```
   .
   .
   .
   <div id="comments_for_post_1">

   </div>

   <div id="add_comment_link_for_post_1">
     <a href="#" onclick="new Ajax.Request('/blogs/1/posts/1/comments/new',
        {asynchronous:true, evalScripts:true, method:'get'});
        return false;">Add a comment</a>
   </div>
   <div id="new_comment_form_for_post_1">
```

```
    </div>
    .
    .
    .
```

We're not in a position to understand all the details, but we can see that an Ajax request has been associated with the `onclick` attribute of the "Add a comment" link, whose target is the RESTful URL for the `new` responder in the Comments controller. This means that when a user clicks on the link, it will send a GET request to that URL. It's important to note that the default method for `link_to_remote` is POST; since `new` responds to GET but not to POST (Figure 16.1), we have to pass `link_to_remote` the option `:method => :get`.

To get the "Add a comment" link to work, we need to define a `new` modifier in the Comments controller that responds to the Ajax request. The first thing to notice is that, just as we used `format.html` to respond to requests for HTML, we can use `format.js` to respond to requests for JavaScript:

Listing 16.11   app/controllers/comments_controller.rb

```
def new
  @comment = Comment.new

  respond_to do |format|
    format.js do
      render :update do |page|
        page.hide "add_comment_link_for_post_#{@post.id}"
        page.replace_html "new_comment_form_for_post_#{@post.id}",
                          :partial => "new"
      end
    end
  end
end
```

The response uses `render :update`, a new aspect of `render` that returns JavaScript to update the page making the XHR request. Here the argument to `render :update` is a block containing *inline RJS*,[6] whose block variable `page` automatically comes equipped with methods for generating JavaScript. In this case, the call to `page.hide` generates JavaScript to hide the comment link, while `page.replace_html` generates JavaScript to replace the (currently blank) HTML inside the new comment form div. Since we have given `page.replace_html` the argument `:partial => "new"`, the replacement

---

[6] See Section 16.3.1 for a second way to use RJS.

HTML will come from the partial _new.rhtml (defined momentarily). In both cases, the first argument to the RJS function is the unique CSS id identifying the relevant HTML element.

As a concrete example of the new responder in action, consider the code returned in response to an XHR request for post 1:

```
page.hide "add_comment_link_for_post_#{@post.id}"
page.replace_html "new_comment_form_for_post_#{@post.id}",
                  :partial => "new"
```

generates the JavaScript[7]

```
Element.hide("add_comment_link_for_post_1")
Element.update("new_comment_form_for_post_1", <HTML from _new.rhtml>)
```

where the second argument to Element.update is the HTML to make a form for posting a new comment. The new responder returns this JavaScript to the browser to be executed, thereby hiding the add comment link and adding a comment creation form to the page.

The form for creating a new post—that is, the HTML used to update the "new_comment_form_for_post_1" div—is straightforward, except for one detail:

Listing 16.12 app/views/comments/_new.rhtml

```
<% remote_form_for(:comment, :url => comments_path) do |form| %>

<fieldset>
  <legend>New Comment</legend>
  <%= form.text_area :body, :rows => 10, :cols => 40 %>
  <%= submit_tag "Create" %>
</fieldset>

<% end %>
```

This is exactly the same kind of form we would define to create a new comment without Ajax, with one crucial difference: Just as we used link_to_remote in place of link_to, we've used remote_form_for in place of the traditional form_for. This arranges to use XHR to submit an asynchronous request to create a comment. As with form_for, remote_form_for submits a POST request by default, which creates a post when it hits the URL comments_path (Figure 16.1).

---

[7] These JavaScript functions are part of Prototype.

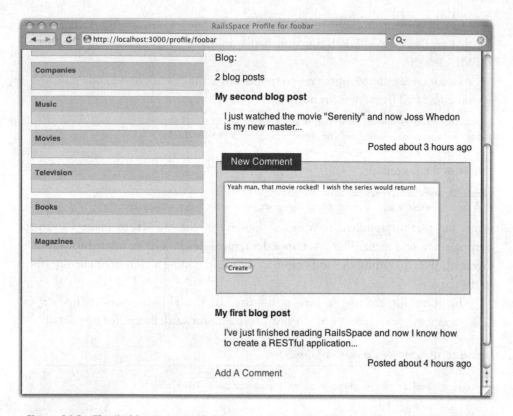

Figure 16.2 The "Add a comment" link becomes the comment form through the magic of Ajax.

Since this section introduced our first Ajax effects, it's taken us awhile to get to the payoff, but it's pretty sweet when we finally arrive. Now clicking on the "Add a comment" link for a particular blog post magically creates a comment form right on the page (Figure 16.2).

16.2.2 Comment creation

The next step is to make the comment form live by defining the `create` action, so that we can create new comments by sending POST requests to URLs such as

```
/blogs/1/posts/99/comments
```

As in the case of the `new` modifier, the `create` action will respond to JavaScript using `format.js`. As with the Posts controller's `create` action (Section 15.3.9), we protect against duplicate comments by using `duplicate?`:

Listing 16.13 app/controllers/comments_controller.rb

```ruby
def create
  @comment = Comment.new(params[:comment])
  @comment.user = User.find(session[:user_id])
  @comment.post = @post

  respond_to do |format|
    if @comment.duplicate? or @post.comments << @comment
      format.js do
        render :update do |page|
          page.replace_html "comments_for_post_#{@post.id}",
                            :partial => "comments/comment",
                            :collection => @post.comments
          page.show "add_comment_link_for_post_#{@post.id}"
          page.hide "new_comment_form_for_post_#{@post.id}"
        end
      end
    else
      format.js { render :nothing => true }
    end
  end
end
```

The `@comment` assignments at the top of `create` ensure that `duplicate?` has all the ids it needs (Section 16.1.2).[8]

The RJS in this case restores the "Add a comment" link using `page.show` (the inverse of `page.hide`) while replacing the HTML in the comments div with the result of rendering all of the comments again. A second possibility would be to use

```ruby
page.insert_html :bottom, "comments_for_post_#{@post.id}",
                 :partial => "comments/comment"
```

to insert the new comment at the bottom of the comments list (Figure 16.3). The reason we elected to rerender all the comments is because someone else might have submitted a comment while we were filling out ours; this way, each user always gets to see *all* the comments.

In the case of an invalid comment (e.g., a blank body), we still need something to respond to the request. Since keeping the form on the page is a sensible behavior, we can just render nothing with

```ruby
render :nothing => true
```

---

[8] As a result, we could actually replace the array append operation `@post.comments << @comment` with a simple `@comment.save`, but we find the former more suggestive.

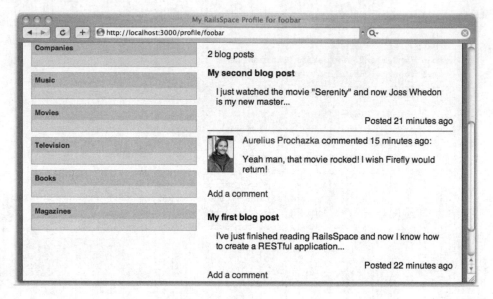

Figure 16.3 The form goes away and the comment shows up.

This silent error assumes that the user can figure out the problem if he tries to submit a blank comment.[9]

16.2.3 Destroying comments

From the typical user's point of view, comments are permanent (be careful what you say!), but we do want to give users control over their own blogs by letting them delete comments. This is easy with `link_to_remote` and `destroy`.

Recall from Section 16.2.1 that we made a link to a new comment form using

```
<%= link_to_remote "Add a comment",
                 :url => new_comment_path(post.blog, post),
                 :method => :get %>
```

This hits URLs of the form

```
/blogs/1/posts/99/comments/new
```

with a GET request. Following the conventions of REST (Figure 16.1), to destroy a comment with id 1, we should submit an HTTP DELETE request to a URL of the form

```
/blogs/1/posts/99/comments/1
```

---

[9] If we wanted to, we could add an errors div above the form div and then use `page.replace_html` to fill it with `error_messages_for(:comment)` to display the Active Record validation errors.

This suggests the code[10]

```
<%= link_to_remote "(delete)",
        :url => comment_path(comment.post.blog, comment.post, comment),
        :method => :delete,
        :confirm => 'Are you sure?' %>
```

Note how easy it is to construct the full RESTful URL using the Comment model associations.[11]

The delete link itself is part of the comment partial; it gets displayed if the user is both logged in and authorized to delete the comment:

Listing 16.14 app/views/comment/_comment.rhtml

```
<div id="comment_<%= comment.id %>" class="comment">
 <hr noshade />
 <% if logged_in? and comment.authorized?(User.find(session[:user_id])) %>
 <span class="edit_link" style="float: right">
 <%= link_to_remote "(delete)",
        :url => comment_path(comment.post.blog, comment.post, comment),
        :method => :delete,
        :confirm => 'Are you sure?' %>
 </span>
 <% end %>
 .
 .
 .

</div>
```

With that code added, a "delete" link appears next to each comment (Figure 16.4). Clicking on it sends a DELETE request to the Comments controller, which gets routed to `destroy`. Before destroying the comment, we first have to check to make sure that the user is authorized—although the link only appears for authorized users, there is nothing to prevent a malicious user from submitting a DELETE request directly. If the user

---

[10] We always have trouble deciding whether to name links such as this "delete" (following the HTTP method and SQL command) or "destroy" (following the Rails REST action). We went with "delete" this time.

[11] Since each comment knows its own post and blog, it would be nice if we could write `comment_path(:id => comment)` and have Rails figure out the rest. We don't see any reason why this couldn't be added to Rails at some point. Such a function wouldn't work in general, though, since it would require each comment to belong to only one post and to only one blog. Rails supports database associations that violate this condition—in particular, `habtm`, or `has_and_belongs_to_many`. (On the other hand, when you think always in terms of CRUD, you usually find `habtm` to be unnecessary.)

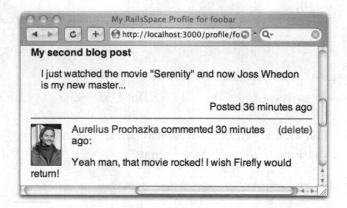

Figure 16.4   Blog post comment with a "delete" link.

is authorized, we destroy the comment and respond to the request with JavaScript to remove the comment from the page:

Listing 16.15   app/controllers/comments_controller.rb

```
def destroy
  @comment = Comment.find(params[:id])
  user = User.find(session[:user_id])

  if @comment.authorized?(user)
    @comment.destroy
  else
    redirect_to hub_url
    return
  end

  respond_to do |format|
    format.js do
      render :update do |page|
        page.remove "comment_#{@comment.id}"
      end
    end
  end
end
```

Here `page.remove` returns a Prototype function to remove the HTML element with the given id. In the user authorization section, note that we `return` after redirecting unauthorized users; recall from Section 6.4.1 that without an explicit return, the code after a redirect still gets executed.

16.3 Visual effects

In an important sense, we are now done with blog comments. It is true, though, that the Ajax effects we've used—showing, hiding, and removing elements, and replacing HTML—are rather simple. In this section we show off some of Ajax's fancier capabilities using script.aculo.us, a collection of visual effects libraries built on top of Prototype. Since these effects lead to slightly longer blocks of RJS, they also provide us with an opportunity to introduce RJS *files*, an alternative to inline RJS.

It's important to realize that JavaScript is executed by the client, not the server, which means that Ajax is subject to the limitations and idiosyncrasies of the client machines and browsers.[12] In particular, script.aculo.us effects can be rather resource-intensive, capable of slowing older computers to a crawl, and they are subject to some of the same browser dependencies that characterized the bad old days before most browsers were (at least minimally) standards-compliant. Sometimes it's hard for programmers to realize this, since we tend to use fast machines and up-to-date browsers, but if you're developing a website for the general public it's a good idea to keep efficiency and browser compatibility in mind. The material in this chapter is intended to show what's possible, not necessarily what's best. With Ajax, as with all other things, *just because you can doesn't mean you should*.

16.3.1 RJS files and the first effect

Currently, the new comment form simply appears immediately upon clicking the link, but in this section we'll give it a more dramatic entrance. Take a look at the script.aculo.us demo page for some of the options:

```
http://wiki.script.aculo.us/scriptaculous/show/CombinationEffectsDemo
```

Since script.aculo.us is integrated with Rails (and has already been included in the RailsSpace layout since it is one of the default JavaScript libraries), we can use script.aculo.us effects through the `page` object's `visual_effect` method. For the comment form, we'll go with the "blind_down" effect, which will make the form appear by sliding down as if it were a window blind:

Listing 16.16 app/controllers/comments_controller.rb

```
def new
  @comment = Comment.new
```

Continues

---

[12] To minimize the effects of these issues, you should make sure that you have the most recent versions of the default JavaScript libraries by running `rake rails:update:javascripts`.

```
respond_to do |format|
  format.js do
    render :update do |page|
      page.hide "add_comment_link_for_post_#{@post.id}"
      form_div = "new_comment_form_for_post_#{@post.id}"
      page.hide form_div
      page.replace_html form_div, :partial => "new"
      page.visual_effect :blind_down, form_div
    end
  end
end
end
```

As in Section 16.2.1, we replace the HTML inside the new comment form div with the form partial, but we've added the additional script.aculo.us effect using

`page.visual_effect :blind_down, form_div`

Note that we hide the form before making it blind down; otherwise, it would flash into existence briefly before disappearing and then sliding down.

In the process of adding the visual effect (and avoiding repeated code using the `form_div` variable), the inline RJS has gotten a little bloated. We can clean up our action by putting the RJS inside an rjs file, in much the same way that we put embedded Ruby in rhtml files. Using files for RJS is conceptually cleaner since RJS is logically part of the view—including RJS in a responder violates MVC by mixing views and controllers. In fact, inline RJS came after RJS files, and was intended for quick one-liners, not blocks of code.

The naming convention for RJS files is the same as for rhtml files, with `rjs` in place of `rhtml`. This means that we can put the RJS for the `new` responder in a file called `new.rjs`:

Listing 16.17 app/views/comments/new.rjs

```
page.hide "add_comment_link_for_post_#{@post.id}"
form_div = "new_comment_form_for_post_#{@post.id}"
page.hide form_div
page.replace_html form_div, :partial => "new"
page.visual_effect :blind_down, form_div
```

Note that there is no `render :update do |page|` here; when using RJS files, Rails automatically creates a `page` object for us.

With `new.rjs` thus defined, `new` is cleaned up considerably:

Listing 16.18 app/controllers/comments_controller.rb

```
def new
  @comment = Comment.new

  respond_to do |format|
    format.js # new.rjs
  end
end
```

In this case, the Rails REST implementation invokes `new.rjs` by default in response to a request for JavaScript, just as it would invoke `new.rhtml` for `format.html`. In fact, because REST can return different formats, we can respond to both kinds of requests appropriately using the same URL; see Section 16.3.4 for an example.

16.3.2 Two more effects

We'll complete the comments machinery for RailsSpace blogs by adding a couple of final visual effects. After comment creation, we'll have the form "blind up"[13] and then briefly highlight the new comment:

Listing 16.19 app/views/comments/create.rjs

```
page.visual_effect :blind_up, "new_comment_form_for_post_#{@post.id}"
page.replace_html "comments_for_post_#{@post.id}",
                  :partial => "comments/comment",
                  :collection => @post.comments
page.show "add_comment_link_for_post_#{@post.id}"
page.visual_effect :highlight, "comment_#{@comment.id}", :duration => 2
```

The final effect here is the (in)famous *yellow fade technique* pioneered by 37signals[14] to show which parts of an Ajaxified page were updated by a particular operation.

As with `new`, putting the RJS commands for `create` in an RJS file simplifies the action:

---

[13] We could get the same blind up/down behavior for the comment form by using `visual_effect :toggle_blind` in both `new.rjs` and `create.rjs`.

[14] This is the company that, as a happy side effect of its Basecamp and Ta-da Lists applications, gave us Ruby on Rails.

Listing 16.20 app/controllers/comments_controller.rb

```ruby
def create
  @comment = Comment.new(params[:comment])
  @comment.user = User.find(session[:user_id])
  @comment.post = @post

  respond_to do |format|
    if @comment.duplicate? or @post.comments << @comment
      format.js # create.rjs
    end
  end
end
```

Finally, we'll delete comments using a "puff" effect (Figure 16.5):

Listing 16.21 app/views/comments/destroy.rjs

```ruby
page.visual_effect :puff, "comment_#{@comment.id}"
```

Here we've put the effect in an RJS file even though it's only one line, so we have to update the `destroy` action:

Listing 16.22 app/controllers/comments_controller.rb

```ruby
def destroy
  @comment = Comment.find(params[:id])
  .
  .
  .
  respond_to do |format|
```

Figure 16.5 With the puff effect, a deleted comment grows in size as it fades away.

```
      format.js # destroy.rjs
    end
  end
```

Though this effect is only a one-liner, and hence is a good candidate for inline RJS, some people prefer to use RJS files for consistency. Also, since one-liners have a tendency to become *n*-liners, it's not a bad idea to start with an RJS file from the start.

16.3.3 A cancel button

Since users might decide not to comment on a post after all, as a final touch to Ajax comments we'll add a "cancel" button to the form. Having to handle a submission from this button on the back-end would be annoying, but thankfully we don't have to if we use `button_to_function`:

Listing 16.23 app/views/comments/_new.rhtml

```
<% remote_form_for(:comment, :url => comments_path) do |form| %>

<fieldset>
  <legend>New Comment</legend>
  <%= form.text_area :body, :rows => 10, :cols => 50 %>
  <%= submit_tag "Create" %>
  <%= button_to_function "Cancel" do |page|
      page.visual_effect :blind_up, "new_comment_form_for_post_#{@post.id}"
      page.show "add_comment_link_for_post_#{@post.id}"
    end
  %>
</fieldset>
<% end %>
```

This creates a button that, rather than submitting to the server, simply calls the JavaScript function defined by the given block, which in this case blinds up the form and restores the comment link.

16.3.4 Degrading gracefully

Before we leave blog comments, there's one more issue we'd like to deal with: What if our users don't have JavaScript enabled in their browsers? (Some individuals and especially companies turn off JavaScript for security purposes.) You will sometimes hear that making a non-Ajax version of an application—that is, degrading gracefully to basic HTML constructs in the absence of JavaScript—is easy, but don't believe it. Supporting

JavaScript-disabled browsers is a pain, and in many cases it's probably not worth the effort, but it is possible. In this section we'll take the first steps toward a non-Ajax version of blog comments.

We'll start by adding an `href` option to the comment link so that non-JavaScript users can click through to a comment form page:

Listing 16.24 app/views/posts/_post.rhtml
___

```
  .
  .
  .
  <div id="add_comment_link_for_post_<%= post.id %>">
    <%= link_to_remote "Add a comment",
                       { :url => new_comment_path(post.blog, post),
                         :method => :get },
                       :href => new_comment_path(post.blog, post) %>
  </div>
  .
  .
  .
```
___

Clicking on this link sends a GET request that expects an HTML response, so we can handle it by defining a `new.rhtml` template:

Listing 16.25 app/views/comments/new.rhmtl
___

```
<div class="post">
  <div class="post_title"><%= sanitize @post.title  %></div>
  <div class="post_body"><%= sanitize @post.body %></div>
</div>
<%= render :partial => "comment", :collection => @post.comments %>
<%= render :partial => "new" %>
```
___

Since our Comments controller is RESTful, the `new` URL is the same as for the Ajax interface—we just respond to a different format:

Listing 16.26 app/controllers/comments_controller.rb
___

```
  def new
    @comment = Comment.new

    respond_to do |format|
      format.html # new.rhtml
      format.js   # new.rjs
```

```
      end
  end

  def create
    @comment = Comment.new(params[:comment])
    @comment.user = User.find(session[:user_id])
    @comment.post = @post

    respond_to do |format|
      if @comment.duplicate? or @post.comments << @comment
        format.html { redirect_to profile_for(@post.blog.user) }
        format.js # create.rjs
      else
        format.html { redirect_to new_comment_url(@post.blog, @post) }
        format.js { render :nothing => true }
      end
    end
  end
end
```

Here the `create` responder just redirects back to the profile for the blog's owner upon successful comment creation.[15]

These non-Ajax comments are far from complete. To finish the implementation, we would have to handle submissions from the cancel button and change all of the delete links to buttons. As it currently stands, though, non-JavaScript users can at least add comments, so they're not completely out of luck.

16.4 Debugging and testing

Because so much of Ajax depends on code executed inside the client's browser, debugging and testing it is rather difficult. Nevertheless, given the importance of Ajax, and its tight integration with Rails, we expect that Ajax testing will continue to improve rapidly. Especially keep an eye on Another RJS Testing System (ARTS),[16] which we hope will evolve into a full-fledged Ajax testing system integrated into Rails. We also recommend taking a look at Selenium, a general test framework for web applications capable of testing Ajax (among other things). For the time being, we can do a serviceable job debugging and testing Ajax using the development server log and functional tests.

---

[15] This won't work well for comments on posts after the first page. It would be better to redirect to the post itself, but the Posts controller's `show` responder is currently protected; we would have to add `show` as an exception in the Posts controller's before filter. We told you supporting non-JavaScript browsers was a pain.

[16] `http://glu.ttono.us/articles/2006/05/29/guide-test-driven-rjs-with-arts`. We had trouble getting ARTS to install, so we haven't used it in RailsSpace.

16.4.1 Another look at `new`

The Rails Ajax support is configured to give helpful alerts for JavaScript errors, but unfortunately Ruby exceptions don't show up in the browser. In other words, when something goes wrong in your application due to an XHR request, the result is usually a silent failure.

For example, consider the `new` responder, where we use a partial to return a form suitable for creating new comments. Suppose that we accidentally typed the wrong name for the partial to render, with `"gnu"` instead of `"new"`:

Listing 16.27 app/views/comments/new.rjs

```
page.hide "add_comment_link_for_post_#{@post.id}"
form_div = "new_comment_form_for_post_#{@post.id}"
page.hide form_div
page.replace_html form_div, :partial => "gnu"
page.visual_effect :blind_down, form_div
```

Now, when we click on the "Add a comment" link, Rails tries to render the gnu partial, which raises an exception since the partial doesn't exist. Unfortunately, the error is silent from the perspective of the browser; as far as the user can tell, the link has simply stopped working.

The way out of this quagmire is to check the server log. If you are running the development server in a terminal window, it's already dumping the log output to the screen; if not, you can look at the file `log/development.log`. This is what you'll see:

```
ActionView::ActionViewError (No rhtml, rxml, rjs or delegate template
found for comments/_gnu in script/../config/../app/views):
  .
  .
  .
```

This identifies our problem as a simple spelling error, which is easy to fix.

The bottom line is that, when developing Ajax applications, it pays to keep an eye on the log. Even if you don't have a terminal window on your desktop, the log should be the first place you look if your Ajax application mysteriously stops responding.

16.4.2 Testing Ajax with `xhr`

Though we don't have tests for the specific Ajax behaviors and effects, we can simulate Ajax requests to the actions and modifiers in the Comments controller and verify that they respond sensibly. The tests in this section parallel those for the Posts controller from Section 15.4, with one crucial difference: Instead of accessing the responders using one of the traditional HTTP methods (`post`, `get`, `put`, or `delete`), we use the `xhr` function to simulate an XHR request.

The `xhr` function takes the HTTP method as an argument, allowing us to send the right request types to test the REST responders. Following the example set by the Posts controller tests (Section 15.4), the Comments controller test suite hits each responder with the right HTTP method and verifies that the basic functionality is correct:

Listing 16.28   test/functional/comments_controller_test.rb

```ruby
require File.dirname(__FILE__) + '/../test_helper'
require 'comments_controller'

# Re-raise errors caught by the controller.
class CommentsController; def rescue_action(e) raise e end; end

class CommentsControllerTest < Test::Unit::TestCase
  fixtures :comments, :posts, :blogs, :users, :specs

  def setup
    @controller = CommentsController.new
    @request    = ActionController::TestRequest.new
    @response   = ActionController::TestResponse.new
    @user = users(:valid_user)
    authorize @user
    @comment = comments(:one)
    @post = posts(:one)
    @valid_comment = { :user_id => @user, :post_id => @post,
                       :body => "Comment Body"}
  end

  def test_new_comment
    xhr :get, :new, :blog_id => @post.blog, :post_id => @post
    assert_response :success
  end

  def test_create_comment
    old_count = Comment.count
    xhr :post, :create, :blog_id => @post.blog,
                        :post_id => @post,
                        :comment => @valid_comment
    assert_response :success
    assert_equal old_count+1, Comment.count
  end

  def test_delete_comment
    old_count = Comment.count
```

Continues

```
    xhr :delete, :destroy, :blog_id => @comment.post.blog,
                            :post_id => @comment.post,
                            :id      => @comment
  assert_response :success
  assert_equal old_count-1, Comment.count
  end

  # Make sure unauthorized users can't delete comments and get redirected.
  def test_unauthorized_delete_comment
    @request.session[:user_id] = 2  # Unauthorized user
    xhr :delete, :destroy, :blog_id => @comment.post.blog,
                            :post_id => @comment.post,
                            :id      => @comment
    assert_response :redirect
    assert_redirected_to hub_url
  end
end
```

Running the suite gives

```
> ruby test/functional/comments_controller_test.rb
Loaded suite test/functional/comments_controller_test
Started
....
Finished in 0.275006 seconds.

4 tests, 7 assertions, 0 failures, 0 errors
```

CHAPTER 17

What next?

In a sense, a web application such as RailsSpace is never *done*—we could always add a feature or two, polish the interface, or improve the test suite—but at some point we have to start thinking about showing it to the world.[1] In this chapter, we briefly discuss several subjects related to application deployment. We can't do the subject justice here, but we can get you started by mentioning some of the techniques and software needed for deploying an application successfully. This is a bit of a whirlwind tour; if the discussion seems rather dense and technical at times, think of it as prime fodder for web searches. Deployment is a rapidly evolving aspect of Rails, and the web is the best and most up-to-date resource.

17.1 Deployment considerations

One benefit of Rails is its weak coupling to the details of any particular deployment architecture—virtually all the deployment-specific aspects of Rails happen automatically upon changing the environment from development to production, and its powerful routing facilities make Rails largely independent of server routing systems such as Apache's `mod_rewrite`. Since it allows us to focus on development rather than deployment, this flexibility is a big win for programmers, but it does mean that we have a dizzying array of options when choosing a deployment architecture.

We'll start this section with a brief overview of some of the software and hardware combinations to consider. Then we'll show how to run the local version of RailsSpace in *production* mode, followed by a description of a minimal production server. Finally, we'll discuss Rails scalability issues and introduce the basics of Rails administration.

---

[1] Of course, before their public debut most sites could use a real web designer at some point, too—this is certainly the case for RailsSpace.

17.1.1   Software and hardware options

When we said that Rails deployment is evolving rapidly, we weren't kidding—when we started writing *RailsSpace* not too many months ago, probably the most common deployment architecture used the lighttpd webserver with FastCGI to process requests. Soon thereafter, the new "standard" deployment architecture became the workhorse Apache webserver combined with Mongrel as an application server,[2] followed by packs of Mongrels running behind Apache's `mod_proxy_balance`. Then came Pound, run as a proxy server between Apache and Mongrel. Nowadays, it seems that many of the cool kids have switched to a webserver called Nginx,[3] used on its own or as a proxy server.

Currently, there are only two things that everyone seems to agree on: Use Mongrel as the Rails application server, and deploy to some flavor of Unix (most commonly Linux). The rest is up to you. One option is to use a shared host, which will probably make the choices for you. Because of the explosive growth of Rails, there are now many shared host options, and a web search for "Rails shared host" provides a cornucopia of possibilities. If you're deploying to your own server, whether it's a rack unit at a colocation facility or the Linux box in your hall,[4] we recommend running Apache in front of a single Mongrel process to start. Unless you expect to get a huge amount of traffic, this setup is probably sufficient for most purposes. (See Section 17.1.4 on scaling if your Rails application does prove outrageously popular.)

17.1.2   Running in production mode

So far in RailsSpace, we've run our application in two different environments: *development* and *test*. Deployed applications run in a third environment, *production*. The purpose of this section is to practice the steps needed to deploy RailsSpace to a production server by running the application in a production environment on the local development machine.

Like the development and test environments, the production environment requires a corresponding database. In fact, you may recall seeing a reference to production in one of our previous encounters with `database.yml`:

---

[2] Recall from Chapter 2 that you can use either WEBrick or Mongrel as the Rails development server; unlike WEBrick, Mongrel is also suitable for production use.

[3] Since much of its documentation is in Russian, Nginx (pronounced "engine X") is relatively obscure, but we've heard great things about it, and it's currently being used by several prominent Rails hosting companies.

[4] In theory, most DSL and cable modem IP numbers are dynamic, but in practice they are often quite stable, so if you just want to deploy a small personal application, this actually isn't a bad option.

Listing 17.1 config/database.yml

```
development:
  adapter: mysql
  database: rails_space_development
  username: root
  password:
  host: localhost

test:
  adapter: mysql
  database: rails_space_test
  username: root
  password:
  host: localhost

production:
  adapter: mysql
  database: rails_space_production
  username: root
  password: <your password>
  host: localhost
```

We can tell Rails how to talk to our production database by filling in the corresponding password field. (For a true deployment, it is probably a good idea to create a special database user just for RailsSpace, with appropriately restricted privileges.)

Of course, to talk to the production database, we first need to have one, so create the `rails_space_production` database using the `mysqladmin` command (or your favorite GUI):

```
> mysqladmin create rails_space_production --user=root --password=my_password
```

Then fill in the database table structure by running the migration with the Rails environment set to `production`:

```
> rake db:migrate RAILS_ENV=production
```

Finally, kill the current development server (if there is one) and start a new server in a production environment using the `-e` flag:

```
> ruby script/server -e production
```

You can see the effect by visiting the RailsSpace home page at `http://localhost:3000`; comparing Figure 17.1 and Figure 6.3, you can see that the debug information no longer appears at the bottom of the page. This is because of the line

```
<% if ENV["RAILS_ENV"] == "development" %>
```

before the debug information in the site layout (Section 4.2.5). Now that we're running in production mode, the debug information automatically disappears.

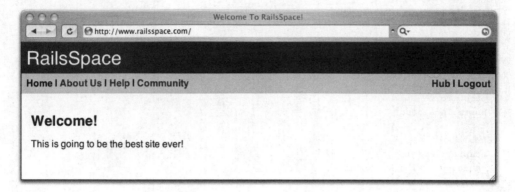

Figure 17.1   The RailsSpace homepage in a production environment, with no debug links.

It's important to note that, in order to incorporate any changes to the application code, in production mode you must always restart the server. Part of what's nice about the development server is that it loads changes immediately, but this feature has a performance penalty, so it is turned off in a production environment.

17.1.3   A minimal production server

Setting up a production server is rather complicated; the details depend on your choice of hardware and software, and even the simplest setup requires a significant amount of experience with things like Linux and Apache. In this section we outline one possible deployment solution. Even if you don't follow these steps exactly, they should give you a good idea of what's involved in deploying a Rails application.

The first step is to install the same software on the server that you have running on your development machine, including Ruby, Rails, and your choice of database, as well as any gems or plugins you might need (such as Ferret). Then, after uploading your Rails project to the server, follow the steps from the previous section to create and configure the production database. Finally, install and configure your choice of application server and webserver. For now, we'll go with Mongrel and Apache.

Installing Mongrel is simple using Ruby gems:

```
> sudo gem install mongrel
```

Then, to start the Mongrel application server for Rails, run `mongrel_rails` in the root directory of your application:

```
> cd rails_space
> mongrel_rails start -d -p 8000 -e production
```

This starts Mongrel running as a daemon (-d) listening on port 8000 (-p 8000) in a production environment (-e production). You can also restart Mongrel (to load application changes, for example) using

```
> mongrel_rails restart
```

or stop it with

```
> mongrel_rails stop
```

As a final step, download and install Apache 2.2 from http://httpd.apache.org/, and then put something like the following in the httpd.conf file:[5]

Listing 17.2 conf/httpd.conf

```
<VirtualHost *:80>
    ServerName railsspace.com
    ServerAlias www.railsspace.com

    ProxyPass / http://www.railsspace.com:8000/
    ProxyPassReverse / http://www.railsspace.com:8000
    ProxyPreserveHost on
</VirtualHost>
```

This arranges for Apache to act as a proxy between port 80 (the default port for web requests) and port 8000 (where the Mongrel process is listening). Now start Apache from the main Apache directory (typically /usr/local/apache2) using

```
> bin/apachectl start
```

With this setup, browser requests to RailsSpace.com will automatically be routed to the Mongrel process listening on port 8000, and the application will be live.

17.1.4 Scaling

Unless your application is likely to get an unexpected spike in traffic from Reddit or Digg, worrying about scaling is probably premature optimization—a single server running a single Mongrel process is probably sufficient for the vast majority of Rails applications. Some sites do become wildly popular, though, and in this case Rails makes it possible to scale to high volume by using a *shared-nothing* architecture. This involves pushing the maintenance of state (such as sessions) into a single location (typically a database) so that the individual Rails servers and processes don't share any data.

---

[5] The exact configuration will depend on your particular Apache setup.

This means that, on a single server, you can just keep adding new Mongrels until you run out of CPU cycles, at which point you can start adding new servers, each with its own complement of Mongrels.

One way to take some of the load off of your web and database servers is to use *caching*. Rails has a powerful caching system to help avoid the computational and database-access expense of generating dynamic HTML. Rails supports three types of caching: *page caching*, *action caching*, and *fragment caching*. Page caching is the most efficient but least flexible form of caching; it simply involves storing the results of rendering a particular page as a plain HTML file, which can be served directly through the webserver as static content. Action caching is similar to page caching, with the results of a particular *action* being cached; the difference is that action caching allows a controller's filters to be run, so that, for example, cached pages can be protected by an authentication before filter.

Because the RailsSpace layout changes depending on login status, we can use neither page caching nor action caching on our site, but we could use fragment caching, which lets us cache fragments of content. For example, we could cache the blog entries for a particular user, so that the entries would be dynamically generated when first hit but would be cached for subsequent requests. Of course, we still need to update the blogs if users make new entries, and Rails lets us *expire* fragments to handle this case. Since the frequency of blog requests is likely to be higher than the frequency of new posts, caching could still give a significant performance boost.

Even with caching to minimize database hits, the database itself might eventually become the application bottleneck. At this point, you could convert to a *memcached* session store,[6] add extra database servers in a master-slave setup, or use some of the VC cash you've no doubt raised by this point to hire yourself a real database/scaling guru.[7] The bottom line is that there's nothing special about scaling Rails applications; by using a shared-nothing architecture, Rails reduces scaling to a previously solved problem.

One important scaling issue has nothing to do with serving pages, but rather is concerned with development and deployment. When developing any large software project, it's practically essential to use a *version control system*, which allows developers to track changes as the code evolves, while making collaboration easier by automatically merging changes. The most popular version control system among Rails developers is

---

[6] memcached is a distributed memory caching system originally developed for the blogging site LiveJournal.

[7] This solution is called *VC cashing*.

almost certainly Subversion, which the authors used to develop RailsSpace. We also recommend darcs, a powerful distributed revision control system based on the linear algebra of software patches.[8]

A particularly convenient complement to a version control system is Capistrano, a system for the automated deployment and rollback of application source code. Capistrano is designed for deployment to multiple servers, with each server being updated with code from a central repository—with a single command, you can push the application you have been running on your modest development machine to a cluster of load-balanced production servers.[9] Though optimized for multiserver deployments, Capistrano is nice enough that many people use it even for single-server systems. Capistrano assumes that you're using version control, and it plays nice with both Subversion and darcs (among others).

In summary, here are our current recommendations for a production Rails application:

- Linux/Apache/Mongrel for deployment
- Caching `mod_proxy_balance` and shared nothing and for scaling
- Subversion or darcs for version control
- Capistrano for automated deployment and rollback

17.1.5 Administration basics

When running an application in production mode, sometimes you want to inspect the Rails internals, and whether you want to track down a bug, view a list of recently updated records, or perhaps update a user's information by hand, the console may be the only tool you need. (You are welcome, of course, to write an administrative interface for the site as well; writing a front-end for RailsSpace administration would be a good thing to put on our to-do list.) Since the console runs in development mode by default, in order to run the console in a production environment, we have to give it an explicit `production` option:

```
> ruby script/console production
```

---

[8] We are not making this up. Originally developed by physicist David Roundy, darcs was inspired by the operator algebras of quantum mechanics. (Incidentally, back in high school David Roundy and Michael Hartl once joined forces to win the gold medal in physics at the California State Science Olympiad.)

[9] No doubt running lighttpd/Nginx/Apache/mod_proxy_balance/Pound/FastCGI/Mongrel/whatever.

When you do this, be careful—using the console in production mode means that any changes you save using Active Record will affect the production database. If you want to be able to inspect your application without having to worry about clobbering production data, you can run the console in a *sandbox*:[10]

```
> ruby script/console production --sandbox
Loading production environment in sandbox.
Any modifications you make will be rolled back on exit.
>>
```

This way, you don't risk doing any permanent damage to your application.

Another key tool for Rails administration is the production log file. This is the production version of the development log file `development.log` mentioned briefly in Section 4.3 (Figure 4.4) and again in Section 16.4.1; both are located (along with a test log) in the `log/` directory. Rails records tons of useful information to the log file, so inspecting it is good for seeing what's going on in your application. For example, this is the log entry when Foo Bar registers (trimmed for brevity):

Listing 17.3 log/production.log

```
Processing UserController#register (for 127.0.0.1 at ...
  Session ID: f20ed0fdfb7db3297095bf2bc5bbc10f
  Parameters: {"user"=>{"password_confirmation"=>"bazquux",
  "screen_name"=>"foobar", "password"=>"bazquux",
  "email"=>"foobar@example.com"}, "commit"=>"Register!",
  "action"=>"register", "controller"=>"user"}
params[:user]: {"password_confirmation"=>"bazquux",
"screen_name"=>"foobar", "password"=>"bazquux",
"email"=>"foobar@example.com"}
Redirected to http://localhost:3000/user
Completed in 0.02988 (33 reqs/sec) | DB: 0.02114 (70%) | 302 Found ...


Processing UserController#index (for 127.0.0.1 at...
  Session ID: f20ed0fdfb7db3297095bf2bc5bbc10f
  Parameters: {"action"=>"index", "controller"=>"user"}
Rendering  within layouts/application
Rendering user/index
Completed in 0.46929 (2 reqs/sec) | Rendering: 0.27744 (59%) |...
```

---

[10] Running in a sandbox has nothing to do with production *per se;* you can run the console in a sandbox in development mode as well.

The log keeps track of which controllers and actions are involved, along with redirects and view renders.

The log keeps track of other things, including SQL queries and, perhaps most importantly, errors. For example, trying to hit the page `http://localhost:3000/fdsa` gives a long series of error messages and a 404 Page Not Found error:

```
Processing ApplicationController#index (for 127.0.0.1 at...
  Session ID: f20ed0fdfb7db3297095bf2bc5bbc10f
  Parameters: {}


ActionController::RoutingError (no route found to match "/fdsa"
with {:method=>:get}):
  .
  .
  .
<long error trace>
  .
  .
  .

Rendering /usr/local/lib/ruby/gems/1.8/gems/actionpack-...
```

Since Ruby exceptions show up in the log, by analyzing it we can discover bugs in our application.

When keeping tabs on an application, it's common to run a `tail` process to monitor the end of the log file continuously:

```
> tail -f log/production.log
```

This won't work on Windows machines since the `tail` command is Unix-specific. (We warned you that no one ever deploys Rails apps to anything but Unix!)

Of course, it's good that errors show up in the log, but in general we don't want to expose errors to users. To this end, Rails serves up customizable error pages instead of showing users an error—though you wouldn't guess that from the error page for an invalid request (Figure 17.2). It turns out that for *local* requests, Rails assumes you want to see the full error, but for any *outside* requests, Rails returns the contents of `public/404.html` (for Page Not Found errors) or `public/500.html` (for application errors). By editing these files, we could arrange for a customized RailsSpace error message. If you are running your development machine (in production mode) on a local network, you can see the public error pages by typing in the IP number rather than `localhost`, as shown in Figures 17.3 and 17.4.

Figure 17.2 The local error page for an invalid request.

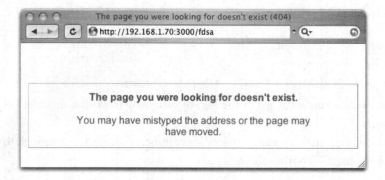

Figure 17.3 The public error page for file not found errors (404).

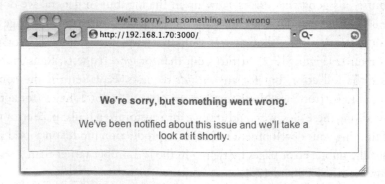

Figure 17.4 The application error page (500) (in this case, a syntax error in the `routes.rb` file).

17.2   More Ruby and Rails

This brings us to the end of RailsSpace. The application we have built is substantial, but in some ways we have only scratched the surface of Ruby on Rails. Active Record, for example, is still full of tricks like observers, `acts_as_tree`, and polymorphic associations. Ajax and RJS alone could fill a book, while the full implications of REST are only beginning to be understood. And, of course, Ruby itself is a full-strength programming language; gaining a deeper understanding of Ruby can do your Rails programming a world of good.

So, where should you go from here? We've already recommended *Programming Ruby* and *The Ruby Way*. Though it's not available as of this writing, we're also excited about the forthcoming book *The Rails Way* by Obie Fernandez (from Addison-Wesley). Unsurprisingly, the Internet is also a rich source of Rails material, with web searches for subjects of interest (including, crucially, error messages) typically producing voluminous and relevant results.[11] There is an especially thriving community of discussion groups and technical blogs covering Rails topics; we won't even try to list all (or even any) of them, but search and ye shall find.

We hope that *RailsSpace* has helped you get on track toward realizing your web dreams with Ruby on Rails. Now go forth and conquer the world!

---

[11] This wasn't always the case, and it is testament to the growing popularity of Rails that nowadays search engines know that Rails programmers aren't particularly interested in trains.

Index

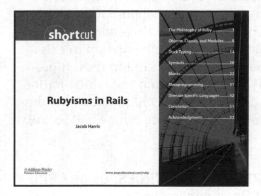
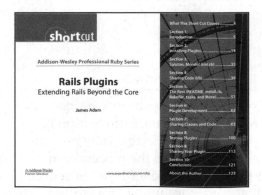

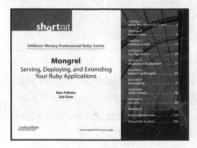

Register
Your Book

at www.awprofessional.com/register

You may be eligible to receive:

- Advance notice of forthcoming editions of the book
- Related book recommendations
- Chapter excerpts and supplements of forthcoming titles
- Information about special contests and promotions throughout the year
- Notices and reminders about author appearances, tradeshows, and online chats with special guests

Contact us

If you are interested in writing a book or reviewing manuscripts prior to publication, please write to us at:

Editorial Department
Addison-Wesley Professional
75 Arlington Street, Suite 300
Boston, MA 02116 USA
Email: AWPro@aw.com

Addison-Wesley

Visit us on the Web: http://www.awprofessional.com